D1555581

READING, LANGUAGE, AND LITERACY:

Instruction for the Twenty-First Century

READING, LANGUAGE, AND LITERACY:

Instruction for the Twenty-First Century

Edited by
FRAN LEHR
JEAN OSBORN
Center for the Study of Reading
University of Illinois at Urbana-Champaign

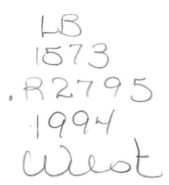

1994

LAWRENCE ERLBAUM ASSOCIATES, PUBLISHERS
Hillsdale, New Jersey   Hove and London

Lawrence Erlbaum Associates, Inc., Publishers
365 Broadway
Hillsdale, New Jersey 07642

Library of Congress Cataloging-in-Publication Data

Reading, language, and literacy : instruction for the twenty-first
   century / edited by Fran Lehr, Jean Osborn.
         p.   cm.
   Includes bibliographical references and index.
   ISBN 0-8058-1166-4
   1. Reading (Elementary) 2. Reading—Language experience approach.
3. Children—Books and reading.   4. Literacy. I. Lehr, Fran.
II. Osborn, Jean.
LB1573.R2795   1993
372.4—dc20   93-4327
                                                                CIP

Printed in the United States of America
10 9 8 7 6 5 4 3 2 1

Contents

Preface

Fran Lehr
Jean Osborn

The impetus for this volume came from a conference entitled "Reading, Language, and Literacy" held in 1989 in Chicago. Sponsored by the School Division of the Association of American Publishers, the International Reading Association, and the Center for the Study of Reading, the conference brought together publishers, reading researchers, and reading educators for the purpose of examining the best available research evidence about what we know—and what we have yet to learn—about the teaching of reading and about how children learn to read. The goal of the conference was to contribute to a sound research base upon which to develop classroom practices that will ensure that every child in America will become fully literate. The conference participants brought with them a commitment to the belief that, in the words of Marilyn Adams, "It is not just that the teaching of reading is more important than ever before, but that it must be taught better and more broadly than ever before" (Adams, 1990, p. 26).

As the presentations were made, the profound commitment of each researcher and practitioner to this belief became clear. At the same time, it was equally clear that the field is still deeply divided over the best ways to translate belief into classroom practice. And so, in preparing this volume, we decided to highlight rather than gloss over these divisions. We know that the problems children have in becoming literate will not go away if we adhere to the status quo. We stress these divisions because we understand that the passion with which proponents present their views indicates a passion for helping children—all children—become competent, enthusiastic readers. We hope that the chapters in this volume will promote thought and discussion that will lead to action in improving reading instruction for children, now and into the new century.

The contributions to *Reading, Language, and Literacy* are arranged according to the following topics: "Learning About Print," "Whole Language," "Children, Adults, Books: Interactive Reading," "The Rediscovery of Literature in the Curriculum," "Reading Research: Implications for Teachers, Policymakers, and Publishers," and "Publishers' Perspectives."

"Learning About Print" focuses on beginning reading instruction. To succeed in school—and beyond—all children must become skillful readers. It is no surprise then, that the content and methods of beginning reading instruction have long been major issues in reading research. Indeed, no area of instruction has received more scrutiny or provoked more controversy. Three of the four chapters in this section deal with key aspects of early instruction: phonics, phonemic awareness, and structural analysis, while the fourth chapter provides a 20-year retrospective of research on the role of phonics in beginning reading.

"Whole Language" focuses on the movement that has generated much discussion and many promises. The four chapters in this section examine the movement from different perspectives. Together, the chapters offer a picture of how well the promises of whole language are being fulfilled.

"Children, Adults, Books: Interactive Reading" contains three chapters that examine the role reading to and with children can play in their reading success. Two of these chapters show that even an issue as seemingly straightforward and as agreed upon as the value of reading to children is subject to controversy. The first chapter reviews the research supporting interactive reading, while the second presents findings from a longitudinal study that raises questions about the value of simply reading aloud to children. The third chapter examines how books are used in the highly regarded Reading Recovery program and offers ideas drawn from that program that can be used in regular classrooms.

The two chapters in "The Rediscovery of Literature in the Classroom" examine another issue that has engendered a great deal of interest in the quality and the kind of texts children should read. One chapter examines narrative text from a psychological and educational perspective; the second points to the lack of multicultural literature available both in our schools and book stores, and argues the importance of providing children with texts that reflect the cultural diversity of the nation.

"Reading Research: Implications for Teachers, Policymakers, and Publishers" contains three chapters that focus on crucial issues in reading research. The first chapter tackles the enormous issue of world illiteracy. By defining illiteracy in various contexts, this chapter offers directions for researchers, practitioners, and publishers to take in addressing the problem. The second chapter looks at the current state of literacy assessment in the United States, highlights the controversies attached to assessment, and offers suggestions for more effective assessment procedures. The third chapter offers an update of the 1985 landmark report, *Becoming a Nation of Readers,* pointing out areas that need more attention from researchers.

Finally, "Publishers' Perspectives" presents the reactions of two well-known educational publishing house executives to issues discussed in the earlier chapters, particularly as those issues affect publishers.

As the chapters in this volume clearly illustrate, reading instruction in the last years of the 20th Century is still characterized by controversy. We hope they also show that rather than prolong that controversy, many researchers, practitioners, and publishers are drawing ideas from it so as to build effective reading instruction for all children.

ACKNOWLEDGMENTS

We offer thanks to the people who have helped us in so many ways. We thank Don Eklund of the School Division of the Association of American Publishers and Dale Johnson of the International Reading Association who organized and conducted the conference that led to this book. We thank Hilary Holbrook for her editorial help and Delores Plowman for her tireless work in preparing the manuscripts. Finally, we most especially thank Dick Anderson, the Director of the Center for the Study of Reading, for his support and guidance throughout the production of this volume.

REFERENCE

Adams, M. J. (1990). *Beginning to read: Thinking and learning about print.* Cambridge, MA: The MIT press.

LEARNING ABOUT PRINT

1 Phonics and Beginning Reading Instruction

Marilyn Jager Adams
Bolt Beranek and Newman
and Center for the Study of Reading

Whatever one's dreams and priorities for America's future might be, finding ways to correct the shortcomings and unevenness of our children's literacy education can only be recognized as an enormous and enormously complicated challenge. Although few cultural requirements are as important to a child's life as that of becoming a reader, it is equally true that few are as complex.

But even while the education community may face no greater challenge in terms of urgency, scope, or importance, efforts toward progress have been broadly deferred to a dispute over a single set of subissues—the role of phonics instruction in beginning reading. Indeed, whether phonics should be taught at all is perhaps the most hotly debated, highly politicized, and divisive issue in elementary education. In essence, the objection to phonics centers on the claim that its instruction impedes development of the attitudes and abilities required for reading with pleasure and comprehension. If correct, this claim can only be seen as a wholly insuperable negative. After all, the very goal of reading instruction is precisely and inarguably to foster the disposition as well as the ability to read purposefully, reflectively, and productively. Rather than dismiss this objection, therefore, I have focused this chapter on its arguments and counterarguments.

FRAMING THE ISSUES

Across the instructional literature, the value of phonics instruction has been demonstrated with sobering consistency across literally hundreds of studies—including small, well-controlled laboratory studies as well as large-scale method comparisons involving hundreds of classrooms and thousands of children. Collectively, these studies argue that, when developed as part of a larger program of reading and writing, phonics instruction leads to higher group achievement at least in word recognition and spelling, at least in the primary grades, and especially for economically disadvantaged and slower students (see Adams, 1990, Chapter 3).

Yet it would be hasty to act on this conclusion without closer analysis. First, neither the well-controlled laboratory studies nor the large-scale classroom studies allow us to pinpoint the source of the phonics advantage. Whereas the laboratory studies provide clean contrasts of whatever variables they were designed to assess, they leave one wondering about the would-be influence of all those factors that were constrained or absent through experimental control: How would the instructional contrasts have held up if the research had been conducted in a real classroom, in the context of a real reading curriculum, with real teachers and students, and over a reasonably realistic time course? The classroom studies, in contrast, offer real-world validity. In doing so, however, they leave one wondering about those many factors that, although unavoidably present, were uncontrolled or unmeasured: Who were the particular students? Who were the particular teachers? What about the specifics of the programs' implementations?

These are not frivolous questions. The phonics advantage documented by this research is neither awesomely large nor comfortably reliable. Even while the studies collectively affirm that phonics instruction is, on average, a positive component of early reading development, they also demonstrate that there are enormous differences in the outcomes of any program depending on the particular schools, teachers, children, and implementation vagaries involved. In particular, even where phonics has been taught, even where it has been taught under the watchful eye of researchers, there have remained many children who nonetheless have experienced difficulty in learning to read.

Why? How can we explain this variability? One possibility is that the effectiveness of phonics instruction depends on individual characteristics of the children. After all, not all children are alike. Some, it has been argued, are global perceivers by nature, and some are analytic; some are auditorily attuned by nature, and some are visual. Phonics, it has been suggested, may well be a good thing for those children who are analytically and auditorily oriented, but what about the others? With global visual predispositions, would they not be fettered, even frustrated and discouraged, with a phonic approach? More generally, would it not be wise to design instructional processes and materials to accommodate such differences in children's perceptual styles or dominant modalities?

In fact, this argument has been quite broadly advocated and adopted. Although today its allure is saliently evidenced by the large following that Carbo, Dunn, and Dunn (1986) have attracted, they did not start it. In a mid 1970s study of special education teachers in Illinois, Arter and Jenkins (1977) found that 95% were familiar with the argument. Of those familiar with it, 99% believed that modality preferences should be a primary consideration in devising instruction for children with learning difficulties.

Arter and Jenkins also found that nearly all the teachers who were familiar with this argument believed it to be well supported by research. But it is not. Over the years, many, many, empirical studies have been conducted on this issue. Despite the energy thereby invested, however, the hypothetical interaction between program effectiveness and preferred modalities is not supported by the data. Instead, working knowledge of phonics seems an asset for all young readers (see Stahl, this volume). Research persistently indicates that weaknesses in basic decoding skills are the most common and can be the most pervasive and debilitating source of reading difficulties (see, e.g., Perfetti, 1985; Stanovich, 1986; Vernon, 1971; Williams, 1991).

The implication, once again, is that there is something about phonics—or, at least, about the knowledge and abilities that phonics is intended to foster—that is of general, substantive, and long-lasting value to all young readers. If so, then the iffiness of its effectiveness would seem to lie in its realization. One clear problem is that phonics is, by no means, all there is to learning to read. Beyond that, however, there exist literally hundreds of "phonic" programs and thousands of "phonic" techniques, and the differences among them are substantial (see, e.g., Aukerman, 1971, 1984). Across instructional programs, for example, the phonic strands differ in starting point as well as stopping point. They differ in the methods, materials, procedures, and progression for everything taught in between. And they differ in fundamental strictures and assumptions about what to and what not to teach, about when to and when not to teach, and about how to and how not to teach. Moreover, whereas some of the differences between programs are just differences, others stand as genuine conflicts and incompatibilities.

Necessarily, then, to ask more precisely why phonics is worthwhile, I must back off one level of abstraction. Instead of focusing on the effectiveness or theoretical promise of particular programs, materials, or techniques, I instead probe the basic assumption that underlies all: namely, that instruction on spelling-sound correspondences is valuable toward helping children learn to read. But neither is this a simple assumption. At the grossest level of analysis, the issues it presupposes are minimally: (a) it is useful for readers to become familiar with the letterwise spelling of words; and/or (b) it is useful for young readers to appreciate the correspondences between spellings and sounds; and (c) it useful to provide instructional support to young readers in these domains. In the balance of this chapter, I examine each of these assumptions in turn.

Is it Useful for Readers to be Familiar with the Letterwise Spellings of Words?

To the extent that our system of writing is alphabetic, its basic symbols—letters, graphemes, or letter patterns—represent phonemes, and its words are represented in their concatenation. To the extent that our system of writing is not alphabetic, words are nonetheless designed by specific and specifically ordered collections of letters. Either way, it would seem, prima facie, that learning to recognize words ought to involve learning to recognize their letterwise composition.

Rational analysis aside, however, this hypothesis is in some deep sense highly counterintuitive. When reading with comprehension and fluency, skillful readers neither look nor feel like they process text in any letter-by-letter fashion. Instead, it is the meaning and message of the text that captures and tracks their attention. Indeed, it is the effective precedence of meaning over mechanics that has fueled virtually every antiphonics movement in history.

In the most recent bout of the "Great Debate," phonics has been held rival to a vision of reading most fully developed by Frank Smith in his seminal book, *Understanding Reading* (1971). Importantly, Smith wrote this book some 20 years ago. At the time, relevant data were scarce. In addition, the dominant theoretical framework of the day was simple and flat; that is, within that prevailing and deeply entrenched framework, and whether working with learning, memory, or perception, the mind was held to work through the pieces one at a time, in series.

Smith's essential thesis was that fluent reading could not be explained within that one-at-a-time serial framework if its units of analysis were either individual letters or individual words. If skilled readers' units of analysis were either single letters or words, he argued, their progress would be far too slow; their memories would too quickly be overloaded; they would be led astray by the unreliability of English spelling–sound correspondences and garden-pathed by the multiple uses, meanings, and pronunciations of the words. Moreover, he argued, if the mind can attend to only one level of processing at a time, then reading must be focused, in process as in outcome, on the meaning and message of the text.

The conclusion, Smith offered, was that skillful readers must work not with letters, not with words, and not even with the left-to-right sequence of print on a line, but with idea units. The speed and cogency of fluent reading could only be explained, he argued, if readers worked from visual features directly to meaning. And he meant this quite literally. Skillful reading does not, he insisted, involve reading just one word in four or one in ten. Instead, he believed, skillful readers utilize just a fourth or a tenth of the information available from every word; they take in several lines of text at once as they have developed the ability to recognize meaning from the scantiest and most efficient sampling of graphic detail.

But what, specifically, could these most useful visual features of text be? Smith (1971) argued that they were necessarily far too diffuse and complex to be consciously known much less taught:

> In one sense, of course, the teacher does "know" what these critical rules of featural and orthographic redundancy are; otherwise, he could not be a fluent reader himself. But this special information about redundancy is not accessible to our aware-

ness, we acquire and use it quite unconsciously, with the unfortunate result that not only can we not pass it on verbally, but we often fail to realize how important it is. And therefore a child may not get the opportunity to acquire a knowledge of redundancy by the only route that is open to him—by experience in reading. (p. 225)

In taking this position, Smith effectively dismissed not only the utility of word- and letter-level instruction but of direct instruction more generally. Children, he concluded, will best learn to read "by experience in reading"—through ample, direct, and unmediated engagement with meaningful text.

To the great benefit of the field, research on meaning and comprehension flourished in the years following publication of Smith's book. On the other hand, many in the instructional field evidently sought something more concrete to grab hold of, and, quite naturally perhaps, what they very often grabbed was whole words. Reading methods texts began to present routines for developing children's strategic ability to use contextual cues (such as syntax, semantics, and pictures) along with the physical envelopes of words (e.g., the words' lengths, shapes, and initial and final letters) so as to "read" them without worrying about their spellings.

To be sure, this focus on words was a compromise, but in many ways it was an uncomfortable kind of a compromise, neutral to the two positions mostly in failing to respect the fundamental issues and claims of either. Against the wisdom of thus displacing attention to phonics are the facts that research has repeatedly shown that word envelopes (for review, see Woodworth, 1938) and context (for review, see Schatz & Baldwin, 1986) just plain do not provide enough information to permit reliable word identification. And on the other side, such focus on word identification is anathema to Smith's position as well. Indeed from within Smith's framework, such recommendations can be seen to amount to an escape from the theoretically unseemable through the theoretically unseemable: Given a flat and serial model of information processing, there can be no mechanism for handling such parallel, multilevel, interactive cues—that, after all, was Smith's basis for dismissing the possibility that reading involved identification of letters and words. And, ultimately, there lay the problem: with the theory.

In fact, Smith was correct in arguing that skillful reading could not proceed through one-at-a-time identification of letters or words. Yet, instead of casting aside the linear one-at-a-time model of behavior and thought that prevailed, he had reached for informational chunks (Miller, 1956)—idea units—big enough to be handled with adequate speed and efficiency within it (note, too, that George Miller was Smith's graduate advisor). Even in retrospect, Smith's analysis of the reading process was tremendously insightful. And, given his starting assumptions, his theory was bold, broad, and creative. But it was also of the day; it was in a real sense a casualty of its own making. Thanks in part to technology, in part to the increased sophistication of the science, but in no small measure to research that Smith's argument provoked, we now know that in skillful reading the mind works interactively and in parallel with as many cues as it can recognize as relevant—and that integrally includes words and their spellings.

Over the last 20 years, research has demonstrated that, for normal adult readers, meaningful text—regardless of its ease or difficulty—is read through what is essentially a left-to-right, line-by-line, word-by-word process. True, the scanning process is somewhat sensitive to the redundancy or predictability of text in the sense that those words that readers do skip over tend to be short function words, such as *in, of, and, to,* and *the* (McClelland & O'Regan, 1981). Nevertheless, when readers skip, they almost never skip more than one word in a row. In the end, many function words and the vast majority of content words receive the reader's direct gaze (Just & Carpenter, 1987).

Moreover, research has demonstrated repeatedly and through a host of different paradigms that skillful readers visually process virtually every letter of every word they read. They do so whether they are reading isolated words or meaningful connected text. They do so regardless of semantic, syntactic, or orthographic predictability of what they are reading. Furthermore, their eye movements indicate that, even in the absence of conscious awareness, the visual system tends to notice the slightest misspelling, even when it involves a visually similar letter and is buried deep in the middle of a long word that is highly predictable from context that precedes it (McConkie & Zola, 1981).

The way this works is schematized in Fig. 1.1. Within each of the "processors," knowledge is represented by constellations of simpler units. Within the orthographic processor, for example, individual letters are represented as interconnected bundles of more elementary visual features, whereas printed words are represented as interconnected bundles of letters. Similarly, the meaning of a familiar word corresponds to some interconnected set of meaning elements, just as its pronunciation corresponds to an interconnected complex of elementary speech sounds.

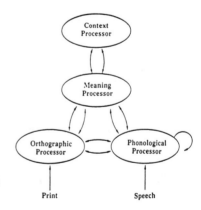

FIG. 1.1. Modeling the reading system: Four processors.

I use the term "processors" in quotes to emphasize that it is mostly in the interest of descriptive convenience that I have separated them, one from another: The functional associations among the pieces of one's knowledge depend, not on the "processor" in which each resides, but on the ways in which they have become interrelated or connected through experience. Indeed, the interconnections among any set of representational units are nothing more than a cumulative record of the ways in which those units have been related to one another in a person's experience. It thus follows that, regardless of the various modalities of its parts, the more frequently that any pattern of activity has been brought to mind, the stronger and more complete will be the bonds that hold it together.

Once the connections have been laid down, they serve the very useful purpose of passing excitation among the elements they link together. For skillful readers, then, even as the letters of a word in fixation are recognized, they activate the spelling patterns, pronunciations, and meanings with which they are compatible. At the same time, using its larger knowledge of the text, the context processor swings its own bias among any rival candidates so as to maintain the coherence of the message. And as each processor hones in on the word's identity, it relays its hypothesis back to all the others such that, wherever hypotheses agree among processors, their resolution is speeded and strengthened. In this way, as initiated by the print on the page and facilitated through feedback and feedforward both within and between the processors, skillful readers come to recognize the spelling, sound, meaning, and contextual role of a familiar word almost automatically and simultaneously, leaving their active attention free for critical and reflective thought.

But here lies a key point: The amount of stimulation that any set of units can pass to any other depends strictly on the strength and completeness of the connections between them. The strength and completeness of the connections between them, in turn, depend strictly on learning. Ultimately, readers come to look and feel like they recognize words holistically because they have acquired a deep, richly interconnected, and ready knowledge of their spellings, sounds, and meanings. However, to the extent that readers make a habit of skipping, glossing, or guessing at unfamiliar words, there can be no opportunity for such knowledge to develop. Skillful readers automatically and quite thoroughly process the component letters of text because their visual knowledge of words is built from memories of the sequences of letters of which the words are comprised. Conversely, because they do so, their orthographic knowledge is reinforced and enriched with each word they read.

Is it Useful for Young Readers to Appreciate the Correspondences Between Spellings and Sounds?

Research demonstrates that, at least at the level of mental activity, skillful readers automatically and rather irrepressibly translate print to speech while they read (for a review, see Patterson & Coltheart, 1987). In Fig. 1.1, this phenomenon is captured by the direct connections between the orthographic and the phonological processors. Yet, the orthographic processor is also directly connected to the meaning processor, indicating that the meaning of a familiar word may be activated just as quickly as its sound.

Given that meaning activation is the whole point of reading a word, we may thus find some motivation for accepting Smith's contention that, "To the fluent reader, the alphabetic principle is completely irrelevant." Yet, Smith's (1973) dismissal of the value of spelling–sound correspondences extended beyond that: "It is sometimes argued that decoding to sound must take place at least when the reader meets a word that he cannot identify on sight. Decoding to sound is the last resort of any reader. Instead the fluent reader ignores the occasional word that is not in his sight vocabulary. He takes advantage of the fact that 1 word in 5 can be completely eliminated from most English text (Shannon, 1951) with scarcely any effect on its overall comprehensibility" (p. 79). To understand the difficulties with this claim, we must back off a moment. Much as Smith argued, thoughtful comprehension is obstructed wherever a reader must deliberate too long or too hard on the identity of the separate words of a text. Not only is active attention limited, but the interfacilitation and coordination of the system depends critically on the speed with which the pieces arrive. Fortunately, then, any word that is highly familiar will be mapped directly, instantly, and effortlessly from sight to meaning. Yet, printed words vary enormously in their frequency of occurrence. By force of probabilities, they must range just as widely in their visual familiarity and accessibility—even for the skillful reader.

To estimate the frequencies with which different words are likely to be encountered by children, Carroll, Davies, and Richman (1971) sampled 5,088,721 words from their school and home reading materials. Counting the number of times each different word occurred, they found that fully 50% of the sample was represented by just 109 very commonly used words. Furthermore, 75% of the sample was made up of only 1,000 different words, and even 90%—or roughly 4,500,000 of the more than 5,000,000 that were sampled—was accounted for by only 5,000 different words.

It is not unreasonable to suppose that, not too far into their school careers and regardless of how they were taught, most children will recognize most of the 5,000 words with no need of phonological medication. However, those 5,000 words represented only a small fraction—about 5%—of the number of *different* words that Carroll et al. encountered. Of the remaining 80,000 or so words— 95% of the total number of different words that were turned up in the sample— each was found to appear no more than a few times per million words of running text.

How infrequently is that? The average fifth-grade student reads approximately 1 million words of text a year, in school and out (Anderson, Wilson, & Fielding, 1988). By implication, she or he must be lucky to encounter any of these words even once in a whole year's worth of reading. It follows that few if any of these less frequent words will be sufficiently familiar to the child to be recognized at a glance.

Is the child's best option really to ignore all such words? It is, in fact, statistically demonstrable that English is sufficiently predictable that an equivalent of 1 word in 5 is informationally redundant (Shannon, 1951). But that is quite different from Smith's suggestion that 1 word—pick a word, any word—in 5 can be eliminated without affecting a text's comprehensibility. The problem is that linguistic information is not evenly distributed across words: Whereas the coherence and connectivity of a text depend strongly on its frequent words, the information in a text derives disproportionately from its less frequent words.

To convince yourself of this, just complete the meaning carried by frequent versus infrequent words in a text, for example:

Frequent Words	Infrequent Words
get	fever
from	disease
or	infection
some	medicine
by	Alexander Fleming
saw	mold
on	melon
was	penicillin
can	protect
from	germs

Can you guess what the passage from which these words were taken was about? Could you guess what it was about by attending only to the frequent words while ignoring the infrequent ones? One point of this example is that the practicality of Smith's recommendation runs wholly counter to its utility: Although the identities of the *frequent* words may be guessable from the *infrequent* ones, the converse is highly unlikely. The larger point is that children cannot gain knowledge from or understanding of a text by reading only its frequent words while ignoring its infrequent ones.

In the end, the meaning of a passage depends integrally on its wording, for in text it is necessarily through wording that authors strive to convey their message. Think about it. For how many and which of the documents you read and write (or ask your students to read and write) in a day would some form of telegraphic language truly be adequate? If only a fraction of the words on a page were functional, why would we struggle so to write them in the first place? Written communication depends on wording (see Rubin, 1980), and toward recognizing visually less familiar words, wherever they occur, working knowledge of spelling-to-sound translations is of vital importance for the reader.

For words that are even vaguely familiar, the process of sounding them out serves at once to turn on their meaning while maintaining activation of their spelling. As a consequence, each such effort serves to strengthen not only the child's knowledge of the word's spelling but also its spelling-to-meaning connections. In keeping with this, phonics instruction has been shown to lead to significantly stronger vocabulary development among young readers (Eldridge, Quinn, & Butterfield, 1990).

Sometimes, of course, children will encounter a word whose meaning is entirely unfamiliar. Even so, if the sounding process is sufficiently rapid, the linkages of the system are such that the word and its pronunciation will become connected to the meaning of the surrounding context; in this way, its meaning will be seeded for future reference and growth. Sometimes, too, the decoding process will be disruptively slow or laborious. In these cases, for the child just as for you, the solution is to reread the sentence from the start once the word has been worked out.

For skillful readers, phonological translations provide an automatic backup system for recognizing visually less familiar words. Even where a word as a whole is not visually familiar, fragments of its spelling almost certainly will be. To the extent that our orthography is alphabetic, after all, speakable syllables are necessarily represented by frequent spelling patterns. Courtesy of the reader's overlearned spelling–sound connections, these spelling patterns will be translated automatically to their phonological equivalents. As a result, even the occasional never-before-seen word may be read off with little outward sign of difficulty. Just try it:

hypermetropical

hackmatack

thigmotaxis

For you, as a skillful reader, such words are easy to decode—so easy, in fact, that if you had known the meanings of these words and if they had appeared in meaningful connected text you might have read right through them without even noticing that you had never seen them before. Indeed, this may well be the greatest benefit of the phonological connections for skillful readers. By meeting, reduplicating, and supplementing the word recognition efforts of the visual system, they ensure that those many words of known meaning but marginal visual familiarity will be recognized with the ease and speed on which fluency and comprehension depend. It is the automaticity of skillful readers' spelling-to-sound translations that saves them from lurching through text with the pace and pause that would otherwise be dictated by the uneven visual familiarity of the words. (And note that the frequency distributions for adult texts are very similar to those for children; Kucera & Francis, 1967.)

In fact, print-to-speech translation meets another need quite independent of word identification. As Smith (1973) pointed out, "many fluent readers tend to subvocalize when confronted with unfamiliar material" (p. 81). In order to interpret a clause or sentence, readers must be able to remember it from beginning to end—they must be able to get the last word of the clause into their memories before the first ones fade away. By thinking or speaking the words to themselves, readers effectively extend the longevity and holding capacity of their verbatim memory (Baddeley, 1986). Preventing skillful readers from subvocalizing does not impair their ability to interpret single familiar words or simple sentences. On the other hand, it severely disrupts their ability to remember or comprehend long or complex sentences (Waters, Caplan, & Hildebrand, 1987). But again, this is a strategy that works effectively only to the extent that it works automatically.

Is it Useful to Provide Instructional Support to Young Readers in Spellings and Spelling–Sound Correspondences?

Across the centuries, methods to help children attend to the sequences of letters and their correspondences to speech patterns have, one way or another, been built into a majority of approaches invented for helping people to read and write alphabetic languages (Feitelson, 1988; Mathews, 1966; Richardson, 1991; Smith, 1974). Even among the Greeks, even with the very advent of the alphabetic system of writing, such methods were core (Mathews, 1966).

For just as long, however, there have periodically cropped up various objections and alternatives to teaching phonics (see Balmuth, 1982). After all, it is argued, if reading for meaning is the very purpose of the exercise, then is it not misguided, even counterproductive, to focus the reader's attention on the individual letters and their sounds? Again, Frank Smith's first book, *Understanding Reading,* offered renewed vigor to these objections through new motivations.

Just a few years before publication of Smith's book, Noam Chomsky (1965) had shaken the psychological world by proving that human language acquisition defied explanations through our standard linear model. Human language was too rich and too varied. Clearly, any speaker could, in principal, produce an infinite number of sentences of infinite length. Whatever the units of learning might be—phonemes, words, or even whole phrases—it was impossible that this capacity could be acquired by learning to imitate and connect them one by one to each other. Furthermore, despite all the complexity of the challenge, despite the noisiness—the blunders, false starts, interruptions, and so forth—of the signal, despite the apparent absence of any universally endorsed instructional science on first-language acquisition, nearly all humans, world around, essentially master their native language within the first few years of life. (As Smith commented,

"There are relatively few books on such topics as 'Why Johnny can't talk,'" p. 49).

The answer, it was proposed, could only be that babies were innately prepared to learn language. With a prewired Language Acquisition Device, or LAD as it was known, human infants were seen to be endowed from birth with a deep knowledge of the essential physical, grammatical, and semantic components of all human languages. To become linguistically competent in their native language, children need only discover which of the various options were operative in their own community of speakers. They did so, it was proposed, through a process of systematically testing, refining, and reformulating their built-in linguistic hypotheses (Chomsky, 1965; McNeil, 1970).

Faced with the seeming inexplicability of written language acquisition, Smith (1971) suggested that it, too, might be governed by the Language Acquisition Device:

> The picture that has been presented shows a child from the very beginning of his life looking for rules that will provide him with the key to the language community in which he finds himself. The child has rules for learning rules, and he tests to see which particular rules apply. We shall see in due course that precisely the same kind of argument may be applied to reading—that basically a child is equipped with every skill that he needs in order to read and to learn to read; all that he needs to discover is the particular rules that apply. When we view the role of the child in this new light, we also see a different role for the adult in the language-learning process. We can perhaps gain some insights into the task of the reading teacher if we understand the function of adults when a child is learning to speak. (p. 55)

Putting it all together, Smith (1971) concluded that, given adequate and motivated experience with meaningful text, learning to read should be as natural as learning to talk. At the same time, he urged against any overemphasis on phonics for three reasons. First, "to a large extent the child has to learn these phonic rules for himself, and he will only acquire them through experience in reading" (p. 226). Second, a child who stops to decode every word of text will read too slowly to capture its meaning, and, within Smith's theory, it is the meaning and flow of text that ultimately support learning about its most useful features. Third, given too much teaching, a child might treat the task of learning to read as one of memorizing isolated instances instead of inducing general rules. Turning to the instructional implications of this view, Smith concluded that, beyond providing materials and opportunities for reading, the teacher's most important job was one of providing feedback. But it must be very sensitive feedback. For, most of all, he argued, the teacher must create the kind of positive and supportive environment that would best encourage students to take on the risky business of testing new hypotheses.

Now, 20 years later, the notion that humans are innately predisposed toward learning to speak has become generally accepted. That is not, however, to say that babies learn to speak without help. To the contrary, research has firmly demonstrated that most parents, perhaps unintentionally but both methodically and effectively, do tutor their babies in the syntax, semantics, and diction of their native language (e.g., Snow, 1986). Even so, with respect to literacy development, the most serious criticism of the let-them-learn-it-through-experience philosophy is that learning to read depends on certain insights and observations that, for many children, are simply not forthcoming without some special guidance.

A major category of such insights and observations pivots on the child's awareness of the word and sound structure of their language. One way or another, a number of different types of linguistic awareness are presupposed in the dialogues and activities of beginning reading instruction. Yet, within this category it is preschoolers' awareness of phonemes (the speech sounds that correspond roughly to individual letters) that has been shown to hold the most impressive predictive power, statistically accounting for as much as 50% of the variance in their reading proficiency at the end of first grade (see, e.g., Blachman, 1984; Juel, 1991; Stanovich, 1986).

Moreover, faced with an alphabetic script, the child's level of phonemic awareness on entering school is widely held to be the strongest single determinant of the success she or he will experience in learning to read and of the likelihood that she or he will fail (see Stanovich, 1986). Measures of preschoolers' level of phonemic awareness strongly predict their future success in learning to read, and this has been demonstrated not only for English but also for Swedish (Lundberg, Olofsson, & Wall, 1980), Spanish (deManrique & Gramigna, 1984), French (Alegria, Pignot, & Morais, 1982), and Russian (Elkonin, 1973). Measures of schoolchildren's ability to attend to and manipulate phonemes strongly correlate with their reading success all the way through the 12th grade (Calfee, Lindamood, & Lindamood, 1973). Poorly developed phonemic awareness distinguishes economically disadvantaged preschoolers from their more advantaged peers (Wallach, Wallach, Dozier, & Kaplan, 1977) and has been shown to be characteristic of adults with literacy problems in America (Liberman, Rubin, Duques, & Carlisle, 1985), Portugal (Morais, Cary, Alegria, & Bertelson, 1979), England (Marcel, 1980), and Australia (Byrne & Ledez, 1983). Indeed, among readers of alphabetic languages, those who are successful invariably have phonemic awareness, whereas those who lack phonemic awareness are invariably struggling (see especially Tunmer & Nesdale, 1985).

To be sure, children's sensitivity to the phonemic structure of words and syllables grows substantially in breadth and depth as their reading and writing skills mature. Yet at its most fundamental level, the basic awareness of the nature and existence of phonemes seems to qualify as a genuine insight. There are wholly understandable reasons for the elusiveness of this insight. For one, phonemes are acoustically sloppy entities (phonemes are cleanly defined not by their sounds, but by their ideal place and manner of articulation). Further, in the course of normal language production or comprehension, people's attention is necessarily trained to the meaning of the message; the processing of individual speech sounds and of gestures of the tongue or lips occurs nearly effortlessly and subattentionally, rather like the processing of individual printed letters by skillful readers.

Understandable or not, however, basic phonemic awareness is an insight that eludes many. Even among eminent Chinese scholars, awareness of phonemes is rare unless they have studied an alphabetic language (Read, Yun-Fei, Hong-Yin, & Bao-Qing, 1986). More to the point, phonemic awareness is shown to escape roughly 25% of American first graders—and were the samples restricted to children from print-poor home environments, that percentage would be substantially larger (Adams, 1990).

Given the indication that so many children lack basic phonemic awareness on one hand and that phonemic awareness is truly so critical for learning to read and write an alphabetic script on the other, it is clearly a domain that begs instructional support. Happily, then, a number of studies have demonstrated that children's awareness of phonemes can be effectively awakened and refined through instruction (for a review, see Adams, 1990). Further, a number of investigators have demonstrated that programs of games and activities designed to develop phonemic awareness result in significant acceleration of the children's subsequent reading and writing achievement (e.g., Ball & Blachman, 1991; Bradley & Bryant, 1983; Lundberg, Frost, & Petersen, 1988; Wallach & Wallach, 1979; Williams, 1980).

In learning to read, the value of phonemes lies in their linkages with spellings and, in keeping with this, preschoolers' familiarity with the letters of the alphabet is also a powerful determinant of the success with which they will learn to read (Bond & Dykstra, 1967; Chall, 1967). Beyond global correlations, young children's knowledge of letter names has been shown to turn spontaneously, or at least easily, into interest in their sounds and in the spellings of words (Chomsky, 1979; Mason, 1980; Read, 1971). In addition, knowing letters is strongly correlated with the ability to remember the forms of written words and the tendency to treat them as ordered sequences of letters rather than holistic patterns (Ehri, 1986, 1987; Ehri & Wilce, 1985), whereas not knowing letters is coupled with extreme difficulty in learning letter sounds (Mason, 1980) and word recognition (Mason, 1980; Sulzby, 1983).

Notably, measures of letter familiarity are losing their predictive potency in large sample investigations because so many children (thanks largely, no doubt, to "Sesame Street") now know their ABCs on first-grade entry (Durrell & Catterson, 1980; McCormick & Mason, 1986; Nurss, 1979). Yet preschoolers' basic familiarity with the letters of the alphabet is still found to be markedly weak in communities with a profile of relatively poor literacy success (Masonheimer, 1982; McCormick & Mason, 1986).

Until letter recognition is reasonably easy, children cannot begin to learn to recognize printed words productively; until letter production is reasonably comfortable, they cannot and/or will not begin to write productively. With respect to the task and for the child, learning to recognize and discriminate printed letters is just too basic, too big, and too fussy a task to be presumed or left alone. Finding ways to ensure that all children are developing a comfortable knowledge of letters should be a priority concern at entry levels.

Lest I be misunderstood, I am not suggesting that either phonemic awareness or letter knowledge be developed to perfection before moving on. Many children will continue to confuse certain letters and "mishear" certain sounds for quite awhile. That is okay. Given sensitive support, both will refine themselves through experience with reading and writing. Indeed, once the children have established a basic awareness of phonemes and a willingness to print, independent writing is an excellent means of further developing both of these capacities. A major advantage of encouraging beginners to write independently is that their products provide an ever-updated and nonintrusive record of their growth or difficulties with print skills, spelling, and phonemic awareness. By monitoring a child's writing, teachers can very often discern both where she or he needs help and when such help might best be offered (see, e.g., Mann, 1986). During those critical "using but confusing" interludes, the formalities of print can be developed with far more efficiency and force than through any arbitrarily scheduled drill and practice.

In a real sense, however, this affordance is but one reflection of a more fundamental, encompassing, and, to my mind, compelling motive for encouraging independent writing. Specifically, in asking children to generate their own spellings, one is effectively challenging them to reflect on the sounds of words and their relations to letters. It is a way of communicating to the children, not that their key job is to memorize a set of individual letter–sound pairings, one by one as revealed by the teacher. It is a way of communicating, instead, that English orthography has a system; that it has a logic that can be understood, by them, through reflection. It is a way of causing the children to think about the sounds of words and their written representations, and there is no more powerful pill for learning than thinking. In keeping with this, children who are given ample opportunity, from the start, to write and spell independently have been shown to exhibit exceptional growth in both word recognition and spelling (Clarke, 1988).

Unfortunately, not all the conventions of English orthography are intuitable. To read or write well, children must eventually learn how to spell correctly, which means that they must sometimes be helped to spell correctly. Although concern is sometimes voiced that independent spelling will interfere with this effort, Uhry and Shepherd (1990) have documented the opposite effect. They presented 6 months of systematic instruction in segmenting and spelling to two groups of children. One group had previously had some phonics instruction along with lots of independent writing; the other had had more phonics but without the independent writing. With Uhry and Shepherd's program, children in the first group grew rapidly such that, by the end, they demonstrated significantly greater proficiency in both word recognition and oral reading fluency than the others. Again, the suggestion is that the children's experience in spelling independently seemed not to obstruct but to promote their ability to internalize the formal spellings.

As valuable as writing is, however, it is not enough. As well known to all who have worked with young writers, children very often cannot read what they can write or even what they have just written (see, e.g., Chomsky, 1979). In the end, reading with fluency and comprehension depends on a prodigious amount of perceptual learning. In significant measure, just as this learning is specific to reading, it can only be gained through reading. Recall the novel word reading challenge that I presented earlier. If you listened to yourself as you read those words *(hypermetropical, hackmatack, thigmotaxis),* you probably heard yourself sounding them in something closer to a syllable-by-syllable than any letter-by-letter process. By comparison, reflect on the difficulty of reading such non-English words as *Wloclawek, Verkhneudinsk, Shihkiachwang,* or *Bydgoszcz.* The ability to decode proficiently and nondisruptively while reading depends integrally on familiarity, not just with individual letter–sound correspondences, but with the spelling patterns from which frequent words and syllables are comprised.

As it happens, the human memory system is designed to learn quite automatically about such sequential patterns—but only to the extent that the perceptual system works with them. The problem is that children's natural tendency seems to be one of examining words more as holistic patterns than as any left-to-right sequence of symbols (Byrne & Fielding-Barnesley, 1989). (After all, this inclination is quite appropriate for virtually all else in their perceptual worlds.)

From this perspective, phonics instruction per se takes on a very special value. To sound out a new word as they read, children must attend to each and every one of its letters, in left-to-right order. Importantly, however, it is not just teaching children phonics that makes a difference but persuading them to use it, and a strong determinant of the latter lies in whether the children find it useful in their earliest efforts after print (Juel & Roper/Schneider, 1985).

Juel and Roper/Schneider (1985) studied two groups of first-grade children across the school year. Both groups received the same program of phonics instruction, and tests indicated that they had learned what they had been taught equally well. However, whereas the first group began reading with preprimers that were built around short decodable words, the other group used a preprimer in which vocabulary was biased instead toward high-frequency words. Although the wordings of the children's books were more or less comparable beyond the preprimer, Juel and Roper/Schneider found distinctive differences in the two groups' word recognition growth. Across the year, the first group showed consistent evidence of using their phonics and even extending it autonomously beyond what they had been taught. The second group, in contrast, tended to depend more on the uniqueness or visual distinctiveness of words for their recognition, showing little tendency to use their phonic knowledge beyond the immediate context of its instruction. By the end of the year, the first group was significantly better than the second at reading new words.

The most frequently cited disadvantage of encouraging children to sound out new words is that it may cause them to become "word-callers"—to become so absorbed in the decoding process that they lose track of meaning. In fact, research affirms that, midway through first grade or so, children tend to shift away from contextually appropriate miscues toward errors that maintain graphemic similarity to the print of the page (Biemiller, 1970; Juel & Roper/Schneider, 1985; Weber, 1970a, 1970b). Yet, these same studies also demonstrate that, as the children's word recognition skills improve, their respect for context returns.

In the end, young readers' tendency to subordinate internal coherence to the external stimulus seems not only temporary but also highly functional (Downing, 1979). As the children internalize the spellings of more and more words, it will happen less and less often. Meanwhile, the only way for them to reach that point is by lending attention to unfamiliar spelling patterns. Indeed, research suggests that, beyond phonemic awareness and sheer bulk of reading experience, readers' inclination to examine rather than gloss the spellings of new words may well be the strongest determinant of their orthographic facility (Stanovich, West, & Cunningham, 1991). And, on the opposite side of the coin, work with second graders shows that, once an unfamiliar word has been decoded and reread just a few times, its recognition remains speeded significantly and quite enduringly (Reitsma, 1983).

SUMMARY

In summary, it is not, as Smith claimed, that skillful readers exploit an automatic ability to recognize the meaning of a text in order to figure out its words. Instead, they depend on automatic recognition of the words of a text so that they can think about its meaning.

Although the orthographic, syntactic, and semantic redundancy of text is highly functional for readers, this is less because it allows readers to skip most of what is printed on the page than because it assists their ability to read it. Unavoidably, text contains polysemous words, homographs, and other forms of ambiguity. Unavoidably, there sometimes occurs a misperceived letter or a glitch in the print. Unavoidably, we encounter words whose meanings are vague to our minds, even words whose meanings we might be unable to retrieve in isolation. Unavoidably, we are sometimes liable to misparsing a sentence or mislinking a pronoun. Indeed, all such types of misses may occur far more often than we ever notice, for normally, by virtue of the redundancy of the text along with the interactive nature of the knowledge and processes involved in reading, such slips are repaired before ever reaching consciousness. The redundancy of text—of its syntax, semantics, and orthography—is highly functional, not because it allows for skipping, but because it supplies the superabundance of information that protects the literal comprehension process from going astray.

But neither is literal comprehension the goal of reading. Rather, the priority issues while reading should include: Why am I reading this and how does this information relate to my reasons for so doing? What are the author's underlying assumptions? Do I understand what the author is saying and why? To what is the author alluding? If I do not know, do I need to? Was it mentioned earlier in the text or is it something the author expects me to know otherwise? Is the text internally consistent? Is it consistent with what I already know and believe or have learned elsewhere? If not, where does it depart, and what can I think about the discrepancy? Attention to such issues is necessarily thought intensive. It requires analytic, evaluative, and reflective access to local and long-term memory. But in it lies the essence of productive reading.

Learning about spellings and spelling–sound relations is a very small component of the literacy challenge. Yet, it is also wholly necessary in meeting that challenge. In the end, the print on the page constitutes the basic perceptual data of reading. Rather than diverting efforts after meaning, the reader's letter- and word-wise processes supply the text-based information on which comprehension depends. As fluent readers move quickly and easily through the print, literal comprehension automatically unfolds apace, leaving their active thoughtful attention free to revel in the knowledge, pleasures, and rewards of literacy.

REFERENCES

Adams, M. J. (1990). *Beginning to read: Thinking and learning about print.* Cambridge, MA: The MIT Press.

Alegria, J., Pignot, E., & Morais, J. (1982). Phonetic analysis of speech and memory codes in beginning readers. *Memory & Cognition, 10,* 451–456.

Anderson, R. C., Wilson, P., & Fielding, L. (1988). Growth in reading and how children spend their time outside of school. *Reaching Research Quarterly, 23,* 285–303.

Arter, J. A., & Jenkins, J. R. (1977). Examining the benefits and prevalence of modality considerations in special education. *Journal of Special Education, 11,* 281–298.

Aukerman, R. C. (1971). *Approaches to beginning reading.* New York: Wiley.

Aukerman, R. C. (1984). *Approaches to beginning reading* (2nd ed.). New York: Wiley.

Baddeley, A. D. (1986). *Working memory.* New York: Oxford University Press.

Ball, E. W., & Blachman, B. A. (1991). Does phoneme segmentation training in kindergarten make a difference in early word recognition and developmental spelling? *Reading Research Quarterly, 26,* 49–66.

Balmuth, M. 1982). *The roots of phonics.* New York: Teachers College Press.

Biemiller, A. (1970). The development of the use of graphic and contextual information as children learn to read. *Reading Research Quarterly, 6,* 223–253.

Blachman, B. A. (1984). Language analysis skills and early reading acquisition. In G. Wallach & K. Butler (Eds.), *Language learning disabilities in school-age children* (pp. 271–287). Baltimore: Williams & Wilkins.

Bond, G. L., & Dykstra, R. (1967). The cooperative research program in first-grade reading instruction. *Reading Research Quarterly, 2,* 5–142.

Bradley, L., & Bryant, P. E. (1983). Categorizing sounds and learning to read—a causal connection. *Nature, 301,* 419–421.

Byrne, B., & Fielding-Barnesley, R. (1989). Phonemic awareness and letter knowledge in the child's acquisition of the alphabetic principle. *Journal of Educational Psychology, 81,* 313–321.

Byrne, B., & Ledez, J. (1983). Phonological awareness in reading disabled adults. *Australian Journal of Psychology, 35,* 185–197.

Calfee, R. C., Lindamood, P. E., & Lindamood, C. H. (1973). Acoustic/phonetic skills and reading: Kindergarten through twelfth grade. *Journal of Educational Psychology, 64,* 293–298.

Carbo, M., Dunn, R., & Dunn, K. (1986). *Teaching students to read through their individual learning styles.* Englewood Cliffs, NJ: Prentice–Hall.

Carroll, J. B., Davies, P., & Richman, B. (1971). *Word frequency book.* Boston: Houghton Mifflin.

Chall, J. S. (1967). *Learning to read: The great debate.* New York: McGraw–Hill.

Chomsky, C. (1979). Approaching reading through invented spelling. In L. B. Resnick & P. A. Weaver (Eds.), *Theory and practice of early reading* (Vol. 2, pp. 43–65). Hillsdale, NJ: Lawrence Erlbaum Associates.

Chomsky, N. (1965). *Aspects of a theory of syntax.* Cambridge, MA: The MIT Press.

Clarke, L. K. (1988). Invented versus traditional spelling in first graders' writing: Effects on learning to spell and read. *Research in the Teaching of English, 22,* 281–309.

deManrique, A. M. B., & Gramigna, S. (1984). La segmentacion fonologica y silabica en ninos de preescolar y primer grado. [Phonological and syllable segmentation among preschool and primary grade children.] *Lectura y Vida, 5,* 4–13.

Downing, J. (1979). *Reading and reasoning.* New York: Springer–Verlag.

Durrell, D. D., & Catterson, J. H. (1980). *Manual directions: Durrell analysis of reading difficulty* (rev. ed.). New York: Psychological Corporation.

Ehri, L. C. (1986). Sources of difficulty in learning to spell and read. In M. L. Wolraich & D. Routh (Eds.), *Advances in developmental and behavioral pediatrics* (Vol. 7, pp. 121–195). Greenwich, CT: JAI Press.

Ehri, L. C. (1987). Learning to read and spell words. *Journal of Reading Behavior, 19,* 5–31.

Ehri, L. C., & Wilce, L. S. (1985). Movement into reading: Is the first stage of printed word learning visual or phonetic? *Reading Research Quarterly, 20,* 163–179.

Eldridge, J. L., Quinn, B., & Butterfield, D. D. (1990). Causal relationships between phonics, reading comprehension, and vocabulary achievement in the second grade. *Journal of Educational Research, 83,* 201–214.

Elkonin, D. B. (1973). USSR. In J. Downing (Ed.), *Comparative reading: Cross-national studies of behaviour and processes in reading and writing.* New York: Macmillan.

Feitelson, D. (1988). *Facts and fads in beginning reading: A cross-language perspective.* Norwood, NJ: Ablex.

Juel, C. (1991). Beginning reading. In R. Barr, M. L. Kamil, P. B. Mosenthal, & P. D. Pearson (Eds.), *Handbook of reading research* (Vol. 2, pp. 759–788). New York: Longman.

Juel, C., & Roper/Schneider, D. (1985). The influence of basal readers on first-grade reading. *Reading Research Quarterly, 20,* 134–152.

Just, M. A., & Carpenter, P. A. (1987). *The psychology of reading and language comprehension.* Boston: Allyn & Bacon.

Kucera, H., & Francis, W. N. (1967). *Computational analysis of present-day American English.* Providence, RI: Brown University Press.

Liberman, I. Y., Rubin, H., Duques, S., & Carlisle, J. (1985). Linguistic abilities and spelling proficiency in kindergartners and adult poor spellers. In D. B. Gray & J. F. Kavanagh (Eds.), *Biobehavioral measures of dyslexia* (pp. 163–176). Parkton, MD: New York Press.

Lundberg, I., Frost, J., & Petersen, O.-P. (1988). Effects of an extensive program for stimulating phonological awareness in preschool children. *Reading Research Quarterly, 23*, 264–284.

Lundberg, I., Olofsson, A., & Wall, S. (1980). Reading and spelling skills in the first school years predicted from phonemic awareness skills in kindergarten. *Scandinavian Journal of Psychology, 21*, 159–173.

Mann, V. A. (1986). Phonological awareness: The role of reading experience. *Cognition, 24*, 65–92.

Marcel, A. (1980). Phonological awareness and phonological representation: Investigation of a specific spelling problem. In U. Frith (Ed.), *Cognitive processes in spelling* (pp. 373–403). New York: Academic Press.

Mason, J. M. (1980). When do children begin to read: An exploration of four-year-old children's letter and word reading competencies. *Reading Research Quarterly, 15*, 203–227.

Masonheimer, P. E. (1982). *Alphabetic identification by Spanish speaking three to five year olds.* Unpublished Manuscript. Santa Barbara: University of California.

Mathews, M. M. (1966). *Teaching to read, historically considered.* Chicago: University of Chicago Press.

McClelland, J. L., & O'Regan, J. K. (1981). Expectations increase the benefit derived from parafoveal visual information in reading words aloud. *Journal of Experimental Psychology: Human Perception and Performance, 7*, 634–644.

McConkie, G. W., & Zola, D. (1981). Language constraints and the functional stimulus in reading. In A. M. Lesgold & C. A. Perfetti (Eds.), *Interactive processes in reading* (pp. 155–175). Hillsdale, NJ: Lawrence Erlbaum Associates.

McCormick, C. E., & Mason, J. M. (1986). Intervention procedures for increasing preschool children's interest in and knowledge about reading. In W. H. Teale & E. Sulzby (Eds.), *Emergent literacy: Writing and reading* (pp. 90–115). Norwood, NJ: Ablex.

McNeil, D. (1970). The development of language. In P. Mussen (Ed.), *Carmichael's manual of child psychology* (Vol. 1, pp. 1061–1162). New York: Wiley.

Miller, G. A. (1956). The magical number seven, plus or minus two. *Psychological Review, 63*, 81–97.

Morais, J., Cary, L., Alegria, J., & Bertelson, P. (1979). Does awareness of speech as a sequence of phonemes arise spontaneously? *Cognition, 7*, 323–331.

Nurss, J. R. (1979). Assessment of readiness. In T. G. Waller & G. E. MacKinnon (Eds.), *Reading research: Advances in theory and practice* (Vol. 1, pp. 31–62). New York: Academic Press.

Patterson, K. E., & Coltheart, V. (1987). Phonological processes in reading: A tutorial review. In M. Coltheart (Ed.), *Attention and performance XII: The psychology of reading.* London: Lawrence Erlbaum Associates.

Perfetti, C. A. (1985). *Reading ability.* New York: Oxford University Press.

Read, C. (1971). Preschool children's knowledge of English phonology. *Harvard Educational Review, 41*, 1–34.

Read, C., Yun-Fei, Z., Hong-Yin, N., & Bao-Qing, D. (1986). The ability to manipulate speech sounds depends on knowing alphabetic writing. *Cognition, 24*, 31–44.

Reitsma, P. (1983). Printed word learning in beginning readers. *Journal of Experimental Child Psychology, 36*, 321–339.

Richardson, S. O. (1991). Evolution of approaches to beginning reading and the need for diversification in education. In W. Ellis (Ed.), *All language and the creation of literacy* (pp. 1–8). Baltimore: Orton Dyslexia Society.

Rubin, A. (1980). A theoretical taxonomy of the differences between oral and written language. In R. J. Spiro, B. C. Bruce, & W. F. Brewer (Eds.), *Theoretical issues in reading comprehension* (pp. 411–438). Hillsdale, NJ: Lawrence Erlbaum Associates.

Schatz, E. K., & Baldwin, R. S. (1986). Context clues are unreliable predictors of word meanings. *Reading Research Quarterly, 21,* 439–453.

Shannon, C. E. (1951). Prediction and entropy of printed English. *Bell Systems Technical Journal, 30,* 50–64.

Smith, F. (1971). *Understanding reading.* New York: Holt Rinehart & Winston.

Smith, F. (1973). *Psycholinguistics and reading.* New York: Holt Rinehart & Winston.

Smith, N. B. (1974). *American reading instruction.* Newark, DE: International Reading Association.

Snow, C. E. (1986). Conversations with children. In P. Fletcher & M. Garman (Eds.), *Language acquisition* (2nd ed., pp. 69–89). New York: Cambridge University Press.

Stanovich, K. E. (1986). Matthew effects in reading: Some consequences of individual differences in the acquisition of literacy. *Reading Research Quarterly, 21,* 360–406.

Stanovich, K. E., West, R. F., & Cunningham, A. E. (1991). Beyond phonological processes: Print exposure and orthographic processing. In S. A. Brady & D. P. Shankweiler (Eds.), *Phonological processes in literacy* (pp. 219–235). Hillsdale, NJ: Lawrence Erlbaum Associates.

Sulzby, E. (1983). A commentary on Ehri's critique of five studies related to letter-name knowledge and learning to read: Broadening the question. In L. M. Gentile, M. L. Kamil, & J. S. Blanchard (Eds.), *Reading research revisited.* (pp. 155–161.) Columbus, OH: Charles E. Merrill.

Tunmer, W. E., & Nesdale, A. R. (1985). Phonemic segmentation skill and beginning reading. *Journal of Educational Psychology, 77,* 417–427.

Uhry, J. K., & Shepherd, M. J. (1990, April). *The effect of segmentation/spelling training on the acquisition of beginning reading strategies.* Paper presented at the annual meeting of the American Educational Research Association, Boston.

Vernon, M. D. (1971). *Reading and its difficulties.* Cambridge: Cambridge University Press.

Wallach, L., Wallach, M. A., Dozier, M. G., & Kaplan, N. E. (1977). Poor children learning to read do not have trouble with auditory discrimination but do have trouble with phoneme recognition. *Journal of Educational Psychology, 69,* 36–39.

Wallach, M. A., & Wallach, L. (1979). Helping disadvantaged children learn to read by teaching them phoneme identification skills. In L. A. Resnick & P. A. Weaver (Eds.), *Theory and practice of early reading* (Vol. 3, pp. 227–259). Hillsdale, NJ: Lawrence Erlbaum Associates.

Waters, G., Caplan, D., & Hildebrand, N. (1987). Working memory and written sentence comprehension. In M. Coltheart (Ed.), *Attention and performance XII: The psychology of reading* (pp. 531–555). Hillsdale, NJ: Lawrence Erlbaum Associates.

Weber, R. M. (1970a). A linguistic analysis of first-grade reading errors. *Reading Research Quarterly, 5,* 427–451.

Weber, R. M. (1970b). First-graders' use of grammatical context in reading. In H. Levin & J. P. Williams (Eds.), *Basic studies on reading* (pp. 147–163). New York: Basic Books.

Williams, J. P. (1980). Teaching decoding with a special emphasis on phoneme analysis and phoneme blending. *Journal of Educational Psychology, 72,* 1–15.

Williams, J. P. (1991). The meaning of phonics base for reading instruction. In W. Ellis (Ed.), *All language and the creation of literacy* (pp. 9–19). Baltimore: Orton Dyslexia Society.

Woodworth, R. A. (1938). *Experimental psychology.* New York: Henry Holt.

2 Phonemic Awareness: A Consideration of Research and Practice

Kathleen Copeland
Center for the Study of Reading

Pamela Winsor
University of Lethbridge

Jean Osborn
Center for the Study of Reading

Erickson (1989) pointed out that, "by age three, almost every human child has learned to speak a language with fluency and appropriateness, which is a task far more cognitively complex than learning to read and write in that language once it has been learned" (p. xiii). In view of this accomplishment in acquiring oral language, it would seem that virtually all children should succeed in acquiring literacy. Yet many children do not learn to read and write. Undoubtedly, an array of factors can hinder children's success, and some of these factors are beyond a teacher's capability to alleviate. On the other hand, there is no doubt that sound instruction can make it possible for children to succeed who traditionally are considered to be at risk (e.g., Heath, 1983; McConnell, 1989).

Although not all questions have been answered, research to date has uncovered a great deal about the process of reading and writing. As well, our field has devoted attention to ways instruction can reflect a sensitivity to insights from theory and research. A primary purpose of this chapter is to cast the light of these insights on one dimension of literacy instruction that is receiving increased attention from researchers trying to understand how children learn to read and write. That dimension is phonemic awareness. Although limiting our focus to this one dimension is both helpful and necessary for our purposes here, we hope this discussion will be considered in a much broader context. All literacy instruction should aim to promote children's understanding and enjoyment of the printed word. Moreover, as we discuss, it is not possible to divorce meaningful experiences with print from sound instruction that helps children acquire the written code.

We begin with a literature review that examines children's movement from spoken to written language. Following the review, we present an analysis that focuses specifically on the instruction provided in eight basal reading programs to help children acquire phonemic awareness. We have chosen the instruction in basal reading programs because research shows that, despite the increasing popularity of incorporating children's literature and of giving children extensive opportunities to write, basal programs continue to dominate, and in many cases embody, classroom reading instruction.

CHILDREN'S MOVEMENT FROM SPOKEN TO WRITTEN LANGUAGE

When children enter school, they already know a great deal about language. Studies of children's oral language acquisition tell us that virtually all children have a considerable control of at least one language by the time they are 5 years old (Lindfors, 1980). Without a special curriculum or training, young children actively construct a knowledge of oral language through meaningful exposure to and interaction through language. And as children experience the surface structure of language, they actually learn much more; they acquire an understanding of the underlying structure or organizing principles of language that enables them to create and understand novel utterances. In addition, children also learn about how to use language for different purposes and in different situations.

Similarly, studies of children's early literacy development that show that children can and do learn written language long before they receive formal instruction challenge the notion that school entry marks the onset of literacy. This research proposes that children's acquisition of literacy is akin to their acquisition of oral language, and that they are capable of building an understanding of written language through meaningful experiences with print, either on their own or with others. Furthermore, because they have genuine reasons for making sense and communicating, children are better able to understand and master the parts of written language. In learning to speak, children begin with meaning or a "whole" message long before they have mastered adult forms of language. For example, a child might say "Katie sock" to communicate "This is Katie's sock" or "Give Katie the sock." In time, children refine their knowledge of language and use forms that rely less on context and that are more easily recognized by adults. In learning to read and write, functional uses of spoken language also enhance their understanding of the forms of written language.

Current language research has yielded a greater appreciation for what children can do and of how amazingly adept they are as language learners. Also, this research has prompted theorists to consider the features and demands of acquiring oral and written language. Smith (1984) pointed out that "language, whether spoken or written, produced or comprehended, always is related to intentions and purposes, and children learn about language as they strive to use it" (p. 144). He added that as compared to oral language development, written language development depends entirely on others to show children how this form of language can be used.

In a literate society, virtually all children enter school knowing some things about the functions and nature of written language. However, there are quantitative and qualitative differences in the early encounters children have with print. Some children enter school already knowing a great deal about the purposes and general nature of written language, knowledge that is critical for learning about the code (Reid, 1983; Wells, 1986). These children become familiar with literacy and see its value because reading and writing are a part of their parents' activities at home and at work (Wells, 1986). In many of these homes, parents engage in reading and writing activities with the children. In contrast, other children come to school knowing comparatively little about literacy.

The longitudinal studies of Wells (1986) and Heath (1983) suggest that children must not only possess concepts about print but that they must also have observed and/or participated in literacy experiences surrounding extended pieces of reading and writing. In this way, some children enter school equipped with literacy experiences that work in concert with the school's instructional practices. Sometimes children are so well equipped that they succeed in spite of inadequate school instruction. On the other hand, children who come to school with many fewer literacy experiences are much more vulnerable, and they rely a great deal on solid instruction to succeed as literacy learners.

Special Demands of Literacy.   An examination of some of the special demands of literacy sheds further light on why the transition from spoken to written language can be less than straightforward. Although spoken and written language share certain features, the two also have differences (Olson, 1984; Vygotsky, 1962; Wells, 1986). In the language they use in their everyday conversations, children construct meaning out of events that they experience with someone else, or out of events about which they have expectations or are familiar with. Therefore, they can draw on context to construct meaning. Furthermore, the participants in a conversation are often face to face, making it possible to use gestures, facial expression, and intonation to help determine meaning. In contrast, written language requires both readers and writers to rely to a much greater extent on words alone as cues to meaning.

In learning to read, children must learn to deal with sustained, less elliptical discourse that presents different demands for comprehension, demands that can increase as texts become longer and more complex in and of themselves. Furthermore, children must learn a different code as a means of understanding the words they encounter; that is, children must learn a new way of responding to a verbal message (Reid, 1983). And so, although oral language remains a storehouse of information on which children may capitalize as they grow as readers, nevertheless, they must acquire new strategies for communicating as they learn to read.

Communicating through reading and writing entails an orientation to language that can differ from the use of oral language. According to Olson (1984), "writing preserves the surface structure, the words themselves, which therefore can be subjected to analysis, study, and interpretation, none of which are encouraged by oral language" (p. 186). Focusing on words themselves and understanding the terms for talking about language (e.g., *letter, word*) do not necessarily accompany learning to speak. Yet children's success in reading and writing entails an increase in their metalinguistic awareness, or their ability to reflect on language itself.

Learning About an Alphabetic Script.   Children who learn to read and write in English must gain mastery of an alphabetic script. They must learn how the sounds of spoken language map onto the sequence of letters within words. Yet as both Reid (1983) and Adams (1990) pointed out, English is not a perfectly alphabetic system in which one letter or a group of letters consistently maps onto a given sound. Rather, children must learn that in English a given letter can function as part of a group (e.g., *c, h,* versus *ch*). They must learn as well that individual letters and groups of letters can have different sounds, depending on the letters around them (e.g., *cap, cape, canal, tail*); that is, in the process of learning to read, children need to know how letters function within a given orthographic environment. Even knowing that a letter can make more than one sound is not always enough, because what is often necessary is the need to "contextualize" the letter (Adams, 1990).

Children's prior knowledge as speakers of English can be brought to bear as they master its alphabetic system. In learning to speak, they have learned about sounds that can be "legally" combined to form words. They also have learned about syntax and semantics, or how words can be combined in ways that are "legal." In learning to read and spell, children must integrate information about a word's orthographic features, or the written symbols for the word (Chomsky & Halle, 1968).

Children build an understanding of the orthography of words through their experiences with print, and they begin to orchestrate this knowledge with their prior knowledge of linguistic properties of words (Adams, 1990; Ehri, 1980). Ehri explained that in the beginning children map a few letters of a word to corresponding sounds. As their familiarity with words increases, so does their knowledge of how spoken words are written, making it easier for them to encounter and retain new words. Adams added that meaningful experiences with print are invaluable in helping children contextualize letters and sounds or become sensitive to the orthography of words. At the same time, reading experiences enable children to "amalgamate" their knowledge of syntax and semantics with their growing knowledge of orthography.

Phonemic Awareness and Sound–Symbol Correspondences.   To internalize orthographic patterns, children must understand the principle that English written words are made up of letters that fairly closely correspond to the phonemes, or sounds, of spoken words (Griffith, 1991). Basic to such an understanding is phonemic awareness, a type of metalinguistic awareness that involves understanding that words are composed of individual distinct sounds, and that these sounds can be manipulated. For example, the three-letter word *cup* is composed of three phonemes and three letters, but the four-letter word *ship* is also composed of three phonemes because the initial letters of this word ("sh") represent one sound.

As we have indicated already, children acquire an *unconscious* understanding of phonemes in learning to speak in that they "know" which sounds and sound combinations are possible. As Adams (1990) pointed out, their attention is focused on the meaning of "the collective, ordered stream of words" (p. 294). Yet what they need to do in learning to read an alphabetic script is to devote *conscious* attention to phonemes, such that they "learn to attend to that which [they] have learned not to attend to" (p. 66); that is, they must come to realize that, in addition to having meaning, words are composed of sounds. Griffith (1991) also offered insight about why phonemic awareness enhances children's ability to internalize orthographic patterns: When children have a high degree of phonemic awareness, they are better prepared to complete an internal analysis of a word, so that "when reading, they have the capacity to focus their attention on individual phonemes in words, thus facilitating the storage of phoneme spellings" (p. 231). Similarly, Adams noted how phonemic awareness plays a role in the learning of sound–symbol correspondences: "To the extent to which children have learned to 'hear' phonemes as individual and separable speech sounds, the system will . . . strengthen their ability to remember or 'see' individual letters and spelling patterns" (p. 304).

We have already commented on the important role meaningful reading experiences play in children's internalization of the orthography of words. Children's early writing experiences also can play a valuable role in enhancing their sensitivity to sound–symbol correspondences and their growth in phonemic awareness. When children attempt to represent ideas through print, they are apt to be consciously aware of how words spoken are represented through letters. Vygotsky (1962) wrote: "Writing also requires deliberate analytical action on the part of the child. In speaking, he is hardly conscious of the sounds he pronounces and quite unconscious of the mental operations he performs. In writing, he must take cognizance of the sound structure of each word, dissect it, and reproduce it in alphabetical symbols, which he must have studied and memorized before" (p. 99). A great deal of evidence indicates that giving children the opportunity to use invented spelling is a prime way to help them develop phonemic awareness and an understanding of the alphabetic principle. This understanding will, in turn, promote growth in word recognition and the conventional spelling of words (Clarke, 1988; Ehri, 1988; Griffith, 1991). When children use invented spelling, they spell words according to the way the words sound to them.

At the outset, children who use invented spelling may have a small measure of phonemic awareness, but in time they are better able to represent the phonemes of words more fully. Research indicates that invented spelling does not hamper children's ability to learn conventional spellings of words. On the contrary, the use of invented spelling is especially helpful in promoting the spelling and recognition of words in lower ability students (Adams, 1990). Another important benefit of invented spelling is that it is an approach to writing many children will use to express their ideas through writing.

In summary, children's movement from spoken to written language includes mastering a written code, which by its very nature requires knowing how spoken sounds are represented by letters. Children must understand this alphabetic principle. Basic to such understanding is phonemic awareness that enables children to attend to letter–sound pairings of words and internalize orthographic representations. Meaningful reading and writing experiences are invaluable ways to help children gain the abilities they need to deal with print. Moreover, meaningful reading and writing experiences provide children real reasons to learn another way to communicate.

PHONEMIC AWARENESS AND EARLY LITERACY INSTRUCTION

To this point, we have referred to phonemic awareness in a global manner. Actually, phonemic awareness can be thought to include several specific types of abilities. Adams (1990) provided a continuum of the kinds of activities associated with phonemic awareness: (a) knowing nursery rhymes; (b) noting similarities and differences among words on the basis of initial, final, or medial sounds; (c) blending given individual sounds to form a word; (d) breaking off the initial phoneme of a word; (e) segmenting a pronounced word into its series of phonemes or indicating how many phonemes are in a pronounced word; (f) manipulating phonemes by pronouncing what a word would become if a given initial, medial, or final sound were removed, or manipulating phonemes by adding phonemes to a word pronounced.

The tasks implied by some of these activities can be too difficult for preschoolers. Segmenting and manipulating phonemes, for example, seem dependent on some progress in reading. Research has shown, however, that acquiring phonemic awareness can be enhanced through instruction (e.g., Bradley & Bryant, 1983; Lundberg, Frost, & Petersen, 1988). And both experimental and longitudinal studies conducted in several countries have shown that some form of phonemic awareness is necessary for learning to read alphabetic languages successfully (see, e.g., Juel, 1988).

Research provides a convincing argument that phonemic awareness is highly correlated with reading success and that it can be taught. What constitutes effective training is less clear, as is whether phonemic awareness is a prerequisite, facilitator, or consequence of reading.

Prerequisite, Facilitator, or Consequence?

Ehri (1980) argued that as children learn to read and spell, they acquire a visual representational system for speech, and that this knowledge of print positively affects their ability to phonemically segment the speech stream. Similarly, Adams (1990) proposed that the pronunciation of a word does not consist of discrete phonemes because, when a word is pronounced, individual phonemes "spill over" into those surrounding them. Thus, knowing that words consist of individual phonemes appears to be learned through literacy experiences.

Morais, Cary, Alegria, and Bertelson (1979) suggested that reading instruction stimulates development of phonemic awareness rather than the reverse. In a study involving illiterate adults and adults who, for social reasons, did not learn to read until adulthood, they found that the illiterate adults performed significantly less accurately on tests of adding and deleting phonemes than did the adults who had learned to read. This suggests that the ability to deal explicitly with phonetic segments is not acquired spontaneously as a consequence of cognitive growth, but rather it is the result of some kind of training. For most people, the necessary training is provided by learning to read.

In her earlier work, Ehri (1979) suggested that phonemic awareness would speed up or ease reading acquisition but was not necessary for learning to read. Williams (1986) also suggested that Mattingly's (1979) proposal of phonemic awareness as a reading readiness requirement might alternatively be interpreted as phonemic analysis being an enabler of faster progress in learning to read.

In a longitudinal study of first graders, Perfetti, Beck, Bell, and Hughes (1987) concluded that initially children can rely on their visual memory of letters, but that eventually success in reading requires phonemic awareness.

It seems evident that dealing with an alphabetic code will be difficult for children who do not progress in their understanding of phonemic awareness. On the other hand, it is not likely that children will acquire phonemic awareness unless they have experiences with an alphabetic script. Thus, withholding instruction from children who are evaluated as "not ready" to read is not called for. Rather, these children must be surrounded with both spoken and written language activities that will contribute to their phonemic awareness.

The Nature of Effective Training

Given that research has shown phonemic awareness to play a critical role in learning to read, it is not surprising that recent attention has been directed to the nature of training phonological skills. Training studies have focused on two questions: (a) What activities are most effective in improving phonemic awareness? and (b) Should training be only oral or should it be accompanied by the presentation of letters?

Effective Training.   In an effort to determine the effectiveness of various training activities, Lewkowicz (1980) categorized 10 phonemic training and testing activities used in research and classrooms according to their usefulness in learning to decode. She determined that two of these activities, blending and segmenting, are basic to decoding. Segmenting entails being able to decompose a word into its individual phonemes or, in other words, to reflect on a word in terms of its individual sounds. Blending entails bringing together isolated sounds to form a word. In a study that confirms the need for children to learn to segment sounds within words, Stanovich, Cunningham, and Cramer (1984) compared children's reading achievement on standardized testing at the end of first grade with their performance on 10 activities similar to those identified by Lewkowicz. They included three activities in a list of those most highly correlated with reading: (a) stating a missing initial consonant, (b) telling which word differs initially from four given words, and (c) indicating which word differs in initial consonant from the first word spoken.

In their study of first graders' acquisition of phonemic awareness and reading skills, Perfetti et al. (1987) demonstrated that blending "taps an essential but primitive knowledge of segmentation" and that "success at reading depends on it" (p. 317).

In a noted study, Williams (1979) found additional support for the training of segmenting and blending. Williams explicitly taught both phoneme analysis and phoneme blending to 7- through 12-year-old children in special classrooms for the learning disabled in New York City. Analysis of the performance of the students who received the training indicated that their reading of not only the trained materials (letter trigrams) but also of transfer materials was superior to that of the control students.

Fox and Routh (1984) also found support for segmenting and blending as valuable training activities. They divided 31 kindergarten children into three groups—one group was trained in both segmenting and blending, another in segmenting only, and a control group received no training. The performance of the children in both segmenting and blending on tasks analogous to reading was superior to both other groups. The segmenting-only group did not differ significantly from the control group. The findings suggest that training in segmenting without blending is insufficient, whereas training in both segmenting and blending is beneficial.

These studies indicate that it is important for children to be able to segment sounds within words and to blend the sounds of words. The next issue to consider is whether these activities should be only oral or involve the use of letters as well.

The Use of Letters in Training Tasks.   Some researchers have used letters in their phonemic awareness training programs with the intent of strengthening children's knowledge of phoneme–grapheme correspondences (Hohn & Ehri, 1983). Yet others have avoided letters on the grounds that their presence detracts from and complicates the auditory segmentation (Lewkowicz, 1980; Roberts, 1975).

Elkonin (1963), whose work provided some very early support for phonemic awareness training, developed a training program that involved the eventual use of letters. His method included a visual model in which a series of connected squares (each square representing a phoneme) represented a word. Initially, he used unmarked tokens to count off the phonemes into the squares, and later the plain tokens were replaced with letters. Elkonin (1963, 1973) reported mastery of phonemic awareness by the children who were taught with this method.

As a part of their longitudinal study, Bradley and Bryant (1983) trained 60 children on tasks of sound organization in four different conditions. The first group used only pictures, the second used pictures and letters, the third learned conceptual categorizing, and the fourth served as the control. Differences in performance were examined in both reading and spelling. No significant differences were found between the pictures-only group and the pictures-and-letters groups on reading tasks, but the group trained with pictures and letters was superior in spelling. The pictures-only group performed significantly better than the no-treatment group on both reading and spelling. The performance of this group was also better, but not significantly so, than that of the conceptual categorizing group. The group trained with pictures and letters significantly outperformed the conceptual and control groups on both reading and spelling. These findings support the use of letters when training for phonemic awareness.

Hohn and Ehri (1983) tested the hypothesis that phonemic segmentation is learned best in the oral mode, and that teaching segmentation with letters confuses learners. Kindergarten children who could not segment phonemically, but who could name at least some letters, were divided into three groups. The first group was taught to segment using letter markers, the second with plain markers, and the third group received no training. Three types of posttests were given: segmenting nonsense words into phonemes, deleting phonemes in nonsense words, and decoding nonsense words. The results did not confirm the researchers' hypothesis but rather favored the use of letter markers in training.

Hohn and Ehri (1983) concluded that letter-using subjects acquired superior segmentation because the letters enabled them to acquire a visual sound-symbolizing system that they could use to distinguish and represent the separate phonemes in memory. The advantage of the letter users over the nonletter-trained group was limited to the training sounds and was not present on the transfer sounds. Both groups, however, outperformed the control group, suggesting that both types of training are effective, but that letters are more effective. In addition, Hohn and Ehri suggested that learning to segment with letters generally promotes knowledge of the alphabetic nature of the language—a concept central to learning to read (Gleitman & Rozin, 1977).

In contrast to studies that support the use of letters in phonemic training,

Lewkowicz (1980) and Roberts (1975) each contended that their use is "a compelling factor" (Roberts, p. 4). We believe that the studies just reviewed put this view in serious question, and we suggest, given the positive effect of letter use on both segmentation and spelling, that a program of effective phonemic awareness training should include letter use.

Some Conclusions and Cautions.   Thus far, we have reached the following conclusions: (a) Phonemic awareness is strongly correlated with reading success and can be acquired through learning to read rather than being a prerequisite to reading; (b) children's early writing experiences can play an invaluable role in the development of phonemic awareness; (c) phonemic awareness can be taught; (d) phonemic awareness associated with blending and segmenting activities is the most highly correlated with reading; and (e) the use of letters contributes to the effectiveness of phonemic awareness training.

On the surface, it might seem that an instructional program that emphasizes phonics would develop phonemic awareness. Research suggests that the situation is not that simple. Juel (1988) studied the literacy development of 54 children from first through fourth grade. In both first and second grades, the children received basal instruction supplemented by a special synthetic phonics program developed by the school district to ensure students received phonics instruction. Juel's data revealed that children who were poor readers in fourth grade had entered school with little phonemic awareness. Although they improved in phonemic awareness over time, they remained far behind the average and good readers in acquiring phonemic awareness. Despite phonics instruction, these poor readers had less phonemic awareness at the end of first grade than did average and good readers when they entered school. Furthermore, children who were poor readers at the end of first grade were likely to remain poor readers at the end of fourth grade. And all but 2 of the 24 poor readers in the fourth grade had poor decoding skills. Thus, the lack of phonemic awareness seemed to hamper the poor readers' learning of sound–symbol relationships. Compounding the problem, poor readers developed negative attitudes toward reading, which is not surprising in view of their failure, and they read less in and out of school.

Tunmer and Nesdale (1985) stated that the method of reading instruction does not affect the development of phonemic awareness, unless, as others, such as Bradley and Bryant (1983) and Williams (1980) have indicated, the instruction includes specific phonemic analysis training.

On the other hand, some children make gains even when phonemic awareness is not explicitly taught. In Juel's study (1988), a considerable percentage of students were average or good readers even without special training in phonemic awareness. Other research also has shown that some children do discover the phonemic structure of language even when it is not explicitly taught. Alegria, Morais, and D'Alimonte (cited in Morais, 1987) found that between the fourth and ninth month of first grade, children taught by a pure whole word method significantly increased their phonemic awareness, apparently through exposure to print. What the research indicates is that we need to make sure all students make steady gains in phonemic awareness once they have embarked on reading instruction so that they can profit from it.

Given that research has indicated that children become aware of phonemes through reading and writing instruction, questions arise as to whether the phonological awareness children acquire before learning to read can play a role. In their research reviews, Adams (1990) and Goswami and Bryant (1990) pointed to the benefits of onsets and rimes, a type of phonological awareness activity that can be described as being in between syllables and phonemes. Onsets are the initial consonant(s) of words, and rimes are the end unit of words. When words contain the same rime, they, in fact, rhyme (e.g., *pat, cat, that*). Research indicates that children are able more easily to divide words into their onset and rime prior to learning to read. Moreover, children who are sensitive to rhyme or who are taught about rhyming are more successful in reading. Goswami and Bryant suggested that from the very beginning of reading instruction children learn to associate onsets and rimes with corresponding letters, capitalizing on their categories of words that rhyme and recognizing that these words can be associated with common spelling patterns. Adams also suggested that onsets and rimes could play an important role, because unlike the awareness of phonemes, children easily acquire understanding of rhyming words. Through working with phonograms, or word families, children can then proceed to noting the phonemes of words much more easily. Also, phonograms offer a means of helping children not only learn about sound–symbol relationships but also sound–symbol relationships as conditioned by the larger orthographic environment.

Some research indicates that children initially approach reading using more global strategies. In the case study of her child's literacy development, Bissex (1980) found that her son analyzed words phoneme by phoneme in his initial spelling, but in reading he relied initially on context clues. After 2 months of invented spelling, her child then seemed to use both context and graphic clues. Similarly, Biemiller (1970) found that in the most advanced stages of beginning reading first graders integrate the use of context clues and graphic clues, following an initial period of relying on context followed by a period of relying on sound–symbol correspondences.

Additionally, Tunmer (1990) purported that beginning readers' ability to use context clues, that is, their syntactic awareness, with "emerging phonological skills" is essential for word recognition development. Relying on findings from a series of studies, Tunmer found that both phonological awareness (which he defines as "the ability to reflect on and manipulate the phonemic segments of speech") and syntactic awareness contribute to "phonological recoding skill—the ability to translate letters and patterns of letters into phonological form." Through using context clues and partial graphophonemic clues, students are able to identify unknown words, thereby learning more about phonological recoding.

Furthermore, Tunmer found that syntactic awareness, another type of meta-linguistic awareness, made a distinct contribution to children's phonological recoding abilities.

Thus, whereas phonemic awareness plays an important role in learning to read, attention to its development in children needs to be kept in perspective. Most importantly, from the outset children need to be exposed to whole, meaningful, reading experiences, so they will see a reason to learn about the code and will be most apt to do so.

Phonemic Awareness Instruction in Basal Reading Programs

To determine the amount and type of phonemic activities in beginning reading programs, we examined the kindergarten and primary levels of eight basal reading programs. (A complete description of this study can be found in Copeland, Winsor, & Osborn, in press.) We selected the programs for review on the basis of their use in large numbers of school districts and/or because they represented a continuum of instructional approaches from scripted lessons to the presentation of language learning as a multidimensional process for which teachers and students share responsibility. The materials examined were the most recently published editions available to us.

Our review of the phonemic awareness-related instruction in these programs involved an examination of the teachers' manuals and student activity books for kindergarten and first grade. The three questions that guided the review were: (a) Are phonemic awareness activities presented? (b) If presented, do phonemic awareness activities include grapheme associations? (c) If presented, what activities are suggested and to what extent are they suggested?

Our identification of activities in the programs was based partially on those identified by Lewkowicz (1980). But because Lewkowicz limited her list to activities that did not involve the use of printed letters or words, we added activities that included the presence of graphemes, and we also considered whether programs advocated invented spelling. Our list of activities, their definitions, and examples of each follows.

1. **Sound–letter correspondences.** These activities directly present or require the association of a letter or letters with the sounds they represent.

Example: When the fish is placed on the hot grill, it makes a sizzling sound, /ss/. Say /ss/ with me. [Letter card is displayed.] The name of this letter is *s*. The letter *s* stands for the /s/ sound in words. When I point to the letter *s*, you say the /s/ sound.

2. **Sound-to-word matching.** These activities require recognition within a word of a previously specified phoneme.

Example: Write the word *rope* on the chalkboard. Read the word slowly emphasizing the vowel sound . . . . Then ask the children to listen for the words with the long /o/ sound as you say these words: *pole, meal, wait, home, bone, bit, nose.*

3. **Word-to-word matching.** These activities require recognition that a word has the same beginning, medial, or final sound as another word.

Example: With a key picture of a tiger above and several other pictures displayed below in a pocket chart, say, "I'll ask someone to name one of these pictures again. If the picture name begins like *tiger,* you may put the picture in the row with the tiger."

4. **Recognition of rhyme.** These activities require recognition that a word is identical to another word except for the portion preceding the stressed vowel, that is, that the words rhyme.

Example: Say the rhyming words *red–shed; fed–led. Red* and *shed* rhyme. *Fed* and *led* rhyme. Do *red* and *fed* rhyme? Repeat these words and tell which pairs rhyme: *red–hit, red–wed, red–mad.*

5. **Sounds in isolation.** These activities involve pronunciation in isolation of a phoneme in the initial, medial, or final position in a word.

Example: Have everyone in the group make the /i/ sound . . . Explain that *i* is a vowel and helps the other letters make their sounds, often in the middle of words. Have students listen for the /i/ in the following words: *pin, hit, lid, pig, bib.* Have them all practice saying the sound of /i/.

6. **Phonemic segmentation.** These activities require a student to discover independently and articulate audibly all the sounds of a word in the correct order.

Example: What are the [three] sounds in *dish*? [The expected response is /d/i/sh/. Incomplete or partial segmentation is also possible, for example *d-ish* or *di-sh.*]

7. **Counting the phonemes.** These activities require the counting and indication of the number of phonemes in a word. The indication is usually by verbal expression, clapping, or tapping.

8. **Blending.** These activities require the students to respond to a sequence of isolated speech sounds by recognizing and pronouncing the word that they constitute.

Example: With *dot* written on the chalkboard, move your hand slowly from left to right as you blend the sounds together to say the word. Then have the children say the word with you.

9. **Deletion of phoneme.** These activities require pronunciation of the new word or syllable that is formed when a designated phoneme of a spoken word is deleted.

Example: Say *dish.* Now say it without the /d/.

10. **Specifying which phoneme has been deleted.** These activities require pronouncing in isolation the phoneme that is left out when two words, differing only by that phoneme, are pronounced.

Example: Say *meat*. Now say *eat*. What phoneme was left out?

11. **Phoneme substitution.** These activities require pronunciation of a new word formed by substituting a specified phoneme for one of the initial, medial, or final sounds in a given word.

Example: Print *keep* on the chalkboard and have it identified, then erase the *k* and substitute *b*. Tell the students that the beginning sound has been changed and ask, "What is the new word?" Continue, substituting the initial consonants *d* and *st* to form the words *deep* and *steep*.

For our analysis, we selected samples from the beginning, middle, and end of each level of the kindergarten and first-grade programs. Each sample consisted of three or four lessons and contained at least three topics in the kindergarten levels and at least three reading selections in the first-grade levels. In a small number of cases when the level involved 10 or fewer lessons, only two selections were made. Introductory and review lessons were avoided to focus on typical lessons.

The occurrence of phonemic awareness activities was rated with the following 4-point scale: no occurrence, occasional, sometimes, and regular. *No occurrence* refers to the absence of relevant instruction or practice of a given activity. *Occasional* refers to instruction prescribed either once or, when more than once, in a whole program, without a discernable schedule. *Sometimes* refers to an activity prescribed twice or more in the samples, and on a noticeable but irregular schedule throughout the program. *Regular* refers to activities prescribed in almost every lesson in the sample and on a regular schedule throughout the program. Table 2.1 shows the final rating that represents the frequency of a given activity in the kindergarten through first-grade programs. It was often necessary to interpret the instructions in manuals in the spirit intended rather than by the actual wording. For example, if a sound–letter correspondence had just been presented and target words were specified, instructions such as "Have children use their knowledge of letter sounds to read the following words" were interpreted as blending practice.

In addition to examining the instruction of the specific activities just discussed, we also pursued one further possible source of phonemic awareness instruction through determining the programs' support for invented spelling.

Findings and Discussion

All eight programs regularly included instruction in sound–letter correspondences. Most programs differed only somewhat in how they presented sound–letter correspondences in that they presented them within a word, as in the letter

TABLE 2.1
Frequency of Activities, K-1

Activity	Program							
	A	B	C	D	E	F	G	H
sound-letter	R	R	R	R	R	R	R	R
sound-to-word matching	R	S	R	N	R	R	R	R
word-to-word matching	N	R	S	N	O	O	R	N
recognition of rhyme	S	R	S	N	O	O	S	N
sounds in isolation	R	N	O	N	O	S	O	R
phonemic segmentation	R	N	N	N	N	N	N	R
counting phonemes	teacher	O	N	N	N	N	N	N
blending[1]	R	R[1]	R[1]	N	N	R	R[1]	R
addition/deletion of phoneme[2]	N	O[2]	S[2]	N	O[2]	S[2]	O[2]	N
specification of deletion	N	N	N	N	N	O	N	N
phoneme substitution	N	O	R	N	S	N	N	N

R = regular within program
S = sometimes
O = occasional
N = no occurrence
[1]Implied blending as in word reading practice, "use what is known about sound–letter correspondences to read."
[2]Includes syllables (e.g., "ing" and "ed"), not just phonemes.

b representing the first sound in *bone*. The presentation of isolated sound–letter correspondences was found regularly in only one program, in which the sound of the phoneme was associated with the symbol. For example, the letter *m* is identified as /m/.

Six of the programs regularly provided sound-to-word matching activities that require children to recognize whether a word contains a given phoneme. One program sometimes did so, and the remaining program provided virtually no activities that promoted phonemic awareness.

Only two programs regularly provided instruction related to word-to-word matching, where students are asked to recognize whether words contain the same initial, middle, or ending sound. Yet, as stated previously, two of the three tasks Stanovich et al. (1984) found to correlate highly with reading were ones that required students to compare words on the basis of their initial consonant sounds.

Only one program regularly featured activities that focused on the recognition of rhyme. Two programs provided such activities occasionally, three did so sometimes, and two programs never devoted attention to recognition of rhyming words.

Only two programs regularly included phonemic segmentation activities. Segmentation activities did not occur in the other programs, and none of the programs encouraged segmentation ability by asking students to count the number of phonemes in a word. This may be because the program developers consider segmentation to be too difficult. As Adams (1990) pointed out, being able to designate the number of phonemes of a word seems dependent on having made some progress in learning to read and, therefore, would be frustrating for many kindergartners. On the other hand, Tunmer and Nesdale (1985) found that among first graders segmentation ability (measured through tapping the number of phonemes of a word) played a critical role in learning to read.

Three programs regularly included teacher directives to encourage blending through prolonged and increasingly more fluent pronunciations; three more had regular activities that implied blending. Two programs had no occurrence of blending activities.

No program focused on deletion activities. However, if the practice given to syllables such as "ing" is added to phoneme deletion, then five programs could be said to have devoted attention to deletion. Virtually no programs devoted attention to specifying which phoneme had been deleted from pairs of words.

Three programs gave some attention to phoneme substitution. In these activities, students identify a new word on the basis of a change in the phoneme of a given word. We included activities in which the words are written on the board. When students are asked to substitute an initial phoneme and letter(s), they are becoming familiar with phonograms, or word families, which as mentioned previously, may be a good route for many students to take in acquiring the alphabetic principle.

When we turned our attention to invented spelling, we found that support ranged from no specific mention of it to a straightforward directive to encourage children to use invented spelling in their writing. Three programs explicitly used the term *invented spelling* and addressed the contribution of student experimentation with sound–symbol correspondences as a preliminary step to gaining mastery over standard spelling. Four programs included description and discussion of writing as a process, but they did not use the term invented spelling. In their discussions, these four programs encouraged teachers to let students first present ideas as they write and attend to editing for mechanics, including spelling, once the content is established. Whereas such directives may make it possible for teachers to foster invented spelling, we felt that they did not adequately help teachers recognize the benefits of invented spelling or alleviate their concerns about students' subsequent mastery of conventional spellings.

CONCLUSION

Our examination of these basal programs has convinced us that, unlike the explicit widespread attention given to sound–symbol correspondences, or phonics, attention to phonemic awareness seems incidental or is lacking overall.

Although some programs provide instructional activities that promote phonemic awareness, generally basal programs do not make consistent concerted efforts in that direction. If they rely on basal programs to call their attention to the importance of developing students' phonemic awareness, teachers most likely will not be conscious of this aspect of literacy development.

What seems most important is that teachers are informed about the role of phonemic awareness so that they can tailor instruction to meet students' interests and needs. We know that many students do acquire phonemic awareness sufficiently in the process of learning to read and write. On the other hand, research indicates that students who are lacking in phonemic awareness experience failure and frustration as they try to learn to read and write in an alphabetic language. If teachers are aware of how phonemic awareness plays a role in successful acquisition of literacy, they can draw on this information as they help students who early on show signs of not succeeding.

Promoting phonemic awareness should not become an excuse for not having time to give students real reading and writing experiences. We know that research shows that less capable readers already do not get as many opportunities to actually read but rather are more apt to spend time on isolated skills and drills (Adams, 1990). Another disturbing scenario is one in which students who do not need special help in acquiring phonemic awareness are required to participate in such instructional activities.

Schickedanz (1989) provided vital examples of how teachers working with young children can help them acquire phonemic awareness in a rich instructional context as opposed to teaching skills in isolation. In the course of natural literacy events, teachers bring speech and print together to help children see that they need to account for the letters in the words they encounter. For instance, in a preschool classroom, the teacher read a note from a child's father with the child, making the sounds within the words explicit and involving the child in looking at the words as they both read them. In another example, the children helped the teacher spell words for a classroom shopping list, with the teacher making the sounds of the words explicit and pausing to give children a chance to name a needed letter. Schickedanz (1989) explained that because the teachers know about the skills their students need to develop, "they know how to make them explicit in the natural course of things, so that children can latch on, instead of getting lost" (p. 104).

Griffith (1991) also pointed out the potential value of whole, meaningful, language activities. In shared readings of enlarged texts, pointing to a word while saying the word can enhance children's knowledge of the spellings of phonemes and of whole words. Similarly, reading books that contain predictable language structures, particularly rhyme, has the potential of helping children move toward focusing on phonemes of words. And, as stated previously, while writing, children are directly confronted with segmenting phonemes. In other words, authentic reading and writing experiences hold a great deal of promise and seem to be especially promising in classrooms where teachers are cognizant of the importance of phonemic awareness but also recognize other critical dimensions of literacy development.

For the purposes of this discussion, we have focused on phonemic awareness at the expense of other critical dimensions of literacy development. However, we also have pointed out that instructional programs must focus on a broader picture. As Erickson (1989) reminds us, children do not come to our classrooms with difficulties in language learning. And research suggests that children can be quite successful if they are given ample opportunities to use language in meaningful ways. Research also indicates that programs should reflect an awareness of the importance of phonemic awareness.

We predict that future editions of basal programs will devote more attention to phonemic awareness. We hope that such instruction will ensure that phonemic awareness is not a stumbling block for children, but that it will provide actual literacy experiences that meet children's interests and needs.

REFERENCES

Adams, M. J. (1990). *Beginning to read: Thinking and learning about print.* Cambridge, MA: The MIT Press.

Biemiller, A. (1970). The development of the use of graphic and contextual information as children learn to read. *Reading Research Quarterly, 6,* 223–253.

Bissex, G. L. (1980). *GYNS at wrk: A child learns to read and write.* Cambridge, MA: Harvard University Press.

Bradley, L., & Bryant, P. E. (1983). Categorizing sounds and learning to read—a causal connection. *Nature, 301,* 419–421.

Chomsky, N., & Halle, M. (1968). *The sound pattern of English.* New York: Harper & Row.

Clarke, L. K. (1988). Invented versus traditional spelling in first graders' writing: Effects on learning to spell and read. *Research in the Teaching of English, 22,* 281–309.

Copeland, K., Winsor, P., & Osborn, J. (in press). *Children's mastery of print: A consideration of instructional practices in view of current theory and research* (Tech. Rep.). Urbana–Champaign: University of Illinois, Center for the Study of Reading.

Ehri, L. C. (1979). Linguistic insight: Threshold of reading acquisition. In T. G. Waller & G. E. MacKinnon (Eds.), *Reading research: Advances in theory and practice* (Vol. 1, pp. 63–84). New York: Academic Press.

Ehri, L. C. (1980). The development of orthographic images. In U. Frith (Ed.), *Cognitive processes in spelling* (pp. 311–338). New York: Academic Press.

Ehri, L. C. (1988). Movement into word reading and spelling: How spelling contributes to reading. In J. Mason (Ed.), *Reading and writing connections* (pp. 65–81). Boston: Allyn & Bacon.

Elkonin, D. B. (1963). The psychology of mastering the elements of reading. In B. Simon & J. Simon (Eds.), *Educational psychology in the USSR* (pp. 165–179). London: Routledge & Kegan Paul.

Elkonin, D. B. (1973). USSR. In J. Downing (Ed.), *Comparative reading: Cross-national studies of behaviour and processes in reading and writing.* New York: Macmillan.

Erickson, F. (1989). Foreword: Literacy risks for students, parents, and teachers. In J. B. Allen &

J. M. Mason (Eds.), *Risk makers, risk takers, risk breakers: Reducing the risks for young literacy learners* (pp. xiii–xvii). Portsmouth, NH: Heinemann.

Fox, B., & Routh, D. K. (1984). Phonemic analysis and synthesis as word attack skills: Revisited. *Journal of Educational Psychology, 76,* 1059–1064.

Gleitman, L. R., & Rozin, P. (1977). The structure and acquisition of reading I: Relations between orthographies and the structure of language. In A. S. Reber & D. L. Scarborough (Eds.), *Toward a psychology of reading* (pp. 1–53). Hillsdale, NJ: Lawrence Erlbaum Associates.

Goswami, U., & Bryant, P. (1990). *Phonological skills and learning to read.* United Kingdom: Lawrence Erlbaum Associates.

Griffith, P. L. (1991). Phonemic awareness helps first graders invent spellings and third graders remember correct spellings. *Journal of Reading Behavior, 23,* 215–233.

Heath, S. B. (1983). *Ways with words: Language, life and work in communities and classrooms.* New York: Cambridge University Press.

Hohn, W. E., & Ehri, L. C. (1983). Do alphabet letters help prereaders acquire phonemic segmentation skill? *Journal of Educational Psychology, 75,* 752–762.

Juel, C. (1988). Learning to read and write: A longitudinal study of 54 children from first through fourth grades. *Journal of Educational Psychology, 80,* 437–447.

Lewkowicz, N. K. (1980). Phonemic awareness training: What to teach and how to teach it. *Journal of Educational Psychology, 72,* 686–700.

Lindfors, J. (1980). *Children's language and learning.* Englewood Cliffs, NJ: Prentice–Hall.

Lundberg, I., Frost, J., & Petersen, O-P. (1988). Effects of an extensive program for stimulating phonological awareness in preschool children. *Reading Research Quarterly, 23,* 265–284.

Mattingly, I. G. (1979). Reading, the linguistic process and linguistic awareness. In J. F. Kavanaugh & I. G. Mattingly (Eds.), *Language by ear and by eye* (pp. 133–147). Cambridge, MA: The MIT Press.

McConnell, B. (1989). Education as a cultural process: The interaction between community and classroom in fostering learning. In J. B. Allen & J. M. Mason (Eds.), *Risk makers, risk takers, risk breakers: Reducing the risks for young literacy learners* (pp. 201–221). Portsmouth, NH: Heinemann.

Morais, J. (1987). Phonetic awareness and reading acquisition. *Psychological Research, 49,* 147–152.

Morais, J., Cary, L., Alegria, J., & Bertelson, P. (1979). Does awareness of speech as a sequence of phonemes arise spontaneously? *Cognition, 7,* 323–331.

Olson, D. R. (1984). "See jumping!" Some oral antecedents of literacy. In H. Goelman, A. A. Oberg, & F. Smith (Eds.), *Awakening to literacy* (pp. 185–192). Portsmouth, NH: Heinemann.

Perfetti, C. A., Beck, I., Bell, L., & Hughes, C. (1987). Phonemic knowledge and learning to read are reciprocal: A longitudinal study of first grade children. *Merrill–Palmer Quarterly, 33,* 283–319.

Reid, J. F. (1983). Into print: Reading and language growth. In M. Donaldson, R. Grieve, & C. Pratt (Eds.), *Early childhood development and education.* New York: Guilford Press.

Roberts, T. (1975). Skills of analysis and synthesis in the early stages of reading. *British Journal of Educational Psychology, 45,* 3–9.

Schickedanz, J. A. (1989). The place of specific skills in preschool and kindergarten. In D. S. Strickland & L. M. Morrow (Eds.), *Emerging literacy: Young children learn to read and write.* Newark, DE: International Reading Association.

Smith, F. (1984). The creative achievement of literacy. In H. Goelman, A. A. Oberg, & F. Smith (Eds.), *Awakening to literacy* (pp. 143–153). Portsmouth, NH: Heinemann.

Stanovich, K. E., Cunningham, A. E., & Cramer, B. B. (1984). Assessing phonological awareness in kindergarten children: Issues of task comparability. *Journal of Experimental Child Psychology, 38,* 175–190.

Tunmer, W. E. (1990). The role of language prediction skills in beginning reading. *New Zealand Journal of Educational Studies, 25,* 95–114.

Tunmer, W. E., & Nesdale, A. R. (1985). Phonemic segmentation skill and beginning reading. *Journal of Educational Psychology, 77,* 417–427.

Vygotsky, L. S. (1962). *Thought and language.* Cambridge, MA: The MIT Press.

Wells, G. (1986). *The meaning makers: Children learning language and using language to learn.* Portsmouth, NH: Heinemann.

Williams, J. P. (1979). The ABD's of reading: A program for the learning disabled. In L. B. Resnick & P. A. Weaver (Eds.), *Theory and practice of early reading* (Vol. 3, pp. 179–196). Hillsdale, NJ: Lawrence Erlbaum Associates.

Williams, J. P. (1980). Teaching decoding with a special emphasis on phoneme analysis and phoneme blending. *Journal of Educational Psychology, 72,* 1–15.

Williams, J. P. (1986). Extracting important information from text. In J. A. Niles & R. V. Lalik (Eds.), *35th National Reading Conference yearbook: Solving problems in literacy: Learners, teachers, and researchers* (pp. 11–29). Rochester, NY: National Reading Conference.

3 Structural Analysis: Some Guidelines for Instruction

William E. Nagy
Center for the Study of Reading

Jean Osborn
Center for the Study of Reading

Pamela Winsor
University of Lethbridge

John O'Flahavan
University of Maryland

THE ROLE OF STRUCTURAL ANALYSIS IN READING

Encountering new words is a normal and necessary part of reading. The vocabulary of written English consists of a relatively small number of words that occur very frequently and an extremely large number of words that occur only infrequently. Hence, in any given sample of text, no matter how large, a substantial proportion of the words will occur only once.

For example, including all reading both in and out of school, the average fifth grader reads somewhere around 1 million words of text in a year (Anderson, Wilson, & Fielding, 1988). Ten thousand of those words will be words that the student sees only once in the year. An avid fifth-grade reader will encounter several times that number. The student will have encountered very few of these low-frequency words in earlier grades; therefore, she or he will be seeing most of them in print for the first time.

Ten thousand words may seem to be an absurdly high estimate for the number of new words the average fifth grader encounters in a school year. To make this figure more understandable, we undertook an analysis of a sample of the words that occurred only once in the corpus collected by Carroll, Davies, and Richman (1971; see Nagy & Anderson, 1984, for a more detailed analysis of the Carroll et al. corpus). On the basis of this analysis, we can account for the composition of the 10,000 "new" words that an average fifth-grade student might encounter as follows:

- About 4,000 are derivatives of more frequent words, for example, *indebtedness, unromantic,* or *metalware.*

• Another 1,300 are inflections of more frequent words (for example, the words *merges* and *merited* occurred only once each in a corpus of 5 million words, although the stems *merge* and *merit* occurred more frequently).

• About 1,500 are proper names.

• About 2,200 words fall into a variety of categories—capitalizations of more frequent words, numbers, deliberate misspellings, algebraic expressions, and other odd things that show up in a large sample of real text that has been sorted by a computer.

• About 1,000 are truly new words, not directly related to more familiar words.

The point is that the 10,000 words seen only once in a year by this student are not all really "new." More than half are clearly related to more familiar words. Skilled readers probably do not even think of a word such as *merited* or *unromantic*, seen only once in a year of reading, as new in any way. They automatically recognize the relationship of these words to their more familiar stems. Readers who cannot discern the relationships, however, face real difficulties in reading.

Skilled reading, therefore, depends not just on knowing a large number of words, but also on being able to deal effectively with new ones. Skilled readers are not readers who never encounter words they do not know but rather are readers who cope effectively with words that are new to them.

How do skilled readers deal with new words? Three sources of information are available. Skilled readers can use (a) context to infer a word's meaning, (b) phonics to determine a word's pronunciation, and (c) structural analysis, or knowledge of word parts, to determine both a word's meaning and pronunciation.

The literature of reading instruction contains a great deal of information about the strategies of context use and phonics, but it contains relatively little information about the contributions of structural analysis instruction to word identification and vocabulary acquisition and about the relative efficacy of different instructional approaches.

One reason for the relative lack of information about structural analysis is lack of research (see, for example, Graves's 1986 review of vocabulary instruction). Another reason seems simply to be lack of attention. A lot of theories, beliefs—and emotional and political energy—have been devoted to the topic of phonics. In contrast, only a little energy—and as far as we can determine, no emotion at all—has been given to structural analysis.

In this chapter, we examine this somewhat unexamined aspect of reading instruction. We start by reviewing what is known about English word structure on the basis of linguistic analysis and about how this structure is acquired and used by readers. Although more research is certainly needed, we have some confidence in laying out guiding principles for evaluating and improving instructional practice in this area.

DEFINING STRUCTURAL ANALYSIS

To begin, we must make clear what we mean by the term *structural analysis.* Structural analysis can most easily be defined as "the use of word parts to help determine the meaning and pronunciation of words." This simple definition, although accurate, does not clearly distinguish structural analysis from phonics, because it does not specify exactly what kinds of "word parts" are used.

To distinguish the domains of structural analysis and phonics, and to make clear distinctions among different kinds of word parts, we need to review the meanings of some of the terminology basic to structural analysis—terms such as *morpheme, affix, prefix, suffix, derivative, root, base, stem,* and *compound.*

Morpheme. Morphemes are usually defined by linguists as "minimal units of meaning." For example, *stoplight* can be broken down into the units *stop* and *light* on the basis of meaning. These units can of course be broken down further in terms of letters or sounds, for example, into onset (the initial consonant or consonant cluster) and rime (the vowel and any following consonants that belong to the same syllable). At this level of analysis, the words *stop* and *light* can be further analyzed as *st/op* and *l/ight.* In fact, the analysis of words into onsets and rimes may be an important step in children's first attempts to break words into smaller pieces and become aware of their individual sounds (Adams, 1990). Some successful spelling programs have capitalized on the onset–rime distinction to help students make more sense out of the apparent irregularities of English orthography. However, the division of a word into onset and rime has nothing to do with its meaning.

Although morphemes are defined as minimal units of meaning, the conception of meaning must be a broad one. For example, it must include what can be called "grammatical meaning." The *s* in *walks* is considered a morpheme, although its contribution to *walks* is in its grammatical function.

Morphemes are categorized into *free* and *bound* morphemes. Free morphemes constitute words in themselves and can occur alone (e.g., *walk, to,* and *below*). Bound morphemes, on the other hand, cannot occur except in combination with other morphemes (e.g., the *s* in *walks,* the *de* in *decontaminate,* and the *cardio* in *cardiovascular*).

Affix. Affixes include *prefixes* and *suffixes.* Affixes are bound morphemes (e.g., *un-* or *-ness*). Not all bound morphemes are affixes, however, For example, the *caut-* in *cautious* and *caution* is a bound morpheme but not an affix.

Among affixes, a distinction can be made between *inflectional* and *derivational* affixes. Inflectional affixes mark number and tense. Words differing only in their inflectional affixes are considered to be different forms of the same word (e.g., *help, helps, helped, helping*). In English, inflections are usually marked by suffixes. On the other hand, derivational affixes appear on both prefixes and suffixes and result in different words *(helpless, unkind)* rather than in different

47

forms of the same word. In English, all prefixes are derivational affixes; for example, *underestimate, disobey,* and *inconsiderate* are considered to be separate words from their stems. We use the term *derivative* for any word containing at least one derivational suffix or prefix.

Neutral affixes are those that can be added only to free morphemes, that is, morphemes that can stand alone as words. For example, *-ness* is a neutral suffix. When you take *-ness* off a word—if it is really a suffix in that word, that is—you always have a word left. Non-neutral affixes, on the other hand, can be added either to free or bound morphemes. The suffix *-ity* is a non-neutral suffix; it can be added to words (as in *rationality*) or to bound morphemes (as in *capacity*). Neutral suffixes do not change the spelling of a word, except for the regular change of *y* to *i* as in *happiness,* and seldom change its pronunciation (the word *business* is an obvious but lone exception). On the other hand, non-neutral suffixes are often associated with changes in both spelling and pronunciation, as can be seen in pairs such as *sane/sanity, profound/profundity,* and *pronounce/pronunciation.* Not surprisingly, there are differences in the way neutral and non-neutral suffixes are learned (Tyler & Nagy, 1989).

Root, Base, Stem.   The terms *root, base,* and *stem* are used more or less interchangeably for what is left when the affixes are removed from a word or when a compound word is divided into parts. To the extent that a distinction is made among these terms, *root* and *base* refer to a single morpheme (i.e., what is left when a word has been exhaustively analyzed). *Stem,* on the other hand, is most often used for what is left when a single particular affix has been removed. For example, *disagree* would be called the stem of the word *disagreement.* The term root or base would be reserved for *agree.*

Compound.   A compound is usually defined as a word made up of two or more other words. In other words, compounds are typically made up of free morphemes (e.g., *keyboard, headache*). However, combinations of bound morphemes such as *petrochemical* or *thermometer* are also usually classed as compounds. The terms *hyphenated compound* and *open compound* are used for compounds in which the parts are separated by a hyphen *(free-lance)* or space *(ice cream),* respectively.

STRUCTURAL ANALYSIS AND PHONICS

The simple definition of structural analysis given previously–the use of word parts to help determine the meaning and pronunciation of words–does not make a clear distinction between structural analysis and phonics.

To some extent, a distinction can be made in terms of purpose. Both structural analysis and phonics instruction have to do with parts of words, and the major goal of both is to enable students to deal with unknown words by breaking them into smaller more familiar parts. The primary goal of phonics instruction, however, is to help students with the pronunciation of unknown words, whereas the primary goal of structural analysis instruction is to give students insight into both the pronunciations *and* the meanings of unknown words.

However, there is still substantial overlap in terms of purpose. Even when the primary goal of structural analysis is figuring out the meaning of an unfamiliar word (that, for example, *botanophobia* means "fear of plants"), the analysis of a word into familiar meaningful parts is a helpful step in determining its pronunciation as well.

The primary difference between structural analysis and phonics is in the nature of the word parts used to analyze the internal structure of words.

Phonics is most often defined as dealing with units of pronunciation (individual letters, digraphs, consonant clusters, and syllables), whereas structural analysis deals with units of meaning, or morphemes. The distinction between units based on meaning and units based on sound or spelling is fundamental. Dividing words into morphemes is not the same as dividing a word into syllables. *Walked* consists of one syllable but two morphemes. *Number* consists of two syllables, but only one morpheme. Students must recognize this distinction in order to understand the concepts prefix and suffix. Otherwise, they may not distinguish between real and "phantom" prefixes (the *re* in *reconsider* and *reality*) and end up looking for "little words in big words"—finding *moth* in *mother* or *fat* in *father*.

Many of the problems that have arisen in trying to clarify the relationship between phonics and structural analysis instruction stem from either a mislabeling of the terms or from the imprecise or ambiguous definition of key definitional concepts. Syllabification, for example, is often labeled as a form of structural analysis, even though syllables are units of pronunciation and not of meaning.

A more basic problem grows out of the definition of morphemes as minimal units of meaning. As we have already noted, "meaningful" in this definition includes the notion of grammatical function. Thus, treating the *s* in *wanders* or the *ness* in *orangeness* as morphemes is not controversial. In fact, dividing these words in this way is intuitively reasonable. How to describe the meanings of such morphemes, however, is usually a problem. Abstract definitions of suffixes, such as defining *-ion* as "the state, condition, or result of," are usually more confusing than helpful to young students.

Furthermore, English does not allow us to draw a clear line between what constitutes a meaningful unit within a word and what does not. The division of *snowman* into *snow* and *man* or *fleeing* into *flee* and *ing* is straightforward (although it is difficult to put into words exactly what the meaning of *ing* is). But the meanings of many words are not so clearly related to the meanings of their parts. English words range over a full continuum—from total semantic regularity (e.g., *sleeplessness*) to complete semantic irregularity (e.g., *understand* or *shiftless*)—with every conceivable intermediate degree of partial regularity.

Words like *foxtrot* and *understand* are obviously not related to the meanings of their parts. Less obvious, and perhaps more troublesome, are words that bear some relationship to the meanings of their parts. The meaning of the compound *waterbed* seems clear enough, but if you did not already know about waterbeds, knowing the meanings of *water* and *bed* might not be sufficient information. You might accept "riverbed" or "bed that has been wet" as equally reasonable meanings.

An even greater problem is posed by words that contain parts that do not have clear-cut meanings. Thousands of English words have parts that are borrowed from Latin or Greek. Some of these have consistent meanings (e.g., the *hemo* in *hemophilia* or *hemorrhage*). On the other hand, many Latin and Greek roots have no discernable core of meaning to those not knowledgeable about their history. The morpheme *ceive* in *deceive* and *conceive, fer* in *confer* and *interfere,* or *duce* in *produce, reduce,* and *deduce* does not transmit meaning to most American students. Latin and Greek prefixes (the *ob* in *obtain,* the *apo* in *apology*) can be even more obscure.

Strictly speaking, then, structural analysis could best be distinguished from phonics by defining it as "the use of *morphemes* to help determine the meaning and pronunciation of words." This definition is more precise than the one utilizing word parts (although *morpheme* is not in everyone's vocabulary). Nevertheless, because of the structure and history of our language, the domain of structural analysis is somewhat vague.

HOW STUDENTS UTILIZE KNOWLEDGE OF WORD STRUCTURE

Word-structure knowledge begins to develop in early childhood. Berko (1958) found that preschool children show some ability to use suffixes and compounding to coin new words; Condry (1979) found second graders able to infer the meanings of new words on the basis of word structure. Word-structure knowledge continues to grow through the school years (Tyler & Nagy, 1989) and continues to increase even after high school (Nagy & Scott, 1990; Sternberg & Powell, 1983).

Different aspects of word-structure knowledge appear to be acquired at different times and at different rates. Tyler and Nagy (1989) investigated the word-structure knowledge of students from fourth grade through college and found that the ability to recognize novel derivatives of familiar stems was already largely in place by fourth grade. However, students' knowledge of the syntactic function of derivational suffixes (e.g., that words ending in *-ness* and *-ion* tend to be nouns) was beginning to develop in fourth grade and increased throughout the school years.

Skilled readers use structural analysis in at least three ways: to recognize known words more efficiently, to remember the meanings and spellings of partially learned words, and to figure out the meanings and pronunciations of new words.

As we have said, the most obvious role of structural analysis is to help students figure out the meanings of new words. Nagy and Anderson (1984) estimated that as many as 60% of English words have meanings that can be predicted from the meanings of their parts, and that for another 10%, word parts may give useful, albeit incomplete, information. In brief, the bulk of new words will be cases like *nontoxicity,* the meaning of which is transparently related to its parts. A smaller number of words will be like *roadrunner*—a case in which the word parts help some with pronunciation, and may have something to do with meaning, but give incomplete or potentially misleading information.

Although students are able to use knowledge of structural analysis to interpret the meanings of new words (Tyler & Nagy, 1989), they often fail to apply knowledge of structural analysis where it would be helpful (White, Power, & White, 1989; Wysocki & Jenkins, 1987). The extent to which they do utilize structural analysis is related to their reading ability (Freyd & Baron, 1982). Instruction in structural analysis therefore can be expected to improve students' ability in interpreting new words.

Structural analysis may also play an important role in remembering the form of new words. Readers encountering the word *electrocution* for the first time may both decode it more accurately and remember it better, if they see its relationship to *electric.* Knowledge of this relationship may also help readers avoid confusing the word *electrocution* with similarly spelled words such as *elocution.*

Structural analysis may also help students remember the meanings of words, even in cases where the meanings of the parts are not sufficient to reveal the meaning of the whole. For example, seeing the *impression* in *Impressionism* will not give a student enough information to pass an art history examination. Knowing why the art movement was called "Impressionism," however, and what this label has to do with impressions may help students remember the rationale for the movement.

Structural analysis can also help with decoding and spelling, even when it does not help with meaning. The word part *ceive,* for example, makes little contribution to the meaning of the word *perceive.* But recognizing that this unit is a recurring element that is also found in *receive, deceive,* and *conceive* may be of help in remembering the spelling of all those words. In this way, knowledge of affixes and roots can be helpful in decoding and spelling words, even where these units do not supply useful information about the meanings of words.

Knowledge of structural analysis also benefits readers by allowing them to recognize words more efficiently. The effects of frequency on word recognition are well documented; words that frequently appear in print are recognized more quickly than less frequent words. However, speed of recognition is determined not just by the frequency of the whole word, but by the frequency of its parts as well. For example, the word *quietness* occurs very seldom in print, about as frequently as the words *sup, matador,* or *brindle.* However, the word *quietness* is likely to be recognized more quickly than these other words, because it consists of parts that are more frequent in the language. Although the results of research on the role of affixes in recognizing familiar words are not unanimous, there is good evidence that the frequency of parts of words plays a role in word recognition (Nagy, Anderson, Schommer, Scott, & Stallman, 1989; Taft, 1979, 1985).

In summary, skilled readers make use of structural analysis to support their word recognition and meaning construction. It follows, then, that effective reading instruction should include measures to help students to gain knowledge of structural analysis and to apply this knowledge while reading.

GUIDING PRINCIPLES FOR INSTRUCTION

Reviews of research related to instruction in structural analysis (Graves, 1986; White et al., 1989) indicate that such instruction is potentially valuable, especially for lower achieving students. It must be acknowledged that relatively few such studies have been conducted—Graves mentions only five—and that there is little, if any, research comparing alternative approaches to structural analysis instruction. Nevertheless, despite the need for more research, we are confident that we can already outline some guiding principles for instruction in structural analysis.

The principles we suggest are based on three sources of information. The first is what we have just covered—what is known about English word structure, and how knowledge of that structure is acquired and utilized by readers. A second source of information is the growing body of knowledge in the field of reading concerning how skilled readers comprehend text and repair comprehension when it breaks down—and also how less skilled readers can learn to do the same. Although this literature has not dealt explicitly with structural analysis, there are a number of points at which more general principles of comprehension instruction have clear and specific implications for instruction in structural analysis.

A third source of information on which we base our suggested guiding principles for structural analysis instruction is a review we conducted of structural analysis instruction and practice in the teachers' manuals and student workbooks of six basal reading programs. The six programs, all with 1989 copyrights, were selected on the basis of their popularity and because they represented a diversity of approaches to instruction. A detailed report of this review is available as a Center for the Study of Reading Technical Report (Winsor, Nagy, Osborn, & O'Flahavan, 1993).

In this review, we focused our attention on instruction relating to prefixes, suffixes, and compound words. Specifically, we looked at lessons in the programs to gather information about four aspects of instruction and application: (a) definition of terms, (b) rationale for instruction, (c) approaches and procedures, and (d) opportunities for application. We did not begin with a set model of ideal instruction against which we measured our observations. However, examination of concrete instructional materials did provide us an opportunity to see how implications based on our first two sources of information might be realized—or not realized—in classroom practice.

Our recommendations for effective instruction in structural analysis can be stated in terms of five guiding principles. We explain each of these in turn, commenting briefly on how each principle appears to be followed, or not followed, in the basal lessons we reviewed.

Provide Explicit Explanations.   Research on comprehension instruction reveals that students often need to be told explicitly *why* they are doing some particular activity. In the case of structural analysis, it is important to make clear both the immediate purpose—determining the meaning and pronunciation of an unfamiliar word—and the ultimate purpose—to construct a coherent meaning for the text. In the basal instruction we reviewed, an explicit statement of the immediate purpose was usually provided. However, neither the explanations suggested for teachers to give to students nor the application activities offered gave much indication of the ultimate purpose. We believe that it is important to convey clearly to students that structural analysis, like other word-level strategies, is subordinate to the goal of gaining meaning from text.

Furthermore, students often also need to be shown clearly *when* and *how* to apply a strategy such as structural analysis. As with instruction in other types of strategies, teacher modeling is very important. For example, the teacher reads aloud a paragraph containing a word to which structural analysis could be applied and "thinks aloud," explaining as thoroughly as possible how to apply knowledge of structural analysis:

> Here's a word I haven't seen before. The first thing I'll do is see whether I recognize any familiar parts—a prefix, stem, or suffix—or maybe it might be a compound. Okay, I see that I can divide this word into a stem I know, and a suffix. So the meaning of this word must have something to do with . . . . Now, I'll see if that meaning makes any sense in this sentence . . . .

Students should then be given guided practice with other paragraphs, with the teacher providing prompts and questions as needed. As students learn how to apply what they have learned, the teacher's prompts can be diminished or withdrawn.

This approach of modeling, guided practice, and gradual release of responsibility to students has been described at length for other aspects of comprehension instruction (Pearson & Dole, 1987); the principles can be applied to instruction in structural analysis in a rather straightforward fashion.

Rely on Examples More than Abstract Rules, Principles, or Definitions. Certainly, concepts such as *prefix, suffix,* and *compounds* must be taught as part of instruction in structural analysis. However, these concepts are more abstract and potentially difficult for students than may be apparent, and they need to be illustrated with numerous examples.

The basal program instruction we reviewed provided examples of these concepts. However, there are three points at which we think special care is needed.

First, although the goal of structural analysis instruction is to help students interpret new words, we believe that initial instruction on concepts such as prefix, suffix, and compound should exemplify these concepts with words that are already familiar to the students; that is, students must be made aware of the internal structure of words they already know before they analyze unfamiliar words. A person may be quite familiar with the word *basement,* for example, and yet never have noticed that it can be analyzed into the stem *base* and the suffix *ment.* If students do not understand the role of an affix in at least some familiar words, it is highly unlikely that they will be able to use this affix as a tool for interpreting the meaning of unfamiliar words. Therefore, we recommend that initial instruction in key concepts of structural analysis be anchored in the known. It should deliberately focus on words that are sure to be familiar to students before any attempt is made to analyze new words.

A second point concerning the use of examples has to do with using nonexamples as well as examples. To learn a concept such as prefix, a student needs to see not just examples of what a prefix is but also examples of what it is not. *Re-* is a prefix in *redo,* but not in *real.* In only three of the six programs we reviewed did we find explicit mention of the possibility that the letters making up a prefix might not actually function as a prefix in some of the words in which they occurred.

Some students may have serious misconceptions about the nature of English morphology and about what constitute effective strategies for utilizing word-structure information. These misconceptions are likely to be exacerbated by poorly conceived instruction. For example, asking students to "look for little words in big words" can turn up *car* in *cargo* and *must* in *muster.* Effective instruction, therefore, must include means for diagnosing the existence of misconceptions and provide examples that explicitly distinguish between the misconceptions and the intended concepts.

A third case in which use of examples is especially important is in teaching the meaning of suffixes. The meanings of suffixes consist primarily in their grammatical function. Such meanings are abstract and cannot be adequately conveyed by short definitions. The suffix *-ed* may mean "past," but *walk* plus *-ed* does not mean "walk past." It is essential, therefore, for structural analysis instruction, and especially instruction on derivational suffixes, to focus on the relationship between a word's structure and its role in a sentence.

Research suggests that the ability to recognize parts of a complex word develops earlier than knowledge of what a derivational suffix such as -*ness* or -*ity* contributes to a word; even in junior high and high school some students may not have a clear grasp of how suffixed words function in sentences or differ from their stems (Freyd & Baron, 1982; Tyler & Nagy, 1989; Wysocki & Jenkins, 1987). Thus, an emphasis on recognizing parts of words is most important for the early grades. As the students get older, there should be an increasing emphasis on grammatical function of suffixes. However, instruction must illustrate the function of suffixes (e.g., by contrasting the use of stem and derivative in sentences) rather than relying on abstract definitions (e.g., defining *frustration* as "the state or condition of being frustrated").

Recognize the Diversity of English Word Structure.   Instruction in structural analysis must deal with the diverse types of word parts. We cannot assume that the instruction that is best for prefixes will necessarily be the best for suffixes, or vice versa. The differences between prefixes and suffixes involve more than just their position with respect to the stem. Prefixes may be processed differently than suffixes (Taft, 1985). Prefixes also differ from suffixes in their content. Suffixes, both inflectional and derivational, tend to convey grammatical information— what part of speech the word is, and how it functions in the sentence. Prefixes tend to convey different kinds of meaning. Several prefixes (e.g., *un-, in-, dis-, a-*) convey negation. Others (e.g., *trans-, in-, re-, sub-*) convey meanings associated with direction. Likewise, instruction about compounds should be different from instruction about affixes.

The distinction between free and bound stems is also important for instruction. Research suggests that students can use knowledge of affixes effectively when the stems are themselves English words; that is, they can find the *confine* in *confinement*. On the other hand, there is little evidence that skilled readers make any use of bound stems (such as *fer* in *transfer*) in recognizing or learning words (Carroll, 1940; Shepherd, 1973). However, it is likely that a distinction should be made between vague Latin roots such as *ceive, lect, fer,* and *mit,* and fairly specific (usually Greek) roots such as *hemo, petro,* or *anthropo.* (Of course, distinctions must also be made among different functions of structural analysis. Latin roots with vague meanings, for example, are conceivably of use in learning to spell, and in some cases in remembering the meanings of new words, even if they are unlikely to function as part of an independent word-learning strategy.)

Instruction should also take into account that affixes and roots differ widely in their frequency in the language, and hence in their potential utility. Some suffixes and prefixes are found on dozens, even hundreds, of words; others occur only infrequently. Some Greek roots are found largely in technical or scientific vocabulary.

A distinction must also be made between different types of knowledge about structural analysis. One part of using structural analysis is the ability to recognize the familiar parts of a complex word, that is, seeing that a new word such as *confinability* is made up of the elements *confine, able,* and *ity.* Another part is knowledge of the function of affixes, that is, knowing that *communicative* is an adjective and hence used in certain ways in a sentence, whereas *communicativity* is a noun and therefore used differently.

Make the Limitations of Structural Analysis Clear.   Part of giving explicit instruction in structural analysis is letting students know its limitations—about how often structural analysis may give incomplete or misleading information, or no information, and what to do in such cases.

As we have mentioned, only half of the basal programs we reviewed warned students about "phantom" affixes, that is, cases like the *re* in *real* or the *ness* in *harness.* Nor was there consistency in warning students about the semantic irregularities associated with structural analysis—for example, the *casual* in *casualty* or the *emerge* in *emergency.* Some of the programs did instruct students to check to see if the meaning derived through structural analysis made sense in the sentence. However, we think that this point needs to be made more frequently, and more forcefully.

Use Extended Text in Opportunities for Application.   Instruction in structural analysis is unlikely to transfer automatically to reading. Just because children have learned how to divide words into roots and suffixes in workbook exercises, we cannot assume that they will apply this skill to the reading of connected text. Instruction in structural analysis must target specifically the kinds of application we expect students to make; therefore, opportunities for applying structural analysis to extended text are an indispensable part of structural analysis instruction. In the lessons we reviewed, however, students were seldom asked to apply what they had learned about structural analysis to extended texts.

Among the reasons for having students practice applying structural analysis to extended texts is the need for them to learn how to coordinate information gained through structural analysis with information from other sources, especially context and background knowledge. Affixed words and compounds do not always mean exactly what one would predict from their parts, and they can mean something quite different; it is therefore essential that students learn to coordinate the information they gain from different sources.

CONCLUSION

Structural analysis information must function to help students develop strategic and flexible use of word parts as a means of constructing word meaning. Because the information in word parts, although usually helpful, can often be incomplete and, in fact, sometimes misleading, structural analysis instruction must also help students become fully aware of its limitations. Structural analysis instruction will be strengthened by closer and more intense alignment with the real task that reading actual text presents to students—that of meaning construction. Specifically, we urge that structural analysis instruction be grounded in context and provide numerous opportunities for students to determine the meanings of prefixed words, derivations, and compound words in extended text.

Effective instruction must aim for strategic use of structural analysis. It is likely that most students have acquired the basic skill of structural analysis— recognizing that a new word can sometimes be broken into familiar parts that reveal something about its meaning—before fourth grade (Tyler & Nagy, 1989). What is less likely to be developed, and more in need of instructional attention, is knowing *when* to use structural analysis. Although some programs warn students about the existence of "phantom" affixes, they offer little, if any, opportunity for students to apply this distinction. We recommend that students be given sentences containing unfamiliar words that could, orthographically at least, be broken down into a familiar stem plus an affix and then asked to decide whether their analysis leads to a meaning compatible with the context.

Strategic use of structural analysis involves using it in concert with other strategies for dealing with new words. Using context to check the plausibility of meanings determined by structural analysis is an important part of coordinating strategies; but we recommend that structural analysis be incorporated into a more comprehensive set of strategies including, for example, deciding how important a word is for understanding the text, when one can get by without knowing the precise meaning of the word, and when using a dictionary or glossary is worth the effort.

REFERENCES

Adams, M. J. (1990). *Beginning to read: Thinking and learning about print.* Cambridge, MA: The MIT Press.

Anderson, R. C., Wilson, P., & Fielding, L. (1988). Growth in reading and how children spend their time outside of school. *Reading Research Quarterly, 23,* 285–303.

Berko, J. (1958). The child's learning of English morphology. *Word, 14,* 150–177.

Carroll, J. B. (1940). Knowledge of English roots and affixes as related to vocabulary and Latin study. *Journal of Educational Research, 34,* 102–111.

Carroll, J. B., Davies, P., & Richman, B. (1971). *Word frequency book.* Boston: Houghton Mifflin.

Condry, S. (1979). *A developmental study of processes of word derivation in elementary school.* Unpublished doctoral dissertation, Cornell University, Ithaca, NY.

Freyd, T., & Baron, J. (1982). Individual differences in acquisition of derivational morphology. *Journal of Verbal Learning and Verbal Behavior, 21,* 282–295.

Graves, M. (1986). Vocabulary learning and instruction. In E. Z. Rothkopf & L. C. Ehri (Eds.), *Review of research in education* (Vol. 13, pp. 49–89). Washington, DC: American Educational Research Association.

Nagy, W., & Anderson, R. C. (1984). How many words are there in printed school English? *Reading Research Quarterly, 19,* 304–330.

Nagy, W., Anderson, R. C., Schommer, M., Scott, J., & Stallman, A. (1989). Morphological families in the internal lexicon. *Reading Research Quarterly, 24,* 262–282.

Nagy, W., & Scott, J. (1990). Word schemas: Expectations about the form and meaning of new words. *Cognition and Instruction, 7,* 105–127.

Pearson, P. D., & Dole, J. A. (1987). Explicit comprehension instruction: A review of research and a new conceptualization of instruction. *Elementary School Journal, 88,* 151–165.

Shepherd, J. S. (1973). *The relations between knowledge of word parts and knowledge of derivatives among college freshmen.* Unpublished doctoral dissertation, New York University.

Sternberg, R., & Powell, J. (1983). Comprehending verbal comprehension. *American Psychologist, 38,* 878–893.

Taft, M. (1979). Recognition of affixed words and the word frequency effect. *Memory and Cognition, 7,* 263–272.

Taft, M. (1985). The decoding of words in lexical access: A review of the morphographic approach. In D. Besner, T. G. Waller, & G. E. MacKinnon (Eds.), *Reading research: Advances in theory and practice* (Vol. 5, pp. 200–252). Orlando: Academic Press.

Tyler, A., & Nagy, W. (1989). The acquisition of English derivational morphology. *Journal of Memory and Language, 28,* 649–667.

White, T., Power, M., & White, S. (1989). Morphological analysis: Implications for teaching and understanding vocabulary growth. *Reading Research Quarterly, 24,* 283–304.

Winsor, P., Nagy, W., Osborn, J., & O'Flahavan, J. (1993). Structural analysis: Toward an evaluation of instruction (Tech. Rep.). Urbana–Champaign: University of Illinois, Center for the Study of Reading.

Wysocki, K., & Jenkins, J. (1987). Deriving word meanings through morphological generalization. *Reading Research Quarterly, 22,* 66–81.

4 Twenty Years of Research on Reading: Answers and Questions

Joanna P. Williams
Teachers College, Columbia University

During the 1960s, a small group of psychologists and linguists at Cornell University, including Eleanor Gibson, Charles Hockett, and Harry Levin, organized Project Literacy. Funded by the United States Office of Education, this consortium of about 20 researchers was dedicated to conducting research on the basic processes of reading rather than on reading pedagogy.

Project Literacy was viewed as a counter to another 1960s' project, the so-called First-Grade Studies (Bond & Dykstra, 1967), which had been designed as the be-all and end-all of method comparisons. The consortium members argued that we needed to know more about the nature of reading itself and about how children learn to read before we could design optimal instructional programs. The assumption was, of course, that once we knew the answers to questions about the processes underlying reading we could—and would—develop methods and materials that were demonstrably effective and that the educational community would be happy to accept.

In 1970, Levin and Williams published *Basic Studies on Reading,* a collection of reports on the projects that had been undertaken under the auspices of Project Literacy. The reports in the collection reflected a variety of disciplines and viewpoints. Among those by linguists, for example, Chomsky's report argued that conventional English orthography is close to optimal as a representation of the spoken language, Venezky's moderated that claim, and Labov's described the complexity of Black English.

Most of the reports dealing with aspects of psychological process focused on the skillful reader. For example, Gibson, Shurcliff, and Yonas addressed issues such as the role of orthographic constraints in word recognition, and Hochberg identified perceptual strategies for sampling text. There was, of course, some attention to children; Weber looked at the reading errors of first graders, and Blom analyzed the social values communicated in school primers. I reported on potential applications for instruction in beginning reading.

Because I was part of Project Literacy, it is satisfying for me to see, many years later, how its work anticipated much of what has happened since. The sheer amount of reading process research that has been conducted is extraordinary, but what is most impressive is the strong theoretical base that underlies much of the work—thanks in large part to the fact that cognitive psychology has found the study of reading to be highly germane to its fundamental concerns about information processing. Marilyn Adams's *Beginning to Read* (1990) reflects the remarkable progress that has been made.

In her book, Adams has given us not only a thorough and well-reasoned discussion of the research itself, but also of how this research might be applied in instruction. Much of the recent research on the reading process has been at a very molecular level of analysis, and it often deals with phenomena that are not amenable to manipulation. Many researchers have turned away from the challenges involved in trying to determine the relevance of this work for education and have addressed more molar topics such as metacognition and problem solving, which hold more immediate promise for instructional applications. But Adams has taken some of the most basic findings in cognitive processing and has shown how they can be valuable not only for understanding the reading process per se but also for identifying a good pedagogical approach.

Adams has also included in her book a discussion of the history of reading instruction and a review of the literature on the effectiveness of various instructional approaches. Many instructional programs are good, she says; specific details within them can vary, but the myriad components of the whole program must be coordinated and integrated. Like so many other thoughtful investigators (e.g., Beck & Juel, in press, Chall, 1967; Liberman, 1990), Adams considers phonics an important part of that whole. She has also considered the arguments of the adherents of the whole language movement (e.g., Teale & Sulzby, 1986); she takes seriously the importance of developing the child's understanding of the purposes and functions of reading. And, of course, throughout the book she maintains a focus on the ultimate goal of reading comprehension. All in all, the book provides a comprehensive, state-of-the-art, and well-balanced presentation of what has become a very popular area of study.

THE PLACE OF PHONICS IN THE CURRICULUM

Although I, and many others, may read Adams as having successfully integrated phonics and the whole language approach, it will not do to leave the matter there. In 1967, Jeanne Chall did much the same in her book, *Learning to Read: The Great Debate*. Chall did not have the sophisticated psychological theory and the extensive body of empirical research that is available today, and she was dealing with a somewhat different issue, in that the 1960s' "alternative" to phonics was the whole word method, not the whole language philosophy. But the thesis of Chall's book was much the same as Adams's conclusion on this point: (a) phonics instruction should be incorporated prominently into beginning reading instruction, and (b) it should by no means be considered the entirety of any reading program. Simply put, phonics is necessary but not sufficient in and of itself.

But consider the huge amount of effort that, since 1967, has gone into what Chall so aptly called The Great Debate. Should we expect that Adams' work—as good as it is—will stop this debate, modify educational practice, and persuade the field to move on to more profitable discussions? I think not, because the simple accumulation of evidence does not in itself necessarily change people's thinking. Other considerations, such as the potential findings promised by new research endeavors, are also important. Investigators continually go to new research topics and even to new research approaches in their attempts to corroborate or refute findings already achieved. What appears to be the likely outcome of the current new research in the field of reading is, in fact, that the conclusions of earlier work will continue to hold.

In this chapter, I want to review the research evidence in favor of a prominent, but not sole, emphasis on phonics (i.e., decoding) in beginning reading instruction. I do not attempt a comprehensive review—it took Adams 424 pages to do that!—but rather, I discuss examples of the several types of evidence available and show that findings from a variety of research approaches all attest to the importance of phonics knowledge, which strengthens the case for decoding instruction. I then discuss in some detail two active research topics I believe hold great promise for the development of effective teaching materials and methods. The fact that both of these promising research areas deal with phonological structure is another argument in favor of phonics instruction. Lastly, I speculate on why some members of the educational community are not pleased with the findings emerging from all this research.

A Variety of Research Approaches

I now review evidence from five different research approaches, each of which indicates the importance of phonics knowledge and decoding instruction.

1. Basic Research. The first approach is the use of psychological theory and laboratory findings to buttress or refute the claims of reading specialists, what we typically label basic research. Although it can be argued that most of this research does not speak directly to the phonics issue, what is important is that the findings do not argue against a recommendation to provide phonics instruction. For example, one of the most persuasive arguments against teaching phonics is that skilled readers could not possibly use phonics, because they recognize words so very rapidly. As a result of technological advances in the study of eye movements, it has been found that proficient readers do recognize a word as a unit; they do have immediate visual access without phonological recording. If this is so, some experts argue, why bother to teach beginning readers something that they will not need later? A traditional but somewhat weak response to this argument has been that knowledge of phonics is always necessary for reading unfamiliar words, such as scientific terminology, even if recognition of familiar words is, in fact, accomplished through some other different process that does not depend on phonics.

Recently, however, that response has given way to an explanation couched in terms of information processing. Seidenberg, Walters, and Barnes (1984) have demonstrated convincingly that there is good empirical evidence that proficient readers can and often (not always) do recognize a printed word by direct visual processing. But one can argue that this purely visual word recognition, unmediated by any phonological processing, is in fact enhanced by giving phonics training to beginning readers. According to Jorm and Share (1983), children who have knowledge of phonics can decode an unfamiliar word. As they sound out the word, its visual pattern becomes more familiar to them. Their repetition of this decoding activity on that particular word leads to direct visual access of it, and the children develop an orthographic image; that is, they can recognize the word immediately, without sounding it out. If, however, they use another strategy besides decoding, for example, if they identify only the first letter and guess the word from that and from context, they will not be paying sufficient attention to the visual features of the word (the letters), and thus they will not develop the ability to recognize it directly. Moreover, decoding also leads to transfer. Because of the fact that the same spelling patterns occur as parts of many different words, decoding practice on one word may enhance recognition of similar words.

Gough and Hillinger (1980) have made a similar argument, emphasizing that whatever strategies a skilled reader actually uses in word recognition, early training in decoding will help to enhance those strategies. Maclean (1988) has called this a "paradox of phonics," that is, that "it is useful to teach beginning readers a skill for which they will have little need as competent readers" (p. 515).

2. Applied Research.   Applied research addresses educational questions directly. One such applied research approach, the laboratory analog, is illustrated by Brendan Byrne's experiments that stimulate the beginning reading process (e.g., Byrne & Fielding-Barnsley, 1989). Byrne taught preliterate preschool children word–picture pairs and found that they learned the pairs by forming associations between the spoken word as a whole and "some aspect" of the print sequence; they did not use an analytic procedure in which they identified and associated phonemes and letters. Byrne also demonstrated that this failure to discover letter–phoneme links was not due to a general deficit in analytic ability.

He concluded that this nonanalytic acquisition procedure is "natural," and that most children will not abandon it unless they are given direct instruction in phonemic segmentation and letter–sound correspondences. Unlike earlier investigators who valued natural acquisition procedures, however, Byrne argued that to become proficient readers children must abandon these natural procedures; and to do this, they must learn phonics.

3. Method Comparisons. The third type of research approach involves method comparisons (which have not been abandoned as a result of the First-Grade Studies mentioned earlier). In 1989, Stahl and Miller published a review of about 50 studies that compared the effects on beginning reading achievement of whole language and language experience approaches and of basal reader approaches, which include some phonics. Overall, Stahl and Miller found the two types of instruction to be approximately equal. Looking more closely, however, they found that the whole language approach may be more effective in kindergarten and less so in first grade. This finding is reasonable in light of the fact that one of the emphases of whole language is on teaching the functional aspects of reading; those insights represent important readiness and early reading goals. But at a later point, instruction must focus children's attention on phonics so that they can master decoding. Finally, Stahl and Miller found that whole language approaches produced weaker effects with disadvantaged students. This confirms all the evidence from the field of special education showing that it is the slower children who are most in need of systematic phonics instruction (Williams, 1987). It is important to note that this effect is demonstrated by "naturalistic" methods of assessment as well as by the more traditional and typical test measures.

Stahl and Miller also found that recent studies showed stronger trends toward the superiority of basal approaches than did earlier ones. This finding may well reflect the recent gradual shift in basals toward the inclusion of more phonics instruction. Although basals have become more phonics oriented over the last few years, they are, as a group, not optimal phonics programs. Many, for example, do not coordinate their phonics lessons with the text that is offered, with the result that children do not get much systematic practice in applying the phonics knowledge they have been taught. Because we know the importance of overlearning in the development of automaticity, this may seriously compromise the phonics training that is being offered. If Stahl and Miller had looked only at basals having serious phonics components, they might have shown even greater differences between basal reader and whole language approaches.

4. Survey Data. Nationwide evaluation of students' performance on reading achievement tests is a relatively new phenomenon. The National Assessment of Educational Progress (NAEP) currently tests the reading achievement of students across the United States every 5 years. From 1970 to 1980, NAEP found an increase in the scores of 9-year-olds, a smaller increase for 13-year-olds, and a decrease for 17-year-olds. According to Chall (1986), these trends are the result of the more challenging beginning reading programs first seen in the late 1960s, programs that included a greater emphasis on phonics. And whereas the 1985 NAEP indicated that the performance of 9-year-olds has tapered off somewhat, Chall suggested that this decline is attributable to the recent emphasis on comprehension in the early grades and the consequent neglect of decoding.

Such surveys, of course, provide only correlational evidence and therefore do not demonstrate causality. Indeed, NAEP's own interpretation of its 1970–1980 data asserts that the 17-year-olds' scores in comprehension, especially inferential comprehension, went down because the students had been exposed to too much decoding in the early grades. Still, data of this kind provide an important basis for evaluation.

5. Observational Studies. The final type of evidence comes from observational and ethnographic studies. This type of research has become much more common over the past few years because of the greater ecological validity of research done in natural contexts. Such work, especially developmental studies of early childhood, is relevant because of the importance of the early years of children's lives to their later reading ability—a point that has been emphasized by whole language proponents. Children must develop an appreciation of the fundamental purpose of reading, that is, that reading is a way of getting meaning and of communicating. This understanding is an important foundation for school instruction.

Whereas most of the studies of the interactions between mothers and very young children do not touch specifically on the issue of phonics, recent work by Bus and IJzendoorn (1988) does. These investigators observed mothers interacting with their 1 1/2-, 3 1/2-, and 5 1/2-year-old children in three tasks: watching "Sesame Street," reading a picture book, and reading a letter book *(B Is for Bear)*. The two older age groups were given tests of both functional and linguistic aspects of written language. These tests measured the children's ability (a) to read (or simulate reading) a favorite book, (b) to construct words from a set of letters, (c) to recognize letter names, (d) to observe reading conventions, and (e) to answer a series of questions dealing with the uses of print. Although almost all the mothers denied ever giving reading instruction to their children, observation indicated that they actually did give instruction in response to expressions of their children's interest. The mothers named letters, tried to make their children recognize sounds in words, and connected letters to well-known words. Moreover, there was a clear relationship between what happened during the mother–child interactions and the test results. The children of mothers who spent more of their time on discussing and interpreting the stories and the illustrations tended to score lower on the tests than did children whose mothers spent more time on specific reading instruction (i.e., making comments relating to formal aspects of written language, such as letter naming, sounds, and word identification). Also, children who spent more of their time during their interactions with their mothers commenting on and asking about the meaning of the stories and the illustrations scored less well on the emergent literacy tasks than did children whose attention was more often focused on letter naming and other such protoreading tasks. In addition, Bus and IJzendoorn (1988) found that the variability in competence among the oldest children was considerably larger than that of the younger groups, suggesting that "competence differences in children grow larger, not only during primary school but during early childhood as well" (p. 1271). It is important to note that there did not seem to be any difference in outcomes between the tests that focused on what might be termed prephonics skills (knowledge of letter names and of conventions, and the ability to construct words out of letters) and those skills that were more related to rudimentary comprehension (the ability to read or simulate reading a story and an understanding of the function of written language).

The Bus and IJzendoorn study suggests that whatever one's frame of reference, that is, whether one sees early literacy acquired during the preschool years on the basis of mother–child interaction as a "natural" developmental process or as an informal teaching–learning process, it is clear that the type of activity addressed in those interactions makes a difference. As in work with older children, attention to specific reading skills that can be characterized as phonics-oriented skills made for better performance.

Two Promising Research Topics

Of the many topics investigated, two—phonemic skills and spelling—stand out as indicating the importance of phonics and decoding in reading instruction and suggesting useful instructional techniques. Both topics relate to phonological structure.

Phonemic Skills.   Over the past several years, the most important advance in our understanding of the decoding process and of effective instructional strategies has come from the study of phonemic analysis. Researchers began to investigate this topic following recommendations by Elkonin (1963) and Zhurova (1963) that phonemic analysis training should precede reading instruction.

Early studies found that proficiency in the analysis of spoken language at both the syllable and the phoneme levels shows a clear developmental progression (Bruce, 1964) and, furthermore, is related to reading achievement (Calfee, Lindamood, & Lindamood, 1973). Liberman, Shankweiler, Fischer, and Carter (1974) asked children to tap out the number of speech segments contained in one- to three-syllable words. The children's performance improved from preschool to first grade and was better on syllable than on phoneme segmentation. Moreover, first graders' scores on the segmentation task were related to their reading achievement in the second grade. The greater difficulty that children experience in performing the phoneme task (Treiman & Baron, 1981) is attributed to the abstract nature of the phoneme.

The results of these, and many other correlational studies encouraged researchers to undertake training studies. As a result, several projects have been devoted to the development of instructional programs that teach phonemic skills. Among the earliest was a program developed by Rosner (1974) that focused on the skills of adding, omitting, substituting, and rearranging phonemes. Rosner found that after 14 weeks of training nonreading first graders outperformed a nontrained control group, not only on reading words that had been used in the training but also on reading transfer words.

Some studies have incorporated phonemic training into comprehensive decoding programs. Williams (1980), for example, developed a decoding program for learning-disabled children to be used as a supplement to their regular classroom instruction. The program taught both phoneme analysis and phoneme blending explicitly. The study showed that children between the ages of 7 and 12 years improved in phoneme segmentation and blending and in decoding skills after using the program. In addition, the training led to significant transfer in decoding unlearned material (novel trigrams, some of which were familiar words, and some of which were nonsense syllables).

Recently, studies have attempted to isolate the effects of phonemic skill training per se. Bradley and Bryant (1985), working with individual children between the ages of 5 and 7 years, showed that training in categorizing words according to phonemes led to higher reading scores than did training in semantic categorization, and, in addition, that phoneme training that included alphabet letters was superior to such training without alphabet letters.

Ball and Blachman (1988) evaluated the effects of 7 weeks of phoneme segmentation training given to groups of kindergarten children in a very low SES school in New Haven, Connecticut. The children who received this training improved more in reading than did a group that received the same instruction in letter names and sounds, along with additional language activities, but no phoneme segmentation training. This study showed not only that phoneme segmentation training has an impact on reading skill (as measured by the Woodcock Word Identification subtest and reading performance on a list of phonetically regular words) but also that phonemic segmentation training had a significantly greater impact than did training in letter–sound correspondences *without* segmentation training.

Lundberg, Frost, and Petersen (1988) designed an 8-month-long training program featuring a variety of phonemic games and exercises and administered it to 6-year-old Danish kindergarten children before they received any reading instruction. In line with the findings of other studies, this study found that the program led to greater proficiency in tasks requiring phonemic manipulation. In addition, Lundberg et al. demonstrated that the training effect was selective, that is, it did not affect linguistic skills such as vocabulary and comprehension of oral instructions. Moreover, this program facilitated reading and spelling acquisition through the second grade.

Is it also true that phonemic skills are a consequence of learning to read? Ehri (1984) has argued that learning to read aids in the development of awareness of the nature of spoken language; that is, when children learn to read and spell, they acquire a visual representation system for speech (i.e., print). The acquisition of this system, because it is built onto children's knowledge of spoken language, may lead to modifications in their speech competencies. In support of this position, Ehri and Wilce (1979) showed that some children used their knowledge of spelling when they were asked to identify the number of phonemes in words. (Indeed, sometimes this strategy backfired: Children claimed that *boat* had four phonemes, because they counted the silent *a*.) Additional evidence comes from a study by Morais, Cary, Alegria, and Bertelson (1979), who found that illiterate adults were not able to delete phonemes from nonsense words, a task that is extremely simple for literate adults. Moreover, it is specifically alphabetic literacy that is important. Read, Yun-Fei, Hong-Yin, and Bao-Qing (1986) showed that Chinese adults literate only in Chinese characters could not delete and add phonemes in spoken Chinese words. These findings confirm the finding of the Byrne and Fielding-Barnsley (1989) study mentioned earlier: Children will not abandon their natural nonanalytic stance unless they are instructed to do so.

The finding that awareness of the phoneme as a linguistic unit is a function of learning to read suggests a further question: Would the type of instruction make any difference? Alegria, Pignot, and Morais (1982) found that first graders who had 4 months of phonics instruction performed better on a phoneme reversal task than did those who had an equivalent amount of whole word instruction. Moreover, performance on the phonemic task was correlated with the teacher's evaluation of the child's reading level only in the phonics-trained group. (See, however, Tunmer & Nesdale, 1985, for data that indicate that the development of phonemic analysis ability is not greatly affected by method of reading instruction.)

The evidence to date is that phonemic skill is both an antecedent to and a consequence of reading instruction, that is, that there is a reciprocal relation between phonemic ability and reading instruction (Ehri, 1979; Perfetti, Beck, & Hughes, 1981). Perfetti (1991) made the further point that the phonemic knowledge a child must have in order to learn to read (i.e., blending phonemes into words) is rudimentary and does not acquire "awareness," whereas the type of phonemic knowledge that children require as a consequence of learning to read is, in fact, the kind that involves "awareness," or reflective analytic ability (phonemic deletion: "Say *cat* without the *c*"). Gains in awareness lead, in turn, to further progress in reading.

Phoneme segmentation and blending activities have not yet been widely incorporated into reading programs. It seems clear, however, that such training is effective and that it should be a part of beginning reading instruction.

Spelling.   The second research topic that relates centrally to the place of phonics in the curriculum is spelling. Spelling was traditionally a common technique in reading instruction (Venezky, 1980), but it became less important when the whole word method came in. Now, however, there is renewed interest in spelling. Read's 1971 analysis of preschoolers' spelling indicated that even before children learn to read they often have some phonemic knowledge. Competence in what are called "invented spellings" is correlated with later reading ability (Mann, Tobin, & Wilson, 1987) and depends on one's phonemic awareness (Liberman, Rubin, Duques, & Carlisle, 1985). Essentially, spelling is a phonics task that involves encoding oral language into written language, rather than decoding writing into speech.

Frith (1986) has proposed that, as children develop some knowledge of spelling–sound relationships and move into the alphabetic stage where they first start utilizing letter–sound correspondences, spelling takes the lead; that is, children start spelling alphabetically while they are still reading according to a logographic strategy that is based on context and purely visual cues. This idea has led people to consider that spelling instruction should be a component of a beginning reading program. In fact, the early programs that followed the Elkonin (1963) design incorporated spelling when they placed letters on the tiles that were used in phoneme analysis and blending training (e.g., Williams, 1980).

Will encoding (spelling) really help reading? Uhry and Shepherd (1990) gave 6 months of segmenting and spelling instruction using blocks and computers to first- and second-grade middle-class children in whole language classrooms that included some phonics training. Not only did the children more quickly gain proficiency in reading both regular and irregular words than did a control group that received only letter–sound training, but they also were better at reading orally, indicating that a gain in fluency had also resulted from the training.

This type of training makes sense when you consider the difference between practicing sound-to-letter (or letter cluster) correspondences on the one hand, and letter-to-sound correspondences on the other. In spelling, the feature that seems to provide the most difficulty—the phoneme—must only be segmented and recognized. It is the letter that must be recalled and produced. In reading, however, the phonemes must be recalled in their segmented representation, produced, and blended.

Spelling instruction offers two advantages: (a) practice on analysis of the phonemes that make up the word, and (b) opportunity to acquire the visual or orthographic image of the word that is essential for proficient reading. (Acquisition of orthographic images based on inaccurately spelled words is not very helpful, of course. In her Reading Recovery program, Marie Clay, 1987, wisely directs teachers to cover up incorrect spellings immediately.)

Beyond Data and Theory

Results from a wide variety of research approaches lead to the conclusion that phonics is an important component of beginning reading instruction and should not be slighted. Moreover, the importance of phonics instruction is also suggested by two topics of research that are currently active and productive.

The importance of being able to buttress conclusions and applications on the basis of several types of research evidence, of course, is that there are inherent limitations in any single type of evidence. Basic research, and even a good deal of what is called applied research, is done outside the true context of the phenomenon of interest, and there are questions of validity and generalization. Comparisons of methods done in actual field settings involve confounding by the many factors that must necessarily go uncontrolled. And the correlational data provided by surveys, not to mention the descriptive data provided by ethnographic studies, are extremely vulnerable to varied and subjective interpretations.

Whereas one can reasonably claim that none of the evidence is perfect, there is no body of evidence showing that instruction that eliminates phonics is superior to other forms of instruction. To make such an argument, one must resort to criteria that we as yet cannot assess, such as the ephemeral "love of reading"—as if, once you learn phonics, you are bound to dislike reading forever.

Why, then, has there been such resistance to phonics? There appear to be several factors involved (Williams, 1987). The first concerns teachers' attitudes. Teachers often consider decoding training to be boring and uncreative, on the grounds that it is "drill oriented" and "mechanical." Teaching decoding is also hard word. Moreover, because thorough training in phonics is far from the norm in teacher education, many teachers may feel ill equipped to teach phonics.

The second factor consists of ideological and political considerations. Phonics is often seen as traditional, authoritarian, and conservative. Indeed, conservative "back-to-basics" movements usually emphasize phonics training. This attitude is being played out today in the political thrust of teacher empowerment.

The third factor is economic. Education is big business, after all, and those who have a vested interest in methods and materials supporting a given approach are often likely to be protective of them no matter what the evidence against the approach.

Lastly, instructional approaches sometimes are rejected even though they are effective because they conflict with, or are perceived to conflict with, other important educational goals. For example, how can you recommend "the one best approach" if you also believe that teachers do a better job if they are allowed to make their own choices about what and how to teach? This is, in fact, what happened with the analysis of the findings from the Follow-Through Planned Variation study, which evaluated several models for educating disadvantaged children. The initial evaluation of the study concluded that the basic skills model was superior to the others (Stebbins, St. Pierre, Proper, Anderson, & Cerva, 1977). However, this evaluation was faulted by House, Glass, McLean, and Walker (1978) on the grounds that the study had shown that the effectiveness of every one of the teaching approaches studied varied widely among school districts, and that this was the finding that should serve as a basis for educational policy; that is, House et al. concluded that local individuality should be honored. This demonstrates a conflict between two quite separate goals, not a judgment about type of instruction.

CONCLUSION

Why are we still hung up on the question of phonics? I suspect, with Adams (1990), that rhetoric is to some extent the villain here; we talk as if there truly were A Great Debate, but we practice sensible moderation. No one would offer phonics lessons as the only form of reading instruction. And, as Adams pointed out, most instructional approaches billed as "nondecoding" (or even "antidecoding") do, in fact, give some, albeit unsystematic, attention to word analysis and letter–sound correspondences. The rhetoric is dangerous, however, because it often leads teachers to believe that they can ignore phonics and decoding. But to be a proficient reader, one must have these skills, regardless of how one acquires them. And many children do not seem able to acquire them without careful, explicit, structured lessons. At the very least, teachers must recognize that these skills must be learned. In addition, they themselves must have a firm grasp of the structure of the English language and of the techniques of teaching phonics as part of their knowledge about reading and their armamentarium of teaching strategies, to be used when required, no matter what their overall instructional method.

Adams has shown persuasively that letter recognition, sound segmentation, letter–sound correspondences, and speedy, accurate word recognition underlie skillful reading. It is too much to hope that her book will convince everyone of the value of phonics training for children, but I do hope that the book will at least help make people aware of the need for teachers to be prepared to teach phonics. In fact, such training is even more essential for teachers who plan to provide their students with only incidental, informal phonics training as opposed to systematic decoding instruction, because it requires considerably greater proficiency and flexibility to respond effectively in the former context. Unfortunately, the conclusion that many people draw from the "antiphonics" or "informal-phonics" whole language movement is not only that phonics training is not a valuable part of the beginning reading curriculum—sad as that may be—but also (and this is perhaps even more serious) that teachers can provide high-quality reading instruction without having been prepared adequately to teach phonics.

REFERENCES

Adams, M. J. (1990). *Beginning to read: Thinking and learning about print.* Cambridge, MA: The MIT Press.

Alegria, J., Pignot, E., & Morais, J. (1982). Phonetic analysis of speech and memory codes in beginning readers. *Memory and Cognition, 10,* 451–456.

Ball, E. W., & Blachman, B. A. (1988). *Phoneme segmentation training: Effect on reading readiness.* Unpublished manuscript.

Beck, I. L., & Juel, C. (in press). The role of decoding in learning to read. In A. R. Farstup & S. J. Samuels (Eds.), *What research has to say about reading instruction* (2nd ed.). Newark, DE: International Reading Association.

Bond, G. L., & Dykstra, R. (1967). The cooperative research program in first-grade reading instruction. *Reading Research Quarterly, 2,* 5–142.

Bradley, L., & Bryant, P. (1985). *Rhyme and reason in reading and spelling.* Ann Arbor: University of Michigan Press.

Bruce, L. J. (1964). The analysis of word sounds by young children. *British Journal of Educational Psychology, 34,* 158–170.

Bus, A. G., & van IJzendoorn, M. H. (1988). Mother–child interactions, attachment, and emergent literacy: A cross-sectional study. *Child Development, 59,* 1262–1272.

Byrne, B., & Fielding-Barnsley, R. (1989). Phonemic awareness and letter knowledge in the child's acquisition of the alphabetic principle. *Journal of Educational Psychology, 81,* 313–321.

Calfee, R. C., Lindamood, P. E., & Lindamood, C. H. (1973). Acoustic/phonetic skills and reading: Kindergarten through twelfth grade. *Journal of Educational Psychology, 64,* 293–298.

Chall, J. S. (1967). *Learning to read: The great debate.* New York: McGraw-Hill.

Chall, J. S. (1986, March/April). New reading trends: The NAEP report card. *Curriculum Review,* 42–44.

Clay, M. M. (1987). *The early detection of reading difficulties* (3rd ed.). Hong Kong: Heinemann.

Ehri, L. C. (1979). Linguistic insight: Threshold of reading acquisition. In T. G. Waller & G. E. MacKinnon (Eds.), *Reading research: Advances in theory and practice* (Vol. 1, pp. 63–84). New York: Academic Press.

Ehri, L. C. (1984). How orthography alters spoken language competencies in children learning to read and spell. In J. Downing & R. Valtin (Eds.), *Learning awareness and learning to read* (pp. 119–147). New York: Springer-Verlag.

Ehri, L. C., & Wilce, L. S. (1979). The mnemonic value of orthography among beginning readers. *Journal of Educational Psychology, 71,* 26–40.

Elkonin, D. B. (1963). The psychology of mastering the elements of reading. In B. Simon & J. Simon (Eds.), *Educational psychology in the USSR* (pp. 165–179). London: Routledge & Kegan Paul.

Frith, U. (1986). A developmental framework for developmental dyslexia. *Annals of Dyslexia, 36,* 69–81.

Gough, P. B., & Hillinger, M. L. (1980). Learning to read: An unnatural act. *Bulletin of the Orton Society, 30,* 179–196.

House, E. R., Glass, G. V., McLean, L. D., & Walker, D. F. (1978). No simple answer: Critique of the Follow Through evaluation. *Harvard Educational Review, 48,* 128–160.

Jorm, A. F., & Share, D. L. (1983). Phonological recoding and reading acquisition. *Applied Psycholinguistics, 4,* 103–147.

Levin, H., & Williams, J. P. (1970). *Basic studies on reading.* New York: Basic Books.

Liberman, I. Y. (1990, March). *Whole language and phonics: A false dichotomy.* Paper presented to the New York branch of the Orton Dyslexia Society, New York.

Liberman, I. Y., Rubin, H., Duques, S., & Carlisle, J. (1985). Linguistic abilities and spelling proficiency in kindergartners and adult poor spellers. In D. B. Gray & J. F. Kavanaugh (Eds.), *Biobehavioral measures of dyslexia* (pp. 163–176). Parkton, MD: New York Press.

Liberman, I. Y., Shankweiler, D., Fischer, F. W., & Carter, B. (1974). Explicit syllable and phoneme segmentation in the young child. *Journal of Experimental Child Psychology, 18,* 201–212.

Lundberg, I., Frost, J., & Petersen, O.-P. (1988). Effects of an extensive program for stimulating phonological awareness in preschool children. *Reading Research Quarterly, 23,* 263–284.

Maclean, R. (1988). Two paradoxes of phonics. *The Reading Teacher, 41,* 514–517.

Mann, V. A., Tobin, R., & Wilson, R. (1987). Measuring phonological awareness through the invented spelling of kindergarten children. *Merrill–Palmer Quarterly, 33,* 365–391.

Morais, J., Cary, L., Alegria, J., & Bertelson, P. (1979). Does awareness of speech as a sequence of phones arise spontaneously? *Cognition, 7,* 323–331.

Perfetti, C. A. (1992). The representation problem in reading acquisition. In P. B. Gough, L. Ehri, & R. Treiman (Eds.), *Reading acquisition* (pp. 145–174). Hillsdale, NJ: Lawrence Erlbaum Associates.

Perfetti, C. A., Beck, I. L., & Hughes, C. (1981, April). *Phonemic knowledge and learning to read: A longitudinal study of first graders.* Paper presented at the biennial meeting of the Society for Research in Child Development, Boston.

Read, C. (1971). Preschool children's knowledge of English phonology. *Harvard Educational Review, 41,* 1–34.

Read, C., Yun-Fei, Z., Hong-Yin, N., & Bao-Qing, D. (1986). The ability to manipulate speech sounds depends on knowing alphabetic writing. *Cognition, 24,* 31–44.

Rosner, J. (1974). Auditory analysis training with prereaders. *The Reading Teacher, 27,* 379–381.

Seidenberg, M. S., Walters, G. S., & Barnes, M. A. (1984). When does irregular spelling or pronunciation influence word recognition? *Journal of Verbal Learning and Verbal Behavior, 23,* 383–404.

Stahl, S. A., & Miller, P. D. (1989). Whole language and language experience approaches for beginning reading: A quantitative research synthesis. *Review of Educational Research, 59,* 87–116.

Stebbins, L. B., St. Pierre, R. G., Proper, E. C., Anderson, R. B., & Cerva, T. R. (1977). *Education as experimentation: A planned variation model. Vol. IV-A. An evaluation of Follow Through.* Cambridge, MA: Abt Associates.

Teale, W. H., & Sulzby, E. (Eds.). (1986). *Emergent literacy: Writing and reading.* Norwood, NJ: Ablex.

Treiman, R., & Baron, J. (1981). Segmental analysis ability: Development and relation to reading ability. In G. E. MacKinnon & T. G. Waller (Eds.), *Reading research: Advances in theory and practice* (Vol. 3, pp. 159–198). New York: Academic Press.

Tunmer, W. E., & Nesdale, A. R. (1985). Phonemic segmentation skill and beginning reading. *Journal of Educational Psychology, 77,* 417–427.

Uhry, J. K., & Shepherd, M. J. (1990, April). *The effect of segmentation/spelling training on the acquisition of beginning reading strategies.* Paper presented at the annual meeting of the American Educational Research Association, Boston.

Venezky, R. L. (1980). From Webster to Rice to Roosevelt: The formative years for spelling instruction and spelling reform in the USA. In U. Frith (Ed.), *Cognitive processes in spelling* (pp. 9–30). New York: Academic Press.

Williams, J. P. (1980). Teaching decoding with a special emphasis on phoneme analysis and phoneme blending. *Journal of Educational Psychology, 72,* 1–15.

Williams, J. P. (1987). Educational treatments for dyslexia at the elementary and secondary levels. In R. F. Bowler (Ed.), *Intimacy with language: A forgotten basic in teacher education* (pp. 24–32). Baltimore: Orton Dyslexia Society.

Zhurova, L. E. (1963). The development of analysis of words into sounds by preschool children. *Soviet Psychology and Psychiatry, 2,* 17–27.

WHOLE LANGUAGE

If It Ain't Whole, It Ain't Language—or Back to the Basics of Freedom and Dignity

Hans U. Grundin
Language and Literacy Consultant

BACK TO FREEDOM AND DIGNITY

Regardless of its "technical merit," an instructional approach, whether in the field of reading or any other field, can only be justified as part of an overall educational philosophy. The subskills-oriented approaches dominating reading instruction in American schools are clearly rooted in a behaviorist philosophy, where concerns about the learner's mind or spirit are dismissed as irrelevant. In the behaviorist philosophy, learning *is* behavior modification, and once the instructor has successfully and lastingly modified the behavior of the learner, education is completed. Nowhere was this basic philosophy expressed more clearly than in B. F. Skinner's book, *Beyond Freedom and Dignity* (1971).

The message of Skinner's book was, to put it very simply, that any concern for the freedom and dignity of the learner interferes with the efficiency of learning— because the learner does not know what is good for him, but the all-knowing instructor does. And if perchance the learner wants to do something other than what the instructor has decided is good for him, then that is irrelevant, because once the instruction is completed, the learner, his behavior suitably modified, cannot help but do what he has been taught.

Authors of modern basal reading programs may not subscribe explicitly to this unashamedly naked expression of pure behaviorism, but the underlying philosophy is still there in their programs. The "scope and sequence" of learning is predetermined; instruction is devised to teach each step in a specified manner; the mind and soul of the learner are not taken into account, other than as objects to be manipulated—"motivated"—to be taught what is preordained, whether or not the learner wants to learn. When this instructional system fails to bring about the required behavior modifications, the object of instruction—the child—is declared deficient and is handed over to another instructional subsystem, the one that deals with the rejects.

Virtually all the research evaluating this type of instructional program seems to have accepted, at least tacitly, the validity of such an educational philosophy. It seems agreed implicitly that Skinner was right, that education does not need to concern itself with the freedom and dignity of human beings, that its task is to shape the required behavior, including thought—for thought is nothing but behavior to the Skinnerians—of the young of the species. This is reflected, not least, in the way success is defined in the research: performance on tasks that the learner has not selected, and that have no intrinsic meaning or value to the learner. The learner is required to show proof of the *skill to read,* without knowing why or for what purpose she or he is reading; and nobody seems interested in whether the learner has the *will to read.*

This educational philosophy is typified in the following quotation from Berliner and Rosenshine (1977), which is cited with approval by Patrick Groff, one of the major Skinnerians in the field of reading: "The classroom behavior of the successful teacher is characterized by direct instruction, whereby students are brought into contact with the curriculum materials *and are kept in contact with them until the requisite knowledge is acquired*" (p. 393, italics added). The italicized clause typifies the relentlessness of those who have followed Skinner all the way—beyond the freedom and dignity of the students.

The Scientificness Myth

The ideology of behaviorism is usually coupled with *empiricism,* the belief that empirical evidence alone can determine what is right or wrong, true or false, regardless of the acceptability of the underlying values. A true empiricist, for example, would expect our society's decision to adopt democracy as a system of government to be based on "empirical evidence" of the superiority of democracy compared to alternative systems. He would also expect the abolition of slavery and the benefits of civil rights to be demonstrated empirically; forgetting or willfully ignoring the fact that democracy and civil rights are "better" than the alternatives *only if one accepts certain basic values as unalienable and axiomatic.* Behaviorism is also likely to be coupled with *scientism,* which is characterized by the dogmatic belief in the infallibility of empiricist and behaviorist science, and the conviction that what the behaviorist holds true is always the result of pure, objective, scientific analysis, unadulterated by "ideas" (which are dismissed as *ideology*).

This combination of behaviorist extremism with empiricism and scientism is typified by Groff (1989) in his defense of basal readers, or rather his attack on the attack on basal readers. For example, he characterized the *Report Card on Basal Readers* (Goodman, Shannon, Freeman, & Sharon, 1988) as "an eccentric, predisposed point of view, a partiality and predilection toward, or preconception of an issue" (p. 38). This is in contrast to "an unbiased, undogmatic, even-handed, and equitable treatment" or "an objective, scientific analysis" (pp. 38–39). Groff is too coy to say it, but he clearly feels the latter description characterizes his own behavior in the basal reader dispute.

To the followers of scientism, there is only one kind of science: the "traditional" one based on empiricism and logical positivism, or in Groff's words, the "controlled experimentation in reading, the type *customarily carried out in most scientific investigations,* in which standardized test data is gathered, analyzed and interpreted" (p. 39).

"Scientismists" will always refuse to discuss the ideas and values underpinning their faith. Any question of the appropriateness of their method and approach is turned into a question of belief in the basic dogma: the superiority and infallibility of The Scientific Method. To people such as Groff, The Scientific Method is not good *for* something; rather is represents an *absolute* good.

Thus, in his spirited defense of basals and the ideology underpinning them, Groff (1989) never said a word about the differing views of the learner and of the fundamental purpose of education that are at the root of the dispute between him and the *Report Card* group. Instead he argued: "Readers of this debate . . . must decide . . . on which side of these differing views as to the relative merit of research models their sympathy lies" (p. 39). In other words, only those who put themselves beyond the pale by rejecting The Scientific Method will have any truck with the *Report Card.*

The Great Debate Among Word Fetishists

Like so many other educational buzz words, whole language is a silly term: Who ever advocated a half-language—or a three-quarter language—approach to literacy? Either language is whole, or it simply is not language.

Everybody agrees that reading is, or at least ought to be, a language art. Reading *is* making sense of printed language. But in most of the reading programs currently in use, the beginning reading instruction deals with words and bits and pieces of words, not with language. This failure to appreciate fully the difference between the concrete, meaning-making, communicative role of language on the one hand and the abstract noncommunicative nature of isolated language fragments on the other is the most serious failing of early reading programs.

Once upon a time, in the Land of The Great Debate, the die-hard "phonicators" tried to make a distinction between *code-emphasis* (i.e., phonics) and *meaning-emphasis* (i.e., everything that was not phonics). Unfortunately, the only alternative to phonics that existed in the minds of the Challs and Flesches of the reading world was "look–say," a method that proposes to teach children a "sight vocabulary" in the hardest way imaginable, by drilling them in a particular variety of the quaint art of barking at print; that is, by recognizing letter combinations "by sight" and proving this recognition by making suitable noises.

"Phonics" is another approach to teaching barking at print. Children are supposed to synthesize the individual letter–sounds *cuh, ah, tuh* to the pronunciation *cat,* which in turn is supposed to evoke in their minds—in the abstract—a notion of some aspects of feline existence. Barking at print is probably protected under the First Amendment as speech that must be free, but it is not reading—it never has been and never will be reading.

The Great Debate was, in fact, a very narrow debate; it dealt with one question only: Should beginning reading start with phonics, or should it start with look–say?

Jeanne Chall (1967) had no doubts about the answer: Phonics is the thing. And aided and abetted by Chall, the members of the Commission on Reading went along with this view in the 1985 report, *Becoming a Nation of Readers* (Anderson, Hiebert, Scott, & Wilkinson). "Keep it simple and do it early" was their advice; given purely on the strength of research in the Skinnerian vein that showed that, on balance, phonics leads to somewhat higher test scores than does look–say.

But those of us who have removed our Skinnerian blinders can see clearly that phonics and look–say are both abstract, language-fragmenting, and meaning-destroying approaches to early reading, which violate everything we know about how children learn—and how they ought to learn.

Learning Without Teaching

To the control-oriented behaviorists there can be no learning without explicit, direct, small-step teaching—or instruction, which is their preferred term. The very thought that the *object of instruction,* which is supposed to be entirely controlled by the *instructor,* actually has the capacity to learn independently of the instructor—and that this independent capacity to learn could be used voluntarily—is probably deeply disturbing to these people.

Again, Groff (1989) gives a very good illustration of this failure to admit even the *possibility* of learning without direct instruction in his defense of basals: "If teachers of reading . . . can arrange for children to get to the meaning of a passage (an ultimate goal of reading instruction) without teaching them how to recognize words, why would these teachers then turn back and teach decoding?" (p. 42). What most advocates of a holistic approach are saying is *not* that children can read without recognizing words. They are saying that children can learn to recognize words *through involvement in an educational curriculum that incorporates carefully designed and selected holistic reading activities.*

Reading Is Mind Over Matter

For those of us who see human learning as the gradual cognitive, social, and emotional development of human beings who deserve both freedom and dignity, it has been known for many decades that the most successful and worthwhile learning does not come about through behavior modification but through the carefully guided and nurtured development of the mind. It is also obvious to us that human growth is so complex and varied that it is folly to pretend that we know exactly how it enfolds—or how it ought to enfold. Only those who reject the basic human rights of freedom and dignity can justify turning young people—and let us remember that children are people—into objects of instruction to be shaped into the preconceived image of the instructor.

Those without Skinnerian blinders also know that human learning always starts with the concrete and the meaningful, things the learner can easily relate to and wants to relate to. And then the learning proceeds gradually toward the more complex, abstract, and sophisticated concepts. This principle applies to all learners, but it is particularly important with young learners. In early literacy learning, the only thing truly concrete and meaningful is language communication; building on young children's command of language as a means of making sense of their world, as a means of telling other people things, and finding out what they have to tell us.

Yet, what do most early reading programs do? They start with the most abstract aspects of language. They have children work extensively with words and bits and pieces of words. It is true that we use words *in* language, but words in isolation—lists of words or stacks of word cards—*do not constitute* language any more than a pile of bricks constitutes a house. With a pile of bricks plus lots of other things plus the knowledge of how to put the pieces together, we can make a house. In the same way, words can be used to *make* language—if we have something to say.

When the old look–say approach was said to have "meaning emphasis," this was based on a confusion of very different kinds of meaning. A word in isolation, say *dog,* only has abstract potential meaning, or rather several abstract potential meanings: its various lexical references. It can refer to any or all the animals of the canine species, that is, the abstract idea of a dog. It can refer to a sausage. It can, as a sexist slang word, refer to women, in phrases like "She's a real dog." But if I were to approach some people and just say "dog," they would feel puzzled to say the least—and probably deeply concerned about my mental health, because I would have told them nothing. "So what's this about a dog?" they would say.

On the other hand, real, concrete, language meaning is created only when words are put together *for a purpose of communication,* when we use language to convey a message. And this is true whether we are dealing with oral or written language. Before there can be language, there must be a message to convey. Call it whole language or call it language plain and simple, but that is what reading and writing are all about—anything else is just meaningless purposeless fragments.

You Cannot Read Words

Trapped in the sterile confines of The Great Debate, many people seem to feel that barking at print is a necessary evil. Of course it is not reading! Of course we do not really like it! Of course we do not believe young children enjoy it! But there is no alternative! That is what the Commission on Reading claims. But the reason the members of the Commission can see no alternative is that they are stuck in their word fetishism. Richard Anderson, Isabel Beck, Jere Brophy, Jeanne Chall, Robert Glaser, Lenore Ringler, David Rumelhart, Dorothy Strickland, Sue Talbot, and Monte Penney—the whole Commission fails to see the language for all the words.

Individually, some of these eminent educators argue for a holistic, language, and literature-based approach to early literacy learning. And in the chapter, "Emerging Literacy," *Becoming a Nation of Readers* shows a thorough understanding of how young children really grow toward literacy. But when it comes to the nitty-gritty of how we ought to *teach reading,* the collective wisdom of the eminent commission is that in the beginning is—and must be—the Word.

The question, they say, is How should children be taught to read words? not, How should children be taught to read? not, How can we help them to become readers? but, How can we teach them words! One wonders if the Commission members have misunderstood the biblical saying, "In the beginning was the word." Do they imagine that in the beginning of the world of literacy there was one gigantic flash card? So it seems, because the high priests of the Cult of the Word have but one concern: How do we get the little children to sound it out? They may sound it out synthetically, analytically, or as a Gestalt. But sound out the Word they must.

Without any kind of linguistic or psycholinguistic argument, it is taken for granted that the word is—and ought to remain—the fundamental unit of early reading. Even after recognizing that young children can have "wholebooksuccess" with repeated reading, that they can "get the satisfaction of reading real books," the Commission quickly brings us back to the straight and narrow path of kowtowing before the Word: "After a story has been read in this fashion, words from the story can be printed on charts . . . so that the children can begin to *recognize the words outside the helpful context of the familiar book*" (Anderson et al., 1985, p. 32, italics added). Real readers never have to recognize words outside context, so why should the beginners be subjected to this most difficult of all barking-at-print skills?

In *Counterpoint and Beyond: A Response to Becoming a Nation of Readers* (1988), Connie Bridge analyzed in some detail the inconsistency between the "interactive constructionist theory of reading and the instructional practices suggested in *Becoming a Nation of Readers.*" She went on: "I have described alternative instructional practices for beginning reading that are compatible with a constructivist view of the reading process and that keep the focus on meaning even during the initial stages of learning. Obviously, research exists to support these beginning reading practices. Why the authors of BNR chose to ignore this body of research is unclear" (p. 59).

In another chapter in *Counterpoint and Beyond,* Mary Anne Hall pointed out the same basic inconsistency between the recognition in *Becoming a Nation of*

Readers of reading as a meaning-making process and its emphasis on phonics and on learning to "read words" in beginning reading instruction. Hall (1988) concluded: "In order for schools to follow the recommendations of *Becoming a Nation of Readers* (other than those on phonics), a *whole language perspective and a program built on that perspective are necessary*" (p. 40, italics added). Contrary to the *Becoming a Nation of Readers* creed, then, the first task is *not* to teach children how to read words—if it were, the Commission's recipe might be all right. The first task in reading is to help children learn what we as literate adults already know: that you only read language—you do not read words.

Language Must Be Put Before Words

I have dwelt at some length on a critique of *Becoming a Nation of Readers* because, since its publication, it has had a tremendous impact on American reading instruction and on published reading programs. In 1985, I went on record (Grundin) with my conclusion that *Becoming a Nation of Readers* gave whole language a raw deal and an unfair deal. Nothing has happened since to make me want to change this conclusion.

Today, the Commission on Reading's attempt to put down whole language can be clearly seen to have been futile. A thumb in a hole in the dike is not doing much good when the tide is sweeping over the top of the dam. Suddenly, everybody is "into" whole language. In the case of publishers, this change was prompted to a large extent by the California Reading Initiative, which undoubtedly has led to considerable improvements in the most recent versions of many reading programs.

But in the early reading instruction in these programs, the new converts to the cause of whole language have not had the courage of their conviction. In the beginning is still the word—and its various bits and pieces, primarily the "letter–sounds." Selections in preprimers and primers are still written, not in English but in that age-old nonlanguage called *Primerese*. In fact, publishers were given a clear license to continue printing Primerese by *Becoming a Nation of Readers* (Anderson et al., 1985): "How can stories be comprehensive when they must be written with a severely limited set of words? . . . The reality is, that because the number of words that beginners can identify is still very limited, . . . the earliest school reading selections cannot . . . tell complete stories. Meaning must be constructed . . . also from picture clues and information provided by the teacher" (p. 44).

So all the concern for meaning and making sense suddenly is allowed to count for nothing, because in the beginning must still be the Word. Never mind the rapidly growing evidence that children can learn to read through reading—through reading language and not just words. It has become an article of faith that reading selections must be written with a severely limited set of words, so limited that the strings of words cease to be language and become the nonlanguage Primerese. And all the tests used to measure the success of such programs are based on the assumption that the word must come before the language.

Some people think that Primerese is actually an impoverished dialect of English, something akin to Pidgin English. I wish it were, because at least Pidgin English is a language used by people who have something to say to each other. This is the true acid test of a language—that it is used for communication, for telling people things. And that is exactly the test that Primerese fails utterly. Primerese writers—there are probably no speakers of Primerese—have one thing in common: They have nothing to tell children. All other writers for children have things to tell them. They may also want to make an honest buck, but they know they can do that only by having something to tell and by telling it well. But not Primerese writers. Their purpose is totally different: to give children the opportunity to recognize words—to decode—to bark at print. Because the only way you prove you have recognized a word is by pronouncing it, making the noise—that is all.

Incidentally, until very recently all Primerese writers used to have one more thing in common: They published their writings anonymously. But for some reason a few brave ones have now started to take public credit for their authorship, although we have yet to see a Preprimer of the Year Award or any other real recognition of achievement.

Why Primerese is Harmful to Young Children

Even Primerese writers recognize the value of children's literature, as long as all the long words and those that are not "phonetic" are excluded. If meaning is thrown out with the nonpermissible words, *tant pis;* the young child simply must not be allowed to see words that cannot be sounded out without the help of context. In case you have not read any good preprimers lately, I shall refresh your memory by giving you an authentic Primerese translation of a children's classic, "Humpty Dumpty" (a / indicates a page ending in the preprimer; taken from *The Piccaninny Readers,* no date):

> Oh Humpty! Oh Humpty Dumpty!/ See, See. See Humpty Dumpty. Oh, Humpty Dumpty. Oh, see. Oh, see./ See, oh See. Humpty Dumpty, Sat on the wall. Oh Humpty Dumpty./ Humpty Dumpty, Sat on the wall. Funny Humpty Dumpty. Look, oh look Funny Humpty Dumpty./ Look Mother, look. See Humpty. See funny Humpty Dumpty. See Humpty on the wall. Funny, funny Humpty./ Oh, Oh, Oh. See Father, see Humpty Dumpty on the wall. Look at Humpty. Funny Humpty Dumpty./ Mother, Father. Look and see On the wall sat Humpty. Oh Humpty, funny Humpty./ Oh, Oh, Oh. Come and see. Mother, Father, come and see. Look at Humpty Dumpty. Oh. Oh. Oh.

If you want to know what this means, you have to look at the pictures.

Many people think this version of "Humpty Dumpty" is funny. Personally, I think it is hilarious. But what about nonliterate 6-year-olds (and many 6-year-olds are nonliterate through no fault of their own)? What about those who have never heard the real thing? Would they find it funny? Would they not instead find it just puzzling, confusing, and totally pointless?

Now, this particular version of "Humpty Dumpty" was published over 50 years ago in Australia, in a series called *The Piccaninny Readers*. Other titles in the series were "Ruff" and "Jack & Jill," and one shudders to think what must have been done to those poor souls. I doubt that *The Piccaninny Readers* would stand much chance of being adopted anywhere in the United States today, but that does not mean that things have changed. The only change is that in the last 10 years I have not read anything remotely as funny as "Humpty Dumpty" in a basal reader. Otherwise, it is as true today as it was 50 years ago: Primerese writers have nothing to tell children. They just expect them to bark at the print. And if the children happen to be interested in what it means, all they can do is look at the pictures.

Anybody who doubts that the previous paragraph is a true statement about preprimers is advised to select a few at random, take them home, and read them aloud to friends and family, including a few young children, and then talk about the "stories," not about the pictures but about the "stories" told in the words.

Through a combination of barking at print and picture analysis, plus explanations from the teacher, children may well get some kind of story from a preprimer selection. A good teacher may even manage to engage the children in some cognitive activity using language. But whatever they are doing, whatever they are learning in the process, *they are not reading*. They cannot be reading, because reading is the process of making sense of printed language—and this presupposes that there is some sense to make in the language.

With their combination of nonlanguage of the Primerese variety and picture comprehension, preprimers virtually force children to take their attention away from the "squiggles" on the paper as soon as they start thinking about what it all means. Children are taught not to expect meaning in the printed words, so that even children who come to school knowing that one can seek meaning in print can very easily be thoroughly confused.

Fortunately, the majority of children get healthy doses of real language and contacts with real literacy; they are read to and see others read—for pleasure, for information, for many reasons, but always for meaning. They are effectively immunized against the nasty side effects of Primerese and phonication. They plod through their preprimers, and when they come to the primer they are rewarded by the odd glimmer of a real story, and after that there is really a great deal of good reading in most basals.

But what about the large number of unfortunate children who come to school without having acquired any sense of what reading is and what it is for, who have not experienced the worthwhileness of reading? These children will take all their ideas about reading from the school reading program. Teachers may know that, although they teach reading as if it were barking at print, they do not really believe that that is all there is to it. A teacher may even tell children good stories with the book open in front of her. She knows that she is reading, but the children may think she is just looking at the pictures and telling stories about them. Because when the reading lesson comes along, these children very quickly learn that, in their books at least, squiggles on paper do not tell stories. Squiggles on paper have to be somehow mysteriously sounded out, barked at: If you get the noise right, the teacher will be pleased; if not, not. But meaning does not come into it. Can one really expect these children to be "turned on" by books and reading? Can one expect them to gather from their meager Primerese diet that reading is, after all, worthwhile? Can one expect them to understand that all this barking at print that has nothing to tell them is but a year-long warming-up exercise before they will be allowed to catch a glimpse of some real reading—and that all the boring meaningless activities will be worth the effort in the long run? If one truly believes this, then preprimers are what these children should have. If not, one must seriously consider the possibility that the early reading books do much more harm than good for precisely those children who most need our help to become literate, to become citizens with full and equal rights in a democratic nation of readers.

The Role of Illustrations in Early Reading

To say that illustrations are prominent in early reading materials seems like a gross understatement. The casual observer opening up a preprimer may think that the illustrations *are* the reading materials. Is it not strange then that, among all the thousands of reading research studies, only a handful have dealt with these illustrations? Even stranger is that what little evidence there is suggests that basaltype reading materials are more effective when the illustrations are removed (Samuels, 1977). Common sense supports the notion that if children have only text to look at, chances are they will pay more attention to the text, so the research findings should not surprise us. What is surprising is that publishers still place an extremely strong emphasis on illustrations in basals, without any clear instructional rationale for doing so.

Becoming a Nation of Readers, however, seems to provide a rationale for using illustrations when it points out that, due to the "severely limited set of words" in early reading materials, "meaning must be constructed . . . also from picture clues" (p. 44). But how does a justification for carefully selected picture clues become a license to cover up to 90% and more of the preprimer pages with rich attractive pictures that, instead of giving clues to the meaning of the text, completely take over the meaning-bearing function: The pictures become the story, and the words are literally relegated to the periphery of the page, as well as to the periphery of the young learner's cognitive attention.

The cognitive take-over by the pictures would, in itself, be very bad for young learners who are unsure of the real nature of writing and reading. The problem is compounded by the fact that not only do they have to look to the pictures for the story that the words fail to tell, but when there is a rudiment of story in the words, this is often contradicted by the pictures.

You Cannot Have a Whole Language Basal

I have concentrated on materials for beginning reading for two reasons: (a) It is by far the stage that is most crucial to long-term reading success; and (b) it is the stage where current programs are at their weakest. If you conclude that current programs would be significantly improved if they were purged of all Primerese and if young nonreaders were spared the traumas of excessive phonication, I would agree wholeheartedly. But if you conclude that we would then have a whole language basal program, you would be wrong. There can be no such thing as a whole language basal. As I have already shown, the basal approach and the whole language approach are rooted in fundamentally different philosophies of learning and education. Even a fully literature-based basal is still a basal, as long as it is designed on the assumption that to learn to read, all children must go through the same scope and sequence of arbitrarily selected fragments of literacy under the name of *subskills,* and that all the children in a class, a school, or a whole district must learn these subskills through working with the same texts, in the same order, with the same ancillary activities—usually in the form of worksheets.

It is surely no coincidence that more and more teachers and children feel that current reading programs and the accompanying tests impose a straitjacket on the learning process. In the early school years, Primerese and phonication cause the most problems, but the rigidity and inflexibility of so many programs, combined with artificiality, are seen by many as affronts to the freedom and dignity of teachers and children alike.

REFERENCES

Anderson, R. C., Hiebert, E. H., Scott, J. A., & Wilkinson, I. A. G. (1985). *Becoming a nation of readers: The report of the Commission on Reading.* Champaign, IL: Center for the Study of Reading; Washington, DC: National Institute of Education.

Berliner, D. C., & Rosenshine, B. (1977). The acquisition of knowledge in the classroom. In R. C. Anderson, R. J. Shapiro, & W. E. Montague (Eds.), *Schooling and the acquisition of knowledge* (pp. 375–396). Hillsdale, NJ: Lawrence Erlbaum Associates.

Bridge, C. A. (1988). Focusing on meaning in beginning reading instruction. In J. L. Davidson (Ed.), *Counterpoint and beyond: A response to Becoming a Nation of Readers* (pp. 51–62). Urbana, IL: National Council of Teachers of English.

Chall, J. S. (1967). *Learning to read: The great debate.* New York: McGraw–Hill.

Goodman, K. S., Shannon, P., Freeman, Y., & Sharon, M. (1988). *Report card on basal readers.* Katonah, NY: Richard C. Owen.

Groff, P. (1989). An attack on basal readers for the wrong reasons. In *ARENA: A debate in print* (pp. 8–13, 23–30, 38–44). Bloomington, IN: ERIC Clearinghouse on Reading and Communication Skills.

Grundin, H. U. (1985). A commission of selective readers: A critique of *Becoming a Nation of Readers*. *The Reading Teacher, 39,* 262–266.

Hall, M. A. (1988). Beyond phonics to language-centered learning. In J. L. Davidson (Ed.), *Counterpoint and beyond: A response to Becoming a Nation of Readers* (pp. 33–42). Urbana, IL: National Council of Teachers of English.

Humpty Dumpty. (no date). *The Piccaninny readers.* Sydney: Atlantic Publications.

Samuels, S. J. (1977). Can pictures distract students from the printed word? *Journal of Reading Behavior, 9,* 361–64.

Skinner, B. F. (1971). *Beyond freedom and dignity.* New York: Knopf.

6 Whole Language: Exploring the Meaning of the Label

Diane Stephens
Center for the Study of Reading

The past 30 years have seen vast changes in literacy education, and within that period the label "whole language" has been used to refer to a group of educators who have advocated particular kinds of change in literacy education. The *whole language* label, however, has been used in a variety of contexts by a variety of individuals. And, as we move across time, contexts, and individuals, it becomes clear that neither the sense (the meaning) of the label nor its referent (that to which it refers) has remained constant.

The effect of this ambiguity is sometimes disconcerting and often problematic. Battles are fought pro and con whole language, and indeed battles are even fought over what each side mistakenly thinks the other means. The reverse is also true. Sometimes language masks differences, and people think they agree about whole language when, indeed, there are major points of disagreement between them.

To understand whole language as it is currently conceptualized, and thus to disambiguate the term, it is first necessary to understand how the field of reading research has changed over the last 30 years and to consider what we have learned during that period. Second, it is essential to understand that whole language is not a particular body of knowledge or a teaching method but rather it is *a response* to our increased knowledge about literacy and how it develops. These understandings, in turn, enable an understanding of whole language as political agenda, provide a foundation for informed consideration of the research that has been conducted on or in whole language classrooms during the last decade, and inform our understanding of, and our own position in, the current debates over whole language.

A BRIEF OVERVIEW OF RECENT READING-RELATED
RESEARCH

As Fig. 6.1 illustrates, prior to 1960, education, psychology, linguistics, sociology, and philosophy were primarily independent fields (hence the vertical lines in the figure). Education was defined *predominately* as method, and within reading education the debate centered on whether to use whole words or phonics to teach reading. Psychology was *predominately* behavioristic (Pavlov, 1927; Skinner, 1957; Thorndike, 1913), and linguistics *generally* concentrated on the surface structure of language (Bloomfield, 1933; Sapir, 1921).

Beginning in the 1960s, both the focus of research within these fields, and the relationships among them, began to change (see Fig. 6.2). The divisions became less rigid, and indeed new fields emerged that represented intersections between disciplines. Educational psychology moved away from behaviorism into cognitive science (Anderson, Reynolds, Schallert, & Goetz, 1977; Brown, 1980; Spiro, 1980), and linguists began to study the "deep structure" of language (Chomsky, 1957). A new field, psycholinguistics, emerged from the common interests of these two groups, and researchers in this field explored how written and oral language were learned (Brown, 1970; Goodman, 1968). Another new field, sociolinguistics, emerged from the interests shared by sociologists and linguists. Michael Halliday, Judith Green, and David Bloome, for example, all explored language as a social construction (Bloome & Green, 1984; Green, 1983; Halliday, 1975).

As psycho- and sociolinguistics emerged and defined themselves, it became

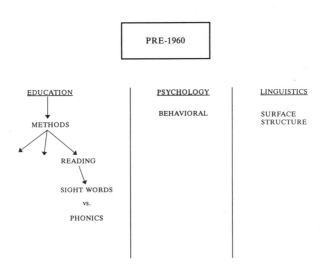

FIG. 6.1.   Reading education in context, pre-1960.

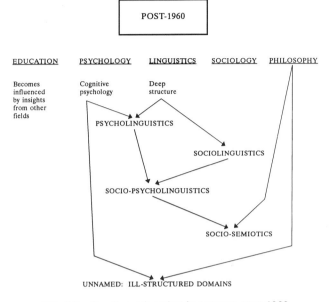

FIG. 6.2. Reading education in context, post-1960.

apparent that these new fields also shared common interests, with the result that some people began to call themselves sociopsycholinguists. Indeed, the Socio-Psycholinguistics Special Interest Group of the International Reading Association (IRA) was established in 1977. More recently, individuals from some of these fields have begun to tap the resources of other fields such as philosophy. Rand Spiro, for example, a cognitive psychologist and a reading researcher, drew from the work of Wittgenstein to talk of criss-crossing landscapes (Spiro, Coulson, Feltovich, & Anderson, 1988). Other researchers, such as Jerome Harste, influenced by work done in semiotics and structuralism, talked of referent and signification and referred to themselves as sociosemioticians (Harste, Woodward, & Burke, 1984).

Thus, rather than remaining separate from other disciplines, reading education has become transdisciplinary. Once limited to one field, reading research has become the domain of many. A number of linguists, cognitive psychologists, sociolinguists, and psycholinguists now consider themselves to be reading researchers; many reading researchers likewise now identify themselves with fields outside the traditional domain of reading education. The cross-disciplinary attention given to reading extends beyond the fields represented here. Some literacy theorists, developmental psychologists, and clinical psychologists now also consider reading as one of their domains.

One result of this multidisciplinary interest is that the meaning of *reading* has

Reading is seen as a cognitive process

Schema

Metacognition

Strategies

Reading is seen as a linguistic process

Cue systems

Rule governed

Learned through
use

Reading is seen as a social process

Contexts

Collaboration

Community

Reading is seen as a meaning-making process

FIG. 6.3. Reading as multi-disciplinary.

Wittgenstein - ill-structured domains

Peirce - signification

been widely expanded (see Fig. 6.3). Reading is now viewed as, at the least, a cognitive process, a languaging process, a social process, and a meaning-making process. From research conducted predominately but not exclusively from a cognitive psychology perspective, for example, we have learned that reading is a cognitive process. We have learned about the importance of background knowledge (e.g., Anderson, Spiro, & Anderson, 1978), of self-monitoring (e.g., Brown, 1980), and of reading as a strategic process (see Goodman, Smith, Meredith, & Goodman, 1976). From research conducted predominately but not exclusively in the field of linguistics, we have learned that reading is a languaging process—that there are cue systems in language (most notably Goodman, 1968), and that written language acquisition is rule governed (Ferriero & Teberosky, 1983; Harste et al., 1984; Read, 1975). We have also come to understand that both written and oral language are learned through use, and that use is driven by the function language serves for the user (Halliday, 1975).

In addition, we have come to understand that reading is a social process. There is now extensive research that documents the significant and necessary contributions to language development and use made by other individuals through collaboration and community (e.g., Bloome & Green, 1984; Green, 1983; Heap, 1980; Heath, 1983). Research within and across these perspectives has deepened our understanding that reading is also a meaning-making process. What we learn is encoded in language, and the meanings we construct both expand and constrain what we know (Halliday, 1975, 1978; Piattelli-Palmarini, 1980; Vygotsky, 1962).

Response To This Research Base

This new knowledge has spurred new debates, perhaps the more public of which has been among those educators whose primary interest is in using new under-standings to improve classroom practice. This debate seems to have emerged as a result of two quite different responses to the expanded knowledge base about reading. One group of educators has tended to focus on devising means for teaching everything that competent readers need to know. These educators con-cern themselves with such issues as how to *teach* students about how language works, how to *teach* self-monitoring, and how to *teach* collaboration. Histori-cally, the approach of this group has been consistent with the education-as-method perspective. I label this approach as the *dominant response*.

A second group of educators has asked different questions. Rather than focus on how to teach all that we now understood about reading and readers, this group asks, "How do we set up classroom environments that will facilitate the learning of these understandings?" I label this approach as the *emergent response*.

The emergent response is not unique to reading education. In mathematics, science, and social studies, educators also ask how to establish classrooms that build on an understanding of how learning occurs outside the classroom. Mathe-matics educators do so when they talk about "authenticity," science educators do so when they talk about "process" and "hands-on" learning, and social studies educators do so when they talk about bringing the community into the classroom.

Within reading education, the emergent response is most often referred to as *whole language*. Consistent with the voices being raised in other curricular areas, whole language represents a commitment to school learning environments in which learning is contextualized, emergent, functional, mediated, and collabora-tive. Whole language advocates, like others with an emergent response perspec-tive, want to take the optimal learning conditions found outside the classroom and make them part of the classroom.

Whole Language as Political Agenda

Until quite recently, many reading educators from both the dominant and emer-gent perspectives primarily debated each other over method, terminology, and materials. One group talked of methods such as "scaffolding," "cognitive ap-prenticeship," and "reciprocal teaching," whereas the other talked of "invita-tions," "demonstrations," "strategy lessons," and "ownership." Some argued for using basal reading programs, and some argued against their use. Both groups claimed "literature-based" programs, and each argued that what it meant by the term was not what the other meant.

And then somewhere in the midst of this often heated debate, some educators began to realize that the debate was not about methods, terminology, or mate-rials; rather, it was about politics and power. Although both groups shared the same long-term goal of improving educational practice, they differed in very important ways. The dominant group was arguing for methods developed outside the classroom that teachers could use to teach what needed to be known; the emergent group was arguing for the enhanced professionalization of teachers so that teachers could serve as mediators and facilitators of learning within environments they designed. The dominant group was attempting to develop methods *drawn from its knowledge base;* the emergent group was attempting to *share the knowledge base* so that teachers could develop their own methods.

To illustrate the differences between these two groups, consider *cooperative learning*. Understanding the importance of learning communities, of cooperation and collaboration, some university educators packaged their knowledge as curricular innovation and began selling "Cooperative Learning" (Johnson & Johnson, 1979). Teachers all over the country attend workshops and inservice sessions based on these programs where, in some instances, they are told how many students to have in a group, what the role of each should be, and how often cooperative learning activities should take place. (After attending one such workshop, one teacher scheduled cooperative learning in her classroom on Fridays at 1:00.)

Such an approach represents the dominant response to new knowledge. Knowledge is held by those outside the classroom, and teachers, rather than being given direct access to that knowledge, are sold curricular innovations. In contrast, those educators whose response can be considered emergent argue against such packages. They argue instead that teachers should have the opportunity to reflect upon and become informed about the importance of learning as a cooperative collaborative activity and of setting up their classrooms as learning communities. With this knowledge base, they maintain, teachers can then make informed decisions about how to help their students learn from and with each other. One decision teachers might make, based on their informed reflections, would be to provide opportunities for students to work together in small groups. Although the particular organization plan would be similar (in both cases students would be doing small-group work cooperatively), from the dominant perspective, teachers would be doing "Cooperative Learning" because they had been told, by outside others, that they should do so and how they should do so; from the emergent perspective, teachers might choose small-group experiences based on their understanding of learning as a social process.

Whether intentional or not, one effect of the dominant response perspective has been to situate authority outside the classroom, whereas the explicit intent of the emergent response perspective is to situate authority within the classroom.

The political ramifications of these differences in perspective are considerable. Many educators, for example, find themselves asking questions such as "What is a teacher's role in the classroom now, and what should that role be in the future?" "Who has, or should have, the power to make these decisions?"

"What are the rules for determining or redistributing this power, and how can the rules be renegotiated?"

University educators, many of whom have become self-conscious about issues of teacher power and authority, are asking serious questions about the role of universities to change agendas and about relationships between universities and the public schools. They also have begun to rethink the concept of *research* and to reconsider what constitutes *proof*. Indeed, they are even raising questions about "authentic" research: Is it more authentic and therefore more useful when teachers conduct research in their own classroom? Is it even necessary to address the issue of proof, or is it enough simply to understand?

The Impact of an Empowerment Perspective

In the midst of this consciousness raising, many, including whole language advocates, are taking the stand that any changes proposed within or about schools should only be considered legitimate and ethical if the changes would empower both teachers and students.

This position rests on the argument that historically teachers have been treated as technicians who transmit information and lessons and vocabulary words to students—who historically have been treated as receivers. We have kept school separate from life and created a school literacy that has no counterpart outside of school. We have attempted to teach the complex by making it simple. The dominant perspective has indeed dominated.

Recent research, however, suggests that when students are empowered—when they are supported as readers, writers, and learners within the school context; when learning in school parallels learning outside of school; when learning is authentic and therefore serves a genuine function—students abandon their passive stance and begin to engage actively as learners. They begin to construct and share and build on knowledge rather than simply receive it. Research findings from social studies and science, from writing and mathematics, from university researchers and from public school educators all attest to the benefits of students as knowledgeable reflective learners. Likewise, findings from research on teachers and teacher education detail the contributions and accomplishments of teachers who are empowered by virtue of their being informed reflective professionals.

In the field of reading education, much of this research has focused on the classrooms of whole language teachers and on the students who learn in those classrooms (see Stephens, 1991). Some of this research has been conducted by the teachers in the classrooms. By empowering themselves with knowledge about learners and how they learn, teachers have begun to test ways of establishing classroom contexts that are consistent with what is known about learning outside of school. These teachers work to ensure that learning in their classrooms is contextualized, emergent, functional, mediated, and collaborative. The knowledge they gain through their research-on-practice contributes, in turn, to their further empowerment by allowing them to modify curriculum, instruction, and assessment. They often share findings with other teachers who then conduct their own research-on-practice.

Sometimes these teacher–researchers share their findings with a broader audience through books, chapters, journal articles, and presentations at conferences. A recent review of the research on whole language (Stephens, 1991) revealed, for example, that 7 of the 38 studies reviewed had been conducted by teachers in their own classrooms. Another 16 studies involved university and public school teachers collaboratively conducting research in the classrooms of public school teachers. These studies document what—once the empowerment perspective is understood—might be considered "common sense": In whole language classrooms, students are actively engaged and therefore experience considerable growth as readers, writers, and learners.

The 10 comparative studies in this review provide several interesting findings. For example, Ribowsky (1986) studied emergent literacy among kindergarten children and compared a "code emphasis" approach with a whole language approach. Analyzing data related to the children's linguistic, orthographic, and graphophonemic literacy, she noted that "ANCOVA results revealed a significant main effect for treatment favoring the whole language group on all dependent measures" (p. 15).

Freppon (1991) studied first-grade children from four classrooms, two of which were considered to be whole language classrooms, and two in which the children received skills-based instruction. Controlling for socioeconomic status, gender, reading ability, and reading instruction, Freppon selected 24 children and studied their beliefs and understandings about reading. She also collected information about the strategies they used as readers. She found significant differences among the children. Ninety-two percent of the children in the whole language group, for example, thought that understanding the story and getting the words right were important; in the skills-based group, only 50% talked about both as important. When trying to figure out unfamiliar words, 34% of the children in the whole language group used what Freppon referred to as a "balanced cuing system" (meaning, structure, and visual cues) compared to 8% of the students in the skills-based group. Freppon also noted that the skills group tried to sound out words twice as often as the whole language group, although, when they did sound out, the whole language group was more successful than their peers in the skills-based group, in spite of the fact that they had not received systematic phonics instruction. Freppon (1991) concluded that "The results . . . revealed differences in the understandings of these two groups of first-grade children. Responses from children in the literature group document a reflective stance, greater depth of understanding reading as a language process involving construction of meaning, and knowledge and use of a balanced cueing system" (p. 159).

Haggerty, Hiebert, and Owens (1989) examined the literacy behaviors of children in whole language and traditional second-, fourth-, and sixth-grade classrooms. They analyzed data from reading comprehension and writing assessment tests, a modification of Burke's Reading Interview (1987), and classroom observations. They found no significant differences on the writing test, although students in the fourth- and sixth-grade whole language classrooms scored approximately one standard deviation higher than the students in the traditional classroom. On the comprehension test, however, students in the whole language classrooms outperformed those in the skills-based classroom. Results from the Reading Interview also favored the students from the whole language classrooms.

CURRENT CONTROVERSIES

Our knowledge about reading and writing, about readers and writers, continues to grow. And although there is still debate about what we know (e.g., "Did so and so's study really prove X?"), and how we come to know it (e.g., "Shouldn't the study have been designed differently?"), the essence of the debate, relative to practice, centers on how that knowledge should be shared. Should teachers have direct access to the knowledge base? Should teachers themselves be the creators of the knowledge base? If so, how can this be done? What would have to change and what would that change process look like?

There are, fortunately, no mandates prescribing how each of us answers these questions. If we want to maintain control of the classroom, if we want expertise to lie outside rather then within, we at the university can continue to debate methods and materials. Teachers can continue to ground their curricular decisions on the information provided in the materials prescribed by their principal, district, or state. And administrators can continue to censor and direct how and what is taught.

If we want control and expertise to lie within the classroom, however, everything, even our questions, change. Decontextualized comparisons between one method and another become irrelevant; teachers will choose for themselves what works best in their situation. One response, one text, will support the learning of one child today; another response or text will support another tomorrow. And comparisons between classrooms driven by publishers' materials and classrooms in which decisions are grounded in the teachers' knowledge base will become embarrassingly silly.

In reading education, whole language is a label that identifies educators who have asked themselves about the roles of teachers and of students in the learning process and have decided in favor of teacher and student empowerment. Whole language thus has come to present a belief that learning in school ought to incorporate what is known about learning outside of school; that teachers should base curricular decisions on what is known; and that teachers as professionals are entitled to a political context that empowers them as informed decision makers (adapted from Stephens, 1991).

I began this chapter by suggesting that disambiguating the term *whole language* requires an understanding of what has happened in the field over the last 30 years—the new knowledge that we have as well as the responses, both dominant and emergent, to that knowledge base. But perhaps the term becomes clear only when we each ask ourselves hard questions: Do we believe that learning in school should be grounded in what we know about learning? That teachers should have access to that knowledge? That they should be empowered to act on their informed reflections? Many have answered *yes* to these questions; some of the many call themselves whole language educators. Together they, and others, are working to achieve a consistency between what they believe should be and what actually is. As John Mayher (*Uncommon Sense, 1990*) reminds us, we believe that to fail to find a way would be to fail ourselves and our students as well as our future.

REFERENCES

Anderson, R. C., Reynolds, R. E., Schallert, D. L., & Goetz, E. T. (1977). Frameworks for comprehending discourse. *American Educational Research Journal, 14,* 367–381.

Anderson, R. C., Spiro, R. J., & Anderson, M. C. (1978). Schemata as scaffolding for the representation of information in connected discourse. *American Educational Research Journal, 15,* 433–440.

Bloome, D., & Green, J. (1984). Directions in the sociolinguistic study of reading. In P. D. Pearson, R. Barr, M. L. Kamil, & P. Mosenthal (Eds.), *Handbook of reading research* (pp. 395–422). New York: Longman.

Bloomfield, L. (1933). *Language.* New York: Henry Holt.

Brown, A. L. (1980). Metacognitive development and reading. In R. J. Spiro, B. C. Bruce, & W. F. Brewer (Eds.), *Theoretical issues in reading comprehension* (pp. 453–482). Hillsdale, NJ: Lawrence Erlbaum Associates.

Brown, R. (1970). *Psycholinguistics.* New York: The Free Press.

Burke, C. (1987). Reading interview. In Y. M. Goodman, D. J. Watson, & C. Burke (Eds.), *Reading miscue inventory: Alternative procedures.* New York: Richard C. Owen.

Chomsky, N. (1957). *Syntactic structures.* The Hague: Mouton

Ferriero, E., & Teberosky, A. (1983). *Literacy before schooling.* Exeter, NH: Heinemann.

Freppon, P. A. (1991). Children's concepts of the nature and purpose of reading in different instructional settings. *Journal of Reading Behavior, 23,* 139–164.

Goodman, K. S. (1968). *The psycholinguistic nature of the reading process.* Detroit: Wayne State University Press.

Goodman, K. S., Smith, E. B., Meredith, R., & Goodman, Y. M. (1976). *Language and thinking in school.* New York: Richard C. Owen.

Green, J. (1983). Research on teaching as a linguistic process: A state of the art. In E. Gordon (Ed.), *Review of research in education* (Vol. 10). Washington, DC: American Educational Research Association.

Haggerty, P. J., Hiebert, E. H., & Owens, M. K. (1989). Students' comprehension, writing, and perceptions in two approaches to literacy instruction. In S. McCormick & J. Zutell (Eds.), *Thirty-eighth Yearbook of the National Reading Conference*. Rochester, NY: National Reading Conference.

Halliday, M. A. K. (1975). *Learning how to mean: Explorations in the development of language*. London: Edward Arnold.

Halliday, M. A. K. (1978). *Language as social semiotic*. Baltimore: University Park Press.

Harste, J. C., Woodward, V. A., & Burke, C. L. (1984). *Language stories and literacy lessons*. Portsmouth, NH: Heinemann.

Heap, J. L. (1980). What counts as reading: Limits to certainty in assessment. *Curriculum Inquiry, 10*, 265–292.

Heath, S. B. (1983). *Ways with words: Language, life and work in communities and classrooms*. New York: Cambridge University Press.

Johnson, D. W., & Johnson, R. T. (1979). Conflict in the classroom: Controversy and learning. *Review of Educational Research, 49*, 51–70.

Mayher, J. (1990). *Uncommon sense*. Portsmouth, NH: Boynton/Cook.

Pavlov, I. P. (1927). *Conditioned reflexes: An investigation of the physiological activity of the cerebral cortex*. London: Oxford University Press.

Piattelli-Palmarini, M. (1980). *Language and learning: The debate between Jean Piaget and Noam Chomsky*. New York: Routledge & Kegan Paul.

Read, C. (1975). Lessons to be learned from the pre-school orthographer. In E. H. Lennenberg & E. Lennenberg (Eds.), *Foundations of language development: A multidisciplinary approach* (Vol. 2, pp. 329–346). New York: Academic Press.

Ribowsky, H. (1986). *The comparative effects of a code emphasis approach and a whole language approach upon emergent literacy of young children*. Unpublished doctoral dissertation, New York University. (ERIC Document Reproduction Service No. ED 269 720)

Sapir, E. (1921). *Language: An introduction to the study of speech*. New York: Harcourt Brace Jovanovich.

Skinner, B. F. (1957). *Verbal behavior*. New York: Appleton-Century-Crofts.

Spiro, R. J. (1980). Constructive processes in prose comprehension and recall. In R. J. Spiro, B. C. Bruce, & W. F. Brewer (Eds.), *Theoretical issues in reading comprehension* (pp. 245–278). Hillsdale, NJ: Lawrence Erlbaum Associates.

Spiro, R. J., Coulson, R., Feltovich, P., & Anderson, D. (1988). *Cognitive flexibility theory: Advanced knowledge acquisition in ill-structured domains* (Tech. Rep. No. 441). Urbana–Champaign: University of Illinois, Center for the Study of Reading.

Stephens, D. (1991). *Toward an understanding of whole language* (Tech. Rep. No. 524). Urbana–Champaign: University of Illinois, Center for the Study of Reading.

Thorndike, E. L. (1913). *The psychology of learning*. New York: Teachers College.

Vygotsky, L. S. (1962). *Language and thought*. Cambridge, MA: The MIT Press.

7

Separating the Rhetoric from the Effects: Whole Language in Kindergarten and First Grade

Steven A. Stahl
University of Georgia

The overheated rhetoric and colorful metaphors used by Hans Grundin obscure the real issue before us. This issue remains: Do young children learn to be better readers in whole language classrooms than in other classrooms? It was to address this issue that Patricia Miller and I (Stahl & Miller, 1989) conducted a review of studies focusing on the effects on beginning reading achievement of whole language and language experience approaches.

In this review, we analyzed data from the five projects of the USOE Cooperative First-Grade Studies and from 46 additional and more recent studies of kindergarten and first-grade reading instruction, using two methods of quantitative synthesis, meta-analysis and vote-counting. In a meta-analysis, each result from a study is converted to an effect size—that is, a measure of how strong an effect is. Vote-counting simply tallies the number of comparisons across studies. (See Light & Pillemer, 1984, for a more extensive discussion of these methods.) For our review, we tallied the number of comparisons that found effects favoring the whole language–language experience approach, those favoring the traditional basal reading program approach, and those finding no significant difference in the two. Our findings provided information that I believe is useful in addressing a number of critical issues that are at the heart of the phonics–whole language debate.

CRITICAL ISSUES: SOME QUESTIONS AND ANSWERS

Overall, do whole language approaches produce better results than basal reading programs in kindergarten and first grade? The answer to this question appears to be no. The vote-counting shown in Fig. 7.1 indicates that, overall, the

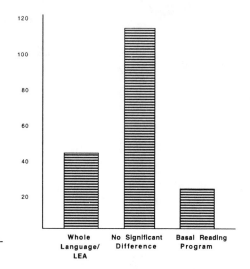

FIG. 7.1.   Overall results: Vote-counting.

effects of whole language–language experience approaches are similar to those of basal reading program approaches, with about as many comparisons favoring whole language approaches as favoring basals, and the vast majority finding no significant differences between them. The comparable meta-analysis found an overall effect size of 0.09, which effectively indicates no overall difference between the two approaches.

On measures of attitude toward reading, the results mirrored the overall findings, with both approaches about equal in their effects on students' attitudes toward reading (see Fig. 7.2). Thus, in spite of the anecdotal reports that say they do (Goodman, 1986), whole language approaches do not seem to produce measurable advantages in attitude toward reading. In fact, students' attitudes toward reading seem generally to be unaffected by the reading approach used (see Stahl, Osborn, Pearson, & Winsor, in press).

Are whole language approaches more effective with disadvantaged students or with students who are placed at risk for reading failure by virtue of conflicts between the culture they belong to and the dominant culture? Whole language theorists argue that such students experience fewer academic problems in whole language classes, because the whole language philosophy more readily accepts differences between people (Edelsky, 1990). However, of the first-grade studies we looked at that used populations labeled "disadvantaged," no comparisons favored whole language approaches (see Fig. 7.3). In fact, some observers (see Delpit, 1989) indicate that such students may benefit from a more structured learning experience than will students who come into school with stronger literacy backgrounds.

Do whole language–language experience approaches have a differential effect on different aspects of reading? We also looked at the effects of these

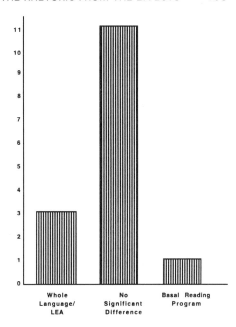

FIG. 7.2.   Attitude measures

approaches on measures of word recognition and comprehension (see Fig. 7.4). The findings were somewhat surprising. Whole language–language experience approaches usually do not teach words in isolation, yet these approaches produce considerably stronger effects on measures of word recognition in isolation than do basal program approaches, which usually *do* teach words in isolation. The whole language–language experience approaches stress comprehension throughout, yet they have a good-sized negative effect on comprehension; that is, basal programs do a better job of improving comprehension than do whole language approaches. These results probably are not due to chance alone.

Let me speculate about why whole language–language experience approaches might have these effects. Perhaps students in basal reading programs have more practice than students in whole language classes on test-like formats—an argument made by a number of whole language theorists (see Goodman, Goodman, & Hood, 1989).

Perhaps students in whole language classes have fewer opportunities to read and comprehend texts than do those in classes using basal reading programs. This seems to be a contradiction, because the whole language philosophy stresses the reading and comprehension of real texts over practice in other aspects of reading. But given that comprehension involves both integrating new information with already known information and summarizing or reducing the information so that it can be remembered, two lines of evidence suggest that students in whole language classes, at least in the early grades, have fewer opportunities to develop comprehension. The first line focuses on the types of texts students in

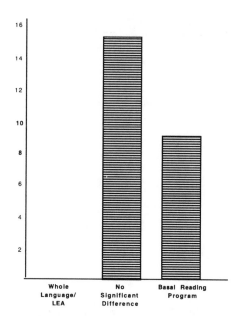

FIG. 7.3. Disadvantaged populations—beginning   reading
studies only.

whole language classes read. In general, these students read more of two types of texts—their own writing and predictable, patterned, language books—than do students in classes that use basal reading programs. Reading their own writing, however, does not require students to integrate new and known information, because the content was known to them before it was written down. Such reading requires only that students recall what they said or intended to say. Reading

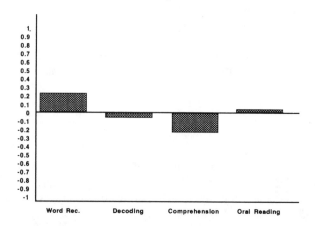

FIG. 7.4. Effects of language experience approaches—meta-analysis.

patterned books presents a different problem. Look at *Brown Bear, Brown Bear, What Do You See?* by Bill Martin (1970). This is a wonderful book, and one that is familiar to almost every child in a whole language classroom. However, it is impossible to come up with a meaningful statement that summarizes the text of the book. The only summary possible is that some animals were looking at each other. Many predictable books have discernable plots. Our observations of the use of these books in first-grade classes, however, suggest that teachers rarely discuss their plots but instead concentrate on oral reading and rereading of the text (Stahl et al., in press). Text and teaching that do not demand attention to plot may hinder students in whole language classes when they encounter the novel passages on comprehension tests.

In contrast, the often impoverished texts of basal reading program preprimers have plots (even if they have to be inferred from both words and pictures), and these plots are discussed by teachers. Through these discussions, students get practice understanding texts. When students do not have to devote attention to comprehension, as when reading *Brown Bear, Brown Bear* or when rereading their own compositions, they can devote more attention to decoding. This, in turn, may contribute to better performance on measures of word recognition in isolation, even though words are rarely, if ever, presented that way in a whole language setting. Thus, the superior results on measures of word recognition in isolation and the negative effects on measures of comprehension can be accounted for by the types of texts that children in whole language classes use.

Do whole language approaches work better than traditional approaches in preparing students for formal reading instruction? Whole language approaches *did* shine in one area. We looked separately at studies to determine whether they compared whole language programs to programs preliminary to a formal reading program (what traditionally have been called "readiness" programs). In this analysis, whole language approaches produced significantly higher achievement at the kindergarten level ($p < .05$) than did basal reading program approaches (see Fig. 7.5). At the first-grade level, the differences between the two approaches were nonsignificant. Thus, whole language approaches seem effective at "setting the stage" for formal reading instruction but do not seem any more effective than basal programs in delivering that instruction.

In particular, whole language programs seemed to be very effective with kindergarten students, perhaps because they provide them with both an overall orientation to what print is used for and how it functions and specific information about the conventions of written language (Clay, 1985). This orientation may reflect a strength of whole language and language experience approaches and fits in well with a stage model of reading acquisition (Chall, 1983b). The stage model suggests that reading develops through several stages, from an awareness of the functions of print, to an awareness of the form of print, to automaticity of decoding, to reading to learn. Before children can understand the significance of letter–sound relationships, they need to understand what reading is and a little

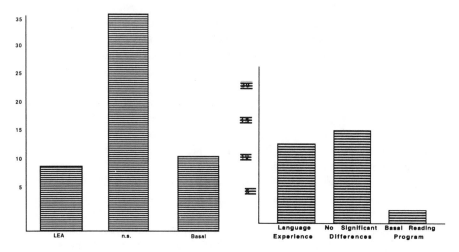

FIG. 7.5.   Beginning reading studies (left) and readiness studies (right) vote-counting.

about how reading functions, and they need to be motivated to learn to read. Once this understanding of the "whole" of reading is accomplished, then, and only then, can a reader focus in on the parts. At this point, children are "ready" for systematic instruction in decoding, and they will focus on the print, whether they are directed to or not. From this model, the question moves from the abstract question "What program is best?" to the more realistic question "Which approaches will help students at a given stage of their reading development?"

A stage model suggests that the big books, experience charts, and book handling experiences that occur in a whole language kindergarten will serve to develop children's understanding of the functions and purposes of reading. These experiences are especially important for children from homes in which little reading takes place. Thus, whole language approaches in kindergarten may provide some of what the years of story book reading and print-related discussions in the home provide (see Adams, 1990). After they gain an understanding of reading functions and purposes, children outgrow the need for such instruction.

Phonics-based programs seem to be more appropriate in first grade, because they clearly and directly instruct students in the code of written language. This seems to be a conclusion, not only in our review but in every major review of beginning reading studies (e.g., Adams, 1990; Chall, 1983a; Williams, 1985). Although many children will develop a knowledge of letter–sound relationships "naturally," through exposure from reading and through invented spellings in writing, some direct instruction will more efficiently help students notice orthographic patterns. Such instruction will lead to better comprehension, at least through the fourth grade, where the evidence stops (Chall, 1983a). There is, however, little agreed-upon evidence about the effectiveness of different types of code-based instruction. It should also be stressed that acceptance of the importance of teaching the code does not mean that teachers are restricted to using endless reams of worksheets, unison responding, or any other "best" method.

Code-based instruction should be given early and quickly. However, children also need ample experience to practice their reading skill in real reading activities (Anderson, Hiebert, Scott, & Wilkinson, 1985). Just as it is counterproductive to ignore letter–sound relationships, it is equally counterproductive to dwell on them. To be a successful reader, a student must learn to decode automatically, without conscious attention to that task. Automaticity comes only with practice. And not just with any practice. Automaticity seems to be best developed through practice reading connected text (Samuels, 1985). Here again may be where whole language approaches shine. As noted earlier, we did not include studies of whole language or literature-based programs at levels higher than second grade in our review. Of the few studies I have seen, the results suggest that whole language approaches may be more effective for students in second grade and beyond than for first-grade students (see, e.g., Haggerty, Hiebert, & Fisher, 1990).

Considering the act of reading through the stage model discussed here, children need to begin with an appreciation of the purposes and functions of the whole task of reading. They then can make sense of its mechanics, especially letter–sound relationships and how such knowledge can be used to understand texts. With this understanding, they can return to the totality of the reading task, reading for meaning or for communication. The overall sequence seems to be the whole-to-part-to-whole sequence argued for by whole language advocates (Goodman, 1986). This sequence is most often discussed as occurring within a single lesson, in which a whole story is presented and the teacher scaffolds children's learning back to an understanding of the functioning of the parts, if needed, but always within the context of the whole story. The sequence that seems to best describe our data is also whole-to-part-to-whole, but this takes place over a curriculum, rather than a lesson (see Stahl, 1992).

Are the effects of whole language approaches best measured by more naturalistic measures rather than by standardized reading tests? Whole language advocates often deride standardized achievement tests as consisting of artificial tasks, different from and unrelated to reading in naturalistic settings. They have suggested that because basal reading materials are designed to give students practice in test-like formats, students who use them have an unfair advantage on standardized tests. They argue that children in whole language classes, who spend their time reading and writing whole texts, have a difficult time with the short fragments of text and the multiple-choice question format of standardized tests (see Goodman et al., 1989). In the seven studies we found that used naturalistic measures, however, six found no significant differences on those measures, and the seventh reported contradictory findings. These measures included free retelling (Ewoldt, 1976), number of oral reading miscues (Ewoldt, 1976; Pollack & Brown, 1980; Ramig & Hall, 1980; Stice & Bertrand, 1987), and the number of predictions made after reading an open-ended story (Farber & Putnam, 1983). Harris, Serwer, Gold, and Morrison (1967) found that in language experience programs, students read more during free reading than did students in basal programs when the number of *books* read was used to measure free reading, but that the reverse was true when the number of *pages* read was used to measure reading.

Could it be that a group of bad studies brought down the mean for the whole language approaches? To answer this question, we devised six criteria for what we thought were the characteristics of the best research in this area and correlated the number of criteria each study met with its effect size. We found that as study quality improved, effect size decreased, with the better designed studies tending to show an effect favoring the basal reading programs (see Fig. 7.6). In other words, the answer is no.

Could it be that the newer studies, under the influence of the whole language movement, produced stronger effects than did the older studies that focused on the language experience approach? Several reviewers have criticized our decision to combine whole language approaches with language experience approaches in our review (Edelsky, 1990; McGee & Lomax, 1990). Our response to this criticism is that the two approaches represent the evolution of a single line of child-centered, meaning-oriented curricula, and that they share many essential features (Stahl, 1990). But to answer the question posed, the answer appears to be no. In fact, as Fig. 7.7 shows, a correlation between date of study publication and effect size indicates that the more recent the studies the *lower* the effect found for the whole language approach. This suggests that the later the study the worse the effect for whole language approaches, and that the earlier language experience approaches actually produced stronger effects.

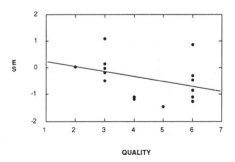

FIG. 7.6. Correlations between study quality and effect size.

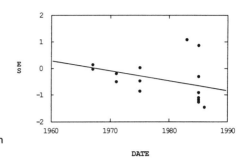

FIG. 7.7. Correlations between
date of study and effect size.

WHAT WE SHOULD TAKE FROM THE WHOLE LANGUAGE MOVEMENT

The evidence from experimental studies has led us to conclude that although whole language is not the panacea its advocates would have us believe, it nonetheless has valuable lessons to teach us.

1. Teachers are a Dominant Factor in Children's Reading Programs. Until recently, the trend was for publishers to make reading programs more and more "teacher-proof" by providing detailed lesson scripts, copious amounts of supplementary materials, and so forth. Trends toward greater accountability combined with a belief that basal materials themselves reflect educational wisdom tended to remove teacher judgment and to put more control into the materials. I know that this was not intended, but I wince every time I hear of a principal, armed with the teacher's manual of a basal program, who observes a teacher and downgrades her every time she strays from the directions; or of a reading coordinator who uses the end-of-unit tests to evaluate teaching effectiveness (when I know that the end-of-unit tests measure little more than whether children have done similar looking worksheets); or of a principal who mandates that every teacher must be on page 129 of the class reader by December 12. The whole language movement is part of the trend toward empowerment of teachers, a trend I heartily support.

The whole language movement sees itself as "child centered" in that children's contributions are valued and that children's curiosity about reading is seen as the engine driving the reading program. Children's understandings need to be valued and responded to, and their interests addressed, whether a program is basal oriented or whole language or something else. However, the teacher is the central figure in the classroom. Successful whole language classrooms seem to be successful as a result of a great deal of teacher planning and effort. But we formally observed one teacher (and have seen others informally) who felt that adopting a whole language approach meant that she was to expose children to books and writing and allow them to absorb reading as "naturally" as they do speaking (Stahl et al., in press). She seldom intervened, and the students were off-task a great deal of the time. The result was disastrous. Over half the students in her class could not read material more difficult than a preprimer by May.

2. *Children Learn to Read by Reading.* Children at all grade levels should read literature, factual articles, poetry, and other types of material, and these should be read to them. Skills instruction should be part of the mixture in a reading program, but it should not dominate the program. Unfortunately, too many children, especially poorer readers, get lots of skills activities and little reading time (Adams, 1990).

3. *Primary-Grade Students Do Too Many Workbook Tasks.* Observations have consistently found that children spend 60% to 70% of their reading instructional time doing workbook or worksheet activities, and as little as 2 to 3 minutes a day reading connected text longer than a paragraph (Anderson et al., 1985). Research has also consistently suggested that the amount of time students spend on reading connected text is related to their gains in reading achievement, whereas the effects of the amount of time spent on workbooks are more equivocal (Leinhardt, Zigmond, & Cooley, 1981).

4. *Reading Time Should Include More Open-Ended, Higher Level Questions Associated with Critical Thinking.* There is no reason why reading time cannot be a time for discussion about a commonly read story or novel rather than recitation. At present, this is something that happens to gifted students if they are lucky. I have found, however, that remedial students also benefit from a guided discussion about a book. There is some evidence that even the children with the lowest initial ability benefit from class discussion (Stahl & Clark, 1987), and that remedial students can make great strides with the help of some instruction in critical thinking (Pogrow, 1990).

5. *Children Should Be Writing Full Sentences, Paragraphs, and Essays.* There is no reason why practice materials must be of a fill-in-the-blank or color-in-the-circle variety. On a simple level, writing full-sentence summaries appears to teach students to summarize more effectively than having them choose, by coloring the circle, the "best" summary. On a higher level, writing a thoughtful response to a story forces students to externalize not only their understanding but also their reactions, both emotional and critical. The use of writing to respond to literature leads to higher level thinking and is closer to what we want students to do in "real" reading situations.

This is not to say that reading and writing and speaking and listening are the same things. They are related, there are connections, but they are not part of one big language process, as whole language people suggest. With my apologies to Dr. Grundin, language comprehension is half of reading comprehension, decoding is the other half (Gough & Tumner, 1986). Indeed, some of the problems I see with the whole language stance come from this notion of one big language process. Whole language is new, so there are not as many whole language horror stories as basal reading horror stories, but let me tell you one about the first-grade teacher who decided that she would conduct a unit on grandparents. She read books about grandparents, talked about grandparents, and so on. The children read very little. In an hour devoted to reading, the children, as a group, read little more than a few dictated lines from an experience chart. What did this do for their reading? Not much. First, they knew a great deal about grandparents to begin with, so this lesson did not add to their background knowledge. Second, they did not read much text; they talked. Observational studies indicate that, although this is a particularly bad example, there is considerably more talk and less reading of written text in many whole language classes (Harris et al., 1967; Stahl et al., in press). The displacement of reading written texts by talk seems to be an unwanted outcome of a whole language philosophy.

WHAT WE SHOULD NOT TAKE FROM THE WHOLE LANGUAGE MOVEMENT

With all these important lessons, however, the whole language movement also has brought a politicization of reading and its education. Whole language advocates (e.g., Edelsky, 1990) have couched their arguments in an either–or framework—either you're with us, or you're against us—arguing that nonwhole language adherents cannot comprehend or criticize the movement. This stridency makes it difficult to bring something from the movement, because the advocates are arguing that one must accept everything about whole language theory or accept nothing. Polarizing the debate adds nothing to our main task, which remains teaching children to read.

My colleagues and I have recently completed a study of first graders learning to read in classes with different philosophies (Stahl et al., in press). In contrast to the rhetoric of whole language, five of the six teachers we observed and interviewed had incorporated some aspect of whole language into their classroom. This group included a DISTAR teacher who added process writing and time for free reading to her direct instruction, synthetic phonics program. In spite of the clear differences in orientation of our teachers, the children had similar orientations toward reading. Looking over a number of interview questions, they seemed to perceive decoding as what was difficult in reading and saw reading as a decoding act. Students in whole language classes were aware of different decoding strategies, such as the use of context to help understand an unknown word, but were not any better at actually using context to aid in decoding than traditionally taught students. All students performed similarly on measures of oral reading and comprehension, differing only on measures of whole recognition and decoding. This finding was essentially confirmed by Freppon (1991), who similarly found that children in whole language and traditional classes showed both an interest in knowing and learning words, including the use of phonics as a reading strategy, but the whole language group tended to demonstrate an understanding of more reading strategies and a somewhat more meaning-oriented view of the reading process. Looking over the data she presents, however, it is clear that the similarities among classes were great and the differences slight.

In our study, we saw first that, in spite of the rhetoric to which teachers are exposed, they are pragmatists and tend to adapt new approaches to what they know rather than begin anew. Second, we found that children tend to view the difficulty inherent in reading in terms of what they do not know—how to decode written words—rather than in terms of what they can do—understand language. Third, we found that differing methods per se had little effect on children's achievement; instead, it seemed that the differences among classes were due to differences in time on task and in the amount of time students spent practicing reading (see Rosenshine & Stevens, 1984).

FINAL COMMENTS

Reading is a textual act; it always involves a text. Children need to learn how to decode that text, so that they can comprehend the language in that text. Without exposure to *written* words, children cannot learn to read them. We know that an early systematic emphasis on the code leads to higher achievement (Adams, 1990; Chall, 1983a). However, it is wrong to equate code instruction with phonics worksheets. To decry code instruction by citing such worksheets is a straw man argument. Good phonics instruction can occur within the context of story reading, as in Reading Recovery (Clay, 1985), a program that is highly regarded by whole language advocates (Pinnell, Fried, & Estice, 1990). Good phonics instruction can also involve direct instruction. However, direct instruction of phonics seems most effective when it is well integrated into a reading program that also stresses meaningful interactions with text and writing (Adams, 1990). Worksheet-only instruction, especially when the worksheets do not relate to the stories read in the rest of the program, does not seem to be as effective (Juel & Roper/Schneider, 1985).

The purpose of good phonics instruction (indeed, good reading instruction) is to enable children to read a wider variety of books, with less vocabulary control, not to have children master certain skills. We educators sometimes forget this, and the whole language movement has arisen partially to remind us. But if we forget that children also need to learn how to deal with the print-specific aspects of reading, we will be equally remiss.

REFERENCES

Adams, M. J. (1990). *Beginning to read: Thinking and learning about print.* Cambridge, MA: The MIT Press.

Anderson, R. C., Hiebert, E. H., Scott, J. A., & Wilkinson, I. A. G. (1985). *Becoming a nation of readers: The report of the Commission on Reading.* Champaign, IL: Center for the Study of Reading; Washington, DC: National Institute of Education.

Chall, J. S. (1983a). *Learning to read: The great debate* (rev. ed.). New York: McGraw–Hill.

Chall, J. S. (1983b). *Stages of reading development.* New York: McGraw–Hill.

Clay, M. M. (1985). *The early detection of reading difficulties.* Portsmouth, NH: Heinemann.

Delpit, L. (1989). The silenced dialogue: Power and pedagogy in educating other people's children. *Harvard Educational Review, 58,* 280–298.

Edelsky, C. (1990). Whose agenda is this anyway? A response to McKenna, Robinson, and Miller. *Educational Researcher, 19,* 7–11.

Ewoldt, C. (1976). *Miscue analysis of the reading of third-grade Follow Through and non-Follow Through children in Wichita, Kansas.* Tucson, AZ: Arizona Center for Educational Research and Development. (ERIC Document Reproduction Service No. ED 236 564)

Farber, F. D., & Putnam, L. P. (1983, October). *Convergent/divergent predictions of urban first graders.* Paper presented at the annual meeting of the College Reading Association, Atlanta.

Freppon, P. A. (1991). Children's concepts of the nature and purpose of reading in different instructional settings. *Journal of Reading Behavior, 23,* 139–164.

Goodman, K. S. (1986). *What's whole about whole language?* Portsmouth, NH: Heinemann.

Goodman, K. S., Goodman, Y. M., & Hood, W. (1989). *The whole language evaluation book.* Portsmouth, NH: Heinemann.

Gough, P. B., & Tunmer, W. E. (1986). Decoding, reading, and reading disability. *Remedial and Special Education, 7,* 6–10.

Haggerty, P., Hiebert, E., & Fisher, C. (1990, December). *Growth in comprehension, metacognition, and writing in literature-based classrooms.* Paper presented at the annual meeting of the National Reading Conference, Austin, TX.

Harris, A. J., Serwer, B. L., Gold, L., & Morrison, C. (1967). *A third progress report on the CRAFT project: Teaching reading to disadvantaged primary-grade urban Negro children.* (ERIC Document Reproduction Service No. ED 015 841)

Juel, C., & Roper/Schneider, D. (1985). The influence of basal readers on first-grade learning. *Reading Research Quarterly, 20,* 134–152.

Leinhardt, G., Zigmond, N., & Cooley, W. W. (1981). Reading instruction and its effects. *American Educational Research Journal, 18,* 343–361.

Light, R. J., & Pillemer, D. B. (1984). *Summing up.* Cambridge, MA: Harvard University Press.

Martin, B. (1970). *Brown bear, brown bear, what do you see?* New York: Holt Rinehart & Winston.

McGee, L. M., & Lomax, R. G. (1990). On combining apples and oranges: A response to Stahl and Miller. *Review of Educational Research, 60,* 133–140.

Pinnell, G. S., Fried, M. D., & Estice, R. M. (1990). Reading Recovery: Learning how to make a difference. *The Reading Teacher, 43,* 282–295.

Pogrow, S. (1990). Challenging at-risk students: Findings from the HOTS program. *Phi Delta Kappan, 71,* 389–397.

Pollack, J. F., & Brown, G. H. (1980). *Observing the effects of reading instruction.* (ERIC Document Reproduction Service No. ED 195 500)

Ramig, C. J., & Hall, M. A. (1980). Reading strategies of first-grade children taught by a language experience and a basal approach. *Reading World, 19,* 280–289.

Rosenshine, B., & Stevens, R. (1984). Classroom instruction in reading. In P. D. Pearson, R. Barr, M. L. Kamil, & P. Mosenthal (Eds.), *Handbook of research in reading* (pp. 745–798). New York: Longman.

Samuels, S. J. (1985). Automaticity and beginning reading. In J. Osborn, P. T. Wilson, & R. C. Anderson (Eds.), *Reading education: Foundations for a literate America* (pp. 215–230). Lexington, MA: Lexington Books.

Stahl, S. A. (1990). Riding the pendulum: A rejoinder to Schickedanz and McGee and Lomax. *Review of Educational Research, 60,* 141–151.

Stahl, S. A. (1992). Saying the "p" word: Exemplary phonics instruction. *The Reading Teacher, 45,* 618–625.

Stahl, S. A., & Clark, C. H. (1987). The effects of participatory expectations in classroom discussion on the learning of science vocabulary. *American Educational Research Journal, 24,* 541–556.

Stahl, S. A., & Miller, P. D. (1989). Whole language and language experience approaches for beginning reading: A quantitative research synthesis. *Review of Educational Research, 59,* 87–116.

Stahl, S. A., Osborn, J., Pearson, P. D., & Winsor, P. (in press). *Six teachers in their classrooms: A closer look at beginning reading instruction* (Tech. Report). Urbana–Champaign: University of Illinois, Center for the Study of Reading.

Stice, C. F., & Bertrand, N. P. (1987, December). *The effects of a whole language program on the literacy development of at-risk children.* Paper presented at the annual meeting of the National Reading Conference, St. Petersburg Beach, FL.

Williams, J. P. (1985). The case for explicit decoding instruction. In J. Osborn, P. T. Wilson, & R. C. Anderson (Eds.), *Reading education: Foundations for a literate America* (pp. 205–214). Lexington, MA: Lexington Books.

8

Creating Optimum Learning Environments: Is Membership in the Whole Language Community Necessary?

Irene W. Gaskins
Benchmark School

Several years ago, a speaker at a national conference I was attending cited the classrooms she visited at Benchmark School, a school for poor readers, as examples of whole language environments. As the director of that school, I was surprised at her remarks—at Benchmark, we do not identify with a particular movement or teaching philosophy. And the question that immediately ran through my mind was whether those identified with whole language would agree with the speaker that what happens in our classrooms is characteristic of whole language instruction.

At Benchmark, decisions about what happens in our classrooms are based on the needs and interests of students and on teachers' knowledge about how children learn. Ours is a student-centered program, in which teachers view all students as capable of learning and seek to set up learning environments in which students can take risks without risking failure. It is an environment in which teachers regard themselves as learners and feel that there is no one best way to teach because students learn differently. Learning at Benchmark is a collaborative venture for both teachers and students. Certainly, whole language advocates would agree that these are characteristics appropriate for whole language environments.

But at Benchmark, children read in basal program readers, and we explicitly teach several strategies for decoding, as well as strategies for active involvement in learning. Would whole language advocates find *these* characteristics appropriate for whole language classrooms?

Prompted by the speaker's comments and by what I saw as contradictions between whole language practices and those used at Benchmark, I later reviewed the literature on whole language to see how well the beliefs put into practice at

Benchmark did fit the whole language philosophy. In the process, I made several discoveries, which are the focus of this chapter.

CHARACTERISTICS COMMON TO WHOLE LANGUAGE ENVIRONMENTS AND BENCHMARK SCHOOL

My first discovery was that the Benchmark program does indeed have a lot in common with whole language environments. Specifically, I identified 10 characteristics common to both.

1. Student-Centered Focus.   In common with whole language environments, teachers at Benchmark begin where the student is (Gaskins, 1980; Gaskins & Baron, 1985; Goodman, 1989a, 1989b). Students who are the same age, and who may even read on the same level, might receive entirely different kinds of support from a teacher. This support can be social, emotional, or academic. In addition, students have the freedom to choose different topics about which to write, and they may read different types of text in class or at home.

Reading group instruction at Benchmark, for example, may take place in basal readers or trade books, depending on what seems most appropriate and acceptable for a particular student. Some poor readers may express a preference for reading in basal readers because these are the kinds of stories they associate with their regular schools or because the basal reader stories are short, and, as a result, the students feel that they are easier to understand. Other students feel that reading predictable books or other kinds of trade books is what helps them become better readers.

2. Process Writing.   In whole language environments, students do a great deal of writing on topics about which they know a lot, and the teacher and peers give feedback, either while the student reads his or her piece orally to others or after the teacher or student has read a draft of a piece (Bergeron, 1990; Gaskins, 1982; Gaskins, 1992). The feedback given by teachers and other students makes it clear that the most important factor in writing is content. At the same time, the teacher fosters a student's growth as a writer by making suggestions about such things as a need for elaboration, organization, and clarity.

Students share, collaborate, and publish. Student-published books are placed in the library for others to read, and student authors are featured each month during a library program that introduces new books. Invented spellings are valued, and concepts about spelling and grammar are taught in the context of a child's own writing. When writing a final draft, for example, a student might be offered graphophonemic hints at an appropriate moment when she or he is not sure how to spell a word. In another instance, the student's use of such cues might be reinforced when she or he has successfully figured out the spelling or reading of an unfamiliar word. In this way, the mechanics of writing are dealt with as part of a whole process.

3. Literature.   Teachers of whole language as well as teachers at Benchmark read literature to their students each day, often featuring a different genre each month (Bergeron, 1990; Gaskins & Elliot, 1983). September might be devoted to realistic fiction, and October might feature fables, science fiction, or biography. The goal is the development of a lifelong awareness and love of literature in all its forms. Students often become interested in the genre the teacher is featuring and select additional books for their independent reading or parent-read-aloud book.

During class discussions, students respond both to the content of the book and to the differences they notice between its language patterns and patterns they have found in other books. In one class students might write for 10 minutes about their feelings in response to what the teacher has read, whereas in another students might evaluate the author's point of view or the lessons for life that can be derived from the piece.

4. Language.   Development of the ability to express oneself well orally is also an important part of both whole language environments and the Benchmark program. At Benchmark, students in the lower school classes look forward to a once-a-week visit from a language therapist who presents whole-class, language-through-literature lessons to enhance their language development (Gaskins & Elliot, 1983). In addition, a few students receive additional assistance during special individual or small-group lessons with a language therapist. Having these lessons taught by a specialist frees the classroom teacher to observe closely each student's use of language, as well as to discover techniques used by the language specialist that can be reinforced throughout the week in the classroom.

As students respond to the literature that is read, the language specialist responds to what they say, valuing each child's contribution, and scaffolds their responses to guide their clarity of expression. As classroom teachers lead discussions in all areas of the curriculum during the remainder of the week, they follow up on the language objectives begun by the language specialists.

5. Reading Instruction.   The use of authentic texts is valued by both whole language and Benchmark teachers. Students at Benchmark spend at least 75% of the time allocated for reading instruction actually reading connected text (Gaskins, 1980; Gaskins & Elliot, 1983). They read a variety of materials, including basal program readers, predictable stories, trade books, magazines, children's weekly newspapers, and other types of informational text.

6. Mediated and Transactive Group Experiences.   Operating on the belief that higher levels of cognitive functioning require a shift from control over learning led by the language of others to learning controlled by the students' own inner language (Vygotsky, 1978), both whole language and Benchmark teachers share with their students strategies for constructing meaning and monitoring progress. Teachers and students discuss the process of reading, as well as model the thinking they use to process information. This open sharing of ways of finding out and knowing is intended to guide students to become more independent and responsible learners. Instruction is scaffolded, with teachers employing responsive and/or cognitive apprenticeship models of instruction (Pressley et al., 1991; Tharp & Gallimore, 1988). In other words, teachers are mediators, not dispensers of learning.

Students meet in groups prior to reading a text to share background information and predictions about the text and to discuss processes for learning from it (Gaskins, 1988c; Gaskins & Elliot, 1991). They are encouraged to become reflective about what they know and how they learn (Newman & Church, 1990).

After the students have completed reading a common text, such as a story book or trade book, they often meet in small groups to share their interpretations. Prior to the small-group meeting, students may write their responses to the text in the form of notes or more formal statements. These written responses may be constructed individually or in collaboration with a classmate, a teacher, or a small group. Whatever the form of the response, students and teachers know they must respect the alternative interpretations provided by others. By this point, Benchmark teachers have relinquished their role as discussion director or interpretive authority and replaced it with the role of facilitator (Pearson & Fielding, 1991). The goal is always the same—the active construction of meaning (Harman & Edelsky, 1989). A safe environment is created where students feel free to take risks in experimenting with interpretations during their reading of new information and relating it to prior knowledge. Meaning is constructed through a transactive process between teacher, students, and text (Edelsky, 1990; Gaskins, Anderson, Pressley, Cunicelli, & Satlow, 1993; Pressley et al., 1992). Teachers and students are responsive to and supportive of the input of others, and meaning is jointly negotiated with each participant constructing a meaning a little different from what he or she would have constructed individually. Students and teachers also discuss the strategies they employed, including how beneficial a particular strategy proved to be in a particular situation and how the strategy was implemented.

7. Independent Reading.   An emphasis on independent reading is common to both whole language environments and to Benchmark. All students at Benchmark choose books, magazines, student newspapers, and so forth to read at home for at least 30 minutes each evening. The next day, they share their thoughts and feelings about their home reading with classmates and/or the teacher, either orally or in writing. For example, in some classrooms, students might write critiques, summaries, or reactions regarding books they have read, and these responses might even be placed on file to be referred to by other students when they want suggestions about good books to read. In other classrooms, teachers might hold small-group sharing sessions where students tell about their home reading. In still other classrooms, teachers might hold individual conferences with each student, whereas others might allow students to share about their home reading in peer conferences.

Some students, both at school and at home, listen to taped books, which are used for repeated readings (Gaskins & Elliot, 1983). Listening to the reading of books and following along in the text is one means of developing fluency and, when these students have learned to read a particular book, it provides an opportunity for them to share with someone else their joy in reading it. The taped-repeated-reading program allows students to read materials at their interest level, a level that might prove too challenging and discouraging if they were to attempt reading without first hearing the tape as they follow along in the book. Reading a book that is at both their interest and conceptual levels proves to be an emotional lift for students who desperately want to read the books being read by their peers who are better readers.

8. Teacher–Student Conferences.   Meeting individually with students is common to both whole language environments and Benchmark. At our school, teachers hold individual conferences with students for a number of reasons (Gaskins & Elliot, 1983). One reason is to discuss what a student has been reading. A guideline we use for these conferences is that the discussion must be of the same authenticity as a discussion a teacher might have with another adult at a social gathering. The conference is not to be an interrogation to see if a student read the book. Rather, the emphasis is on the student's personal reaction to it. During such a conference, a student may also choose a particularly interesting part of the text to read to someone.

A second purpose for individual conferences is for the teacher and student to agree to collaborate on goals. The student and teacher clarify and refine a contract for what the student will accomplish in the classroom during a specified period of time. Other purposes for teacher–student conferences include coaching a student about learning strategies for a specific task, discussing learning styles, or providing positive support.

9. Reflection and Planning.   In both whole language environments and at Benchmark, teachers base the next day's instruction primarily on two pieces of information: (a) what they have discovered about each student's interests, abilities, and needs by watching and learning from the students, and (b) their ever-evolving understanding of theory and research (Gaskins, 1988a, 1988b; Newman & Church, 1990). Although basal program readers are sometimes used as reading material, and teachers sometimes consult the accompanying manuals to gain ideas about related literature and activities, Benchmark teachers tend not to teach as outlined in these manuals. During planning, teachers analyze each student's errors, but they focus on errors not as scores to be recorded in a gradebook but rather as evidence about the student's needs. They also encourage students to self-monitor and self-evaluate their own reading and to regard understanding their errors as a way of learning. As teachers reflect on their teaching each day, they plan questions, procedures, and explorations to enable them to meet each student where he or she is functioning. They plan purposeful activities and carefully structure learning environments so that students will be active participants and learners. The methods they use are dynamic and continually being refined, and their choice of methods is based on the needs of individual students.

10. Cooperation and Collaboration.   In both whole language environments and at Benchmark, learning is viewed as a social activity. In both, students work in cooperative groups, sometimes with other students, sometimes with a teacher and students.

Before cooperative groups meet, our students are explicitly taught both how to collaborate and how to work cooperatively. Learning in the classroom is by collaborative construction, rather than by the transmission of information from an omniscient source. Conversation is the vehicle. For example, students often form dyads to help each other construct an understanding of the meaning of specific learning goals in reading and writing, as well as in science, social studies, and math. Then, after spending a short time collaborating, the groups share and reshape their understandings. This joint construction of meaning is evident in all aspects of the Benchmark curriculum.

CONCERNS ABOUT WHOLE LANGUAGE

My review led me to understand why the speaker identified Benchmark as a whole language environment. Yet it also raised in me several concerns about what I see as deficiencies in whole language instruction, namely, its de-emphasis on explicit strategy instruction, its lack of an explicit, structured, decoding program, and its wholesale rejection of basal reading programs.

The De-emphasis on Explicit Strategy Instruction

The de-emphasis on *explicit* strategy instruction favored by the whole language movement is especially alarming in light of research suggesting that "instruction from teachers remains crucial for students' development of various processes, whether these have to do with reading a new genre, developing new composing techniques such as flashbacks, or understanding patterns of words" (Hiebert, 1991, p. 136). In fact, structured systematic teaching may be particularly crucial in the early grades (Adams, 1990; Chall & Squire, 1991). McCaslin (1989) stated this case most strongly when she said that "lack of instruction is defenseless" (p. 226).

The de-emphasis on teacher-led explicit instruction undoubtedly is an over-reaction to the isolated skills approaches of the past—approaches that *should* be put to rest. However, doing away with skills instruction does not also mean that teachers should no longer explicitly teach students effective and efficient strategies for learning and thinking, nor that they should leave such instruction to incidental teaching or learning from peers. Seizing the opportunity to teach or reinforce a strategy and encouraging peers to learn from one another are components of good teaching; however, learning from peers or discovering language patterns on one's own should not be the only opportunities for becoming strategic constructors of knowledge. Providing students with as many keys as possible to unlocking learning only makes sense, particularly in view of the fact that we do not know of one right key for all students (Newman & Church, 1990).

The Need for a Structured Decoding Program

Another concern related to the de-emphasis on explicit strategy instruction is the lack of explicit, structured, decoding instruction in whole language approaches and the concomitant belief that children will learn to read without benefit of a formal, structured, decoding program. My concern is based on what we have learned from our experience at Benchmark with the successful decoding program we have developed.

Other Concerns

My other lesser concerns about whole language instruction have to do with basal reading programs, the one-program-fits-all-children issue, and whether whole language is a concept with a set definition. With respect to basal programs, there are certainly *aspects* of such programs that are incompatible with the whole language philosophy and with the way we teach at Benchmark. Two of these aspects to which I object are separate skills instruction (resulting in workbook pages, ditto masters, and mastery tests, which suggests that literary development can be reduced to learning discrete skills) and the lack of freedom of choice that is dictated by the lockstep use of the stories (Farr, 1989). I am also uncomfortable with some of the recommendations in the teachers' manuals, particularly ones that suggest that stories should be read over several days rather than read and discussed at a brisk pace, perhaps at the rate of a story a day. On the other hand, like Farr (1989), I find aspects of basal programs that not only seem to fit nicely with whole language, but also with the learning environments we create at Benchmark. These aspects include excellent stories written by outstanding children's authors, which can be used as springboards to a variety of children's literature, and manuals that suggest a choice of activities similar to those encouraged by whole language advocates.

Another issue regarding basal reading programs, and of particular concern to teachers of poor readers, is the condemnation of basal readers because of controlled vocabularies. At Benchmark, we would be the first to agree that there is a wealth of excellent reading material available for children to read that may not be found in basal readers. However, there are clearly some students who have so much difficulty mastering a sight vocabulary and acquiring sound–symbol relationships that they do not feel like competent readers when they struggle through some of the better written, more interesting material containing a wide variety of words. Good literature, when encountered by these students, may present an overwhelming number of unknown words, which not only discourages them but also hampers the development of automaticity, which is so necessary to meaningful reading. In fact, for some students who benefit from reading materials with a controlled vocabulary, the newer basal programs with better literature may prove more difficult than basal programs of the past. Instruction and learning environments cannot be equated with a set of materials. The issue is really what reading material is most appropriate for each student.

A related concern is that a whole language program may not be right for all students. At Benchmark, we believe, like Pinnell (1989), that "neither whole language nor any other kind of classroom literacy program provides the answer for all children" (p. 180). As a result, our staff remains open-minded about the possibility that for some students there may be instructional contexts other than those that fit under the whole language umbrella that are more productive (Freppon & Dahl, 1991).

Yet even making such a determination is difficult, for whole language is not well defined. Hoffman (1989) concurred with other whole language advocates (Goodman, 1989a, 1989b; Harste, 1989) when he stated that "for most, it is a label for a concept that is far from developed" (p. 112).

Training and Support of Teachers

Most of the concerns I have discussed can be addressed by the education and support of teachers before and during the implementation of the whole language philosophy in a classroom.

Teachers are unlikely to be successful as whole language teachers without education in three basic areas: how children learn, how to be responsive to what each child needs, and how to determine what should be taught. Such voids in teacher education are sure to undermine a program in which sound teacher reasoning is a prerequisite for designing successful environments for learning. Teacher education must also involve guidance to help teachers realize that there is not one way of teaching or one set of materials that is best for all children, and that they need to be flexible about instruction for each student and knowledgeable about the possibilities available to them, including explicit and systematic teaching of decoding and other strategies. Ongoing support will also be needed to create an atmosphere for professional growth, where teachers are always in the process of becoming, just as the whole language philosophy of how to teach is constantly evolving.

In addition to the need for teacher education and support, school districts must recognize that effective change takes place slowly. It cannot be mandated to occur over night. As Pearson (1989) has suggested, change occurs "slowly and gradually as we weigh the validity and relevance of accumulating evidence" (p. 239). Whole language programs need to be developed slowly, over several years. It would be overwhelming to initiate all the components of whole language in a year. Such an endeavor would require developing expertise in teaching process writing, mediating the construction of meaning, implementing collaboration and cooperation, learning about children's literature, and developing a background in phonemic awareness and decoding, to mention only a few components of a whole language environment. Further, the ability to make sense of "kid-watching" is based on expertise and experience in each aspect of the whole language curriculum. Teachers need to be given the time and background to understand these components if the goal of improving instruction in our nation's schools is to be achieved.

Without such education, whole language will be just one more great idea that is ultimately abandoned. I believe the whole language philosophy makes too much sense to have it eventually thrown out because teachers are not given the support they need to translate the philosophy into a program.

In the following section, I discuss ideas for developing such a program in the context of the problems and solutions that led to the whole language-like program at Benchmark School.

THE EVOLUTION OF THE BENCHMARK PROGRAM

Benchmark was started as a reaction to the status quo of the late 1960s—a time when children who failed in school had very little chance of ever feeling successful in a school environment. Benchmark's mission then and now is to allow those whom the schools deemed failures in reading (and usually everything else academic) a chance to gain the competencies they need to experience success (Gaskins, 1980).

Number of Words Read Correlates with Progress in Reading

One of the first things we did was to eliminate the traditional classroom activities that our students associated with failure—workbooks, worksheets, skill builders, and reading labs. We reasoned that if the students were behind in reading, they needed the opportunity to read, rather than work on skills in isolation in books that contained very few words. Therefore, we replaced these timeworn means of keeping students busy with lots of easy reading. Our guess was that the number of words read would correlate more highly with progress in reading than would the number of workbook pages completed. We were right (Guthrie & Greaney, 1991; Taylor, Frye, & Maruyasma, 1990).

Phonics Worksheets and Rules Do Not Empower Readers

Phonics workbook pages, accompanied by little if any explicit instruction, or lists of phonics rules to be memorized were common to the programs our students encountered prior to coming to Benchmark. They could quote such rules as, "When two vowels go walking, the first one does the talking," yet they could not decode the word *rain*. Some had even been exposed to a year or two of instruction in the new linguistic reading programs published in the 1960s. These programs featured text such as, "Dan, fan the man on the tan van." We found that the students in the linguistic programs could often read words such as *dinosaur* and *hippopotamus* yet not see the minimal differences in *tan* and *ten* or *fan* and *for*.

Initially, we experimented with a few synthetic phonics programs recommended for children with severe reading problems, but those did not seem to work either. As severe as the decoding problems were within our student population, we decided that the phonics programs of the 1970s just did not seem right for our students. We increasingly became convinced of this as more and more of the students referred to our program were students who had failed in basal programs described as phonics-emphasis. Occasionally these students could identify correctly the sounds associated with the symbols in a word but could not blend these isolated sounds they had decoded back into a whole. We decided to encourage our students to rely on the initial consonant and the sense of the sentence as their cues for decoding unknown words, and, like the whole language advocates, we hoped our students would eventually notice the way our language is structured and apply this understanding to decoding unknown words (Goodman, 1989a).

Children Learn to Write by Writing

In the mid-to-late 1970s we began to receive feedback from the schools to which our students returned that we had done a good job teaching them to read, *but* their writing was often so poorly constructed that teachers had difficulty understanding the points the students were trying to make. We did a literature search to see what we could learn about improving our writing instruction. The exciting idea we encountered was process writing. The name associated with it was Donald Graves, whom we invited to the school to present several inservice programs over the next few years. Under Graves' guidance, process writing was implemented at Benchmark (Gaskins, 1982; Gaskins, 1992). The students loved it. It was the first time they had the opportunity to be experts, for they were writing about familiar and meaningful topics. It was also the first time their written work was free of red marks, for, in early drafts, content was the primary focus, whereas mechanics would be dealt with in later drafts. Students were also reading more because they were reading the pieces written by their classmates as well as reading and rereading drafts of their own pieces. Some classes became so engrossed in process writing that they forgot to go to recess.

Problems and Solutions

So, we eliminated workbooks, busy work, and current phonics programs from our curriculum and emphasized instead lots of easy reading, the use of context in decoding, and process writing. However, all was not as rosy as we would have liked. Two major problems remained that we could not ignore—problems that seemed to suggest solutions that violated our belief that the whole is more than the sum of its parts.

Need for Explicit Decoding Instruction.   One such problem was that many of our poor readers did not infer the structure of the language system through engagement in reading, as we had hoped they would do. For the most part, their independent decoding strategy was to guess what a word was based on the initial consonant and context. If the initial consonant and context did not unlock the pronunciation of the unknown word, students often skipped it. Another strategy they employed was to guess at the unknown word based on its configuration. Interestingly, it appeared that these students were attending to language cues (i.e., initial consonants, context, and configuration) but had not chosen the most productive cues. Further, this misguided attention may have precluded their attending to the phonetic cues they needed to begin reading words reliably (Ehri & Wilce, 1985). These ineffective practices slowed down the reading process, and thus less was read. In addition, these practices interfered with the meaning-construction process. Although other decoding strategies were pointed out to students on an individual basis as the need arose, these minilessons were obviously inadequate. There were a few students who seemed to have figured out the language system on their own, and they seemed able to decode almost anything; but such cases at Benchmark were extremely rare. Like Teale (1991), we were convinced that intensive phonics was the wrong way to teach beginning reading, but we also were discovering that incidental decoding instruction "equates to disaster for beginning reading" (p. 186). We were seeing first hand too much evidence that incidental instruction does not provide the foundation in phonemic awareness and basic decoding strategies that allows beginning readers to develop into proficient readers.

We were learning that Pearson and Fielding's (1991) statement about explicit comprehension strategy instruction is just as true of decoding: "The danger in leaving students to 'their own devices' is that in the process we will do little except exacerbate the already wide gaps between successful and unsuccess-ful . . . ." (p. 851). It was becoming clear that the main difference between our good and poor readers was that the good readers rapidly used spelling–sound knowledge to identify words (Juel, 1991). We also noted that early attainment of decoding skill accurately predicted the students who could give full attention to comprehension (Juel, 1991). Our conclusion was (see Heymsfeld, 1989) that we could not "depend on haphazard amorphous instruction to teach something as critical as the alphabetic code" (p. 66). As Samuels (1988) has suggested, it made sense to explore the possibility of systematically integrating concepts about the code into a holistic approach, particularly in view of the fact that neither phonics nor whole language approaches guarantee success for every student. Others who taught poor readers, specifically those associated with Reading Recovery, seemed to have faced the same dilemma. Pinnell (1989) expressed it as follows: "It is generally recognized that the primary goal of both reading and writing is the communication and construction of meaning, but at times children may need to focus on detail, such as sound–letter relationships or visual features of print, in order to accomplish that goal" (p. 165). We decided that as we continued to focus on comprehension (Teale, 1991), we needed to "build in the learning and teach-ing of decoding at every step" (p. 186).

We began to research how children learn to decode, particularly from the point of view of the linguists. With the help of Patricia Cunningham of Wake Forest University and Richard Anderson of the Center for the Study of Reading, we developed a systematic method for assisting our students in decoding un-known words (Gaskins et al., 1988; Gaskins, Gaskins, & Gaskins, 1991; Gas-kins, Gaskins, & Gaskins, 1992). We taught our students to use words they knew to decode words they did not know. Several factors undoubtedly contributed to the success of this approach with our students. One was that they viewed the approach as easy to learn and use because it was based on what they already knew. Another was that it did not in any way resemble other phonics programs in which they had already failed. And, perhaps most important of all, it met a need that was of concern to them—they knew that they needed a reliable method for decoding if they were going to improve in their ability to read.

By 1985, we were in the midst of a 3-year study with the Center for the Study of Reading regarding the word identification program, whereas on the national scene, whole language discussions were the feature of most professional confer-ences and journals. Our attention to decoding problems seemed totally out of step with the times, certainly contrary to what was being promulgated by whole language advocates. Even though initially we had believed, as the whole lan-guage advocates do, that through a great deal of reading and discussions about reading students would discover how our language works, it had not worked out that way. Such a theory certainly made sense because it was the way most of us learned. Nevertheless, we adapted our program to meet the students where they were. What they seemed to need was explicit instruction about the patterns in our language, patterns that they had not discovered on their own. What we seemed to have ignored was the fact (Schickedanz, 1990) that "print-specific skills rather than oral language development, are necessary for success in beginning reading" (p. 130), particularly for our very verbal and bright underachievers.

Need for Explicit Strategy Instruction.   A second problem that concerned us was our students' seeming lack of knowledge about how to take control of their learning, thinking, and problem solving. Students seemed passive. They did not seem to have any idea how one becomes actively involved in learning. As a result of this concern, we initiated a research and development project to foster strategic learning and thinking across the curriculum (Gaskins & Elliot, 1991). This is a school-wide project to develop actively involved students by helping them develop a conscious awareness of the learning and thinking processes and of how these processes are affected by interaction with personal, environmental, task, and strategy variables. The strategy instruction builds on the students' prior knowledge and language strengths, helps students integrate efficient and effective strategies into their daily learning experiences, and stresses flexibility in the use of strategies.

An important part of our strategies-across-the-curriculum project is sharing with students the rationale for being actively involved in learning. Our goal is to demystify written language, texts, and learning (Harman & Edelsky, 1989). Dubbed Psych 101, these discussions are about *why* students needed to learn how to take charge of their own learning, thinking, and problem solving. Students enjoy these discussions about how the mind works and proudly proclaim that they are receiving a college course in psychology. We have found that one of our students' major fascinations is intelligence. Psych 101 discussions provide an opportunity to dispel students' beliefs that difficulty in learning to read is a sign that they are dumb and that being smart is out of their control.

When teachers give an assignment, they help students analyze the factors affecting successful completion of the task, discuss with students the learning–thinking processes the task entails, and suggest strategies that the students might use to accomplish the task. They share with students why they might choose a particular strategy, other contexts where it could be used, and the thinking process involved in implementing the strategy. Teachers also discuss strategies students can employ to monitor and evaluate their progress in completing tasks. Thus, strategies for constructing meaning are explicitly taught, modeled, and scaffolded because we believe that students profit from this interaction with adults about what works in becoming successful learners.

CREATING OPTIMUM LEARNING ENVIRONMENTS

Instruction at Benchmark is provided by energetic enthusiastic teachers who are empowered by their understanding of children and how they learn and by their understanding of the processes involved in the use of literacy for learning and thinking. The focus is on the learner, not on methods or materials. Benchmark teachers know that central to students' learning are student behaviors and activities, so teachers note how the structure of tasks and students' participation in those tasks affect their learning. Teachers are also interested in how students perceive task difficulty, purpose, and requirements, as well as a teacher's input about these tasks.

As teachers observe their students, they informally assess their progress and roadblocks, as well as what works and does not work. Teachers collaborate with other staff members to create environments that foster optimal learning for every student no matter how different their individual way of learning may be. This can take the form of direct or indirect instruction. The stance may be formal or informal. Each decision is based on what seems to be in the best interest of an individual student, realizing that students are varied and complex and do not respond to one best way of teaching or one best sociopsycholinguistic environment. Ours are students who already have failed in classroom environments where the majority of the students were successful in learning to read; thus we know the learning environments created for the majority may not work for them.

Further, the focus is *not* on providing teachers with the right methods and materials; rather the focus is on how to help teachers acquire the knowledge they need to create learning environments that maximize student learning. We know that this expertise develops slowly and takes nurturing. Optimum learning environments evolve slowly. They are not mandated.

Our Benchmark experience shows that one does not have to be a whole language proponent to feel comfortable with the set of beliefs associated with the whole language philosophy, nor to create optimum learning environments for students. However, it is probable that some whole language proponents will feel that the beliefs associated with instruction at Benchmark are compatible with their philosophy of teaching, for the development of the Benchmark belief system has been influenced in large part by the same theorists who have influenced the development of the whole language philosophy (i.e., Bruner, Dewey, Piaget, Rosenblatt, Schon, Vygotsky). Whether one is a whole language advocate or not, it is clear that the goal of dedicated reflective teachers everywhere is the same—the creation of the best possible learning environment for every student. Those of us with that goal cannot be very far apart in philosophy no matter what we call ourselves.

ACKNOWLEDGMENTS

The author gratefully acknowledges suggestions made about earlier versions of this chapter by Susan Audley, Barbara Barus, Donna Blakeman, Francis Boehnlein, Elizabeth Cunicelli, Marjorie Downer, Thorne Elliot, Mildred Ellison, Renee Erickson, Robert Gaskins, Dorothy O'Donnell, Joyce Ostertag,

Sharon Rauch, and Linda Six. The development of the strategy program discussed in this chapter was supported by a grant from the James S. McDonnell Foundation.

REFERENCES

Adams, M. J. (1990). *Beginning to read: Thinking and learning about print.* Cambridge, MA: The MIT Press.

Bergeron, B. S. (1990). What does the term whole language mean? Constructing a definition from the literature. *Journal of Reading Behavior, 22,* 301–329.

Chall, J. S., & Squire, J. S. (1991). The publishing industry and textbooks. In R. Barr, M. L. Kamil, P. Mosenthal, & P. D. Pearson (Eds.), *Handbook of reading research* (Vol. 2, pp. 120–167). New York: Longman.

Edelsky, C. (1990). Whose agenda is this anyway? A response to McKenna, Robinson, and Miller. *Educational Researcher, 19,* 7–11.

Ehri, L. C., & Wilce, L. S. (1985). Movement into reading: Is the first stage of printed word learning visual or phonetic? *Reading Research Quarterly, 20,* 163–179.

Farr, R. (1989). Reading: A place for basal readers under the whole language umbrella. *Educational Leadership, 46,* 86.

Freppon, P. A., & Dahl, K. L. (1991). Learning about phonics in a whole language classroom. *Language Arts, 68,* 190–197.

Gaskins, I. W. (1980). *The Benchmark story.* Media, PA: Benchmark Press.

Gaskins, I. W. (1982). A writing program for poor readers and writers and the rest of the class, too. *Language Arts, 59,* 854–861.

Gaskins, I. W. (1988a). Helping teachers adapt to the needs of students with learning problems. In S. J. Samuels & P. D. Pearson (Eds.), *Changing school reading programs* (pp. 143–159). Newark, DE: International Reading Association.

Gaskins, I. W. (1988b). Introduction: A special issue on poor readers in the classroom. *The Reading Teacher, 41,* 748–749.

Gaskins, I. W. (1988c). Teachers as thinking coaches: Creating strategic learners and problem solvers. *Journal of Reading, Writing, and Learning Disabilities, 18,* 390–394.

Gaskins, I. W. (1992). And it works for them, too! In J. T. Feeley, D. C. Strickland, & S. B. Wepner (Eds.), *From writing process to reading process: K–8 teachers share their literacy programs.* New York: Teachers College Press.

Gaskins, I. W., Anderson, R. C., Pressley, M., Cunicelli, E. A., & Satlow, E. (1993). The moves and cycles of cognitive process instruction. *Elementary School Journal, 93,* 277–304.

Gaskins, I. W., & Baron, J. (1985). Teaching poor readers to cope with maladaptive cognitive styles: A training program. *Journal of Learning Disabilities, 18,* 390–394.

Gaskins, I. W., Downer, M., Anderson, R. C., Cunningham, P. M., Gaskins, R. W., Schommer, M., & the Teachers of Benchmark School. (1988). A metacognitive approach to phonics: Using what you know to decode what you don't know. *Remedial and Special Education, 9,* 36–41, 66.

Gaskins, I. W., & Elliot, T. T. (1983). *Teaching for success: Administrative and classroom practices at Benchmark School.* Media, PA: Benchmark Press.

Gaskins, I. W., & Elliot, T. T. (1991). *Implementing cognitive strategy instruction across the school: The Benchmark manual for teachers.* Cambridge, MA: Brookline Books.

Gaskins, R. W., Gaskins, J. C., & Gaskins, I. W. (1991). A decoding program for poor readers—and the rest of the class, too! *Language Arts, 68,* 213–225.

Gaskins, R. W., Gaskins, J. C., & Gaskins, I. W. (1992). Using what you know to figure out what you don't know: An analogy approach to decoding. *The Reading and Writing Quarterly.*

Goodman, K. S. (1989a). Whole language is whole: A response to Heymsfeld. *Educational Leadership, 46,* 69–70.

Goodman, K. S. (1989b). Whole language research: Foundations and development. *Elementary School Journal, 90,* 207–221.

Guthrie, J. T., & Greaney, V. (1991). Literacy acts. In R. Barr, M. L. Kamil, P. Mosenthal, & P. D. Pearson (Eds.), *Handbook of reading research* (Vol. 2, pp. 68–96). New York: Longman.

Harman, S., & Edelsky, C. (1989). The risks of whole language literacy: Alienation and connection. *Language Arts, 66,* 392–406.

Harste, J. C. (1989). Commentary: The future of whole language. *Elementary School Journal, 90,* 243–249.

Heymsfeld, C. R. (1989). Filling the hole in whole language. *Educational Leadership, 46,* 65–68.

Hiebert, E. H. (1991). Research directions: Literacy contexts and literacy processes. *Language Arts, 68,* 134–139.

Hoffman, J. V. (1989). Introduction. *Elementary School Journal, 90,* 111–112.

Juel, C. (1991). Beginning reading. In R. Barr, M. L. Kamil, P. Mosenthal, & P. D. Pearson (Eds.), *Handbook of reading research* (Vol. 2, pp. 759–788). New York: Longman.

McCaslin, M. M. (1989). Commentary: Whole language: Theory, instruction, and future implementation. *Elementary School Journal, 90,* 223–229.

Newman, J. M., & Church, S. M. (1990). Myths of whole language. *The Reading Teacher, 44,* 20–26.

Pearson, P. D. (1989). Commentary: Reading the whole language movement. *Elementary School Journal, 90,* 231–241.

Pearson, P. D., & Fielding, L. (1991). Comprehension instruction. In R. Barr, M. L. Kamil, P. Mosenthal, & P. D. Pearson (Eds.), *Handbook of reading research* (Vol. 2, pp. 815–860). New York: Longman.

Pinnell, G. S. (1989). Reading Recovery: Helping at-risk children learn to read. *Elementary School Journal, 90,* 161–183.

Pressley, M., El-Dinary, P. B., Gaskins, I. W., Schuder, T., Bergman, J. L., Almasi, J., & Brown, R. (1992). Direct explanation done well: Transactional instruction of reading comprehension strategies. *Elementary School Journal, 92,* 513–555.

Pressley, M., Gaskins, I. W., Cunicelli, E. A., Burdick, N. J., Schaub-Matt, M., Lee, D. S., & Powell, N. (1991). Strategy instruction at Benchmark School: A faculty interview study. *Learning Disability Quarterly, 14,* 19–48.

Samuels, S. J. (1988). Decoding and automaticity: Helping poor readers become automatic at word recognition. *The Reading Teacher, 41,* 756–760.

Schickedanz, J. A. (1990). The jury is still out on the effects of whole language and language experience approaches for beginning reading: A critique of Stahl and Miller's study. *Review of Educational Research, 60,* 127–131.

Taylor, B. M., Frye, B. J., & Maruyasma, G. (1990). Time spent reading and reading growth. *American Educational Research Journal, 27,* 351–362.

Teale, W. (1991). Dear reader. *Language Arts, 68,* 184–187.

Tharp, R. G., & Gallimore, R. (1988). *Rousing minds to life.* New York: Cambridge University Press.

Vygotsky, L. S. (1978). *Mind in society: The development of higher psychological processes.* Cambridge, MA: Harvard University Press.

III CHILDREN, ADULTS, BOOKS: INTERACTIVE READING

9 Awakening Literacy Through Interactive Story Reading

Bonnie M. Kerr
Jana M. Mason
Center for the Study of Reading

Educational researchers praise the practice of parents and teachers reading to children. In a book aimed at helping parents provide their children with useful learning experiences, for example, Butler and Clay (1979) asserted: "There is no substitute for reading and telling stories to children, from the very earliest days" (p. 17). Based on his review of the literature on reading to children, Teale (1981) concluded that "reading to preschool children . . . is an activity through which children may develop interest and skill in literacy" (p. 902). And in *Becoming a Nation of Readers,* Anderson, Hiebert, Scott, and Wilkinson (1985) cited reading to children as "the single most important activity for building the knowledge required for eventual success in reading" (p. 23). Moreover, a number of correlational studies have linked activities in which adults and preschool children share book reading to the children's beginning reading success in school (Durkin, 1966; Hewison & Tizard, 1980; Moon & Wells, 1979; Walker & Kuerbitz, 1970).

Such unabashed praise for reading to children is intriguing because it begs for elaboration: Why is reading to young children thought to be so beneficial? What knowledge do children acquire from it? Although asserting the value of the practice of reading to children, researchers have given little attention to *what* children learn from it.

Our position is that book reading to children cues many literate behaviors, skills, and dispositions, particularly when an *interactive story reading* approach is used. We define interactive story reading as the joint use of picture books to talk about the pictures, read the text, and discuss the story ideas. Central to this definition is the notion that the adult and child (or group of children) construct an understanding of the book together. It is because of this emphasis on the joint construction of meaning that we prefer this term over others, such as *shared reading, story reading, reading aloud to children,* and *guided reading* that have been used in the research literature to label the event of reading to children.

In this chapter, we specify the concepts, skills, and dispositions that children can acquire from participating in interactive story reading. To do this, we have organized the recent empirical research evidence available on story reading into topics that are likely to affect the emergence of literacy. We first frame this research with Vygotsky's developmental theory of learning, which emphasizes the general social nature of learning.

Theoretical Underpinnings

Vygotsky (1978) postulated that learning precedes development because it "results in mental development and sets into motion a variety of developmental processes" (p. 90). Although learning can begin as exploration, it usually requires adult support to move the child to further learning and development. When the adult support is effective, learning occurs within a region that Vygotsky describes as a "zone of proximal development," the area between what a child can do independently and what she or he can do with adult guidance. This is why Vygotsky emphasized social learning processes, postulating that learning occurs on two planes, the social and the psychological, with social interactions serving as the foundation. Therefore, literacy concepts, skills, and dispositions, being learned behaviors, are socially structured.

Vygotsky (1929) proposed four stages of cultural development, which Mason and Sinha (in press) have applied to literacy learning and development. In the first stage, according to Vygotsky (1929), the child creates "associative or conditional reflexive connections between the stimuli and reactions" (p. 419). At this point, the child is limited by attention, interest, and memory. With respect to literacy, a child in this stage might go through the physical motions of reading and writing, imitating the actions he or she has seen adults perform—holding a book and turning the pages, making up a text, inserting remembered story phrases in talk, scribbling messages with wavy lines, and so forth. Movement into the second stage, although usually beyond the child's memory resources, can occur with the assistance of an adult; that is, within the child's zone of proximal development. In this stage, the child and adult read and write together. The child might memorize texts that were read many times and so appear to be reading. With help, the child might also try to write favorite words. By operating within the child's range of understanding, the adult helps the child see new connections, such as those between letters and their sounds in words, and maintains the child's interest, for example, by reading favorite books and by easing memory demands by rereading stories and pointing to words as they are said. The child achieves new understandings from these learning interactions and so moves into the third stage. This stage is marked by the child figuring out how to use picture, letter, and sound cues to read words, and then practicing that discovery. Much of the learning activity is shifting toward independence. In the fourth stage, the child is freed from external cues, and the process becomes internalized; that is, the child "starts to use the inner schemes, tries to use as signs his remembrances, the knowledge he formerly acquired" (Vygotsky, 1929, p. 427).

These stages should be thought of as specific to each concept and skill, not as general or overarching stages. Thus, a child could be at the first stage with respect to one concept, such as word recognition, but operate at the fourth stage with respect to another, such as letter recognition. Internalization of each concept, however, is dependent on the nature of social functions that envelop and guide learning. The growing point for the child's developing language and literacy is a movement from reacting to surroundings to interacting with family members, and through the interactions with others to understanding the constructs that are used. Through internalization of literacy constructs, the child becomes more aware of their generalizability and applicability to new information.

When children first encounter and notice printed letters and words, for example, they react to them in much the same way as they react to other objects in their surroundings. If, for example, a family is driving past McDonald's, a young child is likely to notice the golden arches. An older sibling or parent who says, "Here's McDonald's," will have labeled it for the youngster. As the family enters and has lunch, the child connects the arches with a place to eat hamburgers. The next time the family passes the arches, the child may remember them and express recognition with "McDonald's." The child may learn that saying "McDonald's" results in getting a hamburger. Logically, the child begins using the name McDonald's to express what he or she wants, and a meaning for the arches is remembered. This insight might spur exploration of other labels or inspire attempts to draw a picture of the arches. Later, the child may realize that the arches are a stylized version of the letter *M,* and later still, that that letter relates to the beginning phoneme in the name McDonald's.

The literacy developmental framework based on Vygotsky, then, has the following pattern. Initially, when children are read words in books, they react by looking at pictures and attending to the story line (Lartz & Mason, 1988; Sulzby, 1985). They also notice the context in which the print is embedded and may connect symbols with meaning (Ferreiro & Teberosky, 1983). By pointing to words as they are read, parents help children to focus on specific words, understand the directionality of reading, connect the words with meaning, and eventually recognize particular words and letter patterns that the parent is saying as certain printed words. When stories are read repeatedly, children expect to hear and see the same words repeated on each page every time the book is opened (and they sometimes admonish parents who try to skip any words on a page!). When parents talk to their children about the story's meaning, children begin to understand how the ideas make a story even though many words are used in new ways, often unlike the oral language they have heard or used (see Chafe, 1985; Perera, 1984), and new words are embellished through picture, story line, or by parents (Bruner, 1990). When parents help children interpret and connect the story to their own experiences, children can focus on story meaning as well as on the way it is communicated and connect their background knowledge to new words and phrases. Interactive storybook reading makes it possible for children to understand written language as an extension of their oral language. It also provides them with a set of new book-related concepts that contributes to their literacy acquisition.

THE PROCESS AND EFFECTS OF INTERACTIVE READING

We have presented the theory underlying our assumption that children learn about a number of literacy concepts when they listen to and discuss stories with adults. We now discuss the research that shows how they learn and then what they learn. We describe the process of interactive reading at home and in school and then examine how interactive reading advances children's (a) written language awareness, (b) knowledge of storybook vocabulary and concepts, and (c) letter and word identification ability. Throughout, our goal is to show how research on reading to children at home or school can be applied to classroom practices.

The Process of Interactive Reading

When adults read stories to young children, they usually do more than read the words aloud. They ask meaningful questions about the stories. To make sure children understand the story, they paraphrase or interpret as needed, and they answer the children's questions about it. From the research that has examined parent–child story reading, it is possible to explain the social nature of the event and to make deductions about what young children learn during it. Because researchers have focused primarily on parent–child book sharing, we look first at these interactions. Then we turn to teacher–group book sharing.

Parent–Child Book Sharing.   The research on parents reading to children is based primarily on middle-class mothers reading to their preschool children at bedtime. Moreover, the studies are often descriptions given by highly educated mothers reflecting on their practices with their children. A seminal work of this type is the Ninio and Bruner (1978) study in which it was found that highly ritualized discussion sequences between parent and child occur during story reading, and that these sequences are the primary means through which toddlers learn to label pictures. Ninio and Bruner found that mothers interpret children's smiling, babbling, vocalizing, reaching, and pointing as either requesting or providing labels. For example, a baby reaches toward one of the pictures in the book, and the mother extends that gesture by saying the name of the picture. Moreover, if the baby vocalizes or gestures toward the picture when the mother gives a label, the mother assumes that the baby is attending to the name she gave, furthering the likelihood that she will continue to provide labels. These parent–child interchanges are orchestrated into turn-taking sessions, with parent or child initiating a communication.

At about the same time that Ninio and Bruner were reporting their work, Snow (1983) began reporting her analyses of mother–child discussion during book sharing. She posited that the features of the interactions that support oral language acquisition are the very same features that promote beginning reading and writing development. She highlighted four such features: (a) *semantic contingency*, or the adult continuing a topic introduced by the child's previous statement through expansions, extensions, clarifications, or answers; (b) *scaffolding*, or the steps the adult takes to minimize the difficulty of the activity; (c) *accountability procedures*, or the way the mother demands the task be finished; and (d) the use of *highly predictable contexts* for language use that help the child move from the concrete here and now to the remote and abstract. Elaborations on these four features illustrate how children learn about reading through social interactions during interactive storybook reading.

The use by adults of *semantic contingency*, or meaningfully extending a child's comment to facilitate oral language acquisition, has been well documented (Cross, 1978). Snow (1983), however, argued that when adults expand on or clarify text during storybook reading, they facilitate the development of literate behavior. For example, adults can answer children's questions about letter names and words, they can clarify story meaning, and they can extend children's understanding of story concepts such as what direction one reads print or where a word begins and ends.

Not only is the discourse during interactive story reading expansive in nature, Snow argued, it is *scaffolded*. Drawing from Bruner (1978), she defined *scaffolding* as the "steps taken to reduce the degrees of freedom in carrying out some task, so that the child can concentrate on the difficult skill he is in the process of acquiring" (p. 170). Scaffolding occurs in oral language development. For example, although young children often say only one word for a whole sentence when they are learning to talk, parents respond by treating the word as a complete and sophisticated statement. In story reading, scaffolding might include parent reminders to the child about the name of the story, who the important characters are, or what the story problem is. The parent might point to a picture and then its printed label, hesitate to see if the child fills in a story word or phrase, or encourage the child to help tell parts of a story.

Snow also argues that parents challenge their children during reading sessions by holding them accountable for what they do to help construct the session.

Ninio and Bruner (1978) have referred to *accountability procedures* as "upping the ante." Like scaffolding, accountability procedures are closely tied to expectations for children to take turns and to perform at their most sophisticated level. So, if a child can use the correct name for an object, parents may not accept pointing to a picture or giving a baby-talk version of the name, or they may refuse to answer a question that the child should be able to answer.

Indeed, the supportive and challenging nature of book reading was confirmed in work by DeLoache and DeMendoza (1987), who studied 30 mothers and their 12- to 18-month-old children. They found that the mothers took responsibility for determining which pictures would be discussed and generally did so by asking for or providing information about the pictures. The decisions a mother used to determine when to tell and when to ask were based on her belief about her child's word knowledge. If she believed the child did not know the word, as was often the case for the youngest children, she provided the information. If she thought the child knew the word, often the case for the older children, the mother would be equally likely to seek the picture label from the child. Moreover, the mothers provided older children with more elaborate information about a picture than younger children. The mothers seemed to evoke optimal performance from the children through these scaffolding techniques.

Finally, Snow argued that parents engage in routines or formats that offer *highly predictable contexts* for children's language and literacy acquisition. A mother caring for an infant may play the same peek-a-boo game whenever she dresses the child. The infant learns the game and will later play it at times other than during dressing. Toddlers and preschoolers are read ABC books, books that use rhythm and rhyme, and predictable books with repeated phrases, all of which help them to recognize and remember letters, to identify a few words, and, later, to associate graphemes with phonemes in words.

Additional support for Snow's argument that interactive story reading promotes literacy comes from her collaborative work. With Goldfield (Snow & Goldfield, 1982), she first characterized the nature of repeated reading sessions with the same book. With Ninio (Snow & Ninio, 1986), she compiled a list of effects of story reading. When Snow and Goldfield examined the nature of the process of learning that occurs with repeated discussions of pictures in a picture book, they observed that, at first, mothers provide both the framework about which questions to ask and the answers needed for those questions. The child uses this information to identify the situation when it occurs again, repeats what the mother has said in previous readings, and eventually supplies it without prompting. Roser and Martinez (1985) support Snow's earlier work. They found that children mimic the adult reader after repeated readings of books.

Snow and Ninio (1986) proposed seven tenets of literate communication from the interactions during the reading event that, although not explicitly taught, help children become literate. These tenets are (a) that a book is for reading rather than manipulating, (b) that a book controls the conversation, (c) that pictures are representations rather than actual objects, (d) that pictures can be named, (e) that pictures and words are static but represent dynamic events, (f) that book events occur outside of real time, and (g) that books are an independent fictional world.

It is clear that parents help children take over storybook-reading talk, and that this practice encourages children's later strategies for talking about and interpreting books. The descriptive research shows clearly that children experience opportunities for learning from engaging in interactive story reading with parents, and that the interactions have characteristic patterns that children imitate and that could promote literacy development. We turn now to interactive reading between teachers and students to see whether similar patterns are evident.

Teacher–Student Story Sharing.   Researchers have only recently begun to look at the exchanges between teacher and students that occur during interactive story reading. Teale, Martinez, and Glass (1989) studied the styles of teacher storybook reading as part of a larger study on implementing an emerging literacy program in kindergarten classrooms. They concluded that teachers do have identifiable, consistent styles of reading storybooks. Mason, Peterman, Powell, and Kerr (1989) reached a similar conclusion when they studied the way teachers read books to their students.

Peterman (1988) empirically tested the influence of teacher reading procedures on kindergartners' literacy learning. Six teachers read to one of their kindergarten classes in the usual way and read to their other class using experimenter-designed story reading procedures. Pretest–posttest comparisons indicated that the new story reading procedures had a significant positive effect on students' story recall, but not on their word reading, story reading, or language. Peterman concluded that students' story recall was enhanced because teachers' story reading procedures emphasized similarities between the characters' and the students' experiences.

Different types of texts have also been found to affect kindergarten children's understanding and recall. Mason et al. (1989) found that the type of text influenced children's story recall, their writing, and even their text reading. Using a predictable book, narrative text, and an expository text, children's responses were more complete or best with the predictable book and least complete or lowest with the expository text. These results were due in part to the way teachers read each text to the children. Teachers read the narrative using discussion of plot features and vocabulary, but when reading the expository text, they focused on demonstrating the main concept and made low-level, picture–text word connections. With the predictable book, the teachers encouraged far more child participation in the actual reading. Thus, it appears that text-type differences affect teachers' presentations of the text, which in turn influences children's recall and ability to read and write about it.

The nature of the dialogue that occurs during interactive book reading is affected by factors that include the size of the group, the competency of the participants, and the familiarity and type of the text. Yet a basic framework can be seen. When parents or teachers model, read, and talk to children about a text, they provide a structure that helps children understand and remember the story content. By promoting socially interactive story reading in which both reader and listener actively participate and cooperatively negotiate what is important and what things mean, teachers engage children in a process of learning through social interaction. It appears that, not only do children internalize the social conventions of stories when they talk with adults about them, they take away specific knowledge from hearing stories, such as the syntax, organization, and word forms used in written language, and knowledge of its elements—words and letters themselves. To confirm this supposition, we turn now to the research that focuses on the effects of interactive reading. We begin with written language awareness and then present evidence that interactive reading also promotes vocabulary growth and letter and word identification ability.

Written Language Awareness

Written language characteristics are evident in analyses of the talk of children during adult–child shared book reading. Moerk (1985) showed how shared picture book reading by a mother and child led to a gradual mastery by the child of book language as well as the development of oral language. The child expanded on the text using a variety of language strategies that were at first very rigid and not fully congruent with the immediate situation but then gradually became more flexible until the borrowed book language was fully incorporated and part of the child's spontaneous production. Lartz and Mason (1988) found that a 4-year-old child asked each week for 8 weeks to retell a story gradually began to replace her oral language-like recall with more written language structures. She mimicked the story dialogue, used phrases that would only be found in books, and repeated seldom-used words from the story.

The effects of interactive story reading appear on performance measures as well as during the reading sessions. Lazzari, Bender, and Kello (1987) studied parental influence on language development by observing parent–child story reading sessions in 38 families. They found that the children of parents who questioned them during story reading had higher language scores on the Peabody Picture Vocabulary Test than did students who were not questioned. Moreover, children who pointed and made text-related comments also had higher scores. Confirming a causal link, an intervention study by Whitehurst et al. (1988) found that parents who were taught to include developmentally sensitive responses, to give feedback, and to ask appropriate questions as they read to their young children had greater effects on the children's language production than did parents who were not so taught.

A case study intervention described by Heath and Branscombe with Thomas

(1986) also supports the idea that the language talk surrounding book reading helps children learn about written language. A 2-year-old African–American child in their study began to use narrative structures such as goal-based stories, physical descriptions, and time-ordered events in everyday conversation after participating in interactive story reading for 10 minutes a day. According to the researchers, "He used items, events, causes, reactions, and comparisons of events to organize factual and fantasized narratives about past, currents, and future events" (p. 31). Heath et al. saw the child developing a perception of himself as a reader and writer, thereby relating the book reading activities to his oral and written language understanding.

Storybook reading also helps children become more proficient in the use of grammatical features of written language. Chomsky (1972) found that children's abilities to understand individual grammatical constructions are significantly related to the amount of story reading they hear. Children in higher linguistic stages had heard more stories. Those stories tended to be more linguistically complex than those heard by children who were at lower linguistic stages. Similarly, Purcell-Gates (1988), studying native English-speaking, nonreading kindergartners who were read to at least five times a week for the 2 years prior to the start of kindergarten, found that these well-read-to children communicated using the linguistic features of oral and written language. Their use of written language constructs, in fact, was comparable to the language use of a group of second-grade students.

Interactive reading that takes place in school also helps children become more aware of written language. Morrow (1988) found that when teachers read and talked to students about stories, their participation in verbal exchanges increased as did their use of the words and phrases from the stories. The students asked more questions and made more comments about the stories read, and the structures of their questions and comments were more complex.

Written language syntactic structures and text structures can be promoted through interactive story reading. The theoretical notion that socially structured learning activities promote development is the driving force (Vygotsky, 1929, 1978). When children hear competent people use novel syntactic structures and stylized text structures, they first mimic them and then begin to understand how these structures and styles fit with their oral language and are meaningful. Thus, they apply that knowledge beyond discussion of a particular story. This is why book language flows into their oral discourse. They may start stories they tell with "once upon a time" and end them with "and they lived happily ever after." In addition, they may use the language from a favorite story when retelling the story, mimic story actions in their play, use story words and phrases in their discourse, and so on. It is apparent that teachers can help students begin learning about written language structures long before the students can read by interactively reading stories to them and providing them with opportunities to discuss and retell the stories.

Vocabulary and Concept Development

Many storybooks contain words that children do not have in their oral vocabulary. These books, however, often contain vivid pictures and clever story lines
that highlight the new words and make them memorable and highly meaningful.
Thus, young children learn about words that are not in their vocabulary when
books are read to them.

The connection between picture book reading to young children and their
vocabulary growth was demonstrated by Ninio (1980), who found that infants
with large vocabularies had mothers who tended to adjust the kind of vocabulary
they used to match the children's abilities and to request more productive and
comprehension-oriented discussion from the children. By contrast, infants with
large imitative vocabularies had mothers who did not adjust questions, talked
less, and provided less varied labels for actions and attributes.

Likewise, Fagan and Hayden (1986) found that vocabulary learning was
enhanced when parents asked children questions such as, "Do you know what a
coach is?" or related a new word to a known concept (i.e., relating the new
concept of *gown* to *dress*). Children responded to these questions with functional
information, and then parents elaborated on the concept. The children were thus
exposed to new vocabulary features and were able to connect these features to
knowledge they already possessed.

Similar findings appear when children hear and discuss books in school. Eller,
Pappas, and Brown (1988) looked at the lexical growth related to picture book
reading. They found that kindergartners were able to learn new words through
hearing stories, and that this acquisition of lexical knowledge was gradual. As
well, Elley (1989) found that children can learn a significant number of new
words when the teacher reads a story straight through, but the effects were even
more profound if the story was read three times with explanations for the key
vocabulary.

The studies relating reading to children with vocabulary development show
that growth in word knowledge occurs from hearing stories, whether they are
shared at home or in the school, but what is learned depends on what is discussed. If adult questions and comments are adjusted to match children's abilities, and if they link the new concept to what children already know, then
learning occurs. However, vocabulary learning is gradual and incidental unless
stories are read more than once and the discussions incorporate explanations.
Repeated readings with explanations of key vocabulary promote more conceptual
and vocabulary development than does reading stories one time. Repeated reading is successful in enhancing comprehension and word recognition with older
students (Amlund, Kardash, & Kulhavy, 1986; Dowhower, 1987; Herman,
1985), and it also proves to be a way to help younger children learn vocabulary.

That repeated reading to children is valuable for vocabulary development is
important for instructional planning because it is a practice that teachers can

incorporate into classroom routines. However, more research is needed to determine how to reread stories in a school setting. Teachers will need to know how to tell what is the optimum number of readings for various types of text, whether to maintain an explanation over readings, and how to assess children's understanding across readings. Thus, although the practice of rereading books seems to be a valuable tool for the classroom, a few strategies still need to be developed.

Letter Awareness and Word Identification

Explanations of how children move into independent word reading have assumed a strong relationship among letter knowledge, phonological awareness, and reading (Ehri, 1989; Mason, 1980, 1989; Mason & Allen, 1986). Reading requires children to attend to the sounds in words and to the letters that symbolize those sounds. New evidence from interactive reading studies suggests that interactive reading may be another way to draw children's attention to print and to the ways that letters sound in words.

Support for this idea was originally tested by McCormick and Mason (1989), who used a book-sharing approach with children in Head Start classrooms. To maximize student involvement, the researchers constructed a four-step reading approach. After encouraging comments and predictions about the text content, teachers read stories to the students, encouraging them to comment or join in. Then, students recited portions of the book collectively and individually, and favorite books were reread. Finally, copies of the books were mailed to students at home. McCormick and Mason found 1 and 2 years later that the book-sharing groups had made significantly greater gains on letter naming, sign and label identification, and book reading than had groups who merely heard teachers read the stories.

This study and the results were replicated with a larger sample of preschool children, identified as at risk for academic failure (Mason, Kerr, Sinha, & McCormick, 1990). With a preschool environment that was already focused on literacy and language development, the inclusion of shared reading in the program significantly increased the amount of letter knowledge the children possessed at the end of the first year. At the end of the kindergarten year, the children could also read more words than children who had been in the regular program.

In a study where a story was read repeatedly, Kawakami (1985) examined story understanding and independent word identification ability. She found that whole-class story reading was useful as an activity for constructing meaning. She also found that kindergartners who participated in three readings of a story had an understanding of critical story elements (main character, setting, problem, and resolution) after the first reading. Then after three readings, they showed an increase in the number of words they knew.

This research indicates that reading and rereading stories to children can help them attend to letter and word information. Yaden, Smolkin, and Conlon (1988) suggested that children's spontaneous questions change from being about illustrations and story meaning to being about print. The shift to print is also enhanced when children are read books with salient print displays (Smolkin, Conlon, & Yaden, 1988). Rereading stories to children can eventually promote beginning levels of letter sound and word awareness, assuming, of course, that children are active participators, that the texts contain effective illustrations and are not overly complex, and that the adult highlights print features.

CONCLUSION

This review of the literature on reading to children shows that through interactive reading, children begin to remember the story dialogues. In the process, they acquire written language structures and new vocabulary and then begin to focus on print and letter concepts. The research documents that these aspects of literacy learning can appear both at home and in the classroom. Therefore, both parents and teachers can promote young children's literacy acquisition through interactive story reading. At home, children can learn at a fairly optimal level because most parents are sensitive to their children's developing abilities in language. Parents can connect book information with their children's background experiences, and they are better attuned to the children's interests and level of understanding. At school, teachers achieve similar effects if they organize the story reading to elicit maximum participation from all students and if they repeatedly read stories.

The theoretical construct posited by Vygotsky helps to explain how learning occurs. When reading to children is a social event, children's book explorations are refined through the verbal and nonverbal interactions that take place during the reading. During the reading, adults highlight and interpret the reality of the book, its written language features, vocabulary, and print forms, and the children mimic and modify the language to fit their understanding. Structured interactions enable children to add these understandings to their current viewpoints through play with the language, questions, comments, and attempts to extend their understandings by making sense of new situations with the book language and print.

From this theoretical perspective, it becomes obvious that reading to children without allowing discussion is not likely to be sufficient for developing the ability to use written language. If the goal is to teach literacy, an adult should mediate the ideas in books by keeping within bounds of children's understandings and by using an interactive story reading approach. Then, story reading becomes a way for young children to acquire knowledge about written language at new levels of understanding. Their face-to-face communication with adults provides a way for them to ask questions, comment about what makes sense, and use book language and book ideas. Although picture books provide essential picture and story line context, the language is without intonation, gestures, and pitch until an adult reads it to the child. But, through mediation of this language, the child learns to interpret, apply, and transfer the sophisticated written language to their own oral language.

Thus, literacy learning opportunities abound in interactive reading sessions. The process takes place through highly structured social interactions, interactions that involve routine joint participation sequences, in which the adults help children make connections to their own knowledge, and in which children make known their old understanding and practice their new understandings. Although this approach is easier for parents who are reading to one child, sufficient evidence now exists that teachers can read to small groups of children in a similar way, particularly in situations where teacher–group interactive language structures are fairly routinized, such as in rereading stories.

Children learn about three aspects of literacy when they engage in interactive reading. First, they acquire knowledge about written language structures from the stories that they read interactively with an adult on a regular basis, and that they can talk about, act out, and use to play with story language. This suggests that teachers need to provide opportunities for children to hear and talk about stories. Second, they acquire new vocabulary from listening to stories. Children's oral language is embellished with new words and book phrases that are drawn from the book they hear read, particularly those they hear read repeatedly. Their attention to story information thereby becomes more focused and their listening comprehension improves. Finally, children learn about the form of print, that is, about how language is graphically represented, when they have opportunities to memorize texts and recite them as though they were reading. Their learning can be heightened when the print in the stories is salient, and when they hear repeated readings. Repeated reading is an activity particularly well suited for preschool and kindergarten classrooms and will foster development of children's letter knowledge and phonological awareness, which can be connected to later word and letter recognition and to decoding.

It is clear from more than a decade of research that interactive story reading is a powerful social avenue for developing language and literacy, and that it can be used as an influential literacy tool both in the home and in the school; that is, as Cochran-Smith (1984) has said, the child and adult bring to life books, and books enrich children's lives.

REFERENCES

Amlund, J. T., Kardash, C. A. M., & Kulhavy, R. W. (1986). Repetitive reading and recall of expository text. *Reading Research Quarterly, 21,* 49–58.

Anderson, R. C., Hiebert, E. H., Scott, J. A., & Wilkinson, I. A. G. (1985). *Becoming a nation of readers: The report of the Commission on Reading.* Champaign, IL: Center for the Study of Reading; Washington, DC: National Institute of Education.

Bruner, J. S. (1978). Learning how to do things with words. In J. S. Bruner & R. A. Garton (Eds.), *Human growth and development*. Oxford, England: Oxford University Press.

Bruner, J. S. (1990). *Acts of meaning*. Cambridge, MA: Harvard University Press.

Butler, D., & Clay, M. (1979). *Reading begins at home: Preparing children for reading before they go to school*. London: Heinemann.

Chafe, W. L. (1985). Linguistic differences produced by differences between speaking and writing. In D. R. Olson, N. Torrance, & A. Hildyard (Eds.), *Literacy language, and learning: The nature and consequences of reading and writing* (pp. 105–123). Cambridge: Cambridge University Press.

Chomsky, C. (1972). Stages in language development and reading exposure. *Harvard Educational Review, 42*, 1–33.

Cochran-Smith, M. (1984). *The making of a reader*. Norwood, NJ: Ablex.

Cross, T. G. (1978). Mother's speech and its association with rate of linguistic development in young children. In N. Waterson & C. Snow (Eds.), *The development of communication*. London: Wiley.

DeLoache, J. S., & DeMendoza, O. A. P. (1987). Joint picture book interactions of mothers and one-year-old children. *British Journal of Developmental Psychology, 5*, 111–123.

Dowhower, S. L. (1987). Effects of repeated reading on second-grade transitional readers' fluency and comprehension. *Reading Research Quarterly, 22*, 389–406.

Durkin, D. R. (1966). *Children who read early*. New York: Teachers College Press.

Ehri, L. C. (1989). Movement into word reading and spelling: How spelling contributes to reading. In J. M. Mason (Ed.), *Reading and writing connections* (pp. 65–82). Boston: Allyn & Bacon.

Eller, R. G., Pappas, C. C., & Brown, E. (1988). The lexical development of kindergartners: Learning from written context. *Journal of Reading Behavior, 20*, 5–24.

Elley, W. B. (1989). Vocabulary acquisition from listening to stories. *Reading Research Quarterly, 24*, 174–187.

Fagan, W., & Hayden, H. (1986). Reading books with young children: Opportunities for concept development. *Australian Journal of Reading, 9*, 11–19.

Ferreiro, E., & Teberosky, A. (1983). *Literacy before schooling*. Exeter, NH: Heinemann.

Heath, S. B., & Branscombe, A., with Thomas, C. (1986). The book as narrative prop in language acquisition. In B. B. Schieffelin & P. Gilmore (Eds.), *The acquisition of literacy: Ethnographic perspectives* (pp. 16–34). Norwood, NJ: Ablex.

Herman, P. (1985). The effect of repeated readings on reading rate, speech pauses, and word recognition accuracy. *Reading Research Quarterly, 20*, 553–565.

Hewison, J., & Tizard, J. (1980). Parental involvement and reading attainment. *British Journal of Educational Psychology, 50*, 209–215.

Kawakami, A. J. (1985, December). *A study of the effects of repeated story reading on kindergarten children's story comprehension*. Paper presented at the annual meeting of the National Reading Conference, San Diego.

Lartz, M. N., & Mason, J. M. (1988). Jamie: One child's journey from oral to written language. *Early Childhood Research Quarterly, 3*, 193–208.

Lazzari, A. M., Bender, W. N., & Kello, M. N. (1987). Parents' and children's behavior during preschool reading sessions as predictors of language and reading skills. *Reading Improvement, 24*, 89–95.

Mason, J. M. (1980). When do children begin to read? An exploration of four-year-old children's letter and word reading competencies. *Reading Research Quarterly, 15*, 203–227.

Mason, J. M. (1989). *Reading and writing connections*. Boston: Allyn & Bacon.

Mason, J. M., & Allen, J. (1986). A review of emergent literacy with implications for research. In E. Z. Rothkopf (Ed.), *Review of research in education* (Vol. 13, pp. 3–47). Washington, DC: American Educational Research Association.

Mason, J. M., Kerr, B. M., Sinha, S., & McCormick, C. (1990). *Shared book reading in an early start program for at-risk children* (Tech. Rep. No. 504). Urbana–Champaign: University of Illinois, Center for the Study of Reading.

Mason, J. M., Peterman, C. L., Powell, B. M., & Kerr, B. M. (1989). Reading and writing attempts by kindergartners after book reading by teachers. In J. M. Mason (Ed.), *Reading and writing connections* (pp. 105–120). Boston: Allyn & Bacon.

Mason, J. M., & Sinha, S. (in press). Emerging literacy in the early childhood years: Applying a Vygotskian model of learning and development. In B. Spodek (Ed.), *The handbook of research on the education of young children*. New York: Macmillan.

McCormick, C., & Mason, J. (1989). Fostering reading for Head Start children with Little Books. In J. Allen & J. Mason (Eds.), *Risk makers, risk takers, risk breakers* (pp. 154–177). Portsmouth, NH: Heinemann.

Moerk, E. L. (1985). Picture book reading by mothers and young children and its impact upon language development. *Journal of Pragmatics, 9,* 547–566.

Moon, C., & Wells, C. G. (1979). The influence of home on learning to read. *Journal of Research in Reading, 2,* 53–62.

Morrow, L. M. (1988). Young children's responses to one-to-one story readings in school settings. *Reading Research Quarterly, 23,* 89–107.

Ninio, A. (1980). Picture book reading in mother-infant dyads belonging to two subgroups in Israel. *Child Development, 51,* 587–590.

Ninio, A., & Bruner, J. (1978). The achievement and antecedents of labelling. *Journal of Child Language, 5,* 1–6.

Perera, K. (1984). *Children's writing and reading: Analyzing classroom language.* New York: Basil Blackwell.

Peterman, C. L. (1988). *The effects of story reading procedures collaboratively designed by teachers and researcher on kindergartners' literacy learning.* Unpublished doctoral dissertation, University of Illinois, Urbana–Champaign.

Purcell-Gates, V. (1988). Lexical and syntactic knowledge of written narrative held by well-read-to kindergartners and second graders. *Research in the Teaching of English, 22,* 128–160.

Roser, N., & Martinez, M. (1985). Roles adults play in preschoolers' response to literature. *Language Arts, 62,* 485–490.

Smolkin, L. B., Conlon, A., & Yaden, D. B. (1988). Print-salient illustrations in children's picture books: The emergence of written language awareness. In J. E. Readence & R. S. Baldwin (Eds.), *Dialogues in literacy research. Thirty-seventh yearbook of the National Reading Conference* (pp. 59–68). Chicago: National Reading Conference.

Snow, C. E. (1983). Literacy and language: Relationships during the preschool years. *Harvard Educational Review, 53,* 165–189.

Snow, C. E., & Goldfield, B. A. (1982). Building stories: The emergence of information structures from conversation. In D. Tannen (Ed.), *Analyzing discourse: Text and talk* (pp. 127–141). Washington, DC: Georgetown University Press.

Snow, C. E., & Ninio, A. (1986). The contracts of literacy: What children learn from learning to read books. In W. H. Teale & E. Sulzby (Eds.), *Emergent literacy: Writing and reading* (pp. 116–138). Norwood, NJ: Ablex.

Sulzby, E. (1985). Children's emergent reading of favorite storybooks: A developmental study. *Reading Research Quarterly, 20,* 458–481.

Teale, W. H. (1981). Parents reading to their children: What we know and need to know. *Language Arts, 58,* 902–912.

Teale, W. H., Martinez, M. G., & Glass, W. L. (1989). Describing classroom storybook reading. In D. Bloome (Ed.), *Classrooms and literacy* (pp. 158–188). Norwood, NJ: Ablex.

Vygotsky, L. (1929). The problem of cultural development of the child. *Journal of Genetic Psychology, 26,* 415–434.

Vygotsky, L. S. (1978). *Mind in society.* Cambridge, MA: Harvard University Press.

Walker, G. H., & Kuerbitz, I. E. (1970). Reading to preschoolers as an aid to successful beginning reading. *Reading Improvement, 16,* 149–154.

Whitehurst, G. J., Falco, F. L., Lonigan, C. J., Fischel, J. E., DeBaryshe, B. D., Valdez-Menchaca, M. C., & Caulfield, M. (1988). Accelerating language development through picture book reading. *Developmental Psychology, 24,* 552–559.

Yaden, D. B., Smolkin, L. B., & Conlon, A. (1988). Preschoolers' questions about pictures, print convention, and story text during reading aloud at home. *Reading Research Quarterly, 24,* 188–214.

10 Student, Text, Teacher: Interactive Learning in the Reading Recovery Program

Gay Su Pinnell
The Ohio State University

Early success in reading is important both for individuals and for society. Yet the population of students considered at high risk of reading failure is increasing (Natriella, McDill, & Pallas, 1990), and the traditional methods of helping these students become readers seem, at best, inadequate. Retention (see Walker & Madhere, 1987) and remediation (see McGill-Franzen & Allington, 1990; Savage, 1987; Slavin, 1987), although well intentioned, have both been largely unsuccessful. However, one early intervention program, Reading Recovery, is providing promising new directions for helping high-risk students.

Like many of the traditional methods for helping high-risk students, Reading Recovery involves a teacher and student working one on one in a tutorial setting. But unlike traditional methods that are based on the assumption that learning to read means teachers guiding students through a series of vocabulary-controlled texts, helping them to learn new words in the process (usually through explicit practice prior to reading) and to acquire the skills necessary to meet increasingly difficult levels of text, Reading Recovery is conceived differently. In Reading Recovery, the key to learning is in the teacher–student interactions that surround encounters with texts.

In this chapter, I look more closely at the student–teacher–text interactions through which Reading Recovery teachers make books available to students. To illustrate the variety of these interactions, I use examples from my work with Michael, a 7-year-old Reading Recovery student. Before I do this, however, I provide a brief overview of the Reading Recovery program.

THE READING RECOVERY PROGRAM

The Reading Recovery program, which grew out of the research of Marie M. Clay (see Clay, 1985, 1991), is based on the idea that, even given good teaching in the first year of school and a rich literacy climate in the classroom, some children will still need extra help to become independent readers. Studies in New Zealand (Clay, 1985, 1987), Australia (Wheeler, 1984), and the United States (Pinnell, 1989) have substantiated the program's immediate and long-term positive effects for children.

Students enter Reading Recovery at about age 6 or 7. They are selected for the program through teacher recommendation and the use of six individually administered diagnostic measures that provide an inventory of what a student knows and can do in reading and writing. Once in the program, students are provided intensive individual help for a relatively short time, usually 12 to 20 weeks, depending on individual needs. During this time, they are expected to make accelerated progress and to develop "self-extending" systems for reading (see Clay, 1991).

Reading Recovery teachers receive special training in how to interact with students as they read and write (see Alvermann, 1990; Pinnell, 1991). The teachers learn to use oral language interactions to support students' problem solving as they read. They consciously act as mediators of the texts students read, and, as they do so, they help students develop implicit knowledge of the complex processes involved in reading, including both constructing the meaning of the text and noticing and using details such as visual features and letter–sound correspondences. When this is achieved, the program is discontinued for the individual student. (More detailed descriptions of Reading Recovery can be found in DeFord, Lyons, & Pinnell, 1991, and Pinnell, Fried, & Estice, 1990.)

In Reading Recovery, teachers select books especially for the students they teach, basing their selections on a thorough knowledge both of the texts and of the students who will use them. Reading Recovery teachers know that it does not matter *which* books they use—as long as the ones chosen meet the goal of helping students learn how to construct meaning from whatever books they encounter. No two Reading Recovery students read the same sequence of books.

The books used in Reading Recovery are organized into 20 levels that provide a slow gradient of difficulty. Level 1 books are very simple patterned texts, usually built around one sentence for each page. Level 20 books are about the level of difficulty that students would be expected to read at the end of the first-grade year. The level of difficulty may vary with the students' backgrounds, cultures, and interests.

According to Peterson (1991), books in Levels 1 through 4 generally have memorable repetitive language and the illustrations strongly support the text. The syntax of these very easy books reflects children's talk, and the content is usually familiar to them. There is no controlled vocabulary except that the books as well as the sentences are short, and the content is simple. The books in Levels 5 through 8 are also patterned, but there are many more variations in the pattern. More literary language is used. Because the texts are longer and more complex, the illustrations cannot cue the entire message, and the students therefore must depend more on the print. The books in Levels 9 through 12 contain repetitive refrains, but there is much variation in language and the sentence length increases. The stories presented in these books are complex events that continue over several pages, and the illustrations assist the students but do not cue the complex messages of the text. The books in Levels 13 through 20 continue to increase in length and complexity.

Peterson (1988, 1991) identified a continuum of patterns that describe how books become progressively more complex but warned that there is no formula to determine a book's "level." Teachers must always accept responsibility for selecting a specific book with a specific student in mind. Therefore, the leveled booklist, consisting of about 1,500 titles, serves only as a guide for teachers. Each year it is reevaluated as more books are tried.

Many books exist on each level, and students are not required to read all the books at each level. Teachers may skip levels or move back to easier levels as they decide what is appropriate for an individual student.

"Little books" from several publishers are used at all levels; but these books blend with works of children's literature as students are able to handle more complex texts. Books such as *Mr. Gumpy's Outing* (Burningham, 1970), *Frog and Toad Are Friends* (Lobel, 1970), *Red is Best* (Stinson, 1982), and *The Fat Cat* (Kent, 1971) are included in the advanced levels.

TEACHER–STUDENT–TEXT INTERACTIONS IN READING RECOVERY—LESSONS WITH MICHAEL

In this section, I provide information about student selection and assessment, a diagnostic period called Roaming Around the Known, and the framework of activities used in formal lessons by using examples from my work with Michael.

Michael was recommended for Reading Recovery by his first-grade teacher. She was concerned not only about his reading difficulties but with the fact that he was a passive child who avoided participating in class activities. As part of the selection process, I had Michael complete two assessments to discover what he knew about reading, the Concepts about Print test (Clay, 1985) and a measure of Text Reading Level.

The Concepts about Print test provides a good idea of what a child knows about how print works. To administer it, the teacher reads aloud a small, specially prepared book and simultaneously asks questions such as, "Where do I start reading?" From Michael's Concepts about Print assessment, I discovered that he knew the front from the back of the book and that print contains the message. He also had good control of left-to-right directionality, and he seemed to know about the use of space to define word boundaries, simple knowledge to be sure, but knowledge that many high-risk students do not possess. In writing my observation summary of Michael's performance, I recorded his knowledge of these areas as his strengths.

The Text Reading Level assessment gives an indication of the limits of a student's reading ability. To gauge this level, the teacher and student interactively read several short patterned books, and the teacher keeps a running record of how the student is able to participate in reading and use predictable patterns. This running record gives the teacher the information necessary to form hypotheses about a student's growing use of reading strategies. (For an in-depth description of running records, see Clay, 1985; DeFord, Lyons, & Pinnell, 1991). As the first step in Michael's Text Reading Level assessment, I chose a text called *Hats* (Scott, Foresman, 1979). In response to the text, Michael produced the sample in Fig. 10.1.

From this sample, I could see that Michael was looking at the pictures and responding to the meaning of the story. Although he did not track words one by one, he did produce language patterns that were similar to the text. He was

Text: The text of *Hats* is: The firefighter has a red hat (p. 2). The pirate has a purple hat (p. 3). The sailor has a white hat (p. 4). The witch has a black hat (p. 5). The woman has a yellow hat (p. 6). Now the monkey has a yellow hat (p. 7). The pictures closely match the text. On page 6, the woman has a yellow hat that has many kinds of fruit on it. The monkey takes the hat and is shown wearing it on page 7.

Teacher: "Let's read this story and find out what colors of hats people wear.

Teacher (reading): The firefighter has a red hat.
                   The pirate . . . You read the rest.

Michael reads: . . . purple. (*He does not point to any words.*)

Teacher reads: The sailor . . .

Michael reads: . . . have white . . .

Teacher reads: The witch . . .

Michael reads: . . . has a black hat.

Teacher reads: The woman . . .

Michael reads: . . . has blue, purple, gold, or yellow . . . (*He points to the fruit in the picture.*

Teacher reads: Now . . .

Michael reads: I have a yellow hat. (*He does not point to anything on the page.*)

FIG. 10.1.   Michael's reading of *Hats*.

"inventing text" and doing so in a competent way, although he paid little attention to the print itself.

As the next step in this assessment, I read another predictable book, *Where's Spot?* (Hill, 1980) and invited Michael to join in. The text of this book begins with Spot's mother, Sally, saying: "That Spot! He hasn't eaten his supper. Where can he be?" Then, on each of the following pages, the text asks a question about the puppy's whereabouts, for example: "Is he behind the door?" Each time, the reader lifts a flap to find an animal that says "No."

Michael was soon readily joining in with me, lifting the flaps and saying, "No." On the seventh page, Sally looks in a box and asks, "Is he in the box?" Lifting the flap reveals three birds, each saying "No." For that page I said, "Point to the words and read." Michael responded, "N–O, no," spelling the word once and then saying it, but he did not point to the words. This suggested to me that Michael was aware of print and knew something about letters but was not attempting to match his spoken language to the printed words.

Roaming Around the Known.   After the assessment is completed, a Reading Recovery teacher works with the student for 10 days in a period called Roaming Around the Known, during which the teacher does not try to teach any new information but instead involves the student in reading, writing, and discussion for 30 minutes each day to explore the full range of what he knows. During this period, the teacher reads selections from children's literature that offer opportunities for the student to participate. There are no prescribed books; the idea is to find books that both the teacher and student enjoy together; books that the student really likes may be read many times. As a part of Roaming Around the Known, a student and teacher may produce collaborative pieces of writing based on favorite selections.

The teacher may also read aloud very simple everyday-language books. Some of these books do not contain stories but instead use photographs of everyday events with informational captions, preferably sentences, that describe them; for example, a picture of a baby crying with a line of print saying, "Baby crying." Other books written in everyday language are organized as stories.

After a few readings of these kinds of texts, the student can join in, point to the words, and eventually read the books independently without actually being able to recognize the words in isolation. The student does not memorize the text in the captions so that she can "say the piece," instead she remembers it as it is cued by the pictures and some features of print.

During Michael's Roaming Around the Known period, he heard and joined in on the reading of, among other books, *Dear Zoo* (Campbell, 1984), *The Chick and the Duckling* (Ginsburg, 1972), *Mrs. Wishy-washy* (Cowley, 1980), and *Who's Counting?* (Tafuri, 1986). On the sixth day, he produced his own book, *Where's Mom?* As the figure shows, Michael clearly based this book on his

Is she in the car?

Page 2. Michael wrote <u>no</u>, a word he had indicated he knew on the Concepts about Print assessment. As in <u>Where's Spot?</u>, he used lift-up flaps for the answers to the questions.

Is she in the garden ?

Page 3. Michael wrote <u>the</u> and <u>no</u>.

Is she under The Bed ?

Page 4. Michael wrote <u>the</u>, <u>yes</u>, and the <u>b</u> in <u>bed</u>.

FIG. 10.2.   Michael's book—*Where's Mom?*

favorite, and often-read book, *Where's Spot?* (Hill, 1980), even down to the lift-up flaps for the answers to the questions.

Formal Lessons.   Formal lessons, which begin on the 11th day, have a more structured framework that includes (a) the student rereading easy texts, (b) the teacher making a running record of a student reading a more difficult text, (c) the student writing and reading a message, and (d) the student reading a new book.

Teachers do not follow a preplanned script in conducting lessons. Instead, they make moment-to-moment decisions based on their knowledge of the individual student, the challenges in the texts, and the student's repertoire of responses.

Rereading Easy Texts.   The student begins each day by reading several selections from the box of books he has read previously. This part of the lesson provides the opportunity for him to read fluently with appropriate phrasing; that is, to behave like a good reader. Some familiar books are very easy for the student; others offer challenges. So, he must solve reading problems (such as figuring out unknown words) and must check on his reading while progressing quickly through a story.

The reading of previously read materials gives the student a chance to use strategies "on the run" while reading. In his second lesson, for example, Michael read several "caption" books, his own *Where's Mom?*, and another book he had produced; and finally, he read *Mouse* (Cowley, 1983b), a predictable storybook. He had begun to point to words consistently, and I complimented him on "making it match."

Making a Running Record.   Each day, the teacher makes a running record of the student's reading of a new book that was introduced and read once the previous day. For this book, the teacher ceases interacting with the student and takes a neutral stance. The goal is to get an idea of how the student performs while reading independently. Once the running record is taken, the new book goes into the student's box to be chosen for rereading during future lessons.

In his second lesson, Michael read *Little Pig* (Melser, 1981). As the analysis indicates, Michael read the book with above 90% accuracy; but it was more important to me to note behavior that indicated he was problem solving with this text that he had read once the previous day. From the analysis, I could see that Michael was able to predict using meaning and language syntax and to cross-check this information with visual cues as evidenced by his self-corrections on *home* and *butcher*. When he had difficulties, Michael tried going back to the beginning of the sentence and reading again. His substitutions reflected an active search for meaning. The running record indicated that this text was a good

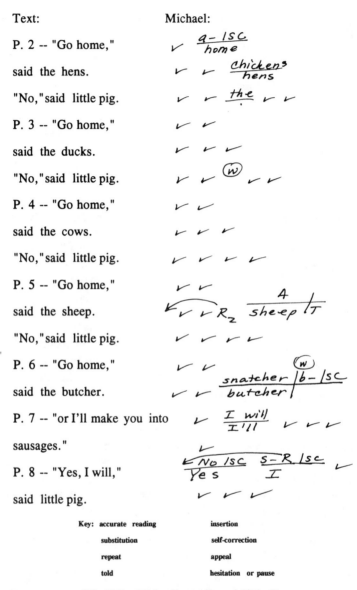

FIG. 10.3. Michael's reading of *Little Pig*.

selection for Michael because it offered enough challenge to allow him to practice "reading work," but it was not so difficult that he got bogged down. The reading task was within his capability so that he could be successful in independent problem solving.

The running record analysis can also indicate that a book is a poor selection or that its meaning and language were not adequately supported when the teacher introduced it. The running record of Michael reading *The Big Toe* (Melser & Cowley, 1980) indicates that the book was not an appropriate selection for him at

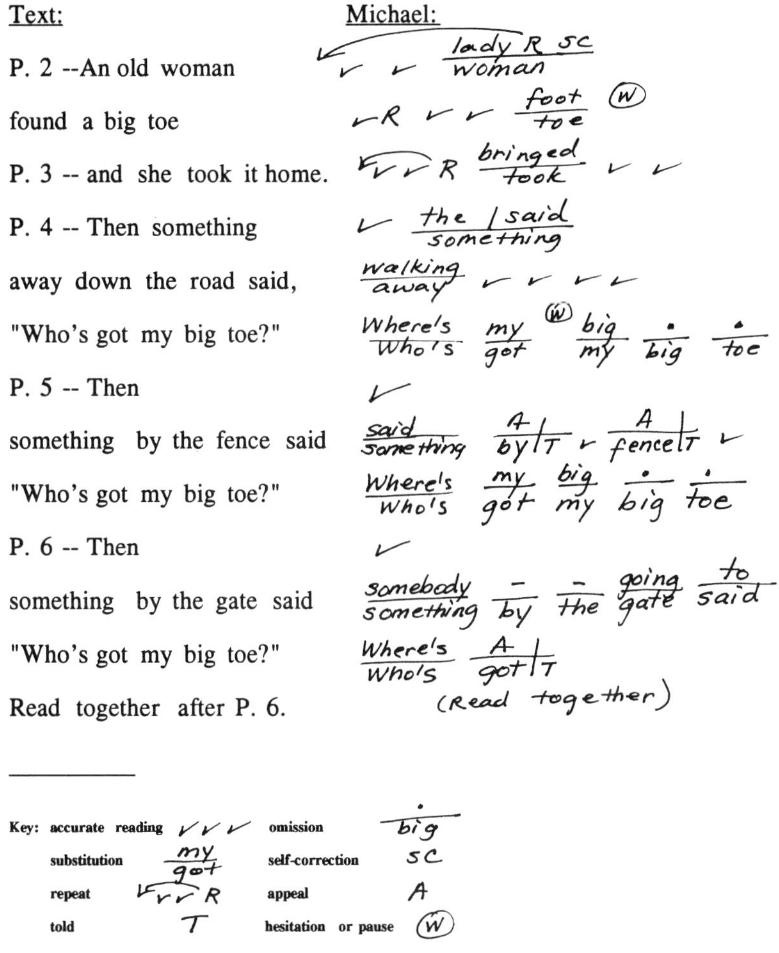

Text: Michael:

P. 2 --An old woman

found a big toe

P. 3 -- and she took it home.

P. 4 -- Then something

away down the road said,

"Who's got my big toe?"

P. 5 -- Then

something by the fence said

"Who's got my big toe?"

P. 6 -- Then

something by the gate said

"Who's got my big toe?"

Read together after P. 6.

Key: accurate reading ✓✓✓   omission   biġ
     substitution my/got   self-correction   SC
     repeat ✓✓✓R   appeal   A
     told   T   hesitation or pause   (W)

FIG. 10.4. Michael's reading of *The Big Toe*.

the time. Whereas the book itself is a good one and is a favorite among children, it was too difficult for Michael. The unfamiliar language patterns got in the way of his attempts to bring meaning to the text. When I realized that the selection had been a poor one, I finished the text by reading with him, and we enjoyed the story together. Even on this difficult text, however, Michael made some good attempts at problem solving, which I noticed and praised.

Examples from running records in subsequent lessons provided further evidence of Michael's growing ability to deal with written texts; these examples also illustrate the types of books he read during his program. The example in Fig. 10.5 shows Michael's ability to predict, check, and confirm his reading of the book *Titch* (Hutchins, 1971). The next day, he was reading *Greedy Cat* (Cowley, 1983a). The example in Fig. 10.6 shows that he could work out language patterns and confirm his reading. He was able to crosscheck using visual information and his own sense of syntax.

Writing and Reading a Message. Writing is an essential component of each Reading Recovery lesson. The teacher and the student engage in a conversation that helps the student compose a message. The constructed message must be in the student's own language; the teacher quickly notes what the message is but does not write it for the student. Then, the message is constructed word by word, with the student producing what she can and the teacher filling in the rest.

Writing is linked to reading in several ways. Generally, writing helps students attend to and use the visual features of print and to become aware of and use sound–letter correspondence in the construction of words. In addition, the written message is always read several times; then, the teacher writes it on a sentence strip that is then cut up for the student to reassemble. Finally, the cut-up sentence is reread in its entirety before it is placed in an envelope for the student to take

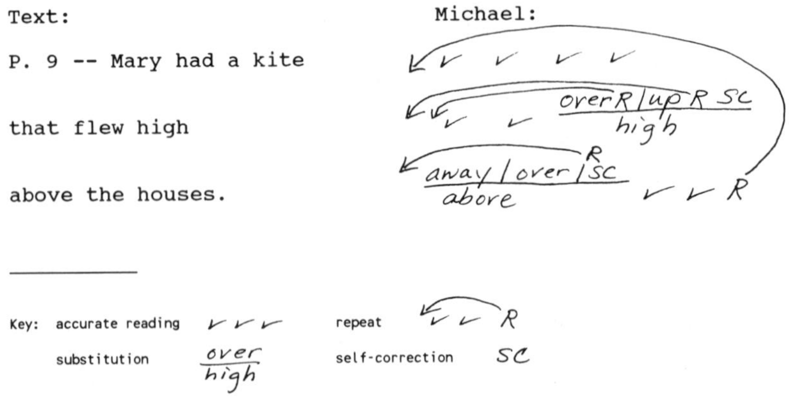

FIG. 10.5. Example from Michael's reading of *Titch*.

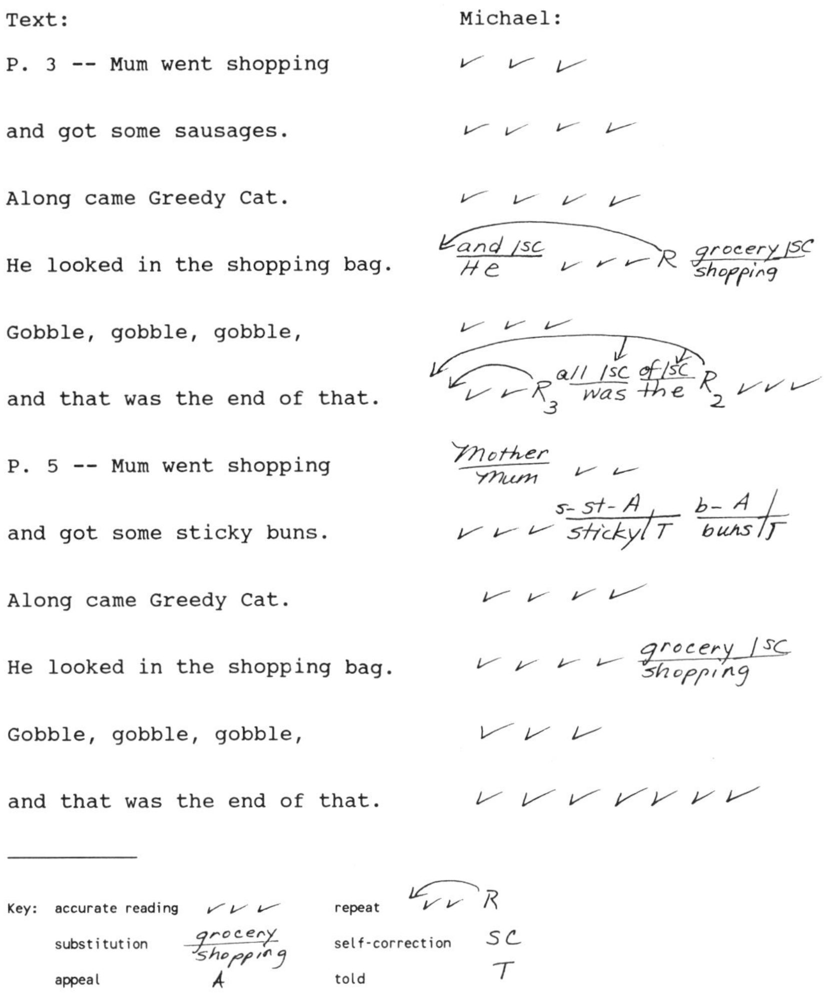

Text: Michael:

P. 3 -- Mum went shopping   ✓ ✓ ✓

and got some sausages.   ✓ ✓ ✓ ✓

Along came Greedy Cat.   ✓ ✓ ✓ ✓

He looked in the shopping bag.   ✓ $\frac{and}{He}$ /SC ✓ ✓ ✓ R $\frac{grocery}{shopping}$ /SC

Gobble, gobble, gobble,   ✓ ✓ ✓

and that was the end of that.   ✓ ✓ ✓ R₃ $\frac{all}{was}$ /SC $\frac{of}{the}$ /SC R₂ ✓ ✓ ✓

P. 5 -- Mum went shopping $\frac{Mother}{Mum}$ ✓ ✓

and got some sticky buns.   ✓ ✓ ✓ $\frac{s-st-A}{sticky}$ /T $\frac{b-A}{buns}$ /T

Along came Greedy Cat.   ✓ ✓ ✓ ✓

He looked in the shopping bag.   ✓ ✓ ✓ ✓ $\frac{grocery}{shopping}$ /SC

Gobble, gobble, gobble,   ✓ ✓ ✓

and that was the end of that.   ✓ ✓ ✓ ✓ ✓ ✓ ✓

Key: accurate reading ✓ ✓ ✓   repeat ✓ ✓ R

      substitution $\frac{grocery}{shopping}$ self-correction SC

      appeal A   told T

FIG. 10.6. Michael's reading of *Greedy Cat*.

home, reassemble, and read. These writing activities help students link oral and written language; the meaning and language syntax are clear and accessible to them because they are their own. Visual print information is also accessible to them because it is examined in a supported context.

Students always have the option of writing about important home events or school events. More often, however, the writing component provides an opportunity to link semantically with the texts the students have read. At first, the teacher may suggest the idea by inviting students to write about a favorite book or a book they read together. In this case, students compose their own versions of a

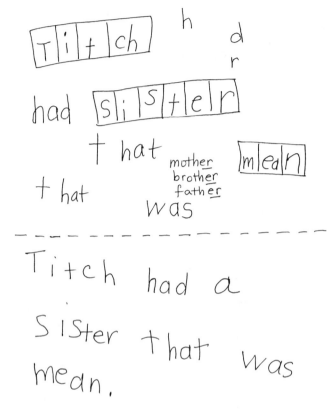

FIG. 10.7.   Michael's story about *Titch*.

story or write about an important or interesting event or character. Sometimes they use the language patterns encountered in books. Occasionally, students write several messages over a period of days that are linked together to extend their understanding of a text.

It is easy to see the source of the message from Michael shown in Fig. 10.7.

The example shows the "story page" below and the "practice page" above. I assisted Michael as he wrote this message word by word. There were opportunities to work out the details of words and letters on the practice page.

The words *Titch*, *sister*, and *mean* were worked out using sound boxes as described by Clay (1985) and as adapted from Elkonin (1975). Michael said each word slowly, producing letters for the sounds that he could hear and represent with a letter, and I filled in the rest. For example, on the word *mean*, he was able to produce the *n*, the *m*, and the *e* in that order. I added the *a*, which is not heard. The word *sister*, after being worked out with the boxes, showed that Michael had internalized the *er* ending and offered an opportunity to think of other words that ended the same way. Michael still had some difficulty writing letters such as *h, d,* and *r,* and I quickly provided models. He jotted down known words *had, that,* and *was* on the practice page just to check on them before putting them on the story page.

Two other examples from Michael's writing show how books often function as the basis for the writing section of the Reading Recovery lesson (see Fig. 10.8). The first sentence shows an extension of *Greedy Cat* (Cowley, 1983a); the second refers to *Rosie's Walk* (Hutchins, 1978), but the language indicates knowledge of other literary texts.

Reading a New Book.   It is important for each student to encounter new and challenging books and to have the opportunity to solve new problems while reading text. The teacher's selection of a new book is most critical, and it must be

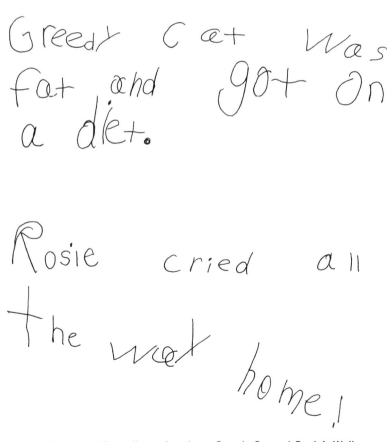

FIG. 10.8.   Michael's stories about *Greedy Cat* and *Rosie's Walk.*

accomplished with the consideration of several factors: (a) the student's background of experience and concepts, (b) the student's own language, (c) the characteristics of the new text and its potential for helping the student learn more about reading, and (d) the general quality of the text.

After a book is selected, the teacher talks briefly with the student about it to provide an oral language framework that will acquaint him or her with the meaning of the whole story prior to reading it. The orientation may also include the use of some of the language patterns that the student will be expected to use while reading. The teacher may ask the student to locate some new and important words, but does not, however, make the text so familiar that it will present no problems.

After the orientation, the student reads the new book with support. The teacher may bring to his or her attention some behaviors that were particularly effective in reading the text. In addition, the teacher can offer specific praise for good problem solving or may challenge the student to resolve discrepancies. The emphasis is also on enjoyment of the story and on talking about what is happening or predicting what might happen. After the new book is read once, sometimes the teacher and student read it together quickly to foster fluency and phrasing.

The lesson usually ends with the student selecting a book to take home from the collection of those previously read. Taking home books is an important part of the program. The student must be able to read the book independently rather than having to depend on busy adults to read it aloud. I am not saying that such a book takes the place of reading to students, but it is also important for first graders to have something they can read by themselves. Research on children's home experiences (see Holland, 1991) indicates that they do read these books to parents, grandparents, younger and older siblings, friends, pets, stuffed animals, and any other person—or thing—who will listen. In some cases, bringing a new book into the home each day greatly adds to the literacy resources of the family.

As he moved through the formal lessons, Michael displayed more and more competence as a reader. After 60 lessons, he was discontinued from the program and returned to his regular classroom. The confidence he had gained as a reader spilled over into his classroom behavior, and his teacher proudly told me that Michael was no longer a passive withdrawn child but now took an active leadership role in class activities!

The Importance of Books in Reading Recovery

Reading Recovery is not a materials program in that students move through a prescribed set of books and/or worksheets. Nevertheless, materials, in the form of a set of good books that reflect increasing levels of difficulty, are essential for the implementation of the program. So much reading takes place in Reading Recovery that there is always a demand for more books.

Reading Recovery demonstrates the value of massive amounts of reading, of having many books at appropriate levels so that young children can read independently, and of connecting books with children's writing. In many places, Reading Recovery has acted as a catalyst for turning the whole school's literacy program toward the provision of more books that children can take on and read at earlier levels. Reading Recovery may help point the way to a future in which the idea of a child spending a whole year going through a few books and many exercises will be rare. Instead, more children, even those considered to be in the lower achievement group, will read more books and in the process learn to enjoy reading from the very beginning days of their schooling.

REFERENCES

Alvermann, D. E. (1990). Reading teacher education. In W. R. Houston, M. Haberman, & J. Sikula (Eds.), *Handbook of research on teacher education: A project of the Association of Teacher Educators* (pp. 687–704). New York: Macmillan.

Clay, M. M. (1985). *The early detection of reading difficulties.* Portsmouth, NH: Heinemann.

Clay, M. M. (1987). Implementing educational Reading Recovery: Systematic adaptations to an educational innovation. *New Zealand Journal of Educational Studies, 22,* 351–358.

Clay, M. M. (1991). *Becoming literate: The construction of inner control.* Portsmouth, NH: Heinemann.

DeFord, D. E., Lyons, C. A., & Pinnell, G. S. (Eds.). (1991). *Bridges to literacy: Learning from Reading Recovery.* Portsmouth, NH: Heinemann.

Elkonin, D. B. (1975). USSR. In J. Downing (Ed.), *Comparative reading: Cross-national studies of behaviour and processes in reading and writing* (pp. 551–579). New York: Macmillan.

Holland, K. (1991). In D. E. DeFord, C. A. Lyons, & G. S. Pinnell (Eds.), *Bridges to literacy: Learning from Reading Recovery* (pp. 119–147). Portsmouth, NH: Heinemann.

McGill-Franzen, A., & Allington, R. L. (1990). Going down the hall for reading: A descriptive study of second graders' experiences. *Journal of Reading, Writing, and Learning Disabilities: International, 14,* 21–30.

Natriella, G., McDill, E. L., & Pallas, A. M. (1990). *Schooling disadvantaged children: Racing against catastrophe.* New York: Teachers College Press.

Peterson, B. L. (1988). *Characteristics of texts that support beginning readers.* Unpublished doctoral dissertation, The Ohio State University, Columbus.

Peterson, B. L. (1991). Selecting books for beginning reading. In D. E. DeFord, C. A. Lyons, & G. S. Pinnell (Eds.), *Bridges to literacy: Learning from Reading Recovery* (pp. 119–147). Portsmouth, NH: Heinemann.

Pinnell, G. S. (1989). Reading Recovery: Helping at-risk children learn to read. *Elementary School Journal, 90,* 161–183.

Pinnell, G. S. (1991). Teachers' and students' learning. In D. E. DeFord, C. A. Lyons, & G. S. Pinnell (Eds.), *Bridges to literacy: Learning from Reading Recovery* (pp. 171–188). Portsmouth, NH: Heinemann.

Pinnell, G. S., Fried, M. D., & Estice, R. (1990). Reading Recovery: Learning how to make a difference. *The Reading Teacher, 43,* 282–295.

Savage, D. G. (1987). Why Chapter 1 hasn't made much difference. *Phi Delta Kappan, 68,* 581–84.

Slavin, R. E. (1987). Making Chapter 1 make a difference. *Phi Delta Kappan, 69,* 110–119.

Walker, E. M., & Madhere, S. (1987). Multiple retentions: Some consequences for the cognitive and affective maturation of minority elementary students. *Urban Education, 22,* 85–102.

Wheeler, H. G. (1984). *Reading Recovery: Central Victorian field trials.* Victoria, Australia: Bendigo College of Advanced Education.

CHILDREN'S BOOKS

Burningham, J. (1970). *Mr. Gumpy's outing.* New York: Holt Rinehart & Winston.

Campbell, R. (1984). *Dear zoo.* New York: Penguin Books.

Cowley, J. (1980). *Mrs. Wishy-washy.* (E. Fuller, Ill.). San Diego: The Wright Group.

Cowley, J. (1983a). *Greedy cat.* (R. Belton, Ill.). Wellington, New Zealand: Ready to Read, School Publications, Department of Education.

Cowley, J. (1983b). *Mouse.* (S. Jordan, Ill.). San Diego: The Wright Group.

Ginsburg, M. (1972). *The chick and the duckling* (J. & A. Aruego, Ills.). New York: Macmillan.

Hill, E. (1980). *Where's Spot?* New York: Putnam.

Hutchins, P. (1971). *Titch.* New York: MacMillan.

Hutchins, P. (1978). *Rosie's walk.* New York: Macmillan.

Kent, J. (1971). *The fat cat.* New York: Scholastic.

Lobel, A. (1970). *Frog and Toad are friends.* New York: Harper & Row.

Melser, J. (1981). *Little pig.* (I. Lowe, Ill.). San Diego: The Wright Group.

Melser, J., & Cowley, J. (1980). *The big toe.* (M. Bailey, Ill.). San Diego: The Wright Group.

Scott, Foresman. (1979). *Hats.* Special Practice Books.

Stinson, K. (1982). *Red is best.* (R. B. Lewis, Ill.). Toronto: Annick Press.

Tafuri, N. (1986). *Who's counting?* New York: Greenwillow.

11

Home and School Influences on Learning to Read in Kindergarten Through Second Grade

Linda A. Meyer
James L. Wardrop
Center for the Study of Reading

The longitudinal study of children's reading development we began in 1983 was prompted by several concerns. First, despite considerable research on ways to improve children's reading performance, standardized test scores and other data indicated that, for some students, low reading achievement continued to be a serious problem. Second, although there had been many individual studies of children's reading, no one had undertaken a study of a large number of children over a period of several years to explain how they learn to read. Last, because of an emphasis on experimental studies, there had been little observational research on reading in more than a decade.

To address these concerns, we undertook a study of approximately 650 children, divided into two cohorts of 325 students each, from kindergarten through sixth grade. Our purpose was to determine which aspects of children's home background, home activities that support reading development, and classroom activities have the greatest influence on their ability to learn to read effectively. In this chapter, we report some of the initial findings from our study of the first cohort of children in kindergarten and first and second grade.

MODEL DESIGN

The model we developed to guide this study reflects the major home and school influences on children's reading development during their early school years. A schematic of this model appears in Fig. 11.1.

The model is composed of eight constructs: home background characteristics, students' ability at the time they began school, the characteristics of instructional

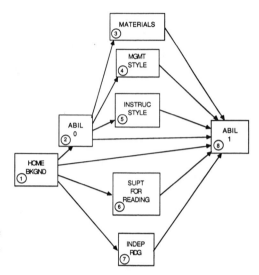

FIG. 11.1. Heuristic model of reading comprehension development.

materials used to teach reading, teachers' management style, teachers' instructional style, home support for reading, student ability at the end of each year, and independent reading.

The following discussion explains how we conceptualized each construct.

1. Home Background. This construct represents the variables of parental occupation and education, the number of adults in the home, the number of older and younger siblings, and the number of hours each parent works outside the home each week.

2. Entering Ability. This construct represents children's verbal abilities on entering a grade that are most likely to affect their reading ability at the end of that grade. Ability 0 on the model represents the children's abilities at the first testing in the fall.

3. Materials. This construct represents the characteristics of instructional materials that may contribute to children's reading development.

Because we believe that teachers do not necessarily manage their classrooms in the same way they instruct, we separated teaching initially into two constructs, management style and instructional style.

4. Management Style. Management style captures teachers' strategies for molding students' general behavior. It is composed of five classroom characteristics: (a) the amount of time teachers allocated to reading instruction; (b) their general praise statements to individual students; (c) their general praise statements to groups of students, such as, "Everyone is working very nicely"; (d) their critical statements directed to individual students, such as "Johnny, sit down and start to work now"; and (e) their critical statements directed to groups of students.

5. *Instructional Style.*   The variables of the instructional style construct are extensions of characteristics reported in research on general teaching effectiveness that have demonstrated the effects produced by instruction. Six classroom process variables compose this construct. Three of these variables are measures of the kinds of interactions teachers initiated with individual students or entire classes; three capture teachers' responses to students who have made errors or who cannot come up with an answer. We also characterized instructional style by the kinds of feedback—sustained, terminating, or confirming—that teachers give.

6. *Home Support for Reading.*   This construct reflects the kinds and amount of activities parents provide to support their children's reading development. The variables differed somewhat in the kindergarten and the first- and second-grade versions of this construct, but, in general, these variables are (a) how much parents read to their children; (b) the amount of reading the children do at home; (c) the resources, such as books and magazines parents make available their children; (d) the kinds of support that parents give to their children to promote literacy, such as taking them to museums, art galleries, or libraries, or playing board and word games with them; (e) the instruction in reading parents provide, such as teaching their young children the names of letters, letter sounds, or words; (f) the amount of homework children bring home and what parents do to help them with it; and (g) the amount of parental support for school activities.

7. *Independent Reading.*   This construct represents reading initiated by the child.

8. *End-of-Year Ability.*   This construct represents students' reading ability in the spring of each school year as measured by a series of tests. Ability 1 on the model represents this construct.

The Setting

While developing the model, we searched for school districts to participate in the study. Because we were asking for a 6-year commitment, we anticipated that it would be difficult to find districts willing to become involved. Furthermore, we decided to use only districts with fairly stable student populations. We knew, for example, about a study at the University of Pittsburgh that started with 300 children and had only 8 children left at the end of 3 years (Lesgold, Resnick, &

Hammond, 1984). This decision meant that we could not work in districts with large numbers of students at risk of school failure because of the typically high rate of student mobility in these districts. We determined, however, that it was more important to have a smaller number of students who would remain in the study throughout its duration than it was to have a larger number whom we would not be able to follow for 6 years. This was clearly a trade-off, but an important one.

Three districts agreed to participate in the study. All these districts are in Illinois, but in very different settings. A description of each district, which we named Poplar, Mahogany, and Evergreen for the purposes of the study, follows.

Poplar.   The Poplar school district is located in a small town about 45 minutes from a larger city. When the study began, there were about 90 children at each grade level. These students, all of whom were White, came mostly from low- and middle-income families.

Poplar was known for the particularly high reading performance of its primary-grade students. The district had a policy of whole-class instruction, even for reading. This policy reflected the district's philosophy that because all children were going to cover the same material, they might as well do it together. Reading instruction in kindergarten emphasized phonics, whereas traditional basal readers were used in first and second grade.

Although Poplar's teachers instructed their classes as a whole, they also typically tailored their instruction to meet the needs of both their highest and lowest performers. Students received a substantial amount of individualized attention. Teachers gave a great deal of feedback to their lowest performers, and they assigned supplementary work to their highest performers.

Two different phenomena indicated the depth of parental interest in and support for their children's education. First, it was not unusual for more than 1,000 people to turn out for school performances put on by the children. Second, almost all the questionnaires we sent to parents were returned within 24 hours.

Poplar's financial resources were limited. With an average annual expenditure of less than $2,800 per pupil, the district's spending on education was among the lowest 10% of the state's unit districts. Just over 50% of the district's revenues came from local resources such as property taxes and bond issues. The ratio of local tax revenues to state aid was 1.2:1, which means that Poplar was highly dependent on state aid to meet its educational expenses.

Mahogany.   The Mahogany district is located in a bedroom community about 20 minutes from a larger town where many parents in the district work. The district also includes the children of farm families from the surrounding areas and children of families living in a large mobile home park. Each grade contained approximately 150 students at the beginning of the study. All the students were White, and they came from a broad range of upper-, middle-, and low-income families. This considerable diversity in socioeconomic status (SES) was mirrored by the widely varying degrees to which Mahogany parents supported their children's education.

Mahogany was known for average to above-average student reading performance, even at the earliest grade levels. Reading instruction relied on traditional basal reading programs. Students were usually taught in groups; in some classrooms, teachers reported they had as many as five different instructional groups.

Whereas each grade was housed in its own separate building, kindergarten and first grade were served by one principal, and another principal was responsible for second grade. The philosophies of these two principals differed, and as a result there was a noticeable shift in the students' schooling experiences between first and second grade during the study. The kindergarten–first-grade principal believed in a more casual and relaxed approach to instruction, and students in these grades spent less time in formal classroom instruction on a daily basis than did those in second grade. The second-grade principal believed that a large part of the day should be devoted to teacher-directed instruction. This principal also encouraged independent reading and the use of the school library.

Mahogany's financial situation was similar to Poplar's. The average annual expenditure per pupil was about $2,950, a figure that put the district in the lowest quarter of Illinois unit districts for educational expenditure. About 65% of the district's revenues came from local sources. The ratio of local receipts to state aid receipts was 1.3:1. Like Poplar, Mahogany was highly dependent on state resources to meet its educational expenses.

Evergreen.   The Evergreen district is located in a suburban area. The school we studied, one of 10 elementary schools in the district, had about 85 children in each grade at the beginning of the study.

The principal of the school described it as a "microcosm of the universe." Forty percent of the student population was White and came from homes in which both parents were employed as professionals. African–American and Hispanic students accounted for 40% and 20%, respectively, of the population; these students came generally from low- and middle-income families. Parental support for their children's education varied widely depending on a complex array of factors. As a general rule, however, the greatest support came from middle-income parents.

Reading performance in the district as a whole was average to above average. However, there was a great deal of variation in student performance. The Evergreen philosophy was that students must be allowed to learn at their own pace. Teachers did not push students to learn to read in the early grades and, in fact, had a rather eclectic approach to reading. Whole language instruction was used primarily in kindergarten, whereas fairly traditional basal reading instruction was used in combined first- and second-grade classes. Teachers also provided direct instruction reading for 30 minutes each day for children with low reading scores.

The school's practice of combining first- and second-grade classes was modeled after the Joplin Plan (Floyd, 1954). First and second graders began the
school day in separate homerooms. They were then grouped together for reading
instruction for most of the morning. They returned to their homerooms shortly
before lunch. This pattern was repeated during the afternoon.

Evergreen was among the top 10% of the state's elementary school districts
for education spending, with annual expenditures of more than $5,800 per pupil.
Local revenues were more than five times those generated by Poplar and Mahogany and accounted for more than 80% of the district's income. The district's ratio
of local revenue to state aid was an impressive 16.3:1. Large local revenues
allowed the district to exercise more independent control of its education resources than was possible in the other two districts.

METHOD

Our model guided the collection of data during each year of the study. Home-
related data were collected by means of a questionnaire sent to parents. School-
related data were gathered through administering a battery of tests twice each
year to reflect students' reading development. Early each fall, we administered
tests of entering ability. Late in the spring, we measured the students' achievement over the school year. In addition, we observed teachers and their classrooms throughout the year.

To capture teachers' management and instructional styles, we observed each
participating teacher for 9 full days each year for the first 3 years of the study,
using an observation system modeled on those used by Stallings and Kaskowitz
(1974) and Barr and Dreeben with Wiratchai (1983). However, our system
differed from these in an important way; in addition to documenting the activities
in which students and teachers engaged and the amount of time they spent in
each, we recorded every instructional interaction the teacher made. It was our
belief that the different kinds of statements teachers made and questions they
asked gave students different kinds of tasks to perform, and that those tasks
reflected different characteristics of teaching. For example, if a teacher prints the
word *girl* on the chalkboard, this activity alone gives no hint as to what task is
required of the students. It is only when the teacher asks, "What word is this?" or
"What are the names of the letters in this word?" that the task becomes clear. We
coded the kind of interactions illustrated in the first question as *whole-word-to-
the-group interactions;* those interactions illustrated in the second question we
coded as *letter–sound interactions.* This system expanded as other kinds of
instructional and procedural interactions (e.g., "Everyone open your book to
page 21 and find the first paragraph.") were observed during classroom instruction. In short, if the teacher did something, we coded it.

When we were unsure about what to call an activity, we asked the teacher what he or she called it and used the same name. Transition periods were coded as the time spent between a teacher's announcement of a change to a new activity and the actual beginning of that activity. If a teacher was not working with an entire class, we looked around the room quickly every 5 minutes to determine the number of students who were on task. We defined being on task as doing whatever the teacher had assigned them to do. For example, if free play was an option and children were playing, they were coded as being on task. On the other hand, if free play was not an option and children were seen playing in any area of the classroom, they were coded as being off task.

Student–teacher interactions were coded on scripts as they occurred. All literacy-related and other relevant lessons were also tape recorded so the observers could complete coding their scripts and double check them later for accuracy. The tapes were also used to prepare written transcripts of entire lessons. These transcripts permitted us to compare the patterns and frequency of instructional interactions across classrooms and districts.

This system was set up so that we could easily identify how many groups a teacher was teaching, how these groups were organized, and how many and what kind of interactions a teacher had with individual students, with groups, or with the entire class. The system also permitted us to identify all the students who participated in a particular instructional interaction. The results provide a picture of instructional style.

Teachers' management statements to students were counted separately from instructional interactions to provide a separate measure of classroom management style. Only the general frequency of these statements was noted; as a result, it was not possible to attribute specific management statements to specific individuals or groups of students. Management statements were coded either as *praise* to an individual and to a group or as *criticism* of an individual student or a group of students.

In the following sections, we focus more specifically on the procedures we used and on the results we obtained at the kindergarten, first-grade, and second-grade levels.

Kindergarten Procedures

During the first week of kindergarten instruction, we administered tests to measure the children's ability to recognize letters and words, their listening comprehension, and their general language proficiency to determine their entering ability. In the middle of the school year, children were tested on their knowledge of letter sounds, word endings, word families, and random words to determine the level of their phonics and word-recognition abilities.

The children were tested again toward the end of the year using reading subtests from two group-administered standardized tests, two individually administered measures of word reading, and an individually administered cloze reading comprehension test to determine which variables in the model best explained differences in their performance at the end of kindergarten.

Between mid-September and mid-April, we observed each kindergarten teacher about once every 3 weeks. During each observation, we documented every literacy-related instructional activity and coded every teacher-initiated interaction and each instance of teacher feedback. We coded more than 50 types of reading interactions, the most frequent of which were initiated by teacher questions about letter sounds, words, sentences, and background knowledge, and requests such as "Open your books to page 29." We coded more than a dozen kinds of teacher feedback, the most frequent of which either *sustained* or *terminated* an interaction or *praised* or *criticized* a child's performance.

Kindergarten Results

Which factors seem to contribute most to children's reading development in kindergarten? In this section, we first consider entering abilities, then home background, home support behaviors, and instruction as these are related to performance on our end-of-year composite measure of reading achievement.

Entering Abilities. Children's beginning-of-year ability to identify the letters of the alphabet and words predicted their end-of-year word-recognition and word-meaning performance. In other words, children with high scores at the beginning of the year also had high scores at the end of the year. Their ability to recognize letters and words was, in turn, predicted by what happened (or perhaps didn't happen) both at home and in the classroom.

Home Background. We used the data on home background collected while the children were in kindergarten for both the kindergarten analysis and the first- and second-grade analyses. Our analysis revealed that most students in all three districts came from two-parent families. Most parents across the three districts had similar educational backgrounds, which included completing 2 years of community college work.

Most of the mothers in the three districts described themselves as homemakers, although 60% of them also worked part time outside the home each week for varying lengths of time (see Table 11.1). Fathers' occupations fell into five general categories: 5% described themselves as unskilled workers, 5% said they were farmers, 21% reported being professionals, 26% were in business, and 42% said they were semiskilled workers. An examination of these occupational data shows there were substantial differences between districts in each category.

We combined four variables (mother's and father's educational and occupational levels) to form an index of home background, a kind of socioeconomic status (SES) variable. The relationship of this index to entry-level ability was strongest in Evergreen, where it accounted for 28% of the variability in chil-

TABLE 11.1
Percentages of Mothers Working Outside the Home and Percentages of Fathers Classified into 5 Levels of Work

District	Mothers	Hours Worked Outside Home						Fathers	Unskilled	Semiskilled	Farming	Business	Professional
		0	1–9	10–19	20–30	31–35	36+						
M	135	52	4	9	23	8	39	133	10	52	6	39	26
	%	39	3	8	17	5	29	%	8	39	4	29	20
P	82	42	1	5	8	5	21	80	3	43	8	13	13
	%	51	1	6	10	6	26	%	4	54	10	15	16
E	52	14	3	4	10	3	18	49	1	14	0	17	17
	%	27	6	7	19	6	35	%	2	28	0	35	35
TOTALS	269	108	8	18	41	16	78	262	14	109	14	69	56
	%	40	3	7	15	6	29	%	5	42	5	26	21

dren's reading ability; not quite so strong in Mahogany (21%); and very weak in Poplar, where only 4% of the variability in entry-level ability was associated with home background.

Home Support for Reading.   Home support was measured on the basis of parents' responses to the questionnaires sent home in the spring, 83% of which were returned. The items measuring home support were clustered into six variables: (a) how much parents read to their children; (b) the amount of reading the children did at home; (c) the resources, such as books and magazines, parents made available to their children; (d) the instruction in reading parents provided; (e) parental support for their children's school activities; and (f) the amount of homework the children had.

Responses varied from district to district, and analyses of these responses revealed that only two home support variables were related significantly to children's reading achievement. Parents from all three districts reported that their children participated regularly in reading at home. However, whereas this variable made significant differences in student achievement in Mahogany and especially in Evergreen, it did not do so in Poplar. The second of these variables, the amount of reading resources parents provided, also was significantly related to achievement in Mahogany, but not in the other two districts.

Home-based influences can have a direct and immediate impact, not only on children's ability to identify letters and words as they enter kindergarten, but also on their performance throughout the school year. The more children read at home, for example, the more developed was their ability to determine the meaning of the words they read. In contrast, however, there was no positive relationship between parents' reading to their children and the children's reading achievement. This may be because parents habitually do not point out print to their children while reading, concentrating instead on the meaning (Phillips & McNaughton, 1990). It should also be noted that our measures were heavily weighted toward coding and print-related skills.

Instruction.   As expected from the differing philosophies of the districts, there were substantial differences in instruction among Poplar, Mahogany, and Evergreen (see Table 11.2). Poplar students received by far the greatest amount of reading instruction in kindergarten. Each child in that district received more than seven whole-word interactions and nearly 4 minutes of reading in text each day, whereas students in Mahogany and Evergreen did not read in text and seldom read whole words.

In Mahogany and Evergreen, the only instructional variable that contributed to end-of-year achievement was teachers' feedback to students about their performance. In Mahogany, the more teachers provided feedback that encouraged children to reconsider their wrong answers, the lower those children's end-of-year achievement. In Evergreen, the more teachers provided feedback that led

TABLE 11.2
Kindergarten Descriptive Statistics: Classroom Process Variables

Variable	Poplar		Mahogany		Evergreen	
	Mean	S.D.	Mean	S.D.	Mean	S.D.
Whole-word Interactions[a]	7.6[c]	.89	0.1[c]	.26	0.8	.98
Feedback: T Encourages[a]	0.5	.27	0.2[c]	.27	0.1	.15
Feedback: T Leads[a]	0.8	.27	0.2	.20	0.1[c]	.07
Time Reading in Text[b]	3.6[c]	.50	0.0	.00	0.0	.00

[a]Variable transformed using square-root transformation for analysis.
[b]Variable transformed using logarithmic transformation for analysis.
[c]Variable appears in final model for this district.

children to the correct answer, the lower those children's end-of-year achievement. In both cases, the result occurred even though we had statistically accounted for the children's entry-level performance, so the observed relationships cannot be explained away by arguing that those types of feedback were provided differentially to the less able children. Perhaps because so little of what we coded as reading instruction took place in these districts, no other classroom instructional variables that we measured were significantly related to end-of-year achievement.

What Do These Results Mean for Kindergartners?

Preschool children's reading development takes place largely in their home environment. Children are best prepared to recognize and comprehend words if they already know some letter names and can read some words when they begin kindergarten. Well-developed language skills also give children a great advantage as they begin to learn how to read. Kindergartners' subsequent ability to recognize letter sounds, word endings, word families, and random words at midyear is closely linked to this beginning-of-the-year knowledge, as is their reading performance at the end of the school year.

These findings indicate that the kindergarten reading programs in the three districts were dramatically different. It should come as no surprise that Poplar students were the highest performing readers at the end of their kindergarten year, and that the frequency of whole-word interactions and the amount of time teachers spent with students reading in text in this district accounted for differences in the performance of these students. In short, students read better at the end of the kindergarten year in the district that focused time and attention on reading instruction. In Mahogany and Evergreen, home background was more strongly related to students' performance at the beginning of the school year than it was in Poplar. Student performance in these two districts at the beginning of the school year was also more strongly related to their performance in the spring than it was in Poplar, where classroom instruction played a bigger role in student performance.

As found in other studies, kindergartners from lower SES homes were less successful at learning to identify and comprehend words and phrases than were kindergartners from higher SES homes. However, regardless of SES, it appears that parents help their children most by focusing their efforts on making them active participants in reading rather than passive receivers. In other words, parents who had their children pick out letters or words, or who reported that their children spent time reading, had children with higher reading performance than parents who simply read *to* their children. Contrary to popular belief, we found no significant relationship at this level between parents reading to their children and their children's print-related skills. On the other hand, we found a positive relationship between the children's participation in reading at home and their end-of-kindergarten reading performance. (Our questionnaire had six components, one of which dealt with reading *to* children, whereas a second dealt with reading actively *with* children: helping them identify the letters and words on the page and understand the meaning of what was being read.) There was, however, a significant relation between parents' reading and children's listening skills, suggesting that the effects of reading to children might be centered on language learning, not on decoding and reading comprehension.

First-Grade Procedures

Pretests.   At the beginning of the school year, we administered three individual performance tests to the first graders who had been studied in kindergarten the year before. These tests, which had also been given in kindergarten, included a test of letter sounds, word endings, word families, and random words; a test of letter names and words; and a test of comprehension in cloze passages.

Posttests.   Near the end of the year, we administered four reading tests. Two of these were individually administered norm-referenced tests, one of which had a series of word lists of graduated difficulty on which students' word-reading accuracy rates were timed. This test also contained a series of passages of graduated difficulty to assess students' reading rate and comprehension accuracy. The other two tests were criterion-referenced measures designed to be particularly sensitive to the reading curricula used in each of the districts. Two of these four tests (the decoding measure and the cloze test) had been used in kindergarten; they were used again to provide continuity in the assessment of students' word-recognition and word-meaning abilities.

We also administered a test developed for this study and designed to measure students' ability to monitor their own comprehension. This measure had two subtests. On the first subtest, students read aloud to an examiner short passages

("The leaves turn red. The leaves turn yellow. The leaves turn blue."), then answered the question "Which word spoiled the meaning?" On the second sub-test, which measured their ability to identify correct sequences of events, the children read aloud short segments of text in which the sequence of events had been scrambled and then answered the question, "What happened at the wrong time?" All the test items were developed from reading vocabulary and concepts found in the children's basal reading programs.

First-Grade Results

Entering Abilities. In each of the districts, children's reading development at the end of first grade was influenced by their ability to recognize letters and words at the beginning of the year. This relationship was especially strong in Evergreen, moderately strong in Poplar, and weak in Mahogany.

Home Background. As with the kindergarten students, parents' level of education and occupation differentially influenced children's reading achieve-ment at the beginning of the year. As in kindergarten, the relationship was stronger in Evergreen (over 37% of the variability in performance was accounted for by home background) than in Mahogany (less than 14%) or Poplar (less than 2%). At the first-grade level, we found that children from single-parent homes performed significantly higher at the end of the school year than did children from homes with two parents. This finding corresponds to Epstein's (1985) finding that single parents give their children more help than parents in two-parent homes. It is also possible that single-parent children may spend more time with their parent than two-parent children spend with their parents because there are no other adults with whom they can readily interact. These interactions may contribute to the children's reading growth.

Home Support for Reading. More than 87% of parents returned the ques-tionnaires sent home with their first graders. The items measuring home support for literacy development on this questionnaire were clustered into five variables instead of the six used for the kindergarten questionnaire: (a) the amount of reading children did at home, (b) the reading-related resources supplied by parents, (c) the amount of activities parents provided to support reading, (d) the instruction in reading supplied by parents, and (e) the amount of homework children brought home and how parents helped with it.

Possibly because the children who were having the most trouble in school needed the most supplemental work at home, we obtained negative correlations with reading growth for the amount of home reading instruction Poplar parents gave to their children, Evergreen parents' support for reading at home, and the amount of homework parents reported their children bringing home in Mahoga-ny. On the other hand, the amount of children's participation in home reading-related activities was positively related to their end-of-year performance in Mahogany. This finding reinforces the findings we obtained with kindergartners in Mahogany and Evergreen, showing the positive effects of children's participation in home reading activities.

None of the other home support variables, including parents reading to their children, had a significant relationship with end-of-year performance. It is also important to note that those variables that did have a significant relationship with end-of-year achievement differed from district to district.

Instruction.   The frequency of the different kinds of teacher–student interactions we observed in first- and second-grade classrooms is summarized in Table 11.3. As these data indicate, there were major differences across districts at these levels. It is also important to note that no single variable common to all three districts significantly predicted reading achievement.

As the figures in Table 11.3 indicate, individual children in Poplar averaged more than 11 whole-word interactions and 23 minutes of reading in a text each day they were observed. They averaged less than 1 turn each on word-comprehension interactions and sounding out words. Individual students received, on average, less than 1 turn each with feedback from teachers leading them through a process to arrive at a correct answer. Their teachers praised their efforts highly about once each day. However, none of these classroom variables significantly accounted for difference in these students' reading performance at the end of first grade.

Each Mahogany student participated in almost 5 whole-word interactions and spent 9 minutes reading in a text. In addition, they averaged less than 1 turn each sounding out words and 1 instance of feedback in which teachers led them through a process to achieve a correct answer. Teachers' whole-word interactions

TABLE 11.3
First-Grade Descriptive Statistics: Classroom Process Variables

Variable	Poplar		Mahogany		Evergreen	
	Mean	S.D.	Mean	S.D.	Mean	S.D.
Whole-World Int.[a]	11.6	11.73	4.9[c]	3.71	5.9	4.13
Time Rdg. in Text[b]	23.5	10.94	8.9[c]	3.72	13.5	6.96
Word Compr. Int.[a]	0.4	0.21	0.21	0.36	0.1[c]	0.16
Sound Out Wds. Int.[a]	0.4	0.53	0.6	1.04	0.3[c]	0.70
Fdbk: Teacher Leads[a]	0.4	0.45	0.6	0.66	0.3[c]	0.40
Fdbk: Lauds Task[a]	0.5	0.60	0.5	0.70	0.4[c]	0.36

[a]Variable transformed using square-root transformation for analysis.
[b]Variable transformed using logarithmic transformation for analysis.
[c]Variable appears in final model for this district.

and the time the students spent reading in text significantly contributed to the student's reading ability at the end of first grade.

Each Evergreen student averaged nearly 6 whole-word interactions and 13.5 minutes reading in a text during first grade and averaged much less than 1 turn per day in each of the four other activities being analyzed. In this district, teachers' word-comprehension and sounding-out interactions, along with feedback that either led the students to correct answers or praised their efforts, significantly predicted their performance at the end of the school year.

These analyses reveal once again that different variables in each school influenced children's reading performance by the end of first grade. In Poplar, none of the instructional variables we measured contributed significantly to their students' performance at the end of first grade. In Mahogany, the number of whole-word interactions and the time children spent reading in a text each day influenced their reading performance at the end of the year. The amount of time spent on homework and reading at home also made a difference in their reading performance. In Evergreen, the number of instructional interactions for sounding out words, word-comprehension activities, leading students to correct answers, and praising them for their efforts had a significant positive effect on their end-of-year reading performance. These were the same variables that were significant in Poplar at the kindergarten level. We interpret this as indicating that Evergreen's policy of delaying reading instruction for a year meant that the children were receiving instruction that children in Poplar had already received in kindergarten. Thus, the same variables that influenced instruction in kindergarten in Poplar influenced instruction with the same goals in Evergreen a year later. In other words, they were simply a year behind the students in Poplar.

What Do These Results Mean For First Graders?

Typically, reading instruction in first grade differs from that in kindergarten in fairly predictable ways. Although there is still an emphasis on letter sounds, there is a much greater emphasis on word reading and sentence reading than had been the case in kindergarten. First graders are also asked more questions and are expected to answer them explicitly.

Children's home lives influenced their reading development in first grade in several ways. Neither home reading-related activities nor home instruction was positively related to children's performance during the school year. The children's participation in reading activities at home, however, was positively related to their performance.

Second-Grade Procedures

Assessment.   At the beginning of second grade, we administered the same four tests we had given at the end of first grade to provide a continuity of scores on key variables. Near the end of the school year, six tests were administered to gauge changes in the children's reading ability during the year. The decoding and cloze comprehension tests were the same ones that had been administered since kindergarten. The other four tests, however, were measures we had not administered before. Two of these were measures of metacognition. The third was a fairly traditional standardized measure of reading ability, whereas the last measure was a relatively new untimed cloze test with passages of graduated difficulty.

Second-Grade Results

Entering Abilities.   As in earlier grades, children's end-of-year reading performance in second grade was most strongly influenced by their entering abilities. This relationship was strongest in Poplar, where over 56% of end-of-year variability in performance was accounted for by initial achievement differences; almost as strong in Mahogany (49%); and much weaker in Evergreen, where only 20% of the variability was accounted for.

Home Background.   As has been already noted, parents' level of education and occupation had a powerful and usually positive influence on children's performance in kindergarten and first grade. During second grade, however, home background had a smaller effect on children's attainment.

Home Support for Reading.   Approximately 90% of the second-grade parents returned our questionnaire. As on the first-grade questionnaire, home support activities encouraging children's literacy development were assessed in terms of five analytical categories.

At the second-grade level, as in kindergarten and first grade, the influence of home activities on the reading performance of second graders varied widely. In Mahogany, for example, we found that none of the home activities parents reported engaging in with their children had a significant influence on the children's reading performance. In Poplar, parents' reading to their children was negatively related to children's reading performance at the end of the school year. However, parental support (which typically meant the time parents spent listening to their children read) had a positive effect on children's performance. By second grade, children should be reading to themselves to get practice and firm up their reading skills (Chall, 1983). In Evergreen, only the children's reading at home was associated with an improvement in their reading performance at the end of the year.

Instruction.   Similar to what we found at the kindergarten and first-grade levels, different variables related to children's end-of-second-grade performance in the three districts (see Table 11.4). We did find some significant instructional variables for second grade in each district. However, because this is a correla-

TABLE 11.4
Second-Grade Descriptive Statistics: Classroom Process Variables

Variable	Poplar		Mahogany		Evergreen	
	Mean	S.D.	Mean	S.D.	Mean	S.D.
Time Rdg. in Text	15.3	6.44	10.2[b]	5.18	12.9	5.76
Letter-Sound Int.[a]	1.0	0.83	0.7[b]	0.67	1.8	3.14
Bkgnd. Knowl. Int.[a]	0.7	0.45	1.0	0.82	1.1[b]	1.10
Whole-Word Int.[a]	5.3[b]	3.48	2.4	2.41	2.7	2.88
Suggest Re-exam. Fdbk[a]	0.1	0.11	0.2[b]	0.27	0.2	0.46
Teacher Encourages Fdbk[a]	0.2	0.18	0.2	0.28	0.4[b]	0.50
Freq. Seatwork	16.0[b]	2.39	22.1	2.13	9.6	2.26

[a]Variable transformed using square-root transformation for analysis.
[b]Variable appears in final model for this district.

tional study, it is difficult to interpret some of these patterns. In Poplar, we found negative correlations between reading growth and the number of whole-word interactions and the amount of seatwork. Did increased seatwork inhibit reading growth or did children who were having problems get additional seatwork to remediate their difficulties? Similarly, did the number of whole-word interactions inhibit growth or did children who were already having problems get more whole-word interactions (Allington, 1983)? The answers are not clear, although the observed relationship was found *after* differences in entry-level performance had been statistically controlled for.

It is important to consider these findings in light of what we found at the other grade levels. Poplar's students clearly gained from work on letter–sound interactions and word reading in kindergarten, and they were the highest performing readers in the study by the end of kindergarten. During first grade, they were not differentially affected by what their teachers did in the classroom. In second grade, however, the time they spent on whole-word interactions and seatwork was negatively related to their performance. This might indicate that these students were ready for reading instruction beyond the word level but did not receive it.

In Mahogany, time spent reading text and letter–sound interactions was positively related to end-of-year reading performance. For all practical purposes, Mahogany students began their reading instruction in first grade rather than in kindergarten. Therefore, it makes sense that they would benefit from reading in text, not only in first grade but also in second grade. Although Evergreen students benefitted from sounding-out-words interactions, word-comprehension interactions, and teacher feedback during first grade, none of the instructional variables we measured in second grade had a differential effect on their reading performance at the end of the school year. In Evergreen, the amount of background knowledge interactions and the number of times teachers provided encouragement when a child did not know an answer were negatively related to achievement, but it is not clear why.

What Do These Results Mean For Second Graders?

In both Poplar and Mahogany, a similar sequence of classroom activities resulted in growth in reading achievement. In this shared sequence, children benefitted first from instruction that focused on whole words. Once they had become familiar with whole words, they benefitted most from reading in texts. Although this simple pattern appeared at different grade levels in these two districts, its prevalence suggests that by second grade children's performance is being shaped more by classroom activities than by other influences from outside the classroom.

Such a finding suggests that, overall, parents' level of education and occupation may have less of an impact by second grade than in kindergarten and first grade. This may be because second grade is a somewhat unique period in children's schooling when tasks particular to school have their greatest impact on children's development. This is especially true if we think of second grade as a period of consolidation, a time when many children can already identify many words and read sentences and understand what they are reading. It is therefore important for teachers to help children focus on text.

Although school factors become more important in second grade, parents do continue to influence performance at this grade level, albeit indirectly, depending on the kind of support and instruction they give their children. Our findings indicate that parental support for reading and children's participation in home reading activities continue to have a positive effect on children's reading performance. The powerful message these findings send about parental involvement at this grade level is that parents need to continue to support their children as they read and encourage them to read at home.

However, the finding from Poplar—that parents' reading to their children was negatively correlated to achievement—suggests that by second grade parental influence on reading becomes more complex and problematic. More specifically, this finding suggests that children learn to read best by engaging in active reading, rather than passive listening. Once children are old enough to learn to read, parents are better off listening to them read and helping them in other supportive ways than they are reading to them.

IMPLICATIONS

First, if we regard the kindergarten, first-, and second-grade years as collectively constituting the foundation of early education, then we must realize that schooling at these grade levels can make a real difference in how well children read by the time they reach third grade. If children are to learn to read, they must be taught how to identify words, and then they must have practice reading text both at school and at home. The words that children read in the first few grades are generally in their spoken vocabularies (Baker & Freebody, 1989). Only by having children reading in texts can word-recognition skills and word-meaning understandings be developed effectively. Curricula and instruction that fail to recognize these essential connections can only shortchange students.

Second, our findings suggest that there should be a hierarchy of instruction for these three grade levels. There first needs to be an emphasis on letter sounds and words composed of those sounds. Word-meaning instruction should then reflect word-recognition development so that, as children are able to identify words, they can focus on the meaning of those same words. This joint focus continues as the text expands. As the children learn to recognize words that make up sentences, they must also focus on the meaning of these larger units of text. To do so, it is essential that they spend time reading in text.

Third, on average, the children do not do a great deal of reading in school. In kindergarten in one district students averaged less than 4 minutes a day reading text, and those in the other two spent no time at all reading text. In first and second grade, students continue to average only 10 to 15 minutes each day reading text, whereas they may spend as much as 1 hour on seatwork. The time spent on reading was correlated to their final achievement (at least in Mahogany and Poplar); the time spent on seatwork was not. Why not let students use at least some of this independent work time for additional text-reading activities?

The small number of teacher–student interactions across categories is equally disturbing. Our study suggests that in kindergarten, for example, individual students average just 2 background-knowledge questions a day, and this figure falls to only 1 question a day in first and second grade. The picture is equally bleak for other instructional activities. The first and second graders in our study averaged only 7 opportunities to read whole words and had only 1 or 2 sentence-level comprehension interactions a day. Surely the number of these interactions can be increased.

Fourth, we need to note that, on the whole, teachers do not manage their classrooms with *supportive* statements about what their students are doing. The tendency to rely increasingly on critical statements to manage classrooms often results in the creation of an unpleasant classroom environment in which, over time, more and more children are encouraged to be disruptive or are dissuaded from viewing learning as a pleasant and rewarding experience.

As we looked at these three grade levels together, another intriguing result emerged. In kindergarten, the correlation between children's knowledge of reading when they entered school and end-of-year reading achievement was lowest in Poplar, the only district in which systematic reading instruction took place. In first grade, Mahogany was the district with the greatest emphasis on reading instruction, and it was also in Mahogany that the beginning- to end-of-year correlation was the lowest. Finally, reading instruction in Evergreen began to receive emphasis in second grade, and at this grade level the beginning-to-end correlation was lowest in that district. If we consider that one of the consequences of effective classroom instruction is to "defeat" our ability to predict end-of-year performance accurately from beginning-of-year performance, then this pattern of correlations leads us to conclude that the most effective reading instruction occurred at different grades in these three districts: kindergarten in Poplar, first grade in Mahogany, and second grade in Evergreen. These findings appear to be consistent with differences in educational philosophy across the three districts. Whether one approach is better than the others is unclear. Is it better to emphasize early instruction, then trust that the foundation that has been provided will carry the children through the grades? Or, should formal reading instruction be postponed a year or two, in the belief that children are more likely to be developmentally ready to profit from instruction when they are older? Answers to such questions must be deferred until we look at how these children perform in subsequent years.

All in all, these findings present a mixed picture of reading instruction in kindergarten through second grade. In Poplar, effective kindergarten instruction gave way to ineffective instruction in first and second grades. In Evergreen, improvements in student performance in these early years rest tenuously on a limited number of instructional characteristics at only one grade level. However, in Mahogany, there appears to be a sustained instructional program, beginning in first grade and carrying on through second grade, at least. It is surely not too much to expect such sustained efforts to be the rule, rather than the exception.

REFERENCES

Allington, R. L. (1983). The reading instruction provided readers of differing reading abilities. *Elementary School Journal, 83,* 549–559.

Baker, C. D., & Freebody, P. (1989). *Children's first school books.* Oxford: Basil Blackwell.

Barr, R., & Dreeben, R., with Wiratchai, N. (1983). *How schools work.* Chicago: University of Chicago Press.

Chall, J. S. (1983). *Stages of reading development.* New York: McGraw–Hill.

Epstein, J. L. (1985). Home and school connections in schools of the future: Implications of research on parent involvement. *Peabody Journal of Education, 62,* 18–41.

Floyd, C. (1954). Meeting children's reading needs in the middle grades: A preliminary report. *Elementary School Journal, 55,* 99–103.

Lesgold, A., Resnick, L. B., & Hammond K. (1984). *Learning to read: A longitudinal study of work skill development in two curricula.* Pittsburgh: University of Pittsburgh, Learning Research and Development Center.

Phillips, G., & McNaughton, S. (1990). The practice of storybook reading to preschoolers in mainstream New Zealand families. *Reading Research Quarterly, 25,* 196–212.

Stallings, J. A., & Kaskowitz, D. (1974). *Follow-through observation evaluation, 1972–1973.* Menlo Park, CA: Stanford Research Institute.

IV THE REDISCOVERY OF LITERATURE IN THE CURRICULUM

12 The Power of the Narrative

Tom Trabasso
University of Chicago

The rediscovery of literature in the curriculum of necessity includes a rediscovery of the narrative as a literary and didactic form. In this chapter, I examine the power of the narrative from a psychological and educational perspective.

THE POWER OF THE NARRATIVE

The narrative is powerful because it is the dominant form of written discourse in the literary, historical, social, and personal texts we encounter throughout our formal schooling. The narrative is especially pervasive in the elementary school curriculum. It has been estimated, in fact, that as much as 90% of what is read by elementary schoolchildren is narrative in form (Stein & Trabasso, 1982). Outside of formal schooling, in the oral tradition, our discourse also is largely narrative in form, serving both to socialize and organize our experience and to provide the main vehicle by which we communicate the past to others (Labov & Waletzky, 1967; Polkinghorne, 1988). The narrative is powerful, then, because of its pervasiveness in usage. This pervasiveness, however, finds its origin in our ability to understand and to produce narrative forms in spoken language. Basic skills in understanding and producing complex narratives develop by the fourth and fifth years of life (Stein, 1988; Stein & Trabasso, 1982; Trabasso & Nickels, 1992; Trabasso, Stein, Rodkin, Munger, & Baughn, 1992; Trabasso, Stein, & Johnson, 1981) and precede and underlie the receptivity to instruction through the more conventional forms that occur in the teaching of reading and writing in school contexts.

The power of the narrative also lies in its ability to make human experience personally meaningful and coherent. The narrative is the primary form by which we interpret our experiences and construct organized unities. We achieve this by cognitive processes that organize experience into causal and temporal episodes and store these in memory for further use. Narratives make individual events, states, and actions interrelated and thematically cohesive (Polkinghorne, 1988). As a consequence, the narrative is powerful because it is so widely used to describe and explain human behavior, both of the self and the other.

Narrative forms are expressed linguistically in early stages of human development and social interaction (Hood & Bloom, 1979; Miller & Sperry, 1988). Historical narrative forms are central to the study of human existence (White, 1981). The fictional narrative is a basic genre in literature (Chatman, 1978). Narratives in child psychology are the primary research tool for studying what children know about what people think, feel, want, perceive, and do (Grueneich & Trabasso, 1981; Schantz, 1975). As such, the narrative is powerful because it spans the realm of human mental and social existence.

The Narrative and Communicative Coherence

The narrative is powerful because it is a prime form of communication. When we use language to communicate, we call it discourse. Discourse consists of language utterances or sentences that cohere or hang together. The linguistic study of discourse concerns itself with the way in which the structures available in a language are used to produce coherence, and how they can be used to signify different meanings at different times. The narrative is a powerful form for producing coherent messages and texts for others to interpret. Because the narrative provides the medium of coherence, this chapter is concerned primarily with the problem of how the narrative does so in its reading or listening or producing. To understand the coherence of a narrative, we need to know what the contents of a narrative text are and how they are structured by the writer and speaker so as to give rise to a perception of coherence in the reader or listener (Trabasso, 1989).

One of the primary implications of focusing on coherence of a text is that it forces us to focus on the quality of the text rather than on the ability of the reader as a source of difficulty in comprehension. The argument can be made that difficulty in reading a text for comprehension may not be because a young reader or writer or speaker is not literate. The difficulty may occur because the writers or speakers whom they are trying to understand have produced discourse or text with content and structure that are simply difficult to process. In short, the texts may lack coherence. The quality of the production and the comprehension must be matched if the communication is to be effective.

If, as a listener, you do not understand what a speaker is saying, you can interrupt and demand a clarification. As a reader, obviously, you cannot do this.

A written text is supposed to be the product of careful planning and revision, and it is supposed to be designed to be intelligible. The importance of producing text that is guaranteed to be intelligible is not to be underestimated.

The Problem of Linear Order of a Discourse

A discourse consists of a sequence of sounds or marks on a page, and it will be either heard or read as a sequence. Ideas themselves may not be sequential, but we have to express and order them as if they were. This problem of the temporal organization of coexisting ideas into a linear sequence faces not just the speaker or the writer but also the listener and the reader.

The narrative is powerful when it allows one to overcome the linear order problem. The narrative allows one to organize ideas temporally into causally meaningful sequences of events, actions, and states and to use this organization in memory to retrieve information from sentences experienced earlier. This retrieval is important in the interpretation of new information as it accrues. The narrative is a powerful means of representing in memory event sequences and of retrieving from that memory representation information that is of value in understanding events as they occur "online."

Narrative Knowledge

The narrative is powerful in that it allows readers to make use of knowledge that is available and appropriate to them. The knowledge I refer to is the knowledge of human intentions, plans, actions, and outcomes, and it is essential to making human experience meaningful. It becomes available to us early in life, and it continues to develop throughout our lives. A writer or speaker assumes what the reader or the listener knows or is capable of knowing. The producer has to have a model of the receiver's knowledge state and uses this in speaking or writing to choose expressions and topics and their organization. This is the well-known background-knowledge problem. A knowledge of what narratives are, of their content, and of how that content is structured can assist writers and speakers in producing texts that lend themselves more readily to coherent interpretation by their readers.

The narrative is powerful when it uses knowledge that children possess: knowledge about events, objects, and states of the world; knowledge about internal reactions such as emotions or cognitions; knowledge about goals, needs, and desires of self and others; knowledge about how these goals are enacted in actions that attempt to achieve them or how a sequence of attempts may follow a plan; knowledge about how attempts or actions effect changes in the world and bring about success or failure of one's goals; and knowledge about how one evaluates the intentions, actions, and outcomes of one's self and others (Stein &

Trabasso, 1982; Trabasso, van den Broek, & Suh, 1989; Trabasso, Stein, & Johnson, 1981).

The background-knowledge problem and the linear-order problem are not independent. In narratives, they can co-occur easily. The writer can introduce new knowledge to the reader and then assume that this is now knowledge that the reader has. The order of presentation of ideas is thus of crucial importance. In fact, everything that is included in the narrative is of potential importance and constrains understanding. Storytellers do not introduce information unless they intend the listener or the reader to use it. Readers and listeners attempt to use each piece of information, whether or not it can be used.

The Linear Structure of Text

Memory and attention to the text are important, and the linear structure of the text can strongly affect them. As the narrative unfolds, the reader will pay attention to certain parts, usually the more recent ones. Events, states, and objects mentioned earlier in a discourse may not be in or available to the reader's working memory or focus of attention later on in time as he or she courses through the text (Fletcher & Bloom, 1988; Kintsch & van Dijk, 1978). When the writer wishes to refer to earlier things, appropriate forms have to be used to reintroduce old ideas (Sanford & Garrod, 1981). The power of the narrative lies in its ability, once interpreted or constructed or produced, to serve as a durable memory representation that can be used for other purposes. These uses may be retrieving earlier text while reading or later in the retelling of the events that took place in the narrative. It can also be used in answering explanatory or descriptive questions about why and how the events occurred, in judging which events were important in the text, in learning and executing plans of action in solving problems, and in evaluating the morality of characters. However, when the narrative is not coherent, online understanding and interpretation suffer. The consequence to the reader is that it is difficult to construct a coherent interpretation, and the consequences to memory and subsequent use of the information are disastrous. One cannot effectively retrieve prior sentences from incoherent text when one is engaged in reading text, and one cannot retrieve later what was not understood and stored in the first place.

What Makes a Text Coherent?

How we construct coherence in understanding a narrative text needs some clarification. When we attempt to understand a series of events, states, and actions in a text, we do not experience them as isolated individual occurrences. Rather we experience them or try to experience them as a coherent sequence of happenings.

We achieve this coherence by making inferences. We make inferences about the time and place in which the action occurs, and about who the characters are and what they are like. We make inferences that interrelate or connect ideas about the events. These inferences are primarily of a causal and logical nature. From these inferences, we construct a memory representation of the text that determines how well we can remember, answer questions, summarize, paraphrase, evaluate, or judge the text. In general, the more coherent the mental representation of the text, the better the comprehension and usage of the text (Trabasso, 1981; Trabasso & van den Broek, 1985; Trabasso, Secco, & van den Broek, 1984; Trabasso & Sperry, 1985).

In what follows, a series of brief narratives are used to illustrate what we mean by coherence and some of the difficulties in achieving it. The narratives are made deliberately simple for purposes of illustration. To the extent that they indicate difficulties in comprehending, imagine what occurs when the text becomes more complicated. Read, therefore, the following narrative and see how coherent an interpretation you can achieve on a single pass through the text (the basic story is taken from van den Broek, 1988).

SCRAMBLED VERSION OF JIMMY STORY

Jimmy bought a beautiful bike. Jimmy asked his mother for some money. Jimmy delivered the newspapers before sunrise without missing a house. Jimmy wanted to get a paper route. Jimmy took the money he had saved. Jimmy went to a newspaper office. Jimmy wanted a 10-speed bike. There once was a boy named Jimmy. Jimmy counted the money he had with him. Jimmy's mother said that he should earn his own money. Jimmy accepted a paper route. Jimmy did not have enough money. Jimmy saw Tom's new 10-speed bike. Jimmy saved $100.

This story is not easy to understand. You can read it. You can understand each sentence. But you cannot understand the story as a whole. Why? Mainly because the states and actions of Jimmy do not occur in a causal and temporal sequence. It is difficult for you to find the causes and consequences that explain Jimmy's behavior. The appropriate or plausible causes are not antecedent and adjacent to their consequences and considerable mental effort is required to find them.

Let us unscramble and rewrite the story so that it becomes intelligible and coherent. Notice now in reading how much easier it is to find meaningful, causal, and temporal relations among the sentences in the text and thereby to construct a coherent memory representation.

HIERARCHICAL VERSION: EXPLICIT GOALS
AND OUTCOMES

There once was a boy named Jimmy. Jimmy saw Tom's new 10-speed bike. Jimmy wanted a 10-speed bike. Jimmy counted the money he had with him. Jimmy did not have enough money. Jimmy wanted to save $100. Jimmy asked his mother for some money. Jimmy's mother said that he should earn his own money. Jimmy wanted to get a paper route. Jimmy went to a newspaper office. Jimmy accepted a paper route. Jimmy delivered the newspapers before sunrise without missing a house. Jimmy saved $100. Jimmy took the money he had saved. Jimmy bought a beautiful bike. Jimmy rode his new bike home.

Most texts should be—but are not—written as fully and coherently as this one. This should be the case, especially for young readers or listeners. The texts need not repeat a character's name in every sentence. Rather, writers can rely on pronouns to achieve this kind of anaphoric reference and cohesion (Sanford & Garrod, 1981). This is not the problem. One can, without difficulty, find texts that (a) separate causes from effects by the inclusion of largely irrelevant information, and (b) omit the information that is necessary to explain events and to infer causes and consequences. Both of these kinds of writing are causes of poor reading comprehension and have untoward effects on the child's retention and use of the material. These kinds of texts are self-defeating not only for learning to read but also for reading to learn.

Let us consider another version of the Jimmy story in which certain information is omitted, then examine what is different about it.

HIERARCHICAL VERSION OF JIMMY STORY:
NO GOALS

There once was a boy named Jimmy. Jimmy counted the money he had with him. Jimmy did not have enough money. Jimmy asked his mother for some money. Jimmy went to a newspaper office. Jimmy accepted a paper route. Jimmy delivered the newspapers before sunrise without missing a house. Jimmy saved $100. Jimmy took the money he had saved. Jimmy bought a beautiful bike.

This story is not hard to read, sentence by sentence, but something is missing that makes it feel less coherent than the previous version. What is missing are Jimmy's goals or motives for doing what he is doing. Narratives are powerful when they provide coherent explanations of human behavior in terms of intentional action. You could, of course, figure out what motivated Jimmy by reading the end of the story, which shows the outcome of his actions. But waiting to the end to provide the reasons for something puts an unnecessary burden on young readers and is a practice to be avoided in good writing.

Let us examine another version of the story with another kind of omission, one that may be more serious.

HIERARCHICAL VERSION OF JIMMY STORY: NO OUTCOMES

> There once was a boy named Jimmy. Jimmy saw Tom's new 10-speed bike. Jimmy wanted a 10-speed bike. Jimmy counted the money he had with him. Jimmy wanted to save $100. Jimmy asked his mother for some money. Jimmy wanted to get a paper route. Jimmy went to a newspaper office. Jimmy delivered the newspapers before sunrise without missing a house. Jimmy took the money he saved.

Narratives are powerful when they tell you about something that happened—what the outcomes were, whether the character succeeded or failed, and how he or she succeeded or failed. This story lacks outcomes. It does not tell you what the consequences of Jimmy's action were. It provides some of the causes, but outcomes as consequences become causes when events follow from them. Jimmy's actions are best understood in terms of the goals and outcomes that precede them. When Jimmy finally attains his highest order goal of buying the bike he desires, the story is finished. This version is unfinished. Incomplete stories of this type occur when pieces of narratives are used in reading. Complete, although brief narratives, are desirable for understanding and for making reading easier.

In the preceding examples, three effects were demonstrated: (a) scrambling a text so that it violates the causal-temporal sequence of the events, (b) omitting the motives and reasons for a character's action, and (c) omitting the outcomes that are both the causes and the consequences of action. All three examples illustrate one central point: When readers or listeners find it difficult to infer the causes and consequences of events, states, and actions, the story lacks coherence. It is difficult to understand because the reader cannot readily or easily find a basis for inferring relations and building a coherent memory representation.

There is abundant experimental evidence that scrambling text or omitting goals and outcomes leads to poor understanding and poor retention of text, independent of the ability of the child to read as measured by conventional measures of reading ability. The message is that writers need to check their material for comprehensibility. They can do this by testing themselves against their own texts for ease of inferring relations and building a coherent mental model of the text. I have found that reading a text aloud to another person or to oneself is a good way to test coherence.

Sequencing Information

Let us return to the linear-order problem or the problem of the sequencing and retrieving and integrating information. The temporal sequence of a series of states and actions is important, not only in terms of placing causes and consequences in adjacent temporal orders but also in terms of the kind of inferences that can be made and the degree to which a text becomes integrated overall. The same sentences, when arranged differently, can give rise to radically different meanings and judgments of what is important (cf. van den Broek, 1988).

Let us now contrast two different versions of the Jimmy story. The first one you have read before; I repeat it here to allow a direct comparison. The second version has all the same sentences as the first, but they appear in a somewhat different order. Both stories are coherent, but one appears to be more coherent than another. Why?

HIERARCHICAL VERSION

There once was a boy named Jimmy. Jimmy saw Tom's new 10-speed bike. Jimmy wanted a 10-speed bike. Jimmy counted the money he had with him. Jimmy did not have enough money. Jimmy wanted to save $100. Jimmy asked his mother for some money. Jimmy's mother said that he should earn his own money. Jimmy wanted to get a paper route. Jimmy went to a newspaper office. Jimmy accepted a paper route. Jimmy delivered the newspapers before sunrise without missing a house. Jimmy saved $100. Jimmy took the money he had saved. Jimmy bought a beautiful bike. Jimmy rode his new bike home.

SEQUENTIAL VERSION

There once was a boy named Jimmy. Jimmy had a lot of spare time. Jimmy wanted to get a paper route. Jimmy went to a newspaper office. Jimmy accepted a paper route. Jimmy did not have enough money. Jimmy wanted to save $100. Jimmy asked his mother for some money. Jimmy's mother said that he should earn his own money. Jimmy delivered the newspapers before sunrise without missing a house. Jimmy saved $100. Jimmy saw Tom's new 10-speed bike. Jimmy wanted a 10-speed bike. Jimmy counted the money he had with him. The money was not enough to buy the bike. Jimmy took the money he had saved. Jimmy bought a beautiful bike. Jimmy rode his new bike home.

The hierarchical version of the story is one in which Jimmy has three goals that are dependent on one another: He wants a job in order to earn money in order to buy a bike. In other words, his goal of wanting the bike motivates his goal to want money. Wanting money motivates his goal of wanting a job. We call this story *hierarchical* because the goals and episodes are arranged into a goal-plan hierarchy. The second story, however, is clearly more linear and sequential. The goals are not related in the same way as before. Rather, here, he gets a job that enables him to earn money that, in turn, enables him to buy a bike. It is not the case that wanting the bike caused wanting money that caused wanting a job. The sequential story portrays three episodes in the life of Jimmy and the three episodes are therefore weakly interrelated. Notice how the meaning of the events differ in the two versions. You can see this by asking yourself why Jimmy wanted a job and wanted money in each version. The answers are quite different.

In a study of the summarizing of these kinds of stories, we (van den Broek, Trabasso, & Thurlow, 1990) found, surprisingly, that adults more than children are likely to read purposes into Jimmy's behavior in *both* stories. Kindergarten and elementary schoolchildren up to the third or fourth grade treat the sequential story as it is: A sequence of three episodes. But children from about the fifth and sixth grades on begin to interpret all of Jimmy's actions in terms of his ultimate goal of buying the bike. This interpretation is actually unwarranted. We have and develop strong propensities to read motives into acts when they are not warranted.

I claimed earlier that the hierarchical version of the Jimmy story in which you are told initially that he wanted to buy a bicycle was more coherent than the sequential version. The reason that it is more coherent is that there are more causal connections between the content of the sentences, both within and between the story's episodes. To the extent that children are better able to remember, retrieve, and integrate the information contained in the sentences into a coherent, functional, memory representation, they should recall the stories better than when they fail to achieve such integration. In a study of memory for these stories by children from 4 to 8 years in age, Liu (1988) found that the hierarchical stories are, in fact, better retained, especially as children become older and are capable of integrating more units of text through inferences. Figure 12.1 shows the differences in recall for the two kinds of stories as a function of age. Note that for the young children there is little difference in recall between the two stories. It

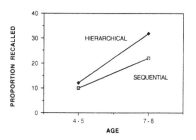

FIG. 12.1. Recall of propositions from stories that differ in structure as a function of age (data from Liu, 1988).

is as if they treat both kinds of text as a linear sequence. However, by the third grade they are differentiating these kinds of stories. The hierarchical story allows more and richer meanings and the children are finding them. This leads to a more coherent story and better retention of the information contained in it.

Promoting Comprehension by Questioning and Inferencing

The data in Fig. 12.1 indicate that very young children do not retain much information from even these simple stories. One reason for this is that they do not make the inferences that are necessary to construct a coherent memory representation of the story. We believed that we could promote understanding and memory by drawing the child's attention to the inferences. We decided to do this by questioning each child as the child listened to or read the text.

The use of questions is a long-standing issue in the literature on reading comprehension. Do questions merely assess, or do they actually facilitate understanding and memory for the text (Anderson & Biddle, 1975; Dillon, 1982)? The data provide a very mixed set of outcomes: Sometimes questions help, sometimes they hinder, and sometimes they have no effect. How can such findings be of value to writers of texts and workbooks? Truthfully, they cannot be of much value. However, when my colleagues and I reflected on the problem (Trabasso, van den Broek, & Liu, 1988), we realized that the questions usually were asked after reading, and that there was no theory of comprehension and coherence of text that guided the prior research. Therefore, we developed systematic procedures for asking questions as the story line is read and constructed and tried to assess and promote causal-temporal inferences by these questions.

Let me illustrate the procedure for the Jimmy story in which there is a hierarchy of goals. The child reads or hears one sentence at a time. At various points we ask explanatory questions that require the child to answer with causes or consequences. The causes and consequences depend on goals, actions, and outcomes. These are the core episodic categories in the story and form the basis for integrating through causal inferences the text into a coherent memory representation while one is trying to understand a text.

The child first reads or hears:

There once was a boy named Jimmy.
Jimmy saw Tom's new 10-speed bike.
Jimmy wanted a 10-speed bike.

Then we ask: "Why did Jimmy want a 10-speed bike?"
Then the child resumes reading or listening:

Jimmy counted the money he had with him.
Jimmy did not have enough money.

Then we ask: "What did Jimmy do so that he found out that he did not have enough money?"

The child resumes reading or listening.

Jimmy wanted to save $100.

We ask: "Why did Jimmy want to save $100?"

This cycle of "Why" and "What did Jimmy do in order to . . . ?" questions continues throughout the story.

Let us examine the effect of this kind of causal-temporal questioning in the context of a story on subsequent retention. Figure 12.2 shows the results, comparing the questioning effects to those children who listened to the stories without questions. These data show that questioning helped retention. In particular, it helped the third-grade children to discover even more relations in the hierarchical stories and to increase their retention to a much higher level. Questioning for these children in the sequential stories did not help as much because there were fewer potential causal inferences to begin with. The younger children benefitted from questions for both kinds of stories. The amount of benefit was, in some cases, to double or increase recall by as much as 100%.

This study demonstrates that questioning, when done in conjunction with reading or listening to a text, can facilitate enormously the comprehension and subsequent retention of the text. We also know that from examining the answers given to the questions that the amount of text information that an individual child can bring forth to answer the question predicts to a very high degree ($r = .80$) subsequent retention for the text. This is an important finding for it suggests that how much information a child can maintain in or retrieve from working memory as the child courses through the text is a predictor of how much information will be integrated into a longer lasting memory representation. Individual differences

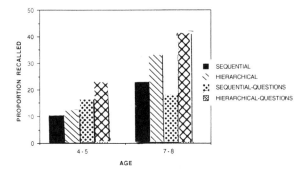

FIG. 12.2. The effect of questioning during listening to stories that vary in structure on retention by children (data from Liu, 1988).

among children in this capacity may be a direct indication of the quality of understanding that children show as they go through a text as well as the quality of the composition of the text. Good texts and good readers lead to good understanding as the text is read and to good memory of the text later in time.

Recently, Suh (1989; Suh & Trabasso, 1993) has studied how people talk aloud about stories as they read them one at a time. In particular, Suh was interested in the kind and number of inferences that people make as they read a story sentence by sentence. Identification of inferences between goals and actions through the talk-aloud protocols predicted where inferences would occur when people read normally. Analyses of the talk-aloud protocols reveal that people are actively retrieving prior text, inferring relations, and integrating these inferences and prior text units into a durable memory representation as they read through a text. The protocols also reveal false starts and failed as well as successful predictions about what is to occur. These kind of data may help us to discern why some texts are difficult to understand and to comprehend the striking individual differences in the ability of readers to maintain, retrieve, and integrate prior text with what they are currently reading.

SOME RECOMMENDATIONS FOR PRODUCING TEXTS, READERS, AND WORKBOOKS

Here, then, are some of the implications of the notions of coherence I have discussed:

1. Writers of narratives or editors who choose to reproduce literary narratives for readers, especially young readers, should be mindful of whether the text produced or chosen is, in fact, readily comprehensible by the intended audience.
2. Comprehensibility and coherence are related. The easier it is for writers or editors to understand a text, the more likely it is that young readers will find it coherent. Writers and editors should read to one another or listen to another reading the texts to make these judgments. We have found in practice that discourse analysis requires high degrees of effort and attention. Passive reading will not allow one to discern difficulties in the coherence of a text or what is making it coherent.
3. As to the extent to which a text is not coherent, it is possible to make it coherent by writing, rewriting, or editing the text. This can be accomplished by (a) ordering events according to when they occur in a causal-temporal sequence; (b) providing explanations, causes, and outcomes where they are missing; (c) making explicit, if need be, the referential and causal relations between sentences; (d) omitting text that is irrelevant to the central story line being developed by a causal chain of events; and (e) providing a single unifying theme.

4. When questions are used to promote and assess comprehension, they should not be used in isolation and should not be placed in separated workbooks. Rather, questions should be placed in the context of the text when students are actively processing it and while they have the appropriate information available. With older children, the process could be a mixture of questions asked during and after the text to promote both short- and long-term retention and availability of the text information for other uses.

5. The questions should be designed to elicit active causal, temporal, and logical inferences that interconnect and relate ideas in the text. They should not be exclusively aimed at information that one finds within a sentence but should draw on information contained across different sentences. They should not be irrelevant to the central theme, causes, and consequences of the text itself. If our goal is to allow narratives to be powerful, we need to design them in such a way as to make them intelligible.

ACKNOWLEDGMENT

The writing of this chapter was supported in part by Grants No. HD25742 and HD17431 from the National Institute of Child Health and Human Development to the author and N. L. Stein.

REFERENCES

Anderson, R. C., & Biddle, W. B. (1975). On asking people questions about what they are reading. In G. Bower (Ed.), *The psychology of learning and motivation* (Vol. 9, pp. 89–131). New York: Academic Press.

Dillon, J. T. (1982). The multi-disciplinary study of questioning. *Journal of Educational Psychology, 74,* 147–165.

van den Broek, P. (1988). The effects of causal relations and hierarchical position on the importance of story statements. *Journal of Memory and Language, 27,* 1–22.

van den Broek, P., Trabasso, T., & Thurlow, R. (1990, April). *The effects of story structure on children's and adults' ability to summarize stories.* Paper presented at the annual meeting of the American Educational Research Association, Boston.

Chatman, S. (1978). *Story and discourse: Narrative structure in fiction and film.* Ithaca, NY: Cornell University Press.

Fletcher, C. R., & Bloom, C. P. (1988). Causal reasoning in the comprehension of simple narrative texts. *Journal of Memory and Language, 25,* 43–58.

Grueneich, R., & Trabasso, T. (1981). The story as a social environment: Children's ability to infer intentions and consequences. In J. Harvey (Ed.), *Cognition, social psychology, and the environment* (pp. 265–288). Hillsdale, NJ: Lawrence Erlbaum Associates.

Hood, L., & Bloom, L. (1979). What, when, and who about why: A longitudinal study of early expressions of causality. *Monograph of the Society for Research in Child Development, 44*(6) (serial no. 181).

Kintsch, W., & van Dijk, T. A. (1978). Toward a model of text comprehension and production. *Psychological Review, 85,* 363–394.

Labov, W., & Waletzky, J. (1967). Narrative analysis: Oral versions of personal experience. In J. Helm (Ed.), *Essays in the verbal and visual arts* (pp. 12–44). Seattle: American Ethnological Society.

Liu, L. G. (1988). *Using causal questions to assess and promote children's understanding and memory for narratives that vary in causal structure.* Unpublished doctoral dissertation, University of Chicago.

Miller, P. J., & Sperry, L. L. (1988). Early talk about the past: The origins of conversational stories of personal experience. *Journal of Child Language, 15,* 293–315.

Polkinghorne, D. E. (1988). *Narrative knowing and the human sciences.* Albany, NY: State University of New York Press.

Sanford, A. J., & Garrod, S. C. (1981). *Understanding written language: Exploration in comprehension beyond the sentence.* New York: Wiley.

Schantz, C. U. (1975). The development of social cognition. In E. Hetherington (Ed.), *Review of child development research* (Vol. 5, pp. 257–324). Chicago: University of Chicago Press.

Stein, N. L. (1988). The development of children's storytelling skill. In M. B. Franklin & S. Barten (Eds.), *Child language: A book of readings* (pp. 282–289). New York: Oxford University Press.

Stein, N. L., & Trabasso, T. (1982). What's in a story? An approach to comprehension. In R. Glaser (Ed.), *Advances in the psychology of instruction* (Vol. 2, pp. 213–268). Hillsdale, NJ: Lawrence Erlbaum Associates.

Suh, S. (1989). *Causal inferences during text comprehension.* Unpublished doctoral dissertation, University of Chicago.

Suh, S., & Trabasso, T. (1993). Inferences during reading: Converging evidence from discourse analysis, talk-aloud protocols, and recognition priming. *Journal of Memory and Language, 32,* 1–22.

Trabasso, T. (1981). On the making and the assessment of inferences during reading. In J. T. Guthrie (Ed.), *Comprehension and teaching: Research reviews* (pp. 56–76). Newark, DE: International Reading Association.

Trabasso, T. (1989). The development of coherence in narrative by the understanding of intentional action. In G. Denhiere & J. P. Rossi (Eds.), *Text and text processing* (pp. 297–314). North Holland Press.

Trabasso, T., & van den Broek, P. (1985). Causal thinking and the representation of narrative events. *Journal of Memory and Language, 24,* 612–630.

Trabasso, T., van den Broek, P. W., & Liu, L. (1988). A model for generating questions that assess and promote comprehension. *Question Exchange, 2,* 25–38.

Trabasso, T., van den Broek, P., & Suh, S. (1989). Logical necessity and transitivity of causal relations in stories. *Discourse Processes, 12,* 1–25.

Trabasso, T., & Nickels, M. (1992). The development of goal plans of action in the narration of a picture story. *Discourse Processes, 15,* 249–275.

Trabasso, T., Secco, T., & van den Broek, P. (1984). Causal cohesion and story coherence. In H. Mandl, N. L. Stein, & T. Trabasso (Eds.), *Learning and comprehension of text* (pp. 83–112). Hillsdale, NJ: Lawrence Erlbaum Associates.

Trabasso, T., Stein, N. L., Rodkin, P., Munger, M. P., & Baughn, C. R. (1992). Knowledge of goals and plans in the on-line narration of events. *Cognitive Development, 7,* 133–170.

Trabasso, T., & Sperry, L. L. (1985). Causal relatedness and importance of story events. *Journal of Memory and Language, 24,* 595–611.

Trabasso, T., Stein, N. L., & Johnson, L. R. (1981). Children's knowledge of events: A causal analysis of story structure. In G. Bower (Ed.), *Learning and motivation* (Vol. 15, pp. 237–282). New York: Academic Press.

White, H. (1981). The value of narrativity in the representation of reality. In W. J. T. Mitchell (Ed.), *On narrative* (pp. 1–23). Chicago: University of Chicago Press.

13 Multiculturalism and Children's Literature

Violet J. Harris
Center for the Study of Reading

Once perceived of as a genteel profession populated by women who dedicated their energies to the creation of whimsical entertaining fare designed to reinforce traditional family and national values, children's literature, so to speak, has grown up. Indeed, we are in the midst of a golden era in terms of the quality and critical recognition of children's literature. Sales of children's books are nearly 1 billion dollars per year (Roback, 1990). Many critically acclaimed authors—Dr. Seuss, Katherine Paterson, Chris Van Allsburg, and Maurice Sendak—routinely appear on best-seller lists. Across the nation, children's bookstores flourish.

In education, children's literature has been presented as the answer to lowered literacy achievement, the method for bequeathing the nation's cultural heritage, and the key to reforming literacy education. Many educators trumpet the benefits—expanded vocabulary, enhanced comprehension skills, and developed sense of story—that children can derive from reading "authentic" literature (Cullinan, 1987; Strickland & Taylor, 1989; Wells, 1986). Children's literature, it seems, has become both cultural treasure and cultural commodity. Therein lies some of its contradictions. In a nation of cultural diversity, children's literature remains largely the domain of middle-class European–Americans.

Consider, for example, the following publishing facts: Fewer than 2% of the nearly 5,000 children's books published in 1990 featured African–Americans (Bishop, 1990b). Even fewer books were published about other racial/ethnic groups (Bishop, 1990b). Of the nearly 375 books considered best sellers for 1990 (sales of 75,000 and up in hardback; 100,000 and up in paperback), only 12 related to people of color—African–American, Asian–American/Pacific Islander, Hispanic, Native American. And several of these, *The Indian in the Cupboard* (Banks, 1982), *The Return of the Indian* (Banks, 1987), *The Secret of the Indian* (Banks, 1989), *The Cay* (Taylor, 1969), and *Sounder* (Armstrong, 1969), generated considerable controversy because of their stereotyped depictions.

Compounding the problem is the lack of access to such literature by people of color. Chain bookstores tend not to locate in communities populated by people of color or to stock extensive materials related to them.

Clearly, this picture suggests limitations that prevent the full flowering of children's literature; limitations that can only be removed by the expansion of the literary canon to include more books by and about people of color, by greater efforts on the part of educators to include more multicultural literature in the classroom, and by greater efforts on the part of publishers and booksellers to make such literature readily available.

In this chapter, I discuss the issues associated with the efforts to include in homes, classrooms, libraries, and bookstores children's literature written by people of color. These efforts are part of a movement often labeled *multicultural-ism* or *cultural diversity.*

MULTICULTURALISM

Multiculturalism has roots in previous educational movements, including global and international studies, pluralism, human relations, and cross-cultural interactions (Banks, 1990). Currently, multiculturalism refers to the idea that a society and its institutions, beliefs, and values should reflect the composition of its members. An additional idea is that members of a culturally diverse society should appreciate, celebrate, understand, and acquire knowledge about the various parallel cultures that exist within its boundaries. It is important to note that parallel cultures overlap, intersect, and diverge; they exert varying degrees of influence on each other and exist, occasionally, in opposition to each other. Rap music, the popular culture art form, signifies the complexities and contradictions evident when parallel cultures co-exist. Rap evolved out of the creativity, frustrations, and political consciousness of African–American youth in urban centers (Powell, 1991; Rose, 1991). The music and lyrics represented in some cases a progressive or radical sociopolitical and cultural stance. Titles such as "Fight the Power," "Fear of a Black Planet," and "911 is a Joke" demonstrate this radical potentiality. The radical potentiality of some rap music has lessened, however, because of the appropriation of the form by commercial entities within the music business. Rap, for instance, has been used in advertising to sell fast food, alcoholic beverages, clothing, and other products.

Various groupings of individuals constitute multicultural entities. The groups include those based on race/ethnicity—African–American, Asian–American/Pacific Islander, Hispanic/Latino, and Native American; religion—Amish, Jewish, and Islamic; gender; language; age; sexual preference; and disability (Banks, 1990; Sleeter & Grant, 1985). Inclusion in one category does not preclude inclusion in others; indeed, the categories can and do overlap and intersect. For instance, a 15-year-old Puerto Rican girl interacts in a variety of worlds, including teen culture, Puerto Rican culture, women's culture, and several geographic cultures. The power commanded by each of these cultures varies. Common to each group, however, is the relative low level of power possessed by each and its marginalization, or placement on the fringes of the dominating or "mainstream" culture. Although writing about African–Americans, hooks' (1984) description of marginalization applies to other nonmainstream groups as well:

> To be in the margin is to be part of the whole but outside the main body. As black Americans living in a small Kentucky town, the railroad tracks were a daily reminder of our marginality. Across those tracks were paved streets, stores we could not enter, restaurants we could not eat in, and people we could not look directly in the face . . . . We could enter that world but we could not live there. We had always to return to the margin, to cross the tracks, to shacks and abandoned houses on the edge of town . . . . There were laws to ensure our return. To not return was to risk being punished. Living as we did—on the edge—we developed a particular way of seeing reality. We looked both from the outside in and from the inside out. We focused our attention on the center as well as on the margin. We understood both. This mode of seeing reminded us of the existence of a whole universe, a main body made up of both margin and center. Our survival depended on an ongoing public awareness of the separation between margin and center and an ongoing private acknowledgment that we were a necessary, vital part of that whole . . . . This sense of wholeness, impressed upon our consciousness by the structure of our daily lives, provided us an oppositional world view—a mode of seeing unknown to most of our oppressors, that sustained us, aided us in our struggle to transcend poverty and despair, strengthened our sense of self and our solidarity. (preface)

This double consciousness adds to literature such emotions and reactions as tension, hope, pain, laughter, succorance, honesty, and understanding— emotions and reactions not necessarily apparent in other literature.

Marginalization can have the effect of silencing the disparate voices that do not conform to or fit mainstream notions of what constitutes culture. Many marginalized authors and illustrators challenge their precarious status in the mainstream through reinterpretations of the "margins." They view the margins as potential spaces of enlightenment and power and, thus, subvert those who view the margins as areas of powerlessness. This seizure of power and reinterpretation of marginalized cultures has always existed among low-status groups, but today's groups seem especially dedicated to challenging mainstream institutions and ideologies.

Multiculturalism and Children's Literature.

Demands for expansion of the literary canon appeared relatively early in the field of children's literature (Harris, 1990), as the title of an 1896 publication "Is Juvenile Literature Demanded on the Part of Colored Children?" illustrates

(Elliot, 1991). In the years since, variations of this question have surfaced and continue to surface among all the groups contained within the category *multicultural* (see, e.g., Asian–American Cooperative Book Project, 1981; Broderick, 1973; Larrick, 1965; Nieto, 1982; Palomino, 1988; Sims, 1982; Slapin & Seale, 1987; Taxel, 1991). Four major factors account for the extension of multiculturalism to children's literature. First, individuals and groups within various ethnic and racial communities have made a conscious choice to voice their concerns and desires for curricula in the schools that include their histories and contributions. Individuals aware of the power of language and pictures have sought to challenge the prevailing, stereotyped, images of themselves in various education media. Some immediate results of their efforts have been the proliferation of ethnic studies courses, insertion of previously excluded writers in literary anthologies and courses, and increased efforts by some publishers to discover authors from excluded groups. Second, many involved in schooling have noted the changing racial/ethnic and linguistic composition of student populations and have concluded that curricula need to include aspects of their various cultures if the students were to achieve. Third, writers such as Virginia Hamilton, Mildred Taylor, Walter Dean Myers, Laurence Yep, Paul Goble, Angela Johnson, Nicholasa Mohr, Gary Soto, Vera Williams, Arnold Adoff, and Crescent Dragonwagon emerged in the 1960s, 1970s, and 1980s. The excellence of their work, and of the work of other writers, demanded their inclusion in the curricula. Moreover, many of these writers articulated a new aesthetic in children's literature that sought to make known the philosophical and creative impulses that suffused their works. Fourth, children's literature critics, awards committee members, librarians, parents, and teachers recognized and celebrated the quality inherent in many of these works and their potential to motivate students.

For the most part, those involved with children's literature duly accept, at least philosophically, the need for it to adopt a multicultural perspective. Others view the issue of expanding the children's literature canon as comparable to or an indication of the "canon" wars waged in adult literature but without the viciousness (Jones, 1991). Nevertheless, some doubts persist, and critics argue against its inclusion in the canon, primarily on the grounds of its quality, appeal, and appropriateness. I address each of these arguments in turn.

The Quality of Multicultural Literature.   Questions about the quality of multicultural literature and the qualifications of its authors arise when discussions center on the literary canon and multiculturalism (D'Souza, 1991). Typically, critics either state or suggest that the canon as currently constituted represents extraordinary works that best capture Western artistic, literary, and intellectual traditions (D'Souza, 1991). Others argue that exhortations for change and expansion represent an assault on intellectual excellence and the encouragement of mediocrity, or that overzealous efforts will lead to balkanization of curricula or multicultural particularism (Ravitch, 1990). In discussions of the adult literature canon, these voices sometimes become quite venal. For example, Paglia suggested that literary awards earned by authors such as Alice Walker and Toni Morrison were examples of literary tokenism, affirmative action, and kowtowing to the demands of special interests groups (cited in Stanfall, 1991).

One hallmark of exceptional literature is its ability to capture universal ideals, values, emotions, beliefs, and conflicts. Traditionally, American critics ascribe these elements to literature written by Europeans or European–Americans. According to some critics, literature written by individuals who do not fit within these categories rarely transcends the limitations of race/ethnicity. Instead, their literature is not perceived of as expressing universal values but rather parochial values circumscribed by the author's own racial/ethnic identity. Arguing for the value of the author's cultural experiences and heritage as a method for conveying universal ideas, Isaac B. Singer (Singer & Burgin, 1985) has contradicted these notions. According to Singer, "individuality is the axiom of literature" (p. 67). Denying one's roots or "spiritual address," he argued, leads to ineffective literature that contains cardboard characters. Roots provide the rich texture needed to individualize a story.

The quality of children's literature produced by Hamilton, Soto, Myers, Yep, Taylor, and others, for example, belies this kind of criticism. Their work, in many cases, expands the aesthetic, intellectual, and artistic boundaries of children's literature. Hamilton, for instance, is the only author writing for children who has won three major children's literature awards—the Newbery Medal, the Boston Globe-Horn Book Magazine Award, and the National Book Award—for one book, *M. C. Higgins, the Great* (1974). The book also received other awards, including the Lewis Carroll Shelf Award and the International Board on Books for Young People Award. Few authors write in as many genres on as many subjects, and with as many experiments with voice, setting, language, and style as Hamilton. Taylor also received the Newbery Medal. Other authors, including the aforementioned Yep and Myers, have won Newbery Honor Medals. Opposition to multicultural literature based on perceived lack of quality, then, has no credence.

The Appeal of Multicultural Literature.   Another argument advanced against including multicultural literature in the literary canon is that it will not appeal to most children—which generally means European–American children. Some argue that these children are simply not interested in reading about people of color. One could argue that this is true because print and electronic media present the lives of people of color as unrelated to the lives of European–Americans. In addition, the negative images of people of color in print and electronic media do not encourage cross-cultural interactions and understanding. Given these images, one might ask why mainstream children would want to develop friendships or read about people portrayed primarily as welfare cheats, athletes, criminals, entertainers, illegal immigrants, and individuals overwhelmed by poverty.

But this argument, too, lacks merit. Children desire stories that are action packed, contain strong characterizations, and have discernible plots with happy, or at least, hopeful endings. Bello (1990) and Spears-Bunton (1990) provided evidence to support the contention that multicultural literature contains many books that embody these elements. They each observed and participated in classrooms (for middle school low achievers and high school English honors students, respectively) that included multicultural literature. Although the students had varying responses to the literature, on the whole their responses were positive. Some difficulties did arise, especially in the high school English class, but they stemmed from the complex sociopolitical interactions of race/ethnicity and class, and the perceptions of people of color held by the students.

Teachers, parents, and librarians will have to make the efforts to select and share literature about people of color that dramatizes a variety of experiences. For example, an adult might share *Me and Neesie* (Greenfield, 1975) as a story about a little girl who must relinquish her imaginary playmate. Many children will relate to this familiar aspect of childhood. One need not necessarily introduce the story as one about an African–American girl; the illustrations make that obvious. However, the girl's race can become one of many foci if a teacher were to say to a group of students something comparable to: "I want to read you a story about a little girl who looks like some of you, talks like you, has a family like yours, and maybe felt about school the same as you."

The Appropriateness of Multicultural Literature.   The third argument against multicultural literature is based on appropriateness. Many adults want children's literature to depict an optimistic, problem-free, patriotic, and ideal world; they argue that children will encounter reality soon enough (Englehardt, 1991). Unfortunately, the experiences of many people of color are not blissful, sugar-coated interludes. They include experiences of poverty, institutionalized racism, and violence. Stories depicting these experiences can help children—all children—to understand that these are not the central experiences of people of color but representative of the experiences of many. In a sense, these stories represent the conferral of historical memory and facts often neglected in social studies texts or other literature. All children also need stories that celebrate the love and laughter found among people of color as a way of presenting a balanced portrait. In fact, the most powerful reasons for including multicultural literature relate to the benefits that all children can derive from its use.

Finally, multicultural literature is a part of the discipline of literature. Fairness should prevail. Children deserve opportunities to sample from a range of authors in order to find the particular words and worlds that touch their lives. In the following section, I discuss several such authors.

MULTICULTURAL AUTHORS: CREATING WORDS
THAT TAKE EFFECT

Several years ago, author Eloise Greenfield (1975) delineated her reasons for writing. She summed up her feelings by stating that she wanted to create words that take effect:

> Writing is my work. It is work that is in harmony with me; it sustains me. I want, through my work, to help sustain children. My attempts and those of other writers to offer sustenance will necessarily be largely ineffectual. Not only do we as human beings have limitations—so also does the written word. It cannot be eaten or worn; it cannot cure disease; it cannot dissipate pollution, defang a racist, cause a spoonful of heroin to disintegrate. But, at the right time, in the right circumstances, falling on the right mind, a word may take effect. (p. 624)

In addition to words that inspired, Greenfield hoped to create works that informed, entertained, and apprised children of the heroic and everyday acts of courage performed by their ancestors, family members, and friends.

> I want to give children a love for the arts that will provoke creative thought and activity; I want to encourage children to develop positive attitudes toward themselves and their abilities, to love themselves; I want to present to children alternative methods for coping with the negative aspect of their lives and to inspire them to seek new ways of solving problems; and I want to give children a true knowledge of Black heritage including both the African and the American experiences among others. (pp. 624–626)

In books such as *Me and Neesie* (1975), *First Pink Light* (1976, 1991), *Honey, I Love* (1978), and *Nathaniel Talking* (1988), she conveys shared experiences that create family ties, forge friendships, and celebrate love, courage, and unity. One stanza from *Honey, I Love* demonstrates these characteristics:

> I love
> I love a lot of things, a whole lot of things
> Like
> My cousin comes to visit and you know he's from the South
> 'Cause every word he says just kind of slides out of his mouth
> I like the way he whistles and I like the way he walks
> But honey, let me tell you that I LOVE the way he talks.

Many regard this small book of poetry a classic in children's literature. Indeed, Greenfield has accomplished her goals with more than 20 books for children and youth.

Yoshiko Uchida, too, writes about the dual consciousness that frames her philosophy. She stated that most readers would have some familiarity with the "American" component of children's literature but not the Japanese–American component. Uchida initially focused on retelling Japanese folk tales but shifted to historical fiction in books such as *Journey to Topaz* (1971) and *A Jar of Dreams* (1981). Of her intentions she wrote (in Commire, 1985):

> Although all of my books have been about the Japanese people, my hope is that they will enlarge and enrich the reader's understanding not only of the Japanese and the Japanese–Americans, but of the human condition. I think it's important for each of us to take pride in our special heritage, but we must never lose our sense of connection with the community of man. And I hope our young people will, through the enriching diversity of the books they read, learn to celebrate our common humanity and the universality of the human spirit. (p. 156)

Again, the emphasis is on entertaining and informing children about people and communities that are similar and less similar to themselves.

Experimentation with form and content are atypical in children's literature. Virginia Hamilton dares to shatter expectations in order to create works that combine verifiable fact, memories, imagination, and something she refers to as the "hopescape"—dreams and hopes of African–Americans. Rarely faltering, she succeeds in expanding our conceptions of what constitutes appropriate children's literature and children's ability to handle her artistic turns. In more than 25 works, she explores what it means to be African–American, Amerind, male, female, famous public figure, ignored historical personage, psychically disturbed prodigy, or grandmother sharing stories with a young charge. Few can match her talent. Hamilton (1983), in numerous essays and articles, discusses the influences on her oeuvre. She had this to say about her artistic intentions.

> I want my books to be read. I want an audience. I struggle daily with literary integrity, black cultural integrity, intellectual honesty, my desire for simplicity in storytelling, and the wish for strong, original characterization, exceptional concepts for plots . . . But when I sit down to write a story, I don't say to myself, now I'm going to write a black story. I've often said, much to the "startlement" of white friends, that black people don't really think about being black. It happens that I know my tribe, as it were, better than any other tribe because I am one of them. I am at ease with being black. The constant in my books is that the characters are black and yet, the emotional content is simply human. The fact that M. C. Higgins sits on a pole in the novel *M. C. Higgins, the Great* has nothing whatever to do with his color, nor does the fact that the sensitive girl in the Justice Cycle books is clairvoyant have anything to do with her race. A pole sitter and a seer might as well be of the black race as any other, since race has nothing to do with either talent. But race can give an added dimension to a story because of the cliches, prejudices, and assumptions many readers bring to stories with some amount of racial content. I love dismantling assumptions. (p. 14)

Always in the vanguard, Hamilton has written biographies of W. E. B. DuBois and Paul Robeson, men shunned because of their color and radical politics, men who otherwise would have enjoyed an exalted position in history and social studies texts. The impetus for sharing historical memories developed on her front porch in sessions with her father. He regaled her with observations and remarks about heroes and heroines that left an indelible impression. The importance of sharing one's culture and history and passing that valued knowledge to future generations is evident in many of her novels, biographies, and essays.

Lately, Hamilton has articulated a philosophy that melds the aesthetic, literary, political, and educational. She does not apologize; rather she encourages others to think about her views. For example, in a presentation before members of the writers' organization, PEN, she (Hamilton, 1986) said:

> Whatever art I possess is a social action in itself. My view is that black people in America are an oppressed people and therefore politicized. All my young characters live within a fictional social order and it is largely a black social order, as is the case in real life. For a score of years I've attempted a certain form and content to express black literature as American literature and to perpetuate a pedigree of American Black literature for the young . . . What being black means is a constant in myself and my work. It is the belief in the importance of past and present Afro–American life to the multi-ethnic fabric of the hopescape and the necessity of making that life known to all Americans. It is the belief in the presentation of the life and literature, the documentary history in schools and libraries for succeeding American generations. It is the imaginative use of language and ideas to illuminate a human condition, so that we are reminded then again to care who these black people are, where they come from, how they dream, how they hunger, what they want. (pp. 16–17)

Inviting readers to understand the American experience through the particulars of the African–American experience is a continuing goal for Hamilton.

Some aspects of Hamilton's philosophy attract support from many, including other authors. Yep (1991) has used Hamilton's metaphor of a "hopescape" to characterize his writing. Yep, too, has remarked on the dual consciousness that shaped his identity and novels. Ever seeking to overcome feelings of being an outsider, he explored similar thoughts in his Newbery Honor Book, *Dragonwings* (1975). An afterword included in the novel explains his reasons for giving voice to the hopescape of Chinese–Americans. Referring to the flier Fung Joe Guey, Yep explains why he attempts to reconcile the duality:

> Like the other Chinese who came to America, he remains a shadowy figure. Of the hundreds of thousands of Chinese who flocked to these shores we know next to nothing. They remain a dull, faceless mass; statistical fodder to be fed to the sociologists, or lifeless abstractions to be manipulated by historians. And yet these Chinese were human beings—with fears and hopes, joys and sorrows like rest of us. In the adventures of the various members of the Company of the Peach Orchard

Vow, I have tried to make some of these dry historical facts become living experiences. . . . At the same time, it has been my aim to counter various stereotypes as presented in the media. Dr. Fu Manchu and his yellow hordes, Charlie Chan and his fortune-cookie wisdom, the laundrymen and the cooks of the movie and television Westerns, and the houseboys of various comedies present an image of Chinese not as they really are but as they exist in the mind of White America. I wanted to show that Chinese–Americans are human beings upon whom America has had a unique effect. I have tried to do this by seeing America through the eyes of a recently arrived Chinese boy, and by presenting the struggles of his father in following his dream. (pp. 247–248)

His other novels, *Child of the Owl* (1977), *Sea Glass* (1979), and *The Serpent's Children* (1984) also convey those dreams. In some ways Yep comes to terms with his dual heritage in *The Lost Garden* (1991a), an autobiography, and *Starfisher* (1991b), a fictionalized account of some of his mother's experiences in West Virginia.

Native Americans must also contend with forces that seek to adapt, reinterpret, and profit from their cultures. Commenting on the renewed interest in artifacts, ceremonies, and spiritual lore as symbolized by workshops, auctions, and sweat lodge ceremonies peopled primarily by non-Native Americans, Aaron Two Elk (Emerson, 1991) said "every 20 years it's fashionable in this country to be an Indian" (p. 1). Fashionable or not, Native Americans remain a staple in children's literature, primarily stereotyped. One need only read the "Indian" series written by Lynn Reid Banks to understand the plight of Native Americans in children's literature. Doris Seale (Slapin & Seale, 1987) criticized the images of Native Americans with these comments:

It doesn't seem to me a lot to ask that the books written about Indians be honest, if nothing else. This is not so simple as it sounds. Very few non-Native writers have bothered to acquire the knowledge to produce meaningful work about our history, culture and lives—although this ignorance does not stop them from doing the books, and getting published . . . . In fact, Indians are the only Americans whose history has been set down almost exclusively by those who are not members of the group about which they are writing. The American literary establishment may pay lip service to ideas of cultural pluralism, but it is nonetheless subject to the same biases that afflict society as a whole. (pp. 6–7)

Several authors have moved beyond quaint Thanksgiving stories, episodes about stolen European–American children, marauding savages, squaws, and nature boys. For example, Virginia Driving Hawk Sneve's books reflect Lakota culture from an insider's perspective, and they have received favorable critical commentary. Authors Paul Goble and Byrd Baylor also portray Native American cultures in a sympathetic fashion. Unfortunately, controversy exists about two authors, previously assumed to be Native American (Emerson, 1991; Harris,

1992). One, Jamake Highwater garnered a Newbery Medal and considerable praise for his books. The other, the late Forest Carter, wrote a book, *The Education of Little Tree* (1976, 1990), that has the distinction of being the number one-selling paperback in the country. Recently, however, it has been discovered that neither Highwater nor Carter are Native Americans. Clearly, their ethnic heritages did not prevent them from creating stories that many considered authentic, but more than a few readers feel exploited.

The statements formulated by the authors reflect several commonalities. Each author felt a need for the creative expression of ideas, emotions, and imagination that only writing provided, or at least, writing became their avenue for self-expression. The need to convey an insider's perspective of a particular culture that would contradict stereotyped depictions also underlies the work of the authors. Equally important is the need for the writer to celebrate and honor the various cultures that nurtured him or her. Further, the authors express a desire to motivate and inspire the children who read their books. These shared objectives suggest the sense of urgency that underlies multicultural literature and provide support for its use.

Implications for Schooling

Writers often portend future sociocultural changes in their works. The philosophies articulated by the authors I have discussed signal the need for continued change in children's literature. First, the cultural diversity apparent in the United States does not indicate any signs of lessening. Indeed, current world conditions suggest that many people around the world will continue to view the United States as a haven. These new immigrants, legal and illegal, will shape the country's culture in myriad ways. Eventually, these citizens, too, will demand a place for their literature in schools. The manner in which we incorporate the diverse stories of today will influence the tenor of discourse in the future.

Second, the influence of the whole language movement and the continued demand for real and not "basalized" literature ensure that children's literature will remain an influential component of literacy education. The increased use of literature, however, will necessarily result in additional confrontations among adults about the appropriateness of selected literature. The battles fought about the Impressions Series and requests for the removal of offensive books from libraries will certainly multiply.

Third, publishers project that the number of children's books published is likely to increase. Given past history, the number of books classified as multicultural will continue to fluctuate. Only consistent demands for the literature and recognition among publishers that a market exists for the books will alter the situation and guarantee a consistent publication rate.

Fourth, teachers and parents need help in acquiring information about the existence of the literature, evaluation of it, and suggestions for use in classes.

Some help is available as evidenced by the number of sessions devoted to the topic at conferences sponsored by the International Reading Association (IRA) and the National Council of Teachers of English (NCTE), the publication of articles in journals such as *Language Arts* and *The Reading Teacher,* and reviews of the literature in a variety of publications. The central task, then, is selecting a book or books that appeal to children at the time that a book is needed.

CONCLUSION

In this chapter I have tried to articulate the position of those of us who want to bring about the full flowering of children's literature. We want *all* children to have experiences with storybook reading and quality literature, not just middle- or upper-class children or those children enrolled in various "whole language" classrooms. We want affordable quality books for *all* children. We want children's bookstores to locate in nonexclusive neighborhoods. Most importantly, we want those political and social figures who command power and influence to read books such as *Tell Me a Story, Mama* (Johnson, 1989), *Yagua Days* (Cruz, 1976), *More, More, More, Said the Baby* (Williams, 1990), and *Tucking Mommy In* (Loh, 1991). We want the inclusion in the literary canon of a broader range of stories that reflect the increasing cultural diversity of the United States. We do not advocate a literary policy of quotas, affirmative action, or political correctness; instead, we urge acknowledgment of the fact that creativity abounds in many people and cultures, and that people of color create exemplary literary texts and artistic products that reflect universal truths and values. All children deserve to encounter a variety of literature, because, as Bishop (1990a) so eloquently put it:

> Books are sometimes windows, offering views of worlds that may be real or imagined, familiar or strange. These windows are also sliding glass doors, and readers have only to walk through imagination to become part of whatever world has been created or recreated by the author. When lighting conditions are just right, however, a window can also be a mirror. Literature transforms human experiences and reflect it back to us, and in that reflection we can see our own lives and experiences as part of the larger human experience. Reading, then, becomes a means of self affirmation, and readers often seek their mirrors in books. (pp. ix–x)

Because we recognize the importance of literature in affirming people and enabling them to move beyond the parochial confines of arbitrary categories, we believe that the chance to enter into the fictive world created by an author, and the possibility of deriving some aesthetic pleasure, entertainment, and intellectual stimulation from that world should not remain the preserve of European–Americans.

REFERENCES

Asian–American Cooperative Book Project. (1981). How children's books distort the Asian–American image. *Interracial Books for Children Bulletin, 7* (2 & 3), 3–33.

Banks, J. (1990). *Teaching strategies for ethnic studies* (5th ed.). Boston: Allyn & Bacon.

Bello, Y. (1990). *Children's responses to African–American children's literature.* Unpublished manuscript.

Bishop, R. (1990a). Mirrors, windows, and sliding glass doors. *Perspectives, 6,* ix–xi.

Bishop, R. (1990b). Walk tall in the world: African–American literature for today's children. *Journal of Negro Education, 59,* 556–565.

Broderick, D. (1973). *Image of the Black in children's literature.* New York: R. R. Bowker.

Commire, A. (Ed.). (1985). *Something about the author: Facts and pictures about contemporary authors and illustrators of books for young people* (Vol. 53, pp. 151–160). Detroit: Gale.

Cullinan, B. (1987). *Children's literature in the reading program.* Newark, DE: International Reading Association.

D'Souza, D. (1991, March). Illiberal education. *The Atlantic,* 51–79.

Elliot, R. (1991, May–June). A literature whose time has come. *Children's Advocate,* 8–9.

Emerson, B. (1991, October 4). The selling of sacred spirits. *Atlanta Constitution,* Section D, 1, 4.

Englehardt, T. (1991, June). Reading may be harmful to your kids. *Harper's,* 55–62.

Greenfield, E. (1975). Something to shout about. *The Horn Book Magazine, 51,* 624–626.

Hamilton, V. (1983). The mind of a novel: The heart of the book. *Children's Literature Association Quarterly, 8,* 10–14.

Hamilton, V. (1986). On being a Black writer in America. *The Lion and Unicorn, 10,* 15–17.

Harris, V. (1990). African–American children's literature: The first one hundred years. *Journal of Negro Education, 59,* 540–555.

Harris, V. (1992). Multiethnic literature. In K. Wood & A. Moss (Eds.), *Exploring literature across the curriculum* (pp. 169–201). Norwood, MA: Christopher-Gordon.

hooks, b. (1984). *Feminist theory: From margin to center.* England: South End Press.

Jones, M. (1991, September 9). It's a not so small world. *Newsweek,* 64–66.

Larrick, N. (1965). The all-white world of children's books. *Saturday Review, 48,* 63–65, 84–85.

Nieto, S. (1982). Children's literature on Puerto Rican themes—Part I: The messages of fiction. *Interracial Books for Children Bulletin, 8* (1 & 2), 3–33.

Palomino, H. (1988). Japanese–American in books or reality? In B. Bacon (Ed.), *How much truth do we tell the children? The politics of children's literature* (pp. 125–134). Minneapolis: MEP Publications.

Powell, C. (1991). Rap music: An education with a beat from the street. *Journal of Negro Education, 60,* 245–259.

Ravitch, D. (1990). Diversity and democracy. *American Educator, 14,* 16–20.

Roback, D. (1990, August 30). Children's book sales: Past and future. *Publishers Weekly,* 30–34.

Rose, P. (1991). "Fear of a Black planet": Rap music and Black cultural politics. *Journal of Negro Education, 60,* 276–290.

Sims, R. (1982). *Shadow and substance.* Urbana, IL: National Council of Teachers of English.

Singer, I., & Burgin, R. (1985). *Conservations with Isaac Bashevis Singer.* Garden City, NJ: Farrar, Strauss & Giroux.

Slapin, B., & Seale, D. (Eds.). (1987). *Books with bias: Through Indian eyes.* Berkeley, CA: Oyate.

Sleeter, C., & Grant, C. (1985). *Making choices for multicultural education.* Columbus, OH: Merrill.

Spears-Bunton, A. (1990). Welcome to my home: African–American and European–American students' responses to Virginia Hamilton's *House of Dies Drear. Journal of Negro Education, 59,* 566–577.

Stanfall, F. (1991, March 4). Woman warrior. *New York*, 22–30.

Strickland, D., & Taylor, D. (1989). Family story book reading. In D. Strickland & L. Morrow (Eds.), *Emerging literacy: Young children learn to read and write* (pp. 27–34). Newark, DE: International Reading Association.

Taxel, J. (1991). On the politics of children's literature. *The New Advocate, 4,* vii–xii.

Wells, G. (1986). *The meaning makers*. Portsmouth, NH: Heinemann.

Yep, L. (1991, April). *Dialogue: The author's perspective*. Paper presented at the annual meeting of the Cooperative Children's Book Center, Madison, WI.

CHILDREN'S BOOKS

Armstrong, W. (1969). *Sounder*. New York: Harper.

Banks, L. (1982). *The Indian in the cupboard*. New York: Avon.

Banks, L. (1987). *The return of the Indian*. New York: Avon.

Banks, L. (1989). *The secret of the Indian*. New York: Avon.

Carter, F. (1976, 1990). *The education of Little Tree*. Albuquerque: University of New Mexico Press.

Cruz, M. (1976). *Yagua days*. New York: Dial.

Greenfield, E. (1976, 1991). *First pink light*. New York: Henry Holt.

Greenfield, E. (1978). *Honey, I love and other poems*. New York: Crowell.

Greenfield, E. (1975). *Me and Neesie*. New York: Harper & Row.

Greenfield, E. (1988). *Nathaniel talking*. New York: Black Butterfly Children's Books.

Hamilton, V. (1974). *M. C. Higgins, the great*. New York: Macmillan.

Johnson, A. (1989). *Tell me a story, Mama*. New York: Orchard Books.

Loh, M. (1991). *Tucking mommy in*. New York: Orchard Books.

Taylor, T. (1969). *The cay*. New York: Avon.

Uchida, Y. (1971). *Journey to Topaz*. New York: Scribner's.

Uchida, Y. (1981). *A jar of dreams*. New York: Atheneum.

Williams, V. (1990). *More, more, more, said the baby*. New York: Greenwillow.

Yep, L. (1975). *Dragonwings*. New York: Harper & Row.

Yep, L. (1977). *Child of the owl*. New York: Harper & Row.

Yep, L. (1979). *Sea glass*. New York: Harper & Row.

Yep, L. (1984). *The serpent's children*. New York: Harper & Row.

Yep, L. (1991a). *The lost garden*. New York: Harper & Row.

Yep, L. (1991b). *Starfisher*. New York: Harper & Row.

V

READING RESEARCH:
IMPLICATIONS FOR
TEACHERS, POLICYMAKERS,
AND PUBLISHERS

14 World Illiteracy

Vincent Greaney
Educational Research Center, St. Patrick's College,Dublin*

At its 1975 meeting in Persepolis, the International Symposium for Literacy (Bataille, 1976) declared literacy a fundamental human right. The important status accorded literacy in the Declaration of Persepolis would have come as a surprise in earlier times. Socrates was not a supporter of reading, contending that it forced a person to follow an argument rather than participate in it. He argued that reliance on writing promoted forgetfulness and the appearance of mastery without substance (Clifford, 1984). Plato observed that the effects of reading, compared to dialogue, were shallow and less enduring. St. Ambrose described reading as the most antisocial behavior yet described by man. In the United States, a preindependence Governor of Virginia remarked (cited in Kozol, 1984), "I thank God that there are no free schools nor printing [in this land]. For learning has brought disobedience, and heresy, and sects into the world and printing hath divulged them. . . . God save us from both" (p. 93). Recently, Frank Smith (1989) has claimed that the concept of literacy has been oversold. He argued that being able to read and write may make people smarter but so does any activity that engages the mind, such as conversation. Furthermore, he argued, achieving literacy does not make anyone a better person.

Ironically, from a historical perspective, the desire to make "better persons" provided a major impetus to the development of widespread literacy. The Reformation with its linking of Biblical reading and living by the Book prompted a mass literacy movement (Ryan, 1982). Subsequently, following the introduction of universal formal education (as early as 1717 in Prussia), the school has taken

---

*Present affiliation: Asia Technical Division, World Bank.

on the role of making people literate. At this point in our history, the ability to read and write has come to be regarded as an essential economic skill, not merely a scholarly attribute. The selection processes used by employers are generally and increasingly based on educational qualifications; those with poor literacy skills have little or no opportunity to acquire the necessary credentials or qualifications. Among developing nations, mass illiteracy has been identified as a serious obstacle to modernization. According to the United Nations (n.d.), illiteracy "affects productivity of workers, hampers the organization of health, sanitation and other public services, complicates the creation of political structures based upon popular consent and in these and other ways, hinders the progress of the individual and the society" (p. 1).

Viewed from an economic perspective, increased levels of literacy within developing countries have been shown to be associated with (a) an increase in worker output, (b) a higher level of life expectancy, and (c) a lower level of fertility (World Bank, 1988). Literacy appears to be a necessary, though not sufficient, condition for economic development. As one commentator (Ryan, 1982) aptly put it, "Literacy is the yeast not the dough of development" (p. 16).

I propose to limit my observations to a number of facets of illiteracy. More specifically, I focus briefly on definitions of literacy, examine the role of the State in promoting literacy, and present international statistics, or more precisely guestimates, of the extent of worldwide illiteracy. I then review some factors associated with illiteracy. Finally, I draw attention to a number of possibilities for tackling the problem.

DEFINITIONS OF LITERACY

Literacy is an elusive concept. A review of definitions over the years suggests that the concept is an ever-expanding moving target. According to Judith Langer (1988), the term literacy is used interchangeably to denote a *skill*, a *state*, and an *action*. Basic word identification and decoding behaviors are examples of *skills* to which the term literacy has been applied. In this instance, the emphasis is on the nature of individual learning and development. Literacy as a *state* of being refers to the knowledge a person has accumulated; it is used as an indicator of achievements or wisdom. From this viewpoint, a literate person is one who is familiar with works of literature and is well read. Literacy *actions* refer to behavior that requires the use of written language. Examples of literacy actions include reading a set of instructions, completing an income tax form, writing a letter, or being able to follow a computer manual.

The broadening of our understanding of the concept of literacy has been reflected in our approaches to assessment. In the United States, for instance, three separate dimensions have been measured in the assessment of the literacy skills of young adults (Kirsch, 1986). The first of these, *prose literacy*, refers to the knowledge and skills needed to understand and use information from texts such as editorials, news stories, and poems. The second dimension, *document literacy*, is concerned with the knowledge and skills required to locate and use information in forms, tables, job applications, and indexes. The third dimension, *quantitative literacy*, relates to a content area that many in the past might consider of little relevance to the development of literacy skills. Quantitative literacy refers to the knowledge and skills needed to apply arithmetic operations to information in printed materials, such as computing a tip or amount of interest.

UNESCO (Morsy, 1987) defines a *functionally illiterate* person as "one who cannot engage in all those activities in which literacy is required for the effective functioning of his group and community and also for enabling him to continue to use reading, writing and calculation for his own and the community's development" (p. 6). Increasingly, it is being accepted that there are no criteria of functional illiteracy that are equally valid for all countries. For instance, a European meeting on illiteracy urged that each government decide its own literacy demands and needs, taking into account the social, educational, and cultural consequences of functional illiteracy (Morsy, 1987). Whereas some governments may be willing to undertake this task, it is reasonable to assume that relatively few of them will be in sympathy with the literacy views of Paulo Freire (1968), the influential Brazilian educator. For Freire, literacy is concerned with equipping people with the necessary skills to enable them to recognize and define social injustice—to read about the world in order to transform it. Obviously, Freire is concerned with much more than reading and writing skills.

ROLE OF THE STATE

Who has the responsibility of making children literate? It is only in comparatively recent times that the State through its educational system has taken on this task. For the Roman father of 2,000 years ago, participation in his son's education came second only to his duty to Rome. Plutarch noted (Mounteer, 1987) that "As soon as the boy showed signs of understanding, his father took him under his own charge and taught him to read" (p. 236). In countries such as Sweden and Scotland, following the Reformation, clergymen played a prominent role in teaching their flocks to read (Johansson, 1981). Within the last 150 years, the Vai, a traditional society in West Africa, have passed on their own writing system from generation to generation without the benefit of a formal educational system (Scribner & Cole, 1981).

It is clearly in the State's self-interest to have a literate population. Through its school system, the State can devise curricula that enable pupils to share common national goals, thereby helping to promote political stability and to build national unity. Napoleon, for instance, never argued that a national curriculum would raise standards in French schools; he saw it as a means of directing political and moral opinion. Some commentators, most notably Illich (1972), have argued that schooling has been used as an instrument of social control. In many countries, the class or basal reader has been used to support the dominant political, religious, and economic values. In the past in the United States, for example, there was virtual unanimity among school textbook authors on the evil results of trade unionism (Elson, 1972). Kaestle (1981) stated that children learning to read and write were "bombarded with messages that were Protestant, nationalist, nativist, racist and vigorously procapitalist" (p. 214).

In the nineteenth century, when Ireland was ruled from London, some of the content of basal readers could hardly be termed politically neutral. (Ireland had been made part of the United Kingdom in 1800. Until late in the first half of the nineteenth century, Irish was the language of the majority of the population.) The following sentence appears in one reader (Commissioners of National Education, 1858): "On the East of Ireland is England, where the Queen lives. Many people who live in Ireland were born in England and we speak the same language and are called one nation" (p. 135).

Following independence in 1921, there was a strong reaction in Ireland to the non-national tone of much of the material in school textbooks. One report (Educational Company, 1921) noted that "the English read in Irish schools should be as far as possible emptied of specifically English thought and culture" (p. 21). In the course of developing a rationale for a distinctly Irish curriculum with a strong emphasis on Irish language and culture, an influential professor of education (Corcoran, 1923) at University College, Dublin, wrote: "Of great dignified national prose writing, Anglo–Irish literature has none to show. In poetry the best is an odd patch of fair, second-rate quality. The cult of such material in Irish educational work would be a real national and linguistic misfortune" (p. 262). It is worth noting that the Anglo–Irish writers of that era featured such "second raters" as James Stephens, John Millington Synge, Sean O'Casey, William Butler Yeats, George Bernard Shaw, Oscar Wilde, and James Joyce. Although English continued to play an important role in the curriculum following Irish independence, the content of basal readers tended to reflect "a simple note of glorification of things Irish" (Coolahan, 1977, p. 22).

In a somewhat similar manner, as countries in Africa achieved independence, the Dick-and-Jane-type stories and European folktales and history used in their schools gave way to some extent to content designed to further the development of African nationalism (Azevedo, 1978–1979; Schmidt, 1985).

The use of textbooks as vehicles for promoting national ideology need not necessarily be confined to class readers or history books. The following problem taken from a Chinese mathematics textbook obviously published before President Nixon's 1972 trip to China shows how pupils were alerted to the decadence of capitalism (Chi Tung-Wei, cited in Swetz, 1978): "In the United States of America, the number of half-starved people is twice the number of unemployed, and is five million less than the number of people who live in slums. As one-half the number of slum dwellers is eleven and a-half million, what is the number of unemployed in the United States" (p. 46).

In the era of glasnost, it came as no surprise to find some educational authorities in the USSR admitting that their school history books served a political purpose. In June 1988, according to Reuters (1989), *Izvestia* denounced those "who deluded generation after generation, poisoning their minds and souls with lies" (p. 11). A Reuters (1989) report stated that high school students in the USSR were given supplements to their history textbooks to allow them to fill in the "blank spots" in their knowledge of history.

Textbook writers universally have tended to attribute god-like qualities to national heroes; far too seldom have these heroes been presented with "warts and all." There is an obvious danger that children fed on a rich diet of nationalistic reading material, especially material of the "drum and trumpet" variety, will have an overdeveloped sense of national pride and a lack of understanding of other nationalities, religions, and political systems. Many may become adults who never outgrow their basic ethnocentrism (Farr, 1985), and many may develop an unhealthy sense of national superiority.

Apart from its role of supporting the acquisition of literacy skills through the provision of schools, the State in many instances has become directly involved in major literacy campaigns. State literacy campaigns appear to have been most successful in countries that have undergone fundamental changes in their social order. Such countries include, most notably, Brazil, Burma, the People's Republic of China, Cuba, Ghana, Somalia, Tanzania, the USSR, and Vietnam. In the USSR, the Soviet Literacy campaign (Ryan, 1985), which commenced in 1919, was faced with a national literacy rate of only 30%, and a widely scattered population who spoke 120 separate languages. A mere 20 years later, 87% of the population was considered literate. The success of this achievement has been attributed to (a) persistence and steadfastness of purpose; (b) effective planning based on a sober evaluation of the difficulties inherent in the exercise, a study of languages, and the preparation of educational materials; (c) provision of schooling for all children; and (d) a political system that created an environment of expectancy and opportunism for all involved in the campaign.

A UNESCO study (Bhola, 1984) of successful national literacy campaigns in the USSR, Vietnam, the People's Republic of China, Cuba, Burma, Brazil, Tanzania, and Somalia concluded that the focusing of national attention on the issue and a strong commitment from national authorities reflected in action, as well as clear goals, were critical factors.

ILLITERACY STATISTICS

Statistics (UNESCO, 1987) related to world illiteracy are complex. This is true for several reasons:

1. As we have noted, different definitions of literacy have been used in different places. These definitions have ranged from the ability to sign a

marriage license to the completion of a level of schooling to performance on objective tests.

2. Procedures for estimating rates of illiteracy vary from nation to nation (UNESCO, 1988). In some countries, estimates have been based on self-assessments during a national census (e.g., United States); other nations have based their estimates on percentage samples of census returns (e.g., China, Guatemala, Korea, Morocco); whereas in others, national authorities have simply provided national estimates (e.g., Brazil, Congo, Equatorial Guinea, Italy, Panama, Philippines, Portugal, Turkey). In countries such as Bermuda and Israel, illiteracy rates are based on the number of persons with no schooling. Other countries exclude segments of their populations in deriving their estimates. For example, Ecuador excludes nomadic Indian tribes, Peru and Venezuela exclude Indian jungle populations, Afghanistan excludes nomads, whereas Puerto Rico excludes members of the armed services.

3. The age used to judge whether people are literate or illiterate varies from nation to nation. Illiteracy estimates for most countries reported by UNESCO (1987, Table 1.3) are based on age 15+. The United States, however, uses the age 14+. A number of countries impose an upper age limit, thereby probably underestimating the extent of adult illiteracy. The former USSR, for example, reported data for the 9 to 49 age group, and Cuba for the 15 to 49 age group. Because illiteracy rates are likely to be higher among the older segments of populations, indices that omit these groups very likely provide underestimations of illiteracy rates.

4. The available evidence suggests that within individual countries, including developed countries, the quality of the available statistical information tends to be poor. For instance, a French governmental investigation concluded that it was not possible to come up with a credible figure of the number of people unable to read or write or who have serious difficulty in making use of these skills, and that the number of persons who were not proficient in reading and writing should be numbered in millions rather than in hundreds of thousands (Esperandieu, Lion, & Benichou, 1984).

Despite the fact that some pupils complete school without learning basic literacy skills, and that a small number relapse into illiteracy after leaving school (Gillette, 1987), school participation rates probably provide one of the more useful international indicators of literacy rates. Let us examine the international data (UNESCO, 1987, Table 2.11) for 1960 and 1985 (see Fig. 14.1). (These statistics do not include data for China and the Democratic Republic of Korea.) In 1960, a total of 62.3% of the 6 to 11 age group in the world was enrolled in school. By 1985, this percentage had increased to 76.8%. There are, however, marked differences in the enrollment data for developed and developing coun-

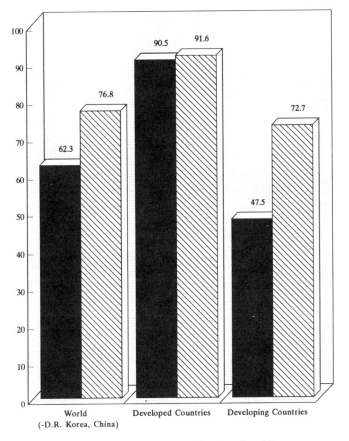

FIG. 14.1. Enrollment ratio: Age 6 to 11.

tries. In developed countries (all European countries, the former USSR, the United States, Canada, Japan, Israel, Australia, New Zealand, and South Africa), the figures were 90.5% for 1960 and 91.6% for 1985. In sharp contrast, fewer than 1 in 2 (47.5%) children in developing countries attended school in 1960. By 1985, there had been a substantial increase to 72.7% in the proportion of 6-to-11-year-olds in these countries who were in school.

Despite this increase, the problems facing the developing countries remain enormous. At the landmark 1990 World Conference on Education for All (WCEFA), it was estimated that there are more than 100 million children, including at least 60 million girls, in developing countries who have no access to primary schooling (WCEFA, 1990). Furthermore, the predicted average annual increase in population in these countries is about three times that of the developed countries (UNESCO, 1987, Table 1.2).

Comparable percentages for Europe (including the former USSR), America, Oceania, Asia, and Africa are depicted in Fig. 14.2. These show that despite a marked improvement over the 25-year period, the percentage of the 6 to 11 age population enrolled in schools is lowest in Asia and Africa.

Published data on school participation rates for various parts of the world

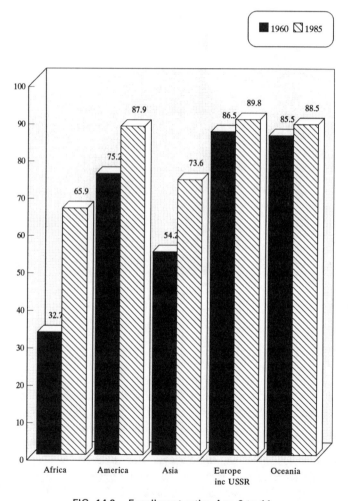

FIG. 14.2.   Enrollment ratio: Age 6 to 11.

indicate that a substantial increase in female rates is required to achieve some measure of social justice. Participation rates for females are almost always considerably lower than those for males (UNESCO, 1987, Table 1.4). In Algeria, for example, the percentage of females over the age of 25 with "no schooling" was well
over 90%; the comparable percentage for males was 71%. Other countries that fall
into the category of having more than 90% of the female population over the age of
25 with "no schooling" include Afghanistan, Egypt, Guatemala, Liberia, Libya,
Morocco, and Pakistan. In each instance, the percentage of males in the no-
schooling category, although still very high, was lower than that for females.

Earlier I noted that the interpretation of data on illiteracy reported by each
nation was a somewhat speculative exercise. Bearing this caveat in mind, let us
direct our attention to the data for the most populous countries for which illiteracy data classified by gender are available (WCEFA, 1990). (Many developed
countries, including the United States, Germany, and the United Kingdom, do
not provide such data.) These data were based on criteria set by the appropriate
national authority. Within this necessarily limited sample of nations, two trends
are apparent. First, illiteracy is more prevalent among females than males (see
Table 14.1). Second, the incidences of illiteracy are more pronounced in Asian
and African countries than in American and European ones.

This latter point is graphically illustrated in Fig. 14.3. The data represented
here summarize the international situation. Even allowing for a possibly sizeable
degree of error in the percentage figures, the international illiteracy data clearly
indicate that by far the greatest number of illiterates reside in Asia. Two Asian
countries alone, China with an estimated 230 million illiterates, and India with
238 million, account for over half the world's estimated illiterates. When populations are taken into account, however, we get a somewhat different picture of
continental differences. Africa (54%) emerges with the highest illiteracy rate and
is followed, in turn, by Asia (36.3%) and Latin America and the Caribbean
(17.3%) (United Nations, n.d.). Overall, the data indicate that the problem is
greatest in the developing countries—countries that have the fewest economic
resources to direct toward the eradication of illiteracy.

FACTORS RELATED TO ILLITERACY

In recent years, research (e.g., Anderson, Hiebert, Scott, & Wilkinson, 1985)
has highlighted the fact that success in reading is dependent on a variety of
factors. Studies have demonstrated the extent to which impoverished home and
environmental circumstances affect the biological, physical, cognitive, emotional, and social development of children (Hamburg, 1988). As we review just a few
of these factors, it should become apparent that, in comparison with their counterparts in the developed world, young children in developing countries are
placed at a considerable disadvantage.

TABLE 14.1
Adult Illiteracy Rate, Age 15+, by Gender

	Pop. (000,000)	Male %	Female %
Asia			
Bangladesh	113	57	78
China	1,122	18	44
India	836	43	71
Indonesia	181	17	35
Pakistan	119	60	81
Europe			
Greece	10	3	12
Italy	57	2	4
Portugal	10	11	20
Spain	39	3	8
Yugoslavia	24	3	14
America			
Argentina	32	4	5
Brazil	147	21	24
Colombia	32	11	13
Mexico	87	8	12
Peru	21	9	22
Africa			
Egypt	51	41	70
Nigeria	105	46	69
Sudan	25	67	86
Tanzania	26	7	12
Zaire	35	21	55

Source: World Conference on Education for All (1990).

Young children brought up in developed countries are much less likely to encounter debilitating or fatal illness than their counterparts elsewhere. Low-income economies (World Bank, 1988) have an infant mortality rate eight times that of the industrial market economies (72 vs. 9 per 1,000, respectively). People brought up in a Western society are likely to be shocked at the realization that in 1980 dehydration caused by diarrhea claimed almost 10,000 young lives every day in the developing countries (Grant, 1989). Whereas the death rate has dropped substantially due to the use of oral rehydration therapy, it still remains a serious problem. In these countries, some 14 million children still die each year from common illnesses and undernutrition, and most of them could be saved by relatively low-cost methods (Grant, 1991). In 1984, low-income countries, apart from China and India, had a physician-unit population ratio of 1:13,910, whereas the healthier industrial market economies had a ratio of 1:470. This ratio is almost 30 times better than that in the poorer countries (World Bank, 1990).

Children in developed countries are more likely to have the educational benefit of supportive parents—parents who first of all, can read and second of all, do read to their young children (Guthrie & Greaney, 1991). They are more likely to be exposed to print both in and out of the home. In contrast, as we have seen, literate parents are the exception rather than the rule in the many developing countries. In many of these countries, the increase in the use of written communication represents a substantial change from the use of oral communication that has been the norm for centuries. In some of these latter countries (e.g., Malaysia, Iran), there is evidence to suggest that parental support for personal reading by a child is lacking (Cheong, 1980; Deckert, 1982). Also, in some African countries, communal life styles frown on solitary behavior such as reading (e.g., Osa, 1986).

Where possible, literacy instruction should be given in the child's first language (Gorman, 1977). It is well nigh impossible, however, to achieve this in many developing countries due to the vast number of languages that exist and also due to national policies of encouraging the development of one official

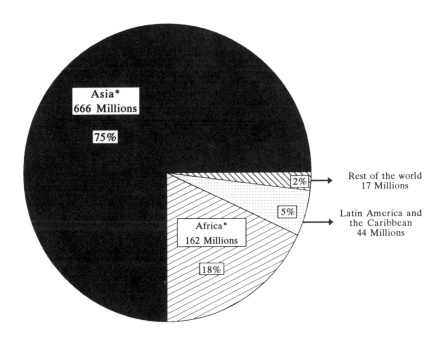

*The Arab States are included in the totals for Asia and Africa

FIG. 14.3.   Illiterates in 1985.

language. Tanzania, for example, has approximately 130 ethnic groups, each with its own language (Clemont & Maimbolwa-Sinyangwe, 1985). Inevitably, given the dearth of resources, it is often not possible to offer instruction in a child's first language. However, Ryan (1982) has emphasized that policy issues over choice of orthography are crucial to the success or failure of literacy campaigns, and some languages used in developing countries do not have alphabets. Furthermore, the 26-letter English alphabet is much easier to master than the minimum of 2,000 characters required to begin to read in Chinese.

The educational disadvantage of children from developing countries does not cease once they begin school. By Western standards, teachers tend to be poorly qualified (Lockheed & Verspoor, 1991). The highest academic "qualification" in some countries, for example, is two years of postprimary school. In 1986, almost half of all primary teachers in Zimbabwe were unqualified (Dorsey, 1989), and in a number of countries, including Kenya (Eshwani, 1985) and Burkina Faso (World Bank, 1988), economic factors have led to recommendations to shorten the preservice training period. Teacher morale is often very low in developing countries (World Bank, 1988). Between 1980 and 1987, whereas primary education personnel in developed countries experienced an average remuneration increase in constant prices of 11%, the corresponding figure for teachers in 56 developing countries was a decrease of 8% (UNESCO, 1990). Some countries, most notably Ghana and Uganda, have witnessed high dropout rates of trained teachers, who had to be replaced by untrained personnel.

School buildings in developing countries tend to be inferior, and expenditures on classroom materials tend to be very low. In 1980, the average expenditure per pupil in industrial market economies was $2,200. Comparative expenditures for East Asia (5 countries) were $190; Latin America (20 countries), $155; and Africa (23 countries), $65 (World Bank, 1988). Currently, per-pupil expenditure in Africa is declining (World Bank, 1988). Heyneman (1984) has calculated that per-pupil expenditure on classroom materials is more than 100 times greater in countries such as Sweden, Norway, Denmark, and Finland than in Bolivia, Malawi, and Indonesia (see Fig. 14.4). He observed that in 1977:

> There were 10 pupils for each available primary school textbook in the Philippines. Thus, pupils in the USA have in the range of 140 times this amount of reading material put at their disposal. In 1979 in Malawi only one pupil in eight had a chair, and only one in 88 had a desk. Primary schools in Malawi—and many other countries are without safety standards. Walls frequently collapse after a rainfall; roofs have holes; wind and storms disrupt classroom activity as a matter of course. The normal classroom is dark and stuffy; students are forced to sit on a bare floor and balance an exercise book on their knees in order to write. (p. 295)

The average expenditure per pupil on books, slates, wall charts, and writing instruments has been estimated at $0.60 for African countries (World Bank, 1988). Furthermore, class sizes tend to be much larger than in developed coun-

FIG. 14.4. Spending on classroom materials and other nonsalary recurrent expenditures per student enrolled in primary school. From Heyneman (1984).

tries. Whereas Australia, for instance, has a pupil–teacher ratio of 18 to 1 at the primary school level (UNESCO, 1987), countries such as Burundi (62), Chad (64), Congo (61), and Mozambique (65) have pupil–teacher ratios of 60 or more to 1 (UNESCO, 1987, Table 3.4).

The lack of appropriate reading materials is a severe stumbling block from the point of view of developing literacy skills in developing countries. Literacy can scarcely be developed and honed in a nonliterate environment. In its recent comprehensive analysis of education in Sub-Saharan Africa, the World Bank (1988) concluded that "the scarcity of learning materials in the classroom is the most serious impediment to educational effectiveness in Africa" (p. 42). The developed world, which has about one quarter of the population of the developing countries, publishes in excess of eight times as many books as do these countries (UNESCO, 1987). Regional data on book production (i.e., of number of titles) and on newsprint consumption are presented in Figs. 14.5 and 14.6. Despite their limitations as indicators, these data strongly suggest that people living in Asia, Africa, and Latin America are much less likely to encounter books or newspapers than those residing in Europe, North America, and Oceania.

The limited figures (UNESCO, 1987) for school textbook production indicate that developing countries have a much lower rate of publication of new titles than do the more developed economies. Furthermore, textbook production in developing countries involves a whole range of problems unlikely to be experienced in the more affluent developed countries. These problems include lack of finance, technology, and raw materials; poor communication; poor distribution and management systems; and storage problems related to unfavorable climatic conditions (tropical humidity).

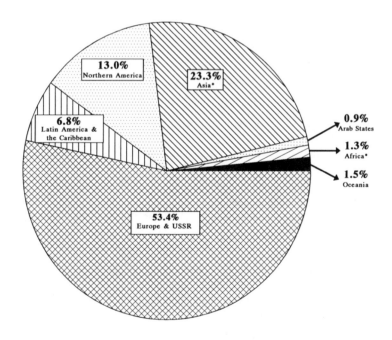

13.0%
Northern America

23.3%
Asia*

6.8%
Latin America &
the Caribbean

0.9%
Arab States

1.3%
Africa*

1.5%
Oceania

53.4%
Europe & USSR

*Excluding Arab States

FIG. 14.5.   Book production in 1985.

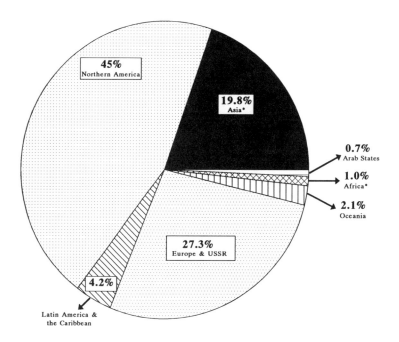

*Excluding Arab States

FIG. 14.6.   Newsprint consumption in 1984.

The importance of an adequate supply of appropriate school textbooks is highlighted by the results of a World Bank program in the Philippines. Over a 5-year period, 97 million secondary school textbooks were produced. This level of production led to the student–textbook ratio being reduced from 10:1 to 2:1. A subsequent study revealed that substantial learning gains were achieved following the program, and that poor students benefitted most from it. It was estimated that the improvement in science scores was equal to twice the impact of reducing class size in North America from 40 to 10 (World Bank, 1987).

Textbooks fill an additional role in developing countries; they enable teachers to overcome uncertainty and to become more confident in their subject areas (Verspoor, 1986). The findings of a study of mathematics textbooks developed for Thailand noted that the books provided teachers with a comprehensive curriculum. The same study concluded that in certain circumstances investment in essential teaching materials such as textbooks may be more effective in improving achievement levels than providing postsecondary education courses for teachers (Lockheed, Vail, & Fuller, 1987).

The results of these two studies suggest that the relationship between the provision of educational materials and student achievement may be quite different in developing than in developed countries. In the United States, for example, these two variables are neither strongly nor systematically related (Hanushek, 1986).

In many countries, the scale of the book-provision problem to be tackled is immense, a point that is graphically borne out by the following Chinese example: When teachers noted that covers were coming off textbooks, it was discovered that the wire staples used to attach the covers were too tight and cut into the 52-gram newsprint used in the books. Correcting the problem would require lengthening the prong of each staple by a mere one millimeter. This seemed to be an obvious solution. However, the additional wire requirement was 4 millimeters for each of the 2.3 billion books for primary and secondary education, an additional requirement of 9,200 kilometers of wire. When higher education titles were added, the total came to 2.7 billion books, which meant an additional 10,800 kilometers of wire was needed (Buchan, personal communication, 1989). In Chinese industrial terms, to produce this amount of wire would require the building of a new factory (Reaching textbook goals, 1987).

All this is not to suggest that illiteracy is confined to the developing countries. A recent report (Chisman, 1989) suggested that in the United States, for instance, as many as 20 to 30 million people "have serious problems with basic skills" (p. iii). In Western societies, increased resources are being spent to tackle the problem of adult illiteracy. I do not wish to focus on this aspect of the illiteracy issue save to mention some of the factors associated with being unable to read. These include specific reading disabilities such as low intelligence, physical handicap, retardation in speech development, and personality, socioenvironmental, and school factors (Malmquist, 1985). In addition, migration to developed countries in search of work has resulted in the creation of large populations of illiterates in many developed countries. To this number we must add the 13.3 million or so refugees reported by the United Nations High Commissioner for Refugees (Cited in Kamm, 1989), some of whom linger in overcrowded camps deprived of many basics, including the opportunity to read.

CAN ANYTHING BE DONE?

At the outset, it is necessary to develop a level of international awareness of the size and dimensions of the illiteracy problem. People need to realize that the figure of 960 million (WCEFA, 1990) represents more than a summary or gross measure of world illiteracy; it represents over one fifth of humankind unable, through no fault of its own, to realize its potential.

International and national efforts are required. International efforts have proved highly successful in the promotion of better health standards, in fighting famine, in lessening global tension, and in limiting the proliferation of nuclear arms. More focused international cooperation is required to tackle the illiteracy problem.

According to a resolution adopted by UNESCO (1978), the struggle against illiteracy is principally a national responsibility. "If it is to be successful, there must be a firm political will exercised with perseverance at the highest level, and all the national resources available must be mobilized" (Document 20 c/71). Given the dearth of resources, declining GNPs, and rising birth rates in many developing countries, the task is enormous. For many, the provision of primary education remains the greatest challenge in the battle against illiteracy.

Apart from highly politicized national campaigns, many of which have achieved notable success, what else can be done? The Philippines experiment highlighted the importance of textbooks. Such books must be of good quality; appropriate in curricula content, language, and design; and affordable. Printing such books in developed countries is hardly an appropriate solution, given delivery and labor costs. Delivery systems must be developed—a complicated task in many regions, especially in rural areas. Teachers have to be educated in the use of new texts.

Consideration might also be given to the possibility of preparing "little books" produced on inexpensive paper. These books, which might consist of no more than 6 to 10 pages stapled together, could be taken home by children and could form the basis of home-literacy activities. Material could be presented in the child's first language. Much of the content of the little books could be made relevant to local circumstances and interests. Little books could be prepared in sites serviced by electricity through the use of desk-top publishing systems. Although the initial investment may appear substantial, the overall cost is likely to be substantially less than that incurred through the use of traditional printing and binding technologies.

In addition to a lack of school-related reading materials, there is a conspicuous shortage of postliteracy materials (e.g., Schmidt, 1985). Having learned to read, many people are being denied the opportunity of reading to learn or of reading for sheer enjoyment. Research has demonstrated that interest plays an important role in developing the reading habit (Guthrie & Greaney, 1991). It would seem not just reasonable but highly desirable to support local publishing efforts to produce material by native authors or at least by authors who have had some immersion in the culture. Children and adults in developing countries should have as much opportunity as their more fortunate counterparts to read about their own cultures, myths, sagas, heroes, and accomplishments.

In the long run, the improvement of literacy rates in developing countries will require substantial investment in terms of school building, teacher training, printing, and publishing and distribution systems. Clearly, many developing countries do not have, or indeed are not likely to have in the near future, the economic freedom to redirect scarce resources to these areas, that is, unless there is a redirection of political priorities. In this respect, it may be noted that a vast amount of scarce resources in developing countries has been directed to the purchase of weapons. The available data for Sub-Saharan African countries, for example, indicate that the level of expenditure on defense exceeds that for health (World Bank, 1988). Virtually all the weapons imported by developing countries come from developed countries. Developed countries have been estimated to account for 97% of major weapons exports (Crow, Thomas, Jenkins, & Kimble, 1986). Within the last decade six countries alone accounted for over 90% of international arms sales. Led by the United States, they are the former USSR, France, Italy, Britain, and West Germany. Ironically and sadly, most of the 65 major wars (those with 1,000 or more deaths) fought between 1960 and 1982 were fought, not in the developed countries but in the less developed ones, presumably with weapons purchased from developed countries.

In 1989, the United States Air Force calculated that each of the 132 B-2 Stealth bombers it wanted would cost more than $530 million (Van Voorst, 1989). A comparison of the price of one of these planes to the amount spent annually on education in individual African countries with populations of at least 1 million (UNESCO, 1988) clearly indicates that considerably less is spent on education in most of these countries than the cost of one of these bombers. In 1986, for instance, Ethiopia, with an estimated population of 44.93 million, spent a total of $184 million on current educational expenditure. With these figures in mind, it is salutary to reflect on the following words (cited in Goodman, 1982): "Every gun made, every warship launched, every rocket fired signifies, in the final sense, a theft from those who hunger and are not fed, those who are cold and are not clothed. This world in arms is not spending money alone. It is spending the sweat of its laborers, the genius of its scientists, the hopes of its children" (p. 4).

The author of this statement is not a spokesman for an antiwar movement nor a left-wing radical. It is, in fact, former United States President and General of the Army, Dwight Eisenhower.

The economic plight facing developing countries provides both a challenge and an opportunity for voluntary organizations, companies, and individuals to make a contribution to the literacy effort. In particular, international educational organizations such as the International Reading Association could provide leadership in this area. The association, along with others, has considerable experience in the area of teacher education. The need for inservice teacher training in many developing countries scarcely needs to be emphasized. The following excerpt taken from Jean Osborn's (1989) detailed description of her visits to a series of schools in Sierra Leone could well be applied to schools in many developing countries: "At least half of the teachers are either unqualified or underqualified . . . By about second grade, [they] teach only in English. Most [teachers] don't speak much English themselves" (p. 25).

On the topic of reading instruction, Osborn noted:

The teacher puts the alphabet or words on the board in the classroom for younger children. One child comes to the board, reads series of letters or a word, the other students then read. Of course the other students can be looking at the ceiling and still say the letters or words. Book reading in the upper grades is the same. Because one reader (and there are no other reading books in the classrooms) is shared by five or six children, the procedure is for each bench load of kids to be put in charge of one child, who is always the best reader. The reading lesson consists of having this child read a sentence, then all the other children in the group read the same sentence. It was evident that this practice develops very good oral statement repetition skills, but for most of the children—since they don't even look at the text as they are repeating the sentence—it doesn't do much for their reading skills. (p. 25)

Osborn concluded "here is a situation, given the terribly limited circumstances, where schooling should not be held up as a promise of a better life for everybody" (p. 25).

Efforts to bring about improvement in teacher education through inservice should be grounded in reality and be sensitive to the level of development of the targeted educational systems. They should also recognize the low level of teacher qualification found in many countries. The process of identifying teacher inservice needs is crucial. It would be rather arrogant and, in the long run, probably ineffective for outside experts to give a series of workshops or lectures based on their analysis of the situation. Inservice volunteers should address the expressed needs of those involved in teaching reading, through offering support in those areas where local teacher educators perceive they are most in need of help. Members who are invited to participate in this form of international inservice training would be expected to familiarize themselves with the curricular goals and also with the local reading materials before travelling.

The International Reading Association could use its vast network of national, state, and provincial organizations to supply appropriate supplementary reading material to schools and local libraries where they exist. A twinning arrangement between a national affiliate, or a province or state association, and a small developing country could provide a vital sense of personal contact between the partners.

Computer companies could be encouraged to donate personal computers with desk-top publishing capabilities.

Publishing companies might be asked to support local writers and to provide expertise in book production and distribution. Suitable existing stock due to be remaindered might be shipped to needy libraries. Other forms of book donor schemes might be undertaken as long as associated expenses including shipping, local transport, and storage were less than the value of the needed donated materials.

Individuals might be approached to support literacy efforts either through direct financial aid or through donating needed materials for reading and writing.

Retiring university personnel, for example, might welcome the opportunity to donate their academic books and journals to the chronically underequipped college libraries in developing countries.

Each of us has the potential to contribute to the worldwide effort to eradicate illiteracy. The effort will require changing our perspective from one concerned with narrow personal, professional, or national interests to a broader international caring perspective. In the past, literacy was the privilege of an elite minority. As beneficiaries of efforts by earlier generations to extend literacy to the masses, surely there is an obligation on us to continue the battle against illiteracy. That is the challenge. Future generations will judge our response.

ACKNOWLEDGMENTS

I am indebted to Grant Cioffi, University of New Hampshire, Durham, and Thomas Kellaghan, Educational Research Centre, St. Patrick's College, Dublin, for their comments.

REFERENCES

Anderson, R. C., Hiebert, E. H., Scott, J. A., & Wilkinson, I. A. G. (1985). *Becoming a nation of readers: The report of the Commission on Reading*. Champaign, IL: Center for the Study of Reading; Washington, DC: National Institute of Education.

Azevedo, M. J. (1978–1979). The legacy of colonial education in Mozambique. *A Current Bibliography on African Affairs, 11*, 3–16.

Bataille, L. (1976). A turning point for literacy. *Proceedings of the International Symposium for Literacy, Persepolis, Iran*. Oxford: Pergamon.

Bhola, H. S. (1984). *Campaigning for literacy*. Paris: UNESCO.

Cheong, C. S. (1980). *The roles of the home and the school in motivating secondary school students to read*. Paper presented at the eighth World Congress on Reading, Manila.

Chisman, F. P. (1989). *Jump start: The federal role in adult literacy*. Southport, CT: Southport Institute for Policy Analysis.

Clemont, C. M., & Maimbolwa-Sinyangwe, I. (1985). Tanzania: System of education. In T. Husen & T. N. Postlethwaite (Eds.), *International encyclopedia of education* (pp. 4987–4992). Oxford: Pergamon.

Clifford, G. J. (1984). Buch und lesen: Historical perspectives on literacy and schooling. *Review of Educational Research, 54*, 472–500.

Commissioners of National Education. (1858). *Second book of lessons*. Dublin: Author.

Coolahan, J. (1977). Three eras of English reading in Irish national schools. In V. Greaney (Ed.), *Studies in reading* (pp. 12–21). Dublin: Educational Company.

Crow, B., Thomas, A., Jenkins, R., & Kimble, J. (1986). *Third World atlas*. Milton Keynes: Open University.

Corcoran, T. (1923). Education through Anglo–Irish literature. *Irish Monthly, 51*, 242.

Deckert, G. D. (1982). Socio-cultural barriers to the reading habit: The case of Iran. *Journal of Reading, 25*, 742–749.

Dorsey, B. (1989). Educational development and reform in Zimbabwe. *Comparative Education Review, 33,* 40–58.

Educational Company. (1921). *Rough draft of Report of National Programme Conference.* Dublin: Author.

Elson, R. M. (1972). *Guardians of tradition: American schoolbooks in the nineteenth century.* Lincoln: University of Nebraska Press.

Eshwani, G. S. (1985). Kenya: System of education. In T. Husen & T. N. Postlethwaite (Eds.), *International encyclopedia of education* (pp. 2803–2810). Oxford: Pergamon.

Esperandieu, V., Lion, A., & Benichou, J. P. (1984). *Des illettres en France.* Paris: La Documentation Francaise.

Farr, R. M. (1985). Social worlds of childhood. In V. Greaney (Ed.), *Children: Needs and rights* (pp. 21–41). New York: Irvington.

Freire, P. (1968). *Pedagogy of the oppressed.* New York: Herder & Herder.

Gillette, A. (1987). Illiteracy in the industrialized nations: Five countries through six books. *Prospects, 17,* 101–109.

Goodman, K. S. (1982). *Celebrate literacy.* Newark, DE: International Reading Association.

Gorman, T. P. (1977). Literacy in the mother tongue: A reappraisal of research and practice. In T. P. Gorman (Ed.), *Language and literacy: Current issues and research* (pp. 271–301). Tehran: International Institute for Adult Literacy Methods.

Grant, J. P. (1989). *The state of the world's children, 1989.* New York: Oxford University Press.

Grant, J. P. (1991). *The state of the world's children, 1991.* New York: Oxford University Press.

Guthrie, J. T., & Greaney, V. (1991). Literacy acts. In R. Barr, M. L. Kamil, P. Mosenthal, & P. D. Pearson (Eds.), *Handbook of reading research* (Vol. 2, pp. 68–96). New York: Longman.

Hanushek, E. A. (1986). The economics of schooling: Production and efficiency in public schools. *Journal of Economic Literature, 24,* 1141–1177.

Hamburg, D. A. (1988). *Fundamental building blocks of early life. Carnegie Corporation of New York: Annual Report, 1987.* New York: Carnegie Corporation.

Heyneman, S. P. (1984). Research on education in developing countries. *International Journal of Educational Development, 4,* 293–304.

Illich, I. (1972). *Deschooling society.* New York: Harper & Row.

Johansson, E. (1981). The history of literacy in Sweden. In H. J. Graff (Ed.), *Literacy and social development in the West* (pp. 151–182). Cambridge: Cambridge University Press.

Kaestle, C. F. (1981). Literacy and mainstream culture in American history. *Language Arts, 5,* 207–218.

Kamm, H. (1989, March 27). Western nations raising barriers to refugees trying to flee poverty. *New York Times,* A1, A13.

Kirsch, I. (1986). *Literacy: Profiles of America's young adults.* Princeton: National Assessment of Educational Progress at Educational Testing Service.

Kozol, J. (1984). *Illiterate America.* New York: Anchor/Doubleday.

Langer, J. A. (1988). The state of research on literacy. *Educational Researcher, 17,* 42–46.

Lockheed, M. E., Vail, S. C., & Fuller, B. (1987). *How textbooks affect achievement. Report No. EDT53.* Washington, DC: World Bank.

Lockheed, M. E., & Verspoor, A. M. (1991). *Improving primary education in developing countries.* Washington, DC: World Bank.

Malmquist, E. (1985). The child and the right to read: Problems in attaining universal literacy. In V. Greaney (Ed.), *Children: Needs and rights* (pp. 153–166). New York: Irvington.

Morsy, Z. (1987). Landmarks. *Prospects, 18,* 5–15.

Mounteer, C. A. (1987). Roman childhood, 200 BC to AD 600. *Journal of Psychohistory, 14,* 233–254.

Osa, O. (1986). The young Nigerian youth literature. *Journal of Reading, 30,* 100–104.

Osborn, J. (1989). *African trip.* Unpublished manuscript.

Reaching textbook goals. (1987). *World Bank Educational News, 1,* 1–3, 8.

Reuters. (1989, February 12). Final exams are back in USSR schools. *Boston Globe,* p. 11.

Ryan, J. W. (1982). *Policies for literacy and numeracy.* Unpublished manuscript. Paris: UNESCO.

Ryan, J. W. (1985). Literacy and numeracy: Policies. In T. Husen & T. N. Postlethwaite (Eds.), *International encyclopedia of education* (pp. 3102–3109). Oxford: Pergamon.

Schmidt, N. J. (1985). *Children's books in Sub-Saharan Africa.* Bloomington: African Studies Program, Indiana University.

Scribner, S., & Cole, M. (1981). *The psychology of literacy.* Cambridge, MA: Harvard University Press.

Smith, F. (1989). Overselling literacy. *Phi Delta Kappan, 70,* 352–359.

Swetz, F. J. (Ed.). (1978). *Socialist mathematics education.* Southampton, PA: Burgundy Press.

UNESCO. (1978). *Resolution 1/6.1/2 of the General Conference. Document 20 C/71.* Paris: Author.

UNESCO. (1987). *Statistical yearbook, 1987.* Paris: Author.

UNESCO. (1988). *Statistical yearbook, 1988.* Paris: Author.

UNESCO. (1990). *Basic education and literacy: World statistical indicators.* Paris: Author.

United Nations. (n.d.) *United Nations proclaims 1990 International Literacy Year.* New York: Author.

Van Voorst, B. (1989, July 31). The stealth takes wing. *Time,* 45.

Verspoor, A. M. (1986). *Textbooks as instruments for the improvement of the quality of education. Report No. EDT50.* Washington, DC: World Bank.

World Bank. (1987). *World development report, 1987.* New York: Oxford University Press.

World Bank. (1988). *Education in Sub-Saharan Africa.* Washington, DC: Author.

World Bank. (1990). *World development report, 1990.* New York: Oxford University Press.

World Conference on Education for All. (1990). *Meeting basic learning needs: A vision for the 1990s.* New York: Inter-Agency Commission.

15 Resistance, Complacency, and Reform in Reading Assessment

P. David Pearson
Anne C. Stallman
Center for the Study of Reading

Assessment figures prominently at all levels of the education system, from the individual student in the classroom to the policy maker in the statehouse. In this chapter, we first characterize the current realities of reading assessment and then explain how these realities evolved. Finally, we offer suggestions for reading educators to consider as they come to grips with assessment's role in shaping the range of students' activities, the quality of teachers' instructional decisions, and the nature of school curricula.

THE CURRENT REALITIES OF ASSESSMENT

Despite the recent and well-publicized calls for performance-based assessment (Wiggins, 1991), standardized, commercially produced paper-and-pencil tests remain the most prevalent form of assessment in the United States. Continuing a tradition that dates to the 1920s, these tests rely almost exclusively on multiple-choice, single-correct-answer formats. They may also contain relatively short, information-laden, story snippets—often about an obscure topic—which are followed by a set of questions requiring students to draw inferences from the most obscure facts in the stories. Such tests pervade the education system: Basal reading program tests tend to be closely modeled on them (although recent editions show some evidence of change), and even in kindergarten testing, multiple-choice items predominate (Stallman & Pearson, 1990). If one considers the various forms of formal and informal tests that a student is likely to encounter from kindergarten through high school, it is well within the realm of possibility that he will complete over 20,000 test items in a school career, or an average of about 46 items per week.

Standardized testing maintains its prominent position in the nation's schools because of both economic and political reasons. For example, as Americans we want our children to receive the best education possible, but we also want to get the most from the education dollars we spend. As a result, we have developed an "accountability mentality" for evaluating the education system, and opinion polls indicate consistently that the general public believes that standardized test scores are the best indicators of the quality of education that children are receiving (Elam, 1990; Elam & Gallup, 1989). The economic force exerted by these scores is evident by uses made of them. In some areas, for example, newspapers publish schools' test scores. Realtors then may quote the scores to prospective property buyers as part of their sales pitch, and, as a result, property values rise and fall according to the quality of the schools—as indexed by test scores (Pearson et al., 1990).

Test scores can take on a political edge when state legislators cite them as the criteria for deciding how special funds will be allocated to schools and school districts.

These economic and political dimensions of testing have serious curricular consequences, causing some educators to assign ever-increasing importance to testing. Some educators make curricular and instructional decisions for the *sole* purpose of improving test scores. Consequently, there is a growing body of evidence that, in many cases, assessment is affecting instruction, both directly and indirectly.

Assessment *directly* affects instruction when educators change their instructional practices for the explicit purpose of improving test scores. The most common example of this is when teachers and students take time from regular instruction to prepare for a particular test. This practice has been well documented in states such as Florida, Texas, and North Carolina, where a great deal of emphasis is placed on assessment, and it continues, not because it produces better educated students, but because it produces higher test scores. This begins the game that we call "high-stakes assessment." Schools with higher test scores gain prestige over those schools with lower scores; instructional programs that demonstrate greater gains are more likely to receive increased financial support; students with higher scores on tests such as the SAT get into better colleges. And so tests and test scores have immediate and direct consequences for the entire education community—districts, schools, teachers, and students.

Assessment *indirectly* affects instruction in a variety of ways. For example, a district may decide to adopt a particular basal reading program on the belief that the new program will somehow raise students' reading test scores. A school may shift the focus of its curriculum to align it more closely with what is covered on tests. These effects stem from the faith that school boards, administrators, and teachers put in test makers. They believe that test makers have some special knowledge of what needs to be taught, and that the tests they create reflect that knowledge. This belief is reinforced by education publishers, who market a particular program by stressing the close ties between its content and what is tested on the most widely used tests. A corollary of this belief in test makers is that if they do not include something on their tests, it must not be important and therefore should not be taught. And so tests have indirect effects on curricula— on both what is and is not taught.

In response to this situation, some educators have argued that because assessment appears to drive instruction, tests should be changed so that, when teachers do teach to them, they will be teaching students the kinds of skills and knowledge that really matter (e.g., Resnick & Resnick, 1990; Wiggins, 1991). Proponents of this argument often call for the use of performance-based forms of assessment in place of standardized tests.

Advocates of standardized tests counter by arguing that performance-based assessment is simply too expensive for education systems that suffer chronically from a lack of financial support. They further argue that standardized tests have many strengths. Unlike time-consuming alternative assessments, they argue, standardized tests are efficient and take very little time away from instruction. They also maintain that standardized tests are fairer than performance-based assessments because they are more objective, free from the biases of any individual, and culturally neutral. Their use, proponents maintain, ensures that everyone will have the same chance for success; that is, the tests provide a "level playing field" for everyone, regardless of income, cultural background, or educational experience.

Thus although standardized tests have been the target of much criticism in the past decade, they nonetheless continue to exert considerable influence.

THE EVOLUTION OF ASSESSMENT

To understand current assessment practices, it is necessary to look to their beginnings in the early years of this century. Edward L. Thorndike's handwriting scale, published around 1914, is considered to be the first standardized test, and it set the stage for the kind of assessment that flourished in the years following. In creating his scale, Thorndike measured the performance on handwriting tasks of thousands of students. He then used their performance scores to establish norms (average levels of performance) for students of various ages. These norms became standards that teachers could use to evaluate the progress of their own students. Our current notion of a "norm-referenced" test stems from these early efforts by Thorndike and others to establish educational standards with reference to the average levels of performance of normal populations of students.

Several factors contributed to a favorable environment for the growth and popularity of the standardized testing movement: the beginning of World War I, the introduction of compulsory education, the growth of the civil service system, and the rise of scientific objectivity as a driving force in the social sciences.

World War I's contribution to the movement came about because of the perceived complexities of "modern warfare." It was deemed important to find ways to determine which recruits had the skills to cope with these complexities. Not surprisingly, norm-referenced, multiple-choice tests of reading and writing skills were adopted as economical and efficient screening mechanisms.

The spread of compulsory education created the need for ways to gather objective evidence to determine which students should be advanced to the next grade and who would get into or out of certain institutions or programs—what is now called gatekeeping. One of the earlier examples of this gatekeeping function occurred with our youngest children. Reading readiness tests were developed in the 1920s in response to educators' concerns about children who were unsuccessful in first grade, usually because they lacked "prereading" skills. Readiness tests were used to determine which children could and should receive regular reading instruction. For those children who were not ready, the tests also served a diagnostic function—to pinpoint the specific skills these children lacked so that teachers could provide appropriate instruction (Stallman & Pearson, 1990).

The most important spur to the standardized testing movement came not from educators, however, but from bureaucrats in charge of the new civil service systems run by federal, state, and local governments. Reform-minded civil service bureaucrats sought ways to determine a worker's capabilities without relying on the interviews and work samples that had been used for years as thinly disguised tools for denying jobs to members of certain racial and ethnic groups. In standardized tests, these bureaucrats found the objectivity and neutrality they were seeking; they had a tool, they thought, that was color blind, culture free, and fair to everyone seeking employment.

The appeal of "objective" testing also reflected the growing influence of the scientific objectivity movement. Because standardized tests were supposed to be based on scientific principles, they were considered free of bias and, as such, inherently fairer to everyone. In short, they were regarded as reliable instruments that could be counted on to yield consistent, objective results over repeated administrations and in a variety of contexts. Although all these factors helped to create a favorable environment for the development of standardized testing, it was a technological innovation that secured its place in American life—the invention of the IBM 805 scanner in 1934. This device cut the cost of scoring tests to one tenth of what it had been and increased the appeal of their use dramatically. Now, not only were the tests objective, they were efficient to administer and score (Pearson & Dunning, 1985; Resnick, 1982).

The 1960s saw two watershed developments in standardized testing. The first of these developments grew out of the passage of the Elementary and Secondary Education Act of 1965, which provided for Title I, now Chapter 1, programs. The reauthorization of this act in the late 1960s contained an important provision:

States had to agree to be accountable for how well the allocated federal funds were spent. By agreeing to test the progress of Chapter 1 students, a major precedent was set. In effect, educators implicitly accepted the premise that student improvement—measured by standardized tests—was the natural outcome of compensatory education. That premise now applies not only to compensatory education but to education in general.

The second watershed development came in the late 1960s, when instruction was linked to assessment in another significant way. Prompted by the egalitarian appeal of concepts such as mastery learning (Bloom, 1968; Carroll, 1963), a whole new approach to assessment was developed (Pearson & Dunning, 1985). Instead of holding instruction constant—by teaching all students in the same way—and allowing achievement to vary, proponents of mastery learning advised teachers to hold achievement constant and allow instruction to vary on a number of dimensions: (a) student time on task (how long students take to achieve mastery), (b) teacher time on task (how much extra instruction teachers provided), and (c) skill prerequisites.

The idea that achievement should be held constant was inconsistent with the philosophy behind norm-referenced tests, which reference achievement to a relative standard (the mean of the distribution) rather than some absolute criterion of achievement. One outgrowth of the mastery learning movement was the development of criterion-referenced tests, which were designed to hold achievement constant by requiring students to achieve a prespecified absolute level of mastery (usually 80% correct) on some target behavior. The mastery notion has had a significant and long-lasting, if unintended, influence on reading assessment. When mastery learning ideas were introduced into the reading field during the 1960s, task-analytic traditions dominated instructional design (e.g., Gagné). Applied to reading, this suggested that the complex task of reading be broken down into component parts so that students could deal with each component separately. Thus, the notion of mastery learning was applied not to *reading itself* as a real-world process but to the *component parts* of reading. Students were tested on their mastery of the subskills of reading such as consonant blends, vowel digraphs, sequencing, and locating the main idea. This led to the powerful assessment practice of skills-management systems. First promoted as free-standing entities, such as the Wisconsin Design, these systems soon became infused into basal reading programs.

In fairness, it must be noted that nothing in Carroll or Bloom's conceptualizations of school learning dictated that mastery notions had to be applied in this way; the notion of mastery could just as easily have been applied to reading as a process. However, the instructional paradigm of the time mandated that the notion of mastery had to be applied at the subskill level. The decision to do so had an incredible impact on the development of reading curriculum and assessment materials during the next two decades.

The most recent important development in standardized testing came in the early 1980s—the development of what is now called outcomes-based education. The basic idea behind outcomes-based education is that schools ought to be willing to hold themselves accountable to specific performance objectives, such as "the mean score of students in District X on Test Y will equal or exceed the 60th percentile." This represents a very different linkage between assessment and instruction than the linkage that stemmed from mastery learning. In the skills management systems that emerged from mastery learning in the late 1960s, assessment and instruction were linked at the level of subskills; within the framework of outcomes-based education, this link was made at a more global level. Spurred by the call to action made by *A Nation at Risk,* and by the apparent success of the outcomes-based programs adopted by states such as Florida, Texas, South Carolina, and Maryland (Popham, Cruse, Rankin, Sandifer, & Williams, 1985), many concluded that teaching to the test was not such a bad practice. If the test scores in a state could be increased significantly by familiarizing teachers with the specifics of what was to be tested, it seemed reasonable to have them teaching to tests that covered what children needed to know.

During the last few years, however, educators have come to realize that teaching to these tests often has the effect of narrowing the curriculum to those outcomes that are easily measurable (Shepard & Dougherty, 1991). Koretz, Linn, Dunbar, and Shepard (1991) have dramatically illustrated this phenomenon. They have worked with a large school district that has assumed a high-stakes assessment profile. Scores there are a matter of public record, and there are consequences for low scores. In 1986, the district used Standardized Test A. In 1987, when it switched to Standardized Test B, average scores, using the norms provided by the new tests, dropped over a half grade level in comparison to the previous year. But then an interesting development occurred. In each year from 1987 to 1990, the average scores, computed at the school level, rose substantially. By 1990, for example, scores for the district's third graders were almost a grade (in grade-norm units) higher than they were in 1987, the first year of the new test. In 1990, the district gave a second test: the old Standardized Test A. Scores on this test were half a grade lower than on the 1990 Test B. (However, this is not really a fair comparison because of the differences in norming populations between Tests A and B.) The 1990 Test A scores were also compared to the 1986 Test A scores. The 1990 scores had dropped a full grade level. These findings strongly suggest that the improved scores on Standardized Test B between 1987 and 1990 were due to teaching to the test.

The researchers made one other comparison. In 1990, they gave alternative tests in both math and reading. The items on the alternative tests were more like everyday classroom assignments (e.g., solving math problems, writing in response to reading, responding to items with multiple correct answers). They also gave these alternative tests, along with Standardized Test B, in a district that, although demographically similar to the first test district, did not assume a high-stakes profile. They compared the performance between these districts on both types of tests. They found that students in the first district performed just as well as those in the second district on the standardized tests but scored consistently below them on the alternative assessments. Again, a conclusion that is hard to avoid is that teaching to the test narrows the curriculum.

NEXT STEPS

Given the current realities of assessment and the historical forces that have brought us to those realities, we see three possible approaches to shaping the future of reading assessment. First, educators and researchers can oppose formal assessments altogether and return to the subjective tradition of a century ago; an approach we characterize as *resistance*. Second, they can learn to live within the parameters of the current situation; an approach we label *complacency*. Or, third, they can try to improve assessment by changing the system from within; an approach we call *reform*. We consider the rationale for, the feasibility of, and the possible consequences of each of these approaches.

Resistance.   There are many powerful arguments for resisting the use of formal assessments as we presently know them—that is, standardized tests. The major argument in favor of resistance is one we described earlier: Teaching to the test has the effect of narrowing the curriculum.

A second argument for resistance is that, when educators use tests to shape instruction, they essentially invalidate test results. Most standardized tests attempt to generalize beyond the sample of items actually found on the test and are predicated on the assumption that educators will *not* teach to them. Classroom realities, however, all too often reveal this to be a false assumption. Imagine, for example, that the test to be given to your class has 40 vocabulary items. Suppose that a worksheet suddenly appears in your mailbox with vocabulary exercises that allow your students to practice those 40 words—and that the mean vocabulary score subsequently jumps from the 47th to the 75th percentile. Do these results lead to the conclusion that your students have a much richer knowledge of vocabulary than they had earlier? Of course not. The students' scores have risen, not because their vocabularies have been developed, but because they have inside information about the test.

A third argument for opposing formal assessments rests on criticism of what the current tests are testing and how they are doing it. Over the past 30 years, there have been many changes in the way in which reading is conceptualized and defined; standardized tests, however, have remained relatively impervious to these new concepts and definitions. Reading is now generally thought of as an interactive process in which the reader uses available resources such as background knowledge, the text, and the context of the situation to construct meaning. Standardized tests, however, continue to be based on the notion that reading is an aggregation of subskills. This mismatch has spawned several criticisms of standardized tests:

1. Standardized tests measure something by using short passages and multiple-choice formats, but what they measure is not what most people now understand reading to entail. Reading is a generative process; moment by moment, readers build and rebuild models of meaning with the thoughts, ideas, and images that come to them. Filling in bubbles on a scannable answer sheet does not capture the dynamic quality of this process.

2. By using so many different short passages, standardized tests mask the inherent, and important, relationship between background knowledge and comprehension. The practice of using short passages more or less guarantees that students with good general verbal ability will do best on standardized tests. Again, test designers need to acknowledge that reading ability is a dynamic, not a static or a general, phenomenon. Different variables, such as student interest and background knowledge, will differentially affect a student's performance.

3. Standardized tests do not contain enough inferential and critical reading items. As a consequence, they provide only a partial picture of what students can do in response to reading passages. Furthermore, as we have already noted, teaching to such trivializing tests will result in simplistic and narrowly focused curricula.

4. Although standardized tests were frequently touted as culturally neutral, contemporary evaluation of these tests has revealed how they are biased against racial and linguistic minorities. Even if the more obvious forms of cultural bias, such as topic selections and ethnic representations, are discounted, these tests are biased in other ways. For example, the performance of Latino students, even those who speak English relatively well, suffers on these tests because of the extra language processing that these students must engage in when reading English. The precise time limits of standardized tests disadvantage them. When given tests in an untimed context, however, their performance increases substantially (Garcia, 1991).

5. The curriculum-narrowing effect of standardized tests is exacerbated for racial and linguistic minorities. Dorr-Bremme and Herman (1986), for example, found that the curriculum of low-income students was influenced by commercial tests to a much greater degree than was true for more affluent children. Low-income students are more likely to be in programs funded by federal entitlement funds, for which commercial assessment is mandatory. Teachers and administrators responsible for these programs understandably want their students to demonstrate progress. However,

because progress is often defined in terms of students' performance on tests of subskills, low-income students are likely to spend their time and energy practicing such skills in the mistaken belief that this will lead them to score higher on the tests (see Garcia & Pearson, 1991).

Taken together, these arguments provide strong evidence that formal assessment as we know it should be eliminated. Before this can be accomplished, however, the demand for accountability means that some other system for evaluating educational practice acceptable to the public must be found. This new system must assure the public that their children are getting a good education and that the money being spent on education is being used effectively. Any new system of accountability must also address the public's concern about fairness and objectivity. We believe that these concerns and demands make it difficult to imagine the complete elimination of standardized testing in the immediate future. The continuing reliance on tests leads us, in turn, to consider the two other approaches to assessment.

Complacency.   The second approach to assessment in the future is complacency. This approach is predicated on the belief that because educators cannot change the political climate and eliminate formal assessments, they should just learn to live with them. Some advocates of this approach argue, in fact, that teaching to tests is not so bad because it forces educators and the educational system to be accountable, even if it does so imperfectly.

Complacency is, probably by default, the approach taken by most educators today. Their reasons for doing so are many and varied. Tests do have political value and they have society's general approval. Parents argue that because they had to take tests their children should have to too, and many educators and politicians view them as an indispensable tool in evaluating program effectiveness.

The net result is a strong rationale for maintaining the status quo. However, there are those who believe that changes need to be made if the present system is to remain credible and that working toward change is a worthwhile enterprise.

Reform.   Reformers acknowledge that formal assessment is deeply entrenched in the American educational system. They believe, however, that changes in test design and in how test results are interpreted and used will make the assessment situation more acceptable.

One means of reforming assessment is to make sure that tests cover what is essential for students to know and be able to do. Some states have adopted this approach with their state reading assessments. Illinois, Michigan, Maryland, Wisconsin, and California, for example, have designed assessments on the assumption that a well-designed test can have a positive influence on school curricula. The basic idea is that if the tests cover what really matters, then teaching to the tests might actually be beneficial. An example of these reforms comes from Illinois, where the state reading assessment developed in the late 1980s was based on the premise that reading is an integrated, constructive, empowering, and meaning-based process. Those of us who helped develop the Illinois assessment anticipated that, if schools developed reading programs in which students spent a lot of time reading, writing, thinking, and evaluating, the students would do just fine on the state tests. Our hopes were borne out; indeed, many districts in Illinois have used the state assessment to convince local educational policy makers of the need to revise school curricula.

In other instances, horror stories testify to the fact that the classroom implementation of reform ideas can be undermined and perverted, either intentionally or unintentionally. As part of the statewide assessment of reading in Illinois, for example, we attempted to measure students' knowledge of the topics of the passages they read as a way to explain their resulting comprehension scores. Had educators responded to this feature of the assessment by developing a range of activities to help students see the connection between what they know and what they read, the outcome would have been positive and appropriate. However, in some school districts, educators prepared students for this part of the assessment by requiring them to complete prior-knowledge worksheets for *every* story they read in their basal reading program. In these districts, what we witnessed was an impulsive response to a surface feature of the test rather than a thoughtful response to the principles on which the test was built.

In addition, we used a structural device, the story map, to develop questions that gave students opportunities to exhibit an integrated understanding of a passage. Under the apparent assumption that if story maps are good for test writers they must also be good for students, educators in some districts required students to write story map summaries of every story they read.

Stories such as these underscore the fact that simply changing tests is, at best, only a partial solution to the current assessment problems. It may be in the nature of such high-stakes assessment that educators will feel pressured to ensure good student performance on the tests and respond to that pressure by overreacting to surface features of the assessment processes rather than their underlying principles.

In recent years, there have been numerous calls for alternative forms of assessment to realign the links between instruction and assessment (Valencia, 1990). Whether they use terms such as informal assessment, portfolio assessment, performance-based assessment, teacher-developed assessment, or student self-assessment, these calls for more authentic forms of assessment have in common a healthy distaste for standardized tests and a conviction that if truly liberating standards of performance—and tests to go with them—can be developed, liberating curricula will follow.

Proponents of authentic assessment argue that the real purpose of classroom assessment is to help teachers make informed instructional decisions (Wixson, 1991) and to inform both teachers and students about achievement and progress in school (Tierney, Carter, & Desai, 1991). Arguments for authentic assessment have at their center the beliefs that if assessments are to be meaningful and useful (a) they must reflect current knowledge about the dynamics of reading; (b) they should yield information about performance on real, not contrived tasks; (c) they should be a natural part of classroom activity, not an intrusion on it; and (d) they should be viewed as beneficial to both teachers and students as they assume joint responsibility for the educational process (Au, Scheu, & Kawakami, 1990; Lipson, 1990; Peters, 1991; Tierney et al., 1991).

Two current assessment efforts typify this version of reform. The New Standards Project (Resnick & Resnick, 1990) has the explicit goal of developing a voluntary national assessment for individual children based on the same logic that underlies many of the new state reading assessments. Project members contend that a national test that measures what matters will spur the development of the kind of curricula that will allow the United States to recapture its position of world economic leadership. It was in response to the calls for reform that developers of the 1992 National Assessment of Educational Progress (NAEP) in reading included an experimental component in which portfolios, individual interviews, and samples of students reading books orally were included in the assessment.

One potential application of the alternative assessment agenda deserves special mention: the call to replace standardized tests with classroom-based assessments. The logic behind this particular proposal runs as follows: What if standardized tests were eliminated in an entire school district? What if they were replaced with some kind of portfolio approach, one in which district administrators, teachers, and students could all have a voice in specifying what would be included in the portfolio? Most educators would agree that such an approach would provide valuable documentation about the progress of individual students, but they are unsure about what it would do to program evaluation at the school and district levels. Is there some way to translate portfolio entries into data for wide-scale evaluation? Perhaps. One way was found by teachers and administrators in a suburban Chicago district, who had convinced the school board to adopt just such an approach. In this district, teachers collect portfolio entries and score them for their own classroom and for individual students. Then, to obtain school- and district-level data, outside auditors are brought in to take a random sample of portfolios and of entries from these portfolios. These samples are then scored independently, and the results are tabulated by school and for the district. The school and district reports contain the kinds of tables and charts that can be constructed from standardized tests, with the obvious omission of comparative state or national norms. However, teachers, administrators, and the local school board can still evaluate what it means, for example, when 74% of the students achieve a competent standard on a writing-in-response-to-reading task. They can also compare the 1992 fifth-grade class with the 1991 class on this, and just about any other criterion. The advantage of using this assessment system is that there are not artificially determined factors present to drive instruction down counterproductive curricular routes. The same data that guide a teacher's decisions within the classroom also provide information that can be used for larger accountability purposes.

Whereas the premise that underlies alternative assessment seems reasonable, several issues still need to be resolved if these new types of measures are to be the future of assessment. The main issue is establishing credibility in the mind of the public: Can the information produced by these alternative measures be trusted? Are they fair to all students, or will they discriminate against particular groups? The importance of establishing credibility with the public cannot be underestimated—for example, an attempt to include a writing sample in the latest version of the SAT was thwarted by an advisory board member who was convinced that essays were biased against Asian students.

Another issue that must be addressed centers on the utility of alternative measures. Whereas they may be very useful for making decisions at the classroom level, can they really be used for making decisions at the larger district, regional, state, or national level? The one successful attempt to do so that we noted is encouraging, but it does not ensure that citizens and policy makers in other settings accept such an approach. Finally, there is the issue of what standards are to be used to evaluate alternative assessments. It is not clear, for example, that the conventional standards of reliability, validity, utility, efficiency, and objectivity are applicable to alternative measures.

CONCLUSION

The current reality of educational politics in the United States means that wide-scale efficient forms of assessment will continue to be needed, or at least mandated by policy makers. Improving the way we assess our students' reading ability, therefore, seems to be a reasonable course of action. Because tests appear to have such a powerful influence on curriculum, we must find a way to come to terms with them—to resist them, accept them, or reform them. Our preference is for reform. And we believe that the development, validation, and evaluation of new performance-based assessments is the most appropriate reform strategy. To remain complacent about our current tests is to doom many children to narrow curricula. To simply resist their use is to ignore their influences, both negative and positive. Our only real option is reforming them, so that they reflect what we know about reading and learning. Only through reform can assessment become a positive force in the lives of children and teachers.

REFERENCES

Au, K. H., Scheu, J. A., & Kawakami, A. J. (1990). Assessment of students' ownership of literacy. *The Reading Teacher, 44,* 154–156.

Bloom, B. S. (1968). *Learning for mastery. Evaluation comment.* Los Angeles: University of California, Center for the Study of Evaluation.

Carroll, J. B. (1963). A model of school learning. *Teachers College Record, 64,* 723–733.

Dorr-Bremme, D. W., & Herman, J. L. (1986). *Assessing student achievement: A profile of classroom practices.* Los Angeles: University of California, Center for the Study of Evaluation.

Elam, S. M. (1990). The 22nd annual Gallup poll of the public's attitudes toward the public schools. *Phi Delta Kappan, 72,* 41–55.

Elam, S. M., & Gallup, A. M. (1989). The 21st annual Gallup poll of the public's attitudes toward the public schools. *Phi Delta Kappan, 71,* 41–54.

Garcia, G. E. (1991). Factors influencing the English reading test performance of Spanish-speaking Hispanic children. *Reading Research Quarterly, 26,* 371–392.

Garcia, G. E., & Pearson, P. D. (1991). The role of assessment in a diverse society. In E. H. Hiebert (Ed.), *Literacy in a diverse society: Perspectives, practices, and policies* (pp. 253–278). New York: Teachers College Press.

Koretz, D. M., Linn, R. L., Dunbar, S. B., & Shepard, L. A. (1991, April). *The effects of high-stakes testing on achievement: Preliminary findings about generalizations across tests.* Paper presented at the annual meeting of the American Educational Research Association and the National Council on Measurement in Education, Chicago.

Lipson, M. Y. (1990). Evaluating the reading context. *The Reading Teacher, 44,* 330–332.

Pearson, P. D., & Dunning, D. B. (1985). The impact of assessment on reading instruction. *Illinois Reading Council Journal, 13,* 18–29.

Pearson, P. D., Stephens, D., Commeyras, M., Roe, M., Shelton, J., Stallman, A. C., & Scharer, P. (1990, May). *Assessment and decision-making in the schools.* Paper presented at the annual meeting of the International Reading Association, Atlanta.

Peters, C. W. (1991). You can't have authentic assessment with authentic content. *The Reading Teacher, 44,* 590–591.

Popham, W. J., Cruse, K. L., Rankin, S. C., Sandifer, P. D., & Williams, P. L. (1985). Measurement driven instruction: It's on the road. *Phi Delta Kappan, 55,* 628–634.

Resnick, D. P. (1982). History of educational testing. In A. K. Wigdor & W. R. Garner (Eds.), *Ability testing: Uses, consequences, and controversies (Part 2).* Washington, DC: National Academy Press.

Resnick, L. B., & Resnick, D. P. (1990). Assessing the thinking curriculum: New tools for educational reform. In B. R. Gifford & M. C. O'Connor (Eds.), *Future assessments: Changing views of aptitude, achievement, and instruction.* Boston: Kluwer.

Shepard, L. A., & Dougherty, K. C. (1991, April). *Effects of high-stakes testing on instruction.* Paper presented at the annual meeting of the American Educational Research Association and the National Council on Measurement in Education, Chicago.

Stallman, A. C., & Pearson, P. D. (1990). *Formal measures of early literacy* (Tech. Rep. No. 511). Urbana–Champaign: University of Illinois, Center for the Study of Reading.

Tierney, R. J., Carter, M. A., & Desai, L. E. (1991). *Portfolio assessment in the reading–writing classroom.* Norwell, MA: Christopher–Gordon.

Valencia, S. W. (1990). Alternative assessment: Separating the wheat from the chaff. *The Reading Teacher, 44,* 60–61.

Wiggins, G. (1991). Standards, not standardization: Evoking quality student work. *Educational Leadership, 48,* 18–25.

Wixson, K. K. (1991). Diagnostic teaching. *The Reading Teacher, 44,* 420–422.

16

Research as We Approach the Millennium: Beyond *Becoming a Nation of Readers*

Judith A. Scott
Simon Fraser University

Elfrieda H. Hiebert
University of Colorado

Richard C. Anderson
Center for the Study of Reading

Becoming a Nation of Readers (Anderson, Hiebert, Scott, & Wilkinson, 1985) was intended to be a policy statement about instruction in reading. It reported conclusions from research about reading and made recommendations about key features of reading instruction based on these conclusions. In this chapter, we use *Becoming a Nation of Readers* as a guidepost to areas of productive inquiry for educators and researchers as we head into the next century.

Becoming a Nation of Readers was not the first report to focus on ways the nation could improve the reading instruction provided in its schools. In 1925, the Committee on Reading of the National Society for the Study of Education compiled a report aimed at improving instruction in reading by providing school officers and teachers with "carefully prepared suggestions based on experimental evidence as far as possible and on expert opinion where such evidence was lacking" (Whipple, 1925). Subsequent reports, also sponsored by the Society, were published in 1937 and 1948 (Henry, 1948, 1949; Whipple, 1937). In 1975, the Committee on Reading of the National Academy of Education issued its report, *Toward a Literate Society* (Carroll & Chall, 1975). Although these reports were aimed at influencing teachers and school officers, they primarily reached the academic community.

The mandate to those preparing *Becoming a Nation of Readers* was to disseminate information about reading to the public—parents, school board members, textbook publishers, test makers, and legislators—as well as to teachers and school personnel, covering issues ranging from how to teach phonics to the role of libraries in schools. The goal of communicating with "the average informed citizen" forced the Commission to synthesize numerous lines of research to create, insofar as possible, a unified policy statement. The Commission often discovered that it wanted to say something about certain issues, but that the research available in 1985 was thin, inconclusive, or nonexistent. In other areas, it found that a great deal of information was available, but that the answers to specific questions about pedagogy or process were in conflict. This created problems for the Commission. On the one hand, it wanted to make strong statements about key issues. On the other hand, the integrity of the report required basing these statements in research.

Careful reading of *Becoming a Nation of Readers* (Anderson et al., 1985) will reveal a number of places where the Commission hedged statements with phrases such as "though research does not prove the point, common sense suggests . . ." (p. 27), "though there is little hard evidence on the point . . ." (p. 67), or "In the judgment of the Commission . . ." (p. 42).

By looking in *Becoming a Nation of Readers* for such statements, it is possible to find issues for future research. Indeed, in the years following the report's publication, some of these issues have been pursued by ourselves and others. Yet three issues in particular deserve a stronger focus: motivation and reading, comprehension instruction, and emergent literacy. We believe these three issues are integral to the improvement of literacy, and that they should be addressed fully in the coming years.

MOTIVATION AND READING

In *Becoming a Nation of Readers,* the Commission identified five principles of skilled reading. One of these principles—skilled reading is a motivated process—was included because the Commission had no doubt that motivation influences reading, even though research on motivation and reading has not been pursued in great depth. Considering the importance that teachers and parents place on motivation to read, it was initially surprising to find so little research in this area. On reflection, the lack of research is attributable both to the difficulty of studying a complex construct such as motivation and to the fact that reading is an interactive skill and a multifaceted subject in schools. Recently, there has been an upsurge of interest in motivation as it relates to general school tasks (Ames & Ames, 1984, 1985, 1989; Ames & Archer, 1988; Levine & Wang, 1983; Newman, 1990; Nicholls, 1984b; Paris, Olson, & Stevenson, 1983; Paris & Winograd, 1990; Shell, Murphy, & Bruning, 1989; Skinner, Wellborn, & Connell, 1990; Winne, 1991). We present some of this work in a framework designed to spur future research on the connections between motivation and reading.

The study of motivation in schools has focused on achievement motivation, that is, individuals' motives for initiating and persisting in behavior that leads to accomplishment in an academic arena. Initially, achievement motivation was viewed in relation to personality traits, with the motive to achieve regarded as a relatively stable and general characteristic of an individual (Atkinson, 1964;

McClelland, 1961). This view held little encouragement for educators, for as long as motivation was viewed as a function of stable personality factors, the ability of educators to influence student motivation is limited.

In the 1970s, Atkinson's model was reinterpreted within a cognitive perspective (Weiner, 1972). Studies showed that people who differ in their achievement needs differ in their perceptions of the reason for success and failure (Weiner & Kukla, 1970). Furthermore, these perceptions vary as a function of the task and the way in which success or failure is defined—also known as the *evaluative setting* of the situation (Ames, 1981, 1984a, 1984b; Maehr & Braskamp, 1986; Nicholls, 1984a). Recent theoretical frameworks portray motivation as an ever-changing fluid process instead of a static system of personality traits or beliefs (Eccles & Wigfield, 1985; Maehr & Braskamp, 1986). A view of motivation that encompasses the task, the situation, and the individual is a provocative view for educators because it suggests avenues for constructive change. The variables of task, situation, and individual are already considered to be important in the process of reading (Barr, Kamil, Mosenthal, & Pearson, 1991). In this section of the chapter, the view of motivation as a fluid process underlies the analysis of each of these variables.

Individual Variables

The poor reader has been described as passive (Johnston & Winograd, 1985). Poor readers often display symptoms of *learned helplessness,* a persistent belief that they are unable to prevent negative outcomes or achieve positive outcomes even when conditions allow them control. They exhibit low persistence, low expectations of success, low self-concept regarding their ability; they attribute success to external unstable factors and failure to internal stable forces; and they fail to use goal-oriented strategies to solve problems (Butkowsky & Willows, 1980; Paris, Wasik, & Turner, 1991). This passive disposition is problematic for growth in reading. Reading is the interactive process of creating meaning from print. When students approach reading passively, they are not likely to engage in the very processes needed to gather meaning from text.

Researchers are now faced with the task of identifying reasons for the passivity of poor readers and providing possible solutions. It is not clear, for example, whether passivity is the cause of poor reading ability or an outcome. Johnston and Winograd (1985) suggested that understanding passive failure in reading is necessary to help students who are poor readers. This makes sense if lack of motivation is seen as a cause of poor reading. Stanovich (1986), however, argued that an initial deficit in an important skill, such as decoding, creates an ever-widening gap between good and poor readers, with academic and motivational consequences.

Most probably, passivity toward reading is both a cause and an effect. Perceptions of ability and the goals students adopt are central in predicting patterns of behavior (Dweck & Leggett, 1988). In an analysis of under and overachievers in reading, Oka and Paris (1987) suggested that students respond to their self-perceptions, attitudes, and skills in a manner that preserves self-worth. Passive responses may be adaptive for certain students who find little value in reading activities, lack specific skills, and believe success is beyond their reach. In fact, manipulating perceived ability by giving prior negative feedback can lead other-wise average fifth graders to display the same negative affect, attributional pat-terns, and strategy deterioration that is characteristic of learned helpless behavior (Elliot & Dweck, 1988).

On the other hand, overachievers in fifth grade are distinguished by their feelings of self-competence and an awareness of how to regulate their skills (Oka & Paris, 1987). But even good readers are not always enthusiastic about the activity called *reading* in school (Durkin, 1982). And students who can read well do not necessarily do so. Studies indicate that most children spend little, if any, time reading on their own (Anderson, Wilson, & Fielding, 1988). Passivity is not the only factor related to motivation to read. Individual variables, including passivity, need to be examined in relation to other mediating factors to explain this complex issue.

Task Variables

Most adults respond differently to different reading tasks. For most people, the motivation to read an introductory statistics text is very different from the mo-tivation to read a novel on the best seller list. Motivation to do a task can be related to the value an individual places on the task. Eccles and Wigfield (1985) have split the value attached to a task into three variables: *attainment* value, *interest* value, and *utility* value. Looking at the profile of values associated with various reading tasks can help clarify the influence of a task on the motivation process.

The attainment value of a task is the value attached to trying to do the task well to affirm self-concept or to fulfill achievement, power, or social needs. For many students, part of the motivation to perform well on school reading tasks could be mediated by the attainment value attached to the act of reading. Reading is a highly valued skill in middle-American society. Children might want to read to prove to others that they are competent, to please parents, or to gain some sense of independence. The converse of this idea is that poor readers might feel that the effort expended is too great in comparison to the value of attaining the skill of reading. This could be a particularly insightful way to view socio-economic, gender, and ethnic differences. Wigfield and Asher (1984) noted that middle-class children, especially girls, are more likely to value reading as an important skill. In subcultures where reading is not as highly valued, children might be less motivated to work hard to read well. In addition, if the attainment of reading skill is tied to self-concept, students may adopt self-defeating strate-gies to preserve self-worth (Covington, 1984; Nicholls & Miller, 1984).

Eccles and Wigfield (1985) defined the enjoyment one receives from doing a task as the interest value of the task. Studies have demonstrated the powerful effect of interest on reading comprehension (Asher, 1979, 1980; Asher, Hymel, & Wigfield, 1978; Asher & Markell, 1974). In the past, these results were viewed with some reservation because of the failure to separate interest from the critical factor of prior knowledge. However, Baldwin, Peleg-Bruckner, and Mc-Clintock (1985) demonstrated that the interest in the topic read about contributes to reading comprehension beyond the contribution of prior knowledge.

Interest in a topic needs to be differentiated from the elements of writing that capture a reader's interest. There are some elements of a story or text that seem to make passages more interesting than others to large groups of readers. Stylistic differences or differences in themes or outcomes have been found to contribute to reading motivation and comprehension. This type of interest has been referred to as *text-based* interest (Hidi, 1990; Hidi & Baird, 1988). For instance, interest ratings for sentences, especially those containing novel ideas or themes that the students could identify with, was far more strongly associated with comprehension than was the readability of the sentences (Anderson, Shirey, Wilson, & Fielding, 1986). Students were much more likely to remember sentences like "The huge gorilla smashed the school bus with his fist" than "The fat waitress poured coffee into the cup." Jose and Brewer's (1984) work suggested developmental differences in children's liking of suspense stories. Younger children were found to prefer stories with happy endings, regardless of the character disposition (*good* or *bad*); older students preferred endings in which good characters were rewarded and bad characters were punished. Hidi (1990) has pointed out that the contribution of individual interest versus the contribution of text-based interest ought to be investigated. Another line of inquiry should systematically investigate factors contributing to text-based interest across different genres, age levels, and cultures.

Although adults usually know the most about topics that interest them, students have been found to know quite a bit about topics that do not hold their interest (Baldwin et al., 1985). Their motivation to learn about these topics may have been derived from the perceived utility value of the task. According to Eccles and Wigfield (1985), the utility value of the task is its usefulness in helping students achieve long- or short-term goals. For example, one goal of reading might be to find out how to do something, such as how to assemble a model airplane by reading directions. The utility value of reading the directions would be high, and students would be motivated to read them if they wanted to complete the model.

Studies have shown that students who understand the utility value of strategies in reading are more likely to apply those strategies on their own (Paris & Jacobs, 1984). Telling students why they should use particular strategies is one way of pointing out the utility value of those strategies in the goal of understanding what they read. However, the goal, in this case, better comprehension, must be regarded by the students as significant or useful if it is to be pursued in the absence of external directives or incentives (Paris, Lipson, & Wixson, 1983). A goal set by a teacher, such as answering comprehension questions, may be seen by some students as useless or unimportant, whereas other students may view it as useful for getting good grades.

Students often do not see the usefulness of tasks they are asked to do in reading (Anderson, 1984). One of the insights in recent years has been that a focus on authentic tasks, such as writing books for publication in a classroom library, as opposed to writing that is only seen by a teacher, enhances student engagement. Restructuring tasks to enhance their perceived utility helps students make sense of and see the significance of their assignments. Research indicates that even subtle changes in utility value, such as having students write a letter to a specific person other than the teacher, result in differences in the amount and quality of participation (Greenlee, Hiebert, Bridge, & Winograd, 1986). Several researchers have described the increased motivation that occurs when students are engaged in authentic tasks (Atwell, 1987; Calkins, 1986; Routman, 1988). It seems that a key element might be the increase in perceived utility value of activities that create legitimate purposes for engagement. Writing to create a school newspaper, to publish a book, or to advertise books for friends could be examined in terms of increased student motivation to participate fully in the classroom. Giving students individual choices in activities might also increase the perceived utility value of learning particular content that is deemed valuable by society. Providing an array of assignments that meet the same instructional goals allows students to choose ones they see as personally relevant.

The most profitable research stance would be to study the profile of values—attainment value, interest value, and utility value—in relation to one another. The values placed on different tasks, such as reading silently or doing workbook exercises, could vary from high to low on all three dimensions. Questions researchers might consider are the relative importance of the three variables, the effects of changing the value of one factor on students' accomplishment of the task, and the nature of individual or developmental differences in perception of task value. It seems reasonable to expect a developmental interaction with the three task mediators. Young students might focus on the attainment value of reading tasks because smart people read and they want to be smart people. Older students, especially those who can do the mechanics of reading, might be motivated by the interestingness or the utility of their school reading tasks. Looking at task values and the interaction of these values should provide interesting instructional insights into motivation for various reading tasks.

The Evaluative Context

Reading activities in school can occur under various conditions, or contexts, that might mediate students' motivation to read. The typical classroom has a strongly evaluative atmosphere in which rewards are based on academic performance

(Levine, 1983). Research on the effect of evaluative systems suggests that competitive situations in which students' skills are evaluated against one another are debilitating for at least some students because they place students in an ego-involved, threatening, self-focused state rather than a task-oriented, effort, or strategy-focused state (Ames, 1984a, 1984b; Covington, 1984; Nicholls, 1984a). The tendency in a competitive situation is to focus on performance judgments and assessment of ability as compared to others. Cooperative situations or situations in which only an individual is involved have been found to be more conducive to goals of learning and mastery (Ames, 1981, 1984a; Ames & Ames, 1981). For example, Elliot and Dweck (1988) found that highly anxious students used appropriate strategies and attributions under nonevaluative conditions, but as soon as evaluative pressure heightened, these same students focused on personal inadequacies, performance deficiencies, and irrelevant aspects of the task.

Much of school reading instruction has occurred traditionally within an evaluative context that could best be characterized as competitive. The conventional reading group format may foster competition rather than cooperation, with comparisons and evaluations made when children read orally or answer questions. Although cooperative learning is gaining support, there is still a sense of competition in many classrooms. One aspect of particular concern is the effect of competitive external reward systems on intrinsic motivation to read. Studies have shown that when external rewards are given for a task that began as intrinsically motivating for students, engagement in that task drops off after the reward is taken away (Lepper, 1983). Yet, in an effort to encourage free reading in schools, many schools and organizations have initiated programs to give away free pizzas, gold stars, and other incentives to readers.

The study of the other mediators of motivation—task and personal characteristics—within the context of the overall evaluative setting is essential. Limited research supports the need for examining complex relationships between these three mediators. Hiebert, Winograd, and Danner (1984), for example, found that students' attributions for their success and failure differed when they were in a personal situation reading for meaning and when they were in a public situation being evaluated for their reading. Investigation of the evaluative context and how it interacts with student and task variables is, like the entire topic of motivation, a promising, indeed, necessary area of study.

COMPREHENSION

Recent studies have provided much information about effective comprehension instruction (for a review, see Pearson & Fielding, 1991). Nonetheless, comprehension and the teaching of comprehension are complex matters and the research needs to be extended in several different ways. In this section of the chapter, we discuss three of these ways.

Direct Instruction

A first major issue is the limits of direct instruction. In direct instruction, the teacher explicitly explains, defines, informs, leads, and models. One achievement of reading research in the last two decades has been to show that direct or explicit instruction works well (Duffy, 1981; Rosenshine & Stevens, 1984). Considering the frailty of educational research methods, the evidence of effectiveness is impressive in breadth and in depth. It comes from both naturalistic and experimental studies. It covers word identification (Becker & Gersten, 1982; Bradley & Bryant, 1983) as well as aspects of comprehension, such as understanding story structure (Fitzgerald & Spiegel, 1983), finding main ideas (Baumann, 1984), summarizing (Hare & Borchardt, 1984), reading critically (Patching, Kameenui, Carnine, Gersten, & Colvin, 1983), and reading strategically (Paris, Cross, & Lipson, 1984).

A problem is that the meaning of the term *direct instruction* is embarrassingly elastic. It is used not only to refer specifically to instruction in which the teacher provides explicit explanations but often seems to include any purposeful, active, concentrated, systematic instruction. For instance, Palincsar and Brown (1984) characterized their very successful technique, reciprocal teaching, as direct instruction. Yet in this technique, the students take turns playing the teacher, so there are long stretches during lessons when the real teacher has a responsive role. Au and her colleagues (Au et al., 1985) described the approach to the teaching of reading used in the highly regarded Kamehameha Early Education Program (KEEP) as direct instruction. Yet a close look at the lessons of KEEP teachers will show that they are masters of indirection; they seldom explain, define, inform, or model. KEEP teachers do not even control turn taking; during guided reading lessons, children speak up when they have something to contribute without so much as raising their hands (Au & Mason, 1981).

The real question for researchers, then, is just what it is about so-called direct instruction that makes it effective? Narrowing the question somewhat, research is needed to figure out what skills, concepts, and strategies benefit from direct instruction in the precise sense.

Research is also needed to determine whether there are any hidden costs of direct instruction. From the student's perspective, perhaps there is an optimal amount of hearing about a task and a point beyond which the teacher talk is redundant and doing the task on one's own becomes the better way. Differences among students at different age or ability levels may condition the effectiveness of direct instruction. Although less able students may be responsive to this kind of instruction, common sense, at least, suggests that more advanced students may become bored with instruction they regard as redundant and obvious. Moreover, direct instruction places students in a passive receptive role. Is it possible that a constant diet of direct instruction will interfere with the development of a propensity for active independent thinking?

The direct instruction motto seems to be: "Tell as much as possible." We are bold enough to suggest that research eventually will show that what may seem to be the opposite motto is the better guide for teachers: "Tell as little possible." By this we mean that students should be left to make any discovery that they can and will figure out for themselves.

Previous research specifically investigating learning by discovery has proved inconclusive. However, this research has had serious weaknesses (Shulman & Keislar, 1966). Several other kinds of evidence suggest that people do learn better when they must work out some aspects of a task for themselves.

From basic research on human learning comes the finding that people consistently learn more when they generate responses or answers to questions (Slamecka & Graff, 1978). To illustrate, Anderson, Goldberg, and Hidde (1971) had college students read aloud highly predictable sentences in which there was a blank in place of the last word, such as *Women carry lots of junk in their* _____. Students who generated the words to complete the blanks were able to recall more sentences than students who read whole sentences, such as *Women carry lots of junk in their purses*. Determining the word that fits in a predictable sentence is a modest discovery at best; however, related research shows the benefits of generating answers when the task is more difficult (Auble, Franks, & Soraci, 1979) or even impossible (Kane & Anderson, 1978).

From applied research on classroom instruction comes the conclusion that students learn more when teachers do not give away the answers to questions or too quickly provide help when a student is faltering. For instance, in a study of reading lessons in 20 first-grade classrooms, Anderson, Evertson, and Brophy (1979) found that growth in reading is positively related to the teacher's providing sustaining feedback—furnishing hints to help students come up with a satisfactory response on their own, but negatively related to the teacher's giving terminal feedback—telling students the correct response or allowing other students to call out the response. In a study of reading lessons in 22 second-grade classrooms that examined in great detail types of oral reading errors and feedback, Hoffman and his colleagues (Hoffman et al., 1984) confirmed that terminal feedback is negatively related to year-to-year growth in reading.

Of course, the whole language movement stresses the value of allowing students to work things out on their own, to the extent that they can, encouraging discoveries rather than always teaching by telling. In Newman's (1990) neat phrase, the skillful whole language teacher "leads from behind." Although there is research that illustrates leading from behind, it barely scratches the surface. We call for research on *indirect* instruction that has the scope and penetration of the research on direct instruction completed during the past two decades.

Background Knowledge

The second set of issues in comprehension concerns the concept of background knowledge. Research establishes that the fund of knowledge a reader already possesses is a critical determiner of comprehension (Anderson & Pearson, 1984).

But exactly what significance this fact has for instruction is far from obvious. Superficially, compelling appeals to background knowledge can be made on both sides of several arguments. For instance, one could argue that the materials students read should concentrate on familiar topics because these will be readily comprehended. At the same time, with seemingly equal force, one could argue that materials should concentrate on unfamiliar topics so as to develop new knowledge.

Becoming a Nation of Readers warned against jumping on the background knowledge bandwagon before the instructional entailments of the concept are clear. Studies should look for instructionally optimal activities to develop appropriate background when students lack prior knowledge. Questions concerning what kinds of topics require activities to develop background knowledge and what types of students need these activities should be answered. Teachers are concerned about activating background knowledge without "giving away" the plot of a story. Is this a valid concern? If the students know the theme, will they be less motivated to read the story? How do teachers decide what to activate in the first place? Studies should look at the effects of activating knowledge relevant to different aspects of a story on the comprehension and motivation of students.

According to schema theory, the essence of knowledge is its organization or structure. Basic research establishes the benefits of possessing a structured body of knowledge as opposed to a basket of facts (see Anderson & Pearson, 1984). As a practical matter, however, not enough is known about the value of techniques that are supposed to help students see the structure of a topic.

One such technique is semantic mapping—that is, drawing diagrams to show how the aspects of a topic are related (Armbruster & Anderson, 1980). Research on semantic mapping and related techniques has yielded promising results (Holley & Dansereau, 1984). A limitation is that most of the research has been done with college students trying to learn difficult technical material, and the students have been required to employ elaborate systems for semantic mapping, systems that are themselves difficult to learn and tedious and time consuming to use. These systems would be daunting for children in the elementary grades.

Informal discussion-based use of semantic mapping, probably inspired by the work of Johnson and Pearson (1978), is increasingly seen in elementary school reading lessons around the country, but casual observation suggests wide variation in the extent to which the structure of a topic actually gets highlighted in these lessons. We call for more research to determine whether such simplified versions of semantic mapping do help elementary schoolchildren grasp the structure of ideas implicit in texts (see Berkowitz, 1986; Darch, Carnine, & Kameenui, 1986).

Vocabulary Growth and Development

The third issue that we touch on in this section is vocabulary growth and development. Durkin's (1978–1979) finding that reading teachers spend alarmingly little time providing comprehension instruction is well known to both scholars and practitioners in the field of reading. Less often quoted is the finding from the same study that less than 5% of reading lesson time is devoted to vocabulary instruction. Durkin's finding is entirely consistent with those of others. In the wake of literature-based instruction, vocabulary instruction may be falling even further behind. Furthermore, according to Graves (1986), authorities who have observed vocabulary instruction in the schools generally agree that it "lacks purpose, breadth, and depth" (p. 78).

Counterbalancing this dismal appraisal is the feeling among vocabulary researchers that, after a long fallow period, the study of vocabulary is undergoing a renaissance. Thanks to recent research, there are now for the first time good, although still provisional, answers to several basic questions about vocabulary: What is a word? How important is word knowledge to comprehension? How many words do children of different ages know? Where do children learn the words they know?

Based on a reanalysis of the major studies of vocabulary size, Nagy and Herman (1987) concluded that the average third- through twelfth-grade student learns about 3,000 new words a year. This compares with the 300 new words a year that Jenkins and Dixon (1983) estimated are taught in the typical reading program. However, the word *taught* must be used advisedly; it would be more accurate to say that most of these words are *introduced*.

Therefore, most of the new words a child learns are not learned from direct instruction. Most new words are learned, it appears, from natural contexts while a child is reading or listening (Nagy, Anderson, & Herman, 1987).

Is there any point to direct vocabulary instruction? We see two possible purposes: The first is to help students with the difficult words they will need to understand a particular selection or series of selections. The second is to help children become better independent word learners.

With respect to the first goal, until just a few years ago, research evidence was equivocal as to whether teaching word meanings even aided comprehension. Now there is a growing body of evidence that teaching difficult vocabulary can help (Beck, Perfetti, & McKeown, 1982; Kameenui, Carnine, & Freschi, 1982; Stahl, 1983; Wixson, 1986). The resulting gains in comprehension are modest, it should be cautioned, and producing these gains requires instruction that is more intensive and systematic than is typically seen in reading programs. The light introduction to unfamiliar words that is typical of reading instruction may sensitize students to these words and increase the odds that the students will learn the words on their own while reading a selection (see Jenkins, Stein, & Wysocki, 1984), but educational research methods are too crude to easily prove a proposition of this subtlety.

With respect to the second goal, helping children become better independent word learners, we believe that eventually it will be possible to prove that this is the sine qua non of vocabulary instruction. It could not be proved at present, however. The conventional wisdom of the field is that children will be helped to acquire vocabulary if they are taught to use context clues and to analyze words into parts. Basically, there is no sound evidence that either practice does very much good (see Graves, 1986; Johnson & Baumann, 1984).

The first step in devising instruction to assist children in becoming independent word learners is to reconceptualize the task. The goal is for children to develop a fulsome word schema—in other words, rich general knowledge about the form, function, and meaning of words. A word schema should be distinguished from a content, or topical, schema, although of course the two types blend together at the boundaries. Although we do not try to develop the concept of a word schema very far in this chapter, a good beginning for instructional practices has been pointed to by Graves (1987), who discussed 16 kinds of knowledge children ought to possess about words (e.g., learning that words may have various meanings, learning to recognize and use figurative language).

The more a person knows about words, the greater the likelihood that he or she will be able to appreciate an additional nuance of meaning of an already partially known word or learn something about the meaning of an entirely unknown word. Discussions of word meanings in reading circles usually focus on context or morphology. Without wishing to suggest that these aspects are unimportant, less often talked about is the deep knowledge that a true word expert will have about semantics—that is, the nature of word meanings.

For instance, a word expert will not only know a great many verbs for characterizing motion but also will tacitly know, at least, the set of distinctions that may be conveyed by a verb of motion (see Miller, 1972). The word expert will know that verbs of motion can be categorized according to whether the movement is across land (*gallops, toddles, marches*), through the air (*flies, soars, swoops*), or through water (*swims, rows, wades*). He or she will know that verbs of motion often mark direction, such as toward or away from the speaker (*come, go; bring, take*), around (*turn, rotate, spin*), or up (*rise, climb, mount*). He or she will know that verbs of motion sometimes indicate whether the movement is fast (*races, scurries, sprints*) or slow (*ambles, creeps, saunters*). It should be obvious that a word expert can readily place a new previously unfamiliar verb of motion within this framework of concepts.

The general point is that sophisticated users of the language have word schemata, or highly developed systems of concepts about words, that probably permit substantial and often rapid learning of word meanings from small amounts of contextual information. Research by Nagy and Scott (1990) indicates that knowledge about typical patterns of word meanings increases from junior high to college. We venture the guess that children can be helped to become word experts—not so much by didactic instruction on context, morphology, and semantics—but by a process of bringing to consciousness, sharpening, and then extending tacit knowledge they already possess about words. The reference source for such instruction will more often be the thesaurus than the dictionary.

In summary, research covering direct and indirect instruction, examination of the concept of background knowledge as it is translated into classroom practice, and understanding of how students become independent word learners should advance the applicability of comprehension research for practitioners. These research extensions of current comprehension research present the challenge in this area for the next few decades.

EMERGENT LITERACY

Since the publication of *Becoming a Nation of Readers,* and even in the short period since we first proposed suggestions for further research (Scott, Hiebert, & Anderson, 1988), scholarly activity in the area of early literacy has blossomed. Several recent reviews on dimensions of early literacy learning or instruction synthesize some of this research (Adams, 1990; Juel, 1991; Stahl & Miller, 1989; Stanovich, 1991; Sulzby & Teale, 1991). Our aim in this section of the chapter is to identify questions and suggest further research based on directions that the field has taken in the past 6 years.

There seem to be three main thrusts in early literacy: whole language, work on phonemic awareness, and early literacy interventions. As all relate to early literacy development, these three directions are not independent. There are, however, different research questions raised by each emphasis.

Whole Language

In *Becoming a Nation of Readers,* we made a distinction between the emerging and extending phases of becoming literate. Since that report, the instructional force of the whole language movement has blurred the distinction. Many of the developments from the area of emergent literacy can now be found in whole language classrooms of all grade levels. Teachers who have seen demands for testing increase considerably through the reform movement of the 1980s (James, 1991), and who have seen textbook manuals give more and more guidance with each new edition (Durkin, in preparation), have enthusiastically embraced whole language principles. Participation in the authentic tasks of reading high-quality literature, writing stories and journals, and talking with one another have been met with resounding acceptance among teachers who see it as their job to be instructional decision makers. Although there is no unanimous agreement as to what constitutes whole language, an operational definition (Froese, 1990) is that whole language is "a child-centered, literature-based approach to language teaching that immerses students in real communication situations whenever possible" (p. 2).

What is it that separates whole language scholars from other researchers in literacy? Some whole language scholars (e.g., Edelsky, 1990; Stephens, this volume) argue that theirs is a different educational paradigm with its own philosophical framework and a particular political ideology. However, it seems that the philosophical underpinning of whole language is similar to the constructivist perspective of learning that has dominated educational theory over the past decade and that guided *Becoming a Nation of Readers*. One might recall that *Becoming a Nation of Readers* recommends increased independent reading of high-quality text, engagement in extensive writing, and the cultivation of a social context that supports reading.

Although a constructivist orientation seems prevalent among researchers who study literacy, those who associate themselves with whole language sometimes seem to claim exclusive ownership over the precepts of constructivism in literacy (see Edelsky, 1990). This is ironic, because whole language scholars, when asked to produce evidence for their claims, generally cite a sampling of existing work from educational research on emergent literacy, literature-based instruction, and writing process (e.g., Shanklin & Rhodes, 1989).

Whole language researchers eschew standardized assessments (e.g., Goodman, 1991). So do many other researchers (e.g., Calfee & Hiebert, 1991; Valencia, McGinley, & Pearson, 1990). "Kid-watching" has been proposed to teachers as a more appropriate way to assess (Goodman, 1991). On the other hand, Au, Scheu, Kawakami, and Herman, (1990), who are not commonly seen as whole language researchers, have identified ownership as a central aspect of literacy and have detailed a portfolio assessment system for a whole literacy curriculum.

Battles in reading methodology are always hard fought. What the whole language advocates fail to realize is that they, to a large extent, have won. Most players in the field of literacy learning have shifted from thinking of reading as hierarchical or skills based to a constructivist paradigm. In addition, numerous studies from mainstream research are consistent with aspects of the whole language philosophy (Brown, Duguid, & Collins, 1989; Hiebert & Fisher, 1992).

One research agenda has already been proposed to pit whole language against other methodologies (McKenna, Robinson, & Miller, 1990). This agenda not only fails to recognize the overall shift to a constructivist paradigm, but it also discounts the nature of teaching, which is a negotiation between teachers, who adapt their instruction from various philosophies (Chall & Feldmann, 1966), and students in a complex social situation. We propose a different agenda.

Whole language advocates have argued that learning to read in schools can be similar to children's language acquisition in home settings. However, the social context, the different functions of literacy in the two settings, and the ratio of adults to children differ enough from oral language learning in the home to warrant further study. A pressing concern is not whether to use authentic literacy experiences but how to embed instruction in authentic literacy experiences for students who are not fluent readers. A long-standing line of research continues to confirm that some attention to word patterns during the early stages of learning to read supports eventual success in reading (Adams, 1990; Juel, 1988). Experimental psychologists have typically conducted research on the identification of words in isolation, whereas whole language scholars typically advocate learning through osmosis during exposure to reading and writing. Teachers are left with little information on how word-level guidance can be presented through authentic literacy tasks, especially in settings where many students have had little prior experience with literacy (Hiebert, 1991).

Although it seems reasonable that word-identification strategies could be learned in authentic tasks, like the repeated reading of predictable text and in writing stories and journals, there is a paucity of convincing research showing that it happens. Work on authentic literacy tasks and instruction is needed with both children who are in the initial stages of learning to read and write and with middle-grade students who are still not reading and writing fluently. This work is particularly important for those children who have not had extensive literacy experience in their homes.

A second question relates to the nature of materials provided for beginning readers. High-quality literature has been repeatedly advocated for instruction (California English/Language Arts Committee, 1987). There can be no doubt that listening to and talking about high-quality literature is essential for developing lifelong literacy. However, it may be dangerous to jump to the further conclusion that the beginning reader's diet should consist solely of high-quality literature. Predictable text appears to assist children at the initial stages of reading (Juel & Roper/Schneider, 1985; Mason & Allen, 1986). Conversely, children may flounder and make poor progress if they regularly receive text that is too difficult. Many predictable books modeled after Bill Martin's *Brown Bear, Brown Bear* (1970) and Dr. Seuss's *The Cat in the Hat* (1957) have been published in the last several years. Whereas some predictable books qualify as "high quality," many do not, and many selections that deserve to be called high quality are unpredictable. We call for a new round of research on the kinds of texts that emergent readers most readily learn from, all things considered.

Another area of research that has opened up in the past decade is that of writing. By their own accounts, teachers who have adopted process writing have dramatically changed their classroom instruction (Atwell, 1987; Routman, 1988). Tierney (1990) suggested that the concept of "reading as a writer" has had a significant impact both on the definition of reading and on instructional practices. Yet most writing research has been conducted with older students. Current work on early writing describes processes such as linguistic or symbolic representation in children's writing (Dyson & Freedman, 1991), yet leaves out connections to reading. Tensions arise between the need to recognize correct spellings of words for reading (Adams, 1990) and the apparent benefits of invented spelling for engagement, creativity, and practice in letter–sound analysis. Will repeated exposure to nonstandard spellings interfere with word recognition? Although some work has begun (e.g., Clarke, 1988), many questions remain concerning the best ways to develop reading proficiency in the early years through writing experiences.

Finally, what can be done with older students who have not yet become fluent in reading and writing? Reyes (1991a) suggested that many native-Spanish-speaking, middle-school students flounder in whole language classrooms. If this is the case, what can be changed to help this group of students? Are there certain types of authentic literacy tasks that will alleviate this problem? Perhaps some students need more initial scaffolding than others before they can become self-directed learners. What shape should this scaffolding take?

Changes in instructional practices have been dramatic over the last few years. Many of the principles that started as the exclusive domain of whole language advocates are widely accepted today. We feel that the articulation of these principles can be facilitated by both qualitative and quantitative research.

Phonemic Awareness

In 1985, our statement in *Becoming a Nation of Readers* that phonics is one of the essential ingredients in teaching children to read was quite controversial, despite an explicit emphasis in the book on reading words in meaningful texts. In the ensuing years, the critical role of phonemic awareness in learning to read has been firmly established (Bradley & Bryant, 1985; Juel, 1990, 1991; Juel, Griffith, & Gough, 1986; Stanovich, 1991). Phonemic awareness appears to be a prerequisite for word identification (Juel et al., 1986; Tunmer & Nesdale, 1985). It is the ability to hear the distinct sounds in words. The construct is not a unitary one but involves different abilities, such as segmenting a phoneme from a word (e.g., dropping the /n/ from *nice* to produce *ice*) or identifying words that rhyme from a set (e.g., *hat, run, bat*) (Cunningham, 1988). Some tasks, like blending phonemes together to produce a word, seem to be more necessary for reading acquisition than others, such as identifying the number of phonemes in a word (Perfetti, Beck, Bell, & Hughes, 1987).

Research substantiates the notion that aspects of phonemic awareness are necessary to read an alphabetic language successfully (for a review, see Juel, 1991). In a longitudinal study, phonemic awareness at the end of first grade contributed to both word recognition (.40) and reading comprehension (.24), even after variance attributed to IQ and listening comprehension was taken into account (Juel et al., 1986).

Training studies on phonemic awareness are beginning to accumulate (Lie, 1991; Lundberg, Frost, & Petersen, 1988). In one study, Lundberg et al. showed that phonemic awareness of preschoolers could be increased substantially through games, nursery rhymes, and listening to rhymed stories. Maclean, Bryant, and Bradley (1987) found that children who are more knowledgeable about nursery rhymes as preschoolers have better phonemic awareness and subsequently perform better in reading and writing.

However, this research has been conducted with preschoolers. It does little to inform teachers about children who enter first grade with low levels of phonemic awareness. Should such children be involved in playing phonemic awareness games, chanting nursery rhymes, and listening to rhymed stories before they read along in shared-book experiences or write in journals? Adams (1990) and Juel (1990) argued against this. However, examples of instruction that develops phonemic awareness while involving children with extensive writing and reading experiences are rare. One unique program that clearly illustrates activities to promote the integration of phonemic awareness with authentic reading and writing tasks is the Reading Recovery program (Clay, 1985), which involves children in reading and writing at the initiation of the program and embeds phonemic awareness activities into reading and, especially, writing activities. For example, if a child cannot spell a word he or she wants to include in a story he or she is composing, the teacher may write a string of boxes on a practice page, one box for each phoneme in the word. The child tries to hear the sounds in the word and to write the corresponding letters in the boxes in the right sequence, with help from the teacher as needed.

The development of phonemic awareness has not been singled out in studies of Reading Recovery. Consequently, it can be difficult to document exactly what Reading Recovery teachers do to promote phonemic awareness and the proportions of lesson time that they spend on this facet of reading. Tunmer (1989) contended that there are inconsistencies in the ways that different Reading Recovery teachers approach phonemic awareness, although Reading Recovery is a flexible responsive program, and it is possible that the apparent inconsistencies were adjustments intended to fit the child and the circumstance.

Other naturalistic contexts that could provide insight into the development of phonemic awareness have yet to be mined. Although writing has been suggested as a context for the development of phonemic awareness (Adams, 1990), there are few researchers who have studied phonemic awareness in this context. One descriptive study indicates that writing alone is not enough; when students wrote frequently but received no guidance in phonemic awareness or in word patterns, low-achieving students' invented spelling quickly reached a plateau (Hiebert, Goudvis, & Burton, 1989). Some guidance in phonemic awareness might have gone a long way to further their strategies.

Phonemic awareness is often discussed as a prerequisite for reading, and we advice caution in interpreting this phrase. Past interpretations of prerequisite have meant that children are denied involvement with meaningful materials until they have mastered the prerequisites. Studies of phonemic awareness in contexts such as Reading Recovery and the many kindergarten and first-grade classrooms in which children are writing extensively (see, e.g., Sulzby, 1992) are needed to determine if and how phonemic awareness is facilitated in contexts other than experimental training studies that have characterized this field (see, e.g., Liberman & Shankweiler, 1985) or the preschool activities that Lundberg et al. (1988) or Maclean et al. (1987) have described. Phonemic awareness may characterize proficient young readers and writers, but the manner in which this knowledge can best be facilitated for children who enter school without it and a host of other understandings about written language and its functions requires speedy attention.

Early Interventions

The importance of early experience with literacy was emphasized in *Becoming a Nation of Readers,* but even more evidence has accumulated since on early experience (Reynolds, 1991). Juel (1988) reported a correlation of .88 between students' literacy levels in first grade and their performance in fourth grade.

The Juel study implies that most children who are behind in the first grade will still lag in the fourth grade. A further implication is that the best time to intervene is early, before a child is too far behind, ineffective strategies are entrenched, and a poor self-concept is endemic. Studies of the best known early intervention, Reading Recovery, have confirmed that students in the bottom 10% to 20% can be brought quickly (12 to 16 weeks for most students) to the average level of literacy of other first graders through daily, especially crafted, intensive, one-on-one tutorials (Clay, 1985; DeFord, Lyons, & Pinnell, 1991). Even several years later, children who received Reading Recovery maintain an edge over peers who started at comparable levels. Whereas some researchers debate these results (see, e.g., Shanahan, 1987; Tunmer, 1989), Madden and Slavin's (1989) review of programs to prevent or ameliorate reading failure identified the one-on-one tutorial model of Reading Recovery as consistently successful with children at risk.

The success of Reading Recovery has spurred a flurry of activity by other research groups. Slavin, Madden, Karweit, Livermon, and Dolan (1990) have integrated tutoring into a school-wide, primary-grade effort entitled Success for All. However, its long-term effects appear to be specific to decoding subtests. This is most likely due to the emphasis the program places on phonics exercises rather than repeated reading of predictable text, a variety of word-level strategies, and writing.

Several other research groups have used a broader set of strategies and authentic tasks across a range of instructional contexts. One of these projects (Juel, 1991) uses tutoring aimed at increasing the literacy levels of both the tutors (university athletes) and the tutees. Other projects involve small-group instruction in Chapter 1 (Hiebert, Colt, Catto, & Gury, 1991) and extra instruction in the classroom (Taylor, Frye, Short, & Shearer, 1990) to restructuring of first-grade classes (Cunningham, Hall, & Defee, 1991). Evaluations of these interventions show that, when provided with instruction, even children with very low literacy levels on entering school can be brought to fluency early in their school careers. However, many questions remain about all these interventions.

Schools are complex organizations where changes in one element affect other elements (Sarason, 1982; Tharp & Gallimore, 1988). With the exception of Slavin et al.'s (1990) programs, where all children received a form of the intervention, interventions have focused on target children, not on the manner in which classroom contexts impact the intervention. Durkin's (1974–1975) classic study showed that, unless adaptations in instruction were made as children progressed through school, the results of an early intervention waned for many children.

The impact of early interventions on classroom instruction and outcomes beyond those of the target children has not yet been considered. When the lowest 20% or 25% of students in a first-grade class are targeted for the intervention, it should be possible for teachers to work with other groups of students who, although not the lowest performing, are still in need of additional support to become fluent readers. When the lowest performing children have become fluent readers and writers as a result of the intervention, classroom experiences in second and third grades might be rearranged to allow more attention to literature (Raphael, Goatley, McMahon, & Woodman, in press) or to literacy activities in social studies and science (Beck & McKeown, 1991).

Such changes by classroom teachers may not happen automatically (Richardson, Anders, Lloyd, & Tidwell, 1991). For example, restructuring instruction to emphasize a particular group of children may go counter to teachers' beliefs (see Allington, 1983). Even teachers who have been participants in the intervention may need additional support. Stephens, Gaffney, Weinzierl, Shelton, and Clark (1991) found that Reading Recovery teachers, at least during their training year, have difficulty making extensions from tutorials to classroom or Chapter 1 settings. This is not surprising in that the Reading Recovery training is focused on individual children and assiduously refrains from extensions to other settings. However, when Reading Recovery teachers were asked to adapt the tutoring techniques to group settings, their students' performances were not as high as those of tutored students but were better than those of students in a typical Chapter 1 program (Pinnell, Lyons, DeFord, Bryk, & Seltzer, 1991). Apparently, extensions can be made, with encouragement and at least a minimal amount of support.

How an early intervention relates to larger school settings should also be examined in contexts where a majority of students could benefit from support in literacy learning. Clay (1985) has been adamant that the techniques of Reading Recovery are appropriate only for the lowest 10% to 20% of a school. This statement begs many questions. In many large North American school districts, significant numbers of children could benefit from systematic support in literacy. This context is quite different from the social context of typical New Zealand schools (Goldenberg, 1991). In literacy, a treatment typically produces higher gains than status quo practices (Pflaum, Walberg, Karegianes, & Rasher, 1980). The novelty for teachers and, presumably, the added work and renewed energy that comes from such an effort may be difficult to maintain over time.

Summary

The rhetoric surrounding emergent literacy instruction has changed significantly since the publication of *Becoming a Nation of Readers*. Many teachers have abandoned ability grouping, worksheets, and basal readers. We celebrate the change to constructivist notions of learning. We also caution against an entrenchment of forces and the rejection of quantitative research. There are still many administrators, policy makers, and parents who need to be convinced that constructivist notions of learning will translate into increased learning for children. There are also many teachers who have embraced aspects of a whole language perspective but who need support to translate these notions into appropriate action. The few completed studies of whole language instruction (e.g., Hiebert, Potts, Katz, & Rahm, 1989) suggest that teachers who identify themselves as having a whole language philosophy are unlikely to provide scaffolding for groups of children who require support in reading strategies. The first- and third-grade teachers observed by Hiebert et al. modeled their literacy activities after Atwell's (1987) work with middle-school students. Some first-grade teachers expressed concern about appropriate instruction for nonfluent readers but admitted that they knew of few alternatives other than ability grouping or Atwell's "reader's workshop" model. Similarly, Reyes (1991b) has described the "one size fits all" mentality of whole language implementations with language-minority students. If instruction is truly child centered, then the needs of some children for scaffolded instruction should be taken into account.

Early interventions can provide some models for systematic instruction with authentic tasks to first-grade children who are low in literacy levels (Hiebert et al., 1991; Taylor et al., 1990). The manner in which these interventions can guide classroom teachers in everyday settings is a question of critical importance. For the many additional children who require support, instructional opportunities such as the ones currently given to a portion of low-proficiency children need to become common fare for at least part of the school day. Research that documents intensive focused instruction as part of classroom practice for beginning readers would integrate the three areas that often have been studied separately over the past several years—whole language, phonemic awareness, and early interventions.

CONCLUDING REMARKS

In this chapter, we have attempted to explicate some research questions that deserve the attention of researchers in the next few years. We have discussed three aspects of reading research—motivation, comprehension instruction, and emergent literacy—in depth. The issues we covered are obviously only a small subset of the issues included in *Becoming a Nation of Readers*. In addition to providing a focus for the areas discussed in this chapter, we hope that a larger purpose has been served. When *Becoming a Nation of Readers* appeared in 1985, it was hailed as the definitive statement about reading and dubbed the "Surgeon General's Report on Reading." To date more than 300,000 copies of the report have been sold.

In the years since its appearance, however, the field of reading research has changed tremendously. As research is conducted, as papers are written, as talks are given, our knowledge base increases and our thoughts change. Some people seemed to think that, with the report written, research had resolved all the important issues in reading. Reality is far different. The agonizing process of trying to give clear, unequivocal answers to the questions addressed in *Becoming a Nation of Readers* only made us more aware of how much remains to be learned—of how many other issues remain to be addressed. Recent research has focused on some of these issues. But others, such as those touched on in this chapter, must also be addressed if we truly want to become a nation of readers.

REFERENCES

Adams, M. J. (1990). *Beginning to read: Thinking and learning about print*. Cambridge, MA: The MIT Press.

Allington, R. L. (1983). The reading instruction provided readers of differing reading abilities. *Elementary School Journal, 83,* 549–559.

Ames, C. (1981). Competitive versus cooperative reward structures: The influence of individual and group performance factors on achievement attributions and affect. *American Educational Research Journal, 18,* 273–287.

Ames, C. (1984a). Achievement attributions and self-instruction under competitive and individualized goal structures. *Journal of Educational Psychology, 76,* 478–487.

Ames, C. (1984b). Competitive, cooperative, and individualistic goal structure: A cognitive-motivational analysis. In R. Ames & C. Ames (Eds.), *Research on motivation in education: Student motivation* (Vol. 1, pp. 177–207). Orlando: Academic Press.

Ames, C., & Ames, R. (1981). Comprehension vs. individual goal structures: The salience of past performance information for causal attributions and affect. *Journal of Educational Research, 73,* 411–418.

Ames, C., & Archer, J. (1988). Achievement goals in the classroom: Students' learning strategies and motivation processes. *Journal of Educational Psychology, 80,* 260–267.

Ames, R., & Ames, C. (Eds.). (1984). *Research on motivation in education: Student motivation* (Vol. 1). Orlando: Academic Press.

Ames, R., & Ames, C. (Eds.). (1985). *Research on motivation in education: The classroom milieu* (Vol. 2). Orlando: Academic Press.

Ames, R., & Ames, C. (Eds.). (1989). *Research on motivation in education: Goals and cognitions* (Vol. 3). Orlando: Academic Press.

Anderson, L. (1984). The environment of instruction: The function of seatwork in a commercially developed curriculum. In G. G. Duffy, L. R. Roehler, & J. Mason (Eds.), *Comprehension instruction: Perspectives and suggestions* (pp. 93–103). New York: Longman.

Anderson, L. M., Everston, C. M., & Brophy, J. (1979). An experimental study of effective reading in first-grade reading groups. *Elementary School Journal, 79,* 193–223.

Anderson, R. C., Goldberg, S. R., & Hidde, J. L. (1971). Meaningful processing of sentences. *Journal of Educational Psychology, 62,* 193–223.

Anderson, R. C., Hiebert, E. H., Scott, J. A., & Wilkinson, I. A. G. (1985). *Becoming a nation of readers: The report of the Commission on Reading.* Champaign, IL: Center for the Study of Reading; Washington, DC: National Institute of Education.

Anderson, R. C., & Pearson, P. D. (1984). A schema-theoretic view of basic processes in reading comprehension. In P. D. Pearson, R. Barr, M. L. Kamil, & P. Mosenthal (Eds.), *Handbook of reading research* (pp. 255–292). New York: Longman.

Anderson, R. C., Shirey, L., Wilson, P., & Fielding, L. (1986). Interestingness of children's reading material. In R. Snow & M. Farr (Eds.), *Aptitude, learning and instruction: Cognitive and affective processes analysis* (Vol. 3, pp. 287–299). Hillsdale, NJ: Lawrence Erlbaum Associates.

Anderson, R. C., Wilson, P., & Fielding, L. (1988). Growth in reading and how children spend their time outside of school. *Reading Research Quarterly, 23,* 285–303.

Armbruster, B. B., & Anderson, T. H. (1980). *The effect of mapping on the free recall of expository text* (Tech. Rep. No. 160). Urbana–Champaign: University of Illinois, Center for the Study of Reading. (ERIC Document Reproduction Service No. ED 182 735)

Asher, S. R. (1979). Influence of topic interest on black children's and white children's reading comprehension. *Child Development, 50,* 686–690.

Asher, S. R. (1980). Topic interest and children's reading comprehension. In R. Spiro, B. Bruce, & W. Brewer (Eds.), *Theoretical issues in reading comprehension* (pp. 525–534). Hillsdale, NJ: Lawrence Erlbaum Associates.

Asher, S. R., Hymel, S., & Wigfield, A. (1978). Influence of topic interest on children's reading comprehension. *Journal of Reading Behavior, 10,* 35–47.

Asher, S. R., & Markell, R. A. (1974). Sex differences in comprehension of high- and low-interest reading material. *Journal of Educational Psychology, 66,* 680–687.

Atkinson, J. W. (1964). *An introduction to motivation.* Princeton, NJ: D. Van Nostrand.

Atwell, N. (1987). *In the middle: Writing, reading, and learning with adolescents.* Portsmouth, NH: Heinemann.

Au, K. H., & Mason, J. M. (1981). Social organizational factors in learning to read: The balance of rights hypothesis. *Reading Research Quarterly, 17,* 115–152.

Au, K. H., Scheu, J. A., Kawakami, A. J., & Herman, P. A. (1990). Assessment and accountability in a whole literacy curriculum. *The Reading Teacher, 43,* 574–578.

Au, K. H., Tharp, R., Crowell, D., Jordan, C., Speidel, G., & Calkins, R. (1985). KEEP: The critical role of research in the development of a successful reading program. In J. Osborn, P. Wilson, & R. C. Anderson (Eds.), *Reading education: Foundations for a literate America* (pp. 275–289.) Lexington, MA: D. C. Heath.

Auble, P. M., Franks, J. J., & Soraci, S. A. (1979). Effort toward comprehension: Elaboration or "aha!"? *Memory & Cognition, 7,* 426–434.

Baldwin, R. S., Peleg-Bruckner, Z., & McClintock, A. (1985). Effects of topic interest and prior knowledge on reading comprehension. *Reading Research Quarterly, 20,* 497–504.

Barr, R., Kamil, M. L., Mosenthal, P. B., & Pearson, P. D. (Eds.). (1991). *Handbook of reading research* (Vol. 2). New York: Longman.

Baumann, J. F. (1984). The effectiveness of a direct instruction paradigm for teaching main idea comprehension. *Reading Research Quarterly, 20,* 93–115.

Beck, I. L., & McKeown, M. G. (1991). Research directions: Social studies texts are hard to understand: Mediating some of the difficulties. *Language Arts, 68,* 482–490.

Beck, I. L., Perfetti, C. A., & McKeown, M. G. (1982). Effects of long-term vocabulary instruction on lexical access and reading comprehension. *Journal of Educational Psychology, 74,* 506–521.

Becker, W. C., & Gersten, R. (1982). A follow up of follow through: The later effects of a direct instruction model on children in the fifth and sixth grades. *American Educational Research Journal, 19,* 75–92.

Berkowitz, S. J. (1986). Effects of instruction in text organization on sixth-grade students' memory for expository reading. *Reading Research Quarterly, 21,* 161–178.

Bradley, L., & Bryant, P. E. (1983). Categorizing sounds and learning to read: A casual connection. *Nature, 301,* 419–421.

Bradley, L., & Bryant, P. E. (1985). *Rhyme and reason in reading and spelling.* Ann Arbor: University of Michigan Press.

Brown, J. S., Duguid, P., & Collins, A. (1989). Situated cognition and the culture of learning. *Educational Researcher, 18,* 32–42.

Butkowsky, I. S., & Willows, D. M. (1980). Cognitive-motivational characteristics of children varying in reading ability: Evidence for learned helplessness in poor readers. *Journal of Educational Psychology, 72,* 408–422.

Calfee, R. C., & Hiebert, E. H. (1991). Classroom assessment of reading. In R. Barr, M. L. Kamil, P. B. Mosenthal, & P. D. Pearson (Eds.), *Handbook of reading research* (Vol. 2, pp. 281–309). New York: Longman.

California English/Language Arts Committee. (1987). *English-language arts framework.* Sacramento: California State Department of Education.

Calkins, L. M. (1986). *The art of teaching writing.* Portsmouth, NH: Heinemann.

Carroll, J., & Chall, J. S. (Eds.). (1975). *Toward a literate society: The report of the Committee on Reading of the National Academy of Education.* New York: McGraw–Hill.

Chall, J. S., & Feldmann, S. (1966). First grade reading: An analysis of the interactions of professed methods, teacher implementation, and child background. *The Reading Teacher, 19,* 569–575.

Clarke, L. (1988). Invented versus traditional spelling in first graders' writings: Effects on learning to spell and read. *Research in the Teaching of English, 22,* 281–309.

Clay, M. M. (1985). *The early detection of reading difficulties* (3rd ed.). Portsmouth, NH: Heinemann.

Covington, M. V. (1984). The motive for self-worth. In R. Ames & C. Ames (Eds.), *Research on motivation in education: Student motivation* (Vol. 1, pp. 77–113). Orlando: Academic Press.

Cunningham, A. E. (1988, April). *A developmental study of instruction in phonemic awareness.* Paper presented at the annual meeting of the American Educational Research Association, New Orleans.

Cunningham, P. M., Hall, D. P., & Defee, M. (1991). Non-ability grouped, multilevel instruction: A year in a first-grade classroom. *The Reading Teacher, 44,* 566–571.

Darch, C. B., Carnine, D. W., & Kameenui, E. J. (1986). The role of graphic organizers and social structure in content area instruction. *Journal of Reading Behavior, 18,* 275–296.

DeFord, D. E., Lyons, C. A., & Pinnell, G. S. (Eds.). (1991). *Bridges to literacy: Learning from Reading Recovery.* Portsmouth, NH: Heinemann.

Duffy, G. G. (1981). Teacher effectiveness research: Implications for the reading profession. In M. Kamil (Ed.), *Directions in reading: Research and instruction: Thirtieth yearbook of the National Reading Conference* (pp. 113–136). Washington, DC: National Reading Conference.

Durkin, D. (1974–1975). A six-year study of children who learned to read in school at the age of four. *Reading Research Quarterly, 10,* 9–61.

Durkin, D. (1978–1979). What classroom observations reveal about reading comprehension instruction. *Reading Research Quarterly, 14,* 481–533.

Durkin, D. (1982). *A study of poor black children who are successful readers* (Reading Ed. Rep. No. 33). Urbana–Champaign: University of Illinois, Center for the Study of Reading.

Durkin, D. (in preparation). *How the new basal reader series are affecting teachers' behavior: Grades 1, 3, and 5.* Urbana–Champaign: University of Illinois, Center for the Study of Reading.

Dweck, C. S., & Leggett, E. L. (1988). A social-cognitive approach to motivation and personality. *Psychological Review, 95,* 256–273.

Dyson, A. H., & Freedman, S. W. (1991). Writing. In J. Flood, J. M. Jensen, D. Lapp, & J. R. Squire (Eds.), *Handbook of research on teaching the English Language arts* (pp. 754–774). New York: Macmillan.

Eccles, J., & Wigfield, A. (1985). Teacher expectations and student motivation. In J. B. Dusek (Ed.), *Teacher expectancies* (pp. 185–226). Hillsdale, NJ: Lawrence Erlbaum Associates.

Edelsky, C. (1990). Whose agenda is this anyway? A response to McKenna, Robinson, & Miller. *Educational Researcher, 19,* 7–11.

Elliot, E. S., & Dweck, C. S. (1988). Goals: An approach to motivation. *Journal of Personality and Social Psychology, 54,* 5–12.

Fitzgerald, J., & Spiegel, D. L. (1983). Enhancing children's reading comprehension through instruction in narrative structure. *Journal of Reading Behavior, 15,* 1–17.

Froese, V. (1990). *Whole-language practice and theory.* Scarborough, Ont: Prentice–Hall Canada.

Goldenberg, C. (1991). *Learning to read in New Zealand: Some observations and possible lessons for American educators.* Unpublished manuscript, University of California at Los Angeles.

Goodman, Y. M. (1991). Informal methods of evaluation. In J. Flood, J. M. Jensen, D. Lapp, & J. R. Squire (Eds.), *Handbook of research on teaching the English language arts* (pp. 502–509). New York: Macmillan.

Graves, M. F. (1986). Vocabulary learning and instruction. In E. Rothkopf (Ed.), *Review of research in education* (Vol. 13, pp. 49–90). Washington, DC: American Educational Research Association.

Graves, M. F. (1987). The roles of instruction in fostering vocabulary development. In M. McKeown & M. Curtis (Ed.), *The nature of vocabulary acquisition* (pp. 165–184). Hillsdale, NJ: Lawrence Erlbaum Associates.

Greenlee, M. E., Hiebert, E. H., Bridge, C. A., & Winograd, P. N. (1986). The effects of different audiences on young writers' letter writing. In J. A. Niles & R. V. Lalik (Eds.), *Solving problems in literacy: Learners, teachers, and researchers: Thirty-fifth yearbook of the National Reading Conference* (pp. 281–289). Rochester, NY: The National Reading Conference.

Hare, V. C., & Borchardt, K. M. (1984). Direct instruction of summarization skills. *Reading Research Quarterly, 20,* 62–78.

Henry, N. B. (Ed.). (1948). *Forty-seventh yearbook of the National Society for the Study of Education: Reading in the elementary school and college.* Chicago: University of Chicago Press.

Henry, N. B. (Ed.). (1949). *Forty-eighth yearbook of the National Society for the Study of Education: Reading in the elementary school.* Chicago: University of Chicago Press.

Hidi, S. (1990). Interest and its contribution as a mental resource for learning. *Review of Educational Research, 60,* 549–571.

Hidi, S., & Baird, W. (1988). Strategies for increasing text-based interest and students' recall of expository texts. *Reading Research Quarterly, 23,* 465–483.

Hiebert, E. H. (1991). The development of word-level strategies in authentic literacy tasks. *Language Arts, 68,* 234–240.

Hiebert, E. H., Colt, J. M., Catto, S., & Gury, E. (1991, December).*The impact of consistent, authentic literacy experiences on Chapter 1 students' literacy growth.* Paper presented at the annual meeting of the National Reading Conference, Palm Springs, CA.

Hiebert, E. H., & Fisher, C. W. (1992). The tasks of school literacy instruction: Trends and tensions. In J. Brophy (Ed.), *Advances in research on teaching: Planning and managing learning tasks and activities* (Vol. 3, pp. 191–223). Greenwich, CT: JAI Press.

Hiebert, E. H., Goudvis, A., & Burton, N. (1989, December). *Knowing about reading and writing: Strategies of students in whole language classrooms.* Paper presented at the annual meeting of the National Reading Conference, Austin, TX.

Hiebert, E. H., Potts, T., Katz, H., & Rahm, D. (1989, December). *Characteristics of reading and writing instruction in whole language classrooms.* Paper presented at the annual conference of the National Reading Conference, Austin, TX.

Hiebert, E. H., Winograd, P. N., & Danner, F. W. (1984). Children's attributions for failure and success in different aspects of reading. *Journal of Educational Psychology, 76,* 1139–1148.

Hoffman, J. V., O'Neal, S. F., Kastler, L. A., Clements, R. O., Segel, K. W., & Nash, M. F. (1984). Guided oral reading and miscue focused verbal feedback in second-grade classrooms. *Reading Research Quarterly, 19,* 367–384.

Holley, C. D., & Dansereau, D. F. (Eds.). (1984). *Spatial learning strategies.* New York: Academic Press.

James, T. (1991). State authority and the politics of educational change. In G. Grant (Ed.), *Review of research in education* (Vol. 17, pp. 169–224). Washington, DC: American Educational Research Association.

Jenkins, J., & Dixon, R. (1983). Vocabulary learning. *Contemporary Educational Psychology, 8,* 237–260.

Jenkins, J., Stein, M., & Wysocki, K. (1984). Learning vocabulary through reading. *American Educational Research Journal, 21,* 767–788.

Johnson, D. D., & Baumann, J. F. (1984). Word identification. In P. D. Pearson, R. Barr, M. L. Kamil, & P. Mosenthal (Eds.), *Handbook of reading research* (pp. 583–608). New York: Longman.

Johnson, D., & Pearson, P. D. (1978). *Teaching reading vocabulary.* New York: Holt Rinehart & Winston.

Johnston, P. H., & Winograd, P. N. (1985). Passive Failure in reading. *Journal of Reading Behavior, 17,* 279–301.

Jose, P., & Brewer, W. (1984). Development of story liking. Character identification, suspense, and outcome resolution. *Developmental Psychology, 20,* 911–924.

Juel, C. (1988). Learning to read and write: A longitudinal study of fifty-four children from first through fourth grade. *Journal of Educational Psychology, 80,* 437–447.

Juel, C. (1990). The role of decoding in early literacy instruction and assessment. In L. M. Morrow & J. K. Smith (Eds.), *Assessment for instruction in early literacy* (pp. 135–154). Englewood Cliffs, NJ: Prentice–Hall.

Juel, C. (1991). Beginning reading. In R. Barr, M. L. Kamil, P. B. Mosenthal, & P. D. Pearson (Eds.), *Handbook of reading research* (Vol. 2, pp. 759–788). New York: Longman.

Juel, C., & Roper/Schneider, D. (1985). The influence of basal readers on first grade reading. *Reading Research Quarterly, 20,* 134–152.

Juel, C., Griffith, P. L., & Gough, P. B. (1986). Acquisition of literacy: A longitudinal study of children in first and second grade. *Journal of Educational Psychology, 78,* 243–255.

Kameenui, E. J., Carnine, D. W., & Freschi, R. (1982). Effects of text construction and instructional procedures for teaching word meanings on comprehension and recall. *Reading Research Quarterly, 17,* 367–388.

Kane, J. H., & Anderson, R. C. (1978). Depth of processing and interference effects in learning and remembering of sentences. *Journal of Educational Psychology, 70,* 626–635.

Lepper, M. R. (1983). Extrinsic reward and intrinsic motivation: Implications for the classroom. In J. M. Levine & M. C. Wang (Eds.), *Teacher and student perceptions: Implications for learning* (pp. 281–317). Hillsdale, NJ: Lawrence Erlbaum Associates.

Levine, J. M. (1983). Social comparison and education. In J. M. Levine & M. C. Wang (Eds.), *Teacher and student perceptions: Implications for learning* (pp. 29–55). Hillsdale, NJ: Lawrence Erlbaum Associates.

Levine, J. M., & Wang, M. C. (Eds.). (1983). *Teacher and student perceptions: Implications for learning.* Hillsdale, NJ: Lawrence Erlbaum Associates.

Liberman, I. Y., & Shankweiler, D. (1985). Phonology and the problems of learning to read and write. *Remedial and Special Education, 6,* 8–17.

Lie, A. (1991). Effects of a training program for stimulating skills in word analysis in first-grade children. *Reading Research Quarterly, 26,* 234–250.

Lundberg, I., Frost, J., & Petersen, O.-P. (1988). Effects of an extensive program for stimulating phonological awareness in preschool children. *Reading Research Quarterly, 23,* 263–284.

Maclean, M., Bryant, P., & Bradley, L. (1987). Rhymes, nursery rhymes, and reading in early childhood. *Merrill–Palmer Quarterly, 33,* 255–281.

Madden, N. A., & Slavin, R. E. (1989). Effective pullout programs for students at risk. In R. E. Slavin, N. L. Karweit, & N. A. Madden (Eds.), *Effective programs for students at risk* (pp. 52–72). Boston: Allyn & Bacon.

Maehr, M. L., & Braskamp, L. A. (1986). *The motivation factor: A theory of personal investment.* Lexington, MA: Lexington Press.

Martin, B. (1970). *Brown bear, brown bear, what do you see?* New York: Holt Rinehart & Winston.

Mason, J., & Allen, J. (1986). A review of emergent literacy with implications for research and practice in reading. *Review of Research in Education, 13,* 3–47.

McClelland, D. C. (1961). *The achieving society.* Princeton, NJ: Van Nostrand.

McKenna, M. C., Robinson, R. D., & Miller, J. W. (1990). Whole language: A research agenda for the nineties. *Educational Researcher, 19,* 3–6.

Miller, G. A. (1972). English verbs of motion: A case study in semantics and lexical memory. In A. Melton & E. Martin (Eds.), *Coding processes in human memory* (pp. 335–372). New York: Wiley.

Nagy, W. E., Anderson, R. C., & Herman, P. A. (1987). Learning word meanings from context during normal reading. *American Educational Research Journal, 24,* 237–270.

Nagy, W. E., & Herman, P. A. (1987). Breadth and depth of vocabulary knowledge: Implications for acquisition and instruction. In M. McKeown & M. Curtis (Eds.), *The nature of vocabulary acquisition* (pp. 19–30). Hillsdale, NJ: Lawrence Erlbaum Associates.

Nagy, W., & Scott, J. (1990). Word schemas: Expectations about the form and meaning of new words. *Cognition and Instruction, 7,* 105–127.

Newman, R. S. (1990). Children's help-seeking in the classroom: The role of motivational factors and attitudes. *Journal of Educational Psychology, 82,* 71–80.

Nicholls, J. G. (1984a). Conceptions of ability and achievement motivation. In R. Ames & C. Ames (Eds.), *Research on motivation in education: Student motivation* (Vol. 1, pp. 39–73). Orlando: Academic Press.

Nicholls, J. G. (Ed.). (1984b). *Advances in motivation and achievement: The development of achievement motivation* (Vol. 3). Greenwich, CT: JAI.

Nicholls, J. G., & Miller, A. T. (1984). Development and its discontents: The differentiation of the concept of ability. In J. G. Nicholls (Ed.), *Advances in motivation and achievement: The development of achievement motivation* (Vol. 3, pp. 185–218). Greenwich, CT: JAI.

Oka, E. R., & Paris, S. G. (1987). Patterns of motivation and reading skills in underachieving children. In S. J. Ceci (Ed.), *Handbook of cognitive, social, and neuropsychological aspects of learning disabilities* (Vol. 2, pp. 115–145). Hillsdale, NJ: Lawrence Erlbaum Associates.

Palincsar, A. S., & Brown, A. L. (1984). Reciprocal teaching of comprehension fostering and monitoring activities. *Cognition and Instruction, 1,* 117–175.

Paris, S. G., Cross, D. R., & Lipson, M. Y. (1984). Informed strategies for learning: A program to improve children's reading awareness and comprehension. *Journal of Educational Psychology, 76,* 1239–1252.

Paris, S., & Jacobs, J. E. (1984). The benefits of informed instruction for children's reading awareness and comprehension skills. *Child Development, 55,* 2083–2093.

Paris, S. G., Lipson, M. Y., & Wixson, K. K. (1983). Becoming a strategic reader. *Contemporary Educational Psychology, 8,* 293–316.

Paris, S. G., Olson, G. M., & Stevenson, H. W. (Eds.). (1983). *Learning and motivation in the classroom.* Hillsdale, NJ: Lawrence Erlbaum Associates.

Paris, S. G., & Winograd, P. (1990). How metacognition can promote academic learning and instruction. In B. F. Jones & L. Idol (Eds.), *Dimensions of thinking and cognitive instruction* (pp. 15–51). Hillsdale, NJ: Lawrence Erlbaum Associates.

Paris, S. G., Wasik, B. A., & Turner, J. C. (1991). The development of strategic readers. In R. Barr, M. L. Kamil, P. Mosenthal, & P. D. Pearson (Eds.), *Handbook of reading research* (Vol. 2, pp. 609–640). New York: Longman.

Patching, W., Kameenuni, E., Carnine, D., Gersten, R., & Colvin, G. (1983). Direct instruction in critical reading skills. *Reading Research Quarterly, 18,* 406–418.

Pearson, P. D., & Fielding, L. (1991). Comprehension instruction. In R. Barr, M. L. Kamil, P. B. Mosenthal, & P. D. Pearson (Eds.), *Handbook of reading research* (Vol. 2, pp. 815–860). New York: Longman.

Perfetti, C. A., Beck, I., Bell, L., & Hughes, C. (1987). Phonemic knowledge and learning to read are reciprocal: A longitudinal study of first-grade children. *Merrill–Palmer Quarterly, 33,* 283–319.

Pflaum, S. W., Walberg, H. J., Karegianes, M. L., & Rasher, S. P. (1980). Reading instruction: A quantitative analysis. *Educational Researcher, 9,* 12–18.

Pinnell, G. S., Lyons, C. A., DeFord, D. E., Bryk, A. S., & Seltzer, M. (1991). *Studying the effectiveness of early intervention approaches for first grade children having difficulty in reading* (Educational Rep. #16). Columbus, OH: Martha L. King Language and Literacy Center.

Raphael, T. E., Goatley, J. J., McMahon, S. I., & Woodman, D. A. (in press). Teaching literacy through student book clubs. In B. E. Cullinan (Ed.), *Literature across the curriculum: Making it happen.* Newark, DE: International Reading Association.

Reyes, M. (1991a). A process approach to literacy using dialogue journals and literature logs with second language learners. *Research in the Teaching of English, 25,* 291–313.

Reyes, M. (1991b, April). *The "one size fits all" approach to literacy.* Paper presented at the annual meeting of the American Educational Research Association, Chicago.

Reynolds, A. J. (1991). Early schooling of children at risk. *American Educational Research Journal, 28,* 392–422.

Richardson, V., Anders, P. L., Lloyd, C., & Tidwell, D. (1991). The relationship between teachers' beliefs and practices in reading comprehension research. *American Educational Research Journal, 28,* 559–586.

Rosenshine, B., & Stevens, R. (1984). Classroom instruction in reading. In P. D. Pearson, R. Barr, M. L. Kamil, & P. Mosenthal (Eds.), *Handbook of reading research* (pp. 745–799). New York: Longman.

Routman, R. (1988). *Transitions: From literature to literacy.* Portsmouth, NH: Heinemann.

Sarason, S. B. (1982). *The culture of the school and the problem of change* (2nd ed.). Boston: Allyn & Bacon.

Scott, J. A., Hiebert, E. H., & Anderson, R. C. (1988). *From present to future: Beyond Becoming a Nation of Readers* (Tech. Rep. No. 443). Urbana–Champaign: University of Illinois, Center for the Study of Reading.

Seuss, Dr. (1957). *The cat in the hat.* New York: Random House.

Shanahan, T. (1987). Review of *The early detection of reading difficulties* (3rd ed.). *Journal of Reading Behavior, 19,* 117–119.

Shanklin, N., & Rhodes, L. (1989). *Bibliography on whole language.* Denver: University of Colorado.

Shell, D. F., Murphy, C. C., & Bruning, R. H. (1989). Self-efficacy and outcome expectancy mechanisms in reading and writing achievement. *Journal of Educational Psychology, 81,* 91–100.

Shulman, L. S., & Keislar, E. R. (1966). *Learning by discovery: A critical appraisal.* Chicago: Rand-McNally.

Skinner, E., Wellborn, J., & Connell, J. (1990). What it takes to do well in school and whether I've got it: A process model of perceived control and children's engagement and achievement in school. *Journal of Educational Psychology, 82,* 22–32.

Slamecka, N. J., & Graff, P. (1978). The generation effect: Delineation of a phenomenon. *Journal of Experimental Psychology: Human Learning and Memory, 4,* 592–604.

Slavin, R. E., Madden, N., Karweit, N. L., Livermon, B. J., & Dolan, L. (1990). Success for all: First-year outcomes of a comprehensive plan for reforming urban education. *American Educational Research Journal, 27,* 255–278.

Stahl, S. (1983). Differential word knowledge and reading comprehension. *Journal of Reading Behavior, 15,* 33–50.

Stahl, S., & Miller, P. (1989). Whole language and language experience approaches for beginning reading: A quantitative research synthesis. *Review of Educational Research, 59,* 87–116.

Stanovich, K. E. (1986). Matthew effects in reading: Some consequences of individual differences in the acquisition of literacy. *Reading Research Quarterly, 21,* 360–406.

Stanovich, K. E. (1991). Word recognition and changing perspectives. In R. Barr, M. L. Kamil, P. B. Mosenthal, & P. D. Pearson (Eds.), *Handbook of reading research* (Vol. 2, pp. 418–452). New York: Longman.

Stephens, D., Gaffney, J. S., Weinzierl, J., Shelton, J., & Clark, C. (1991). *Five teachers teaching: Beliefs and practices of Reading Recovery teachers-in-training.* Unpublished manuscript, University of Illinois, Center for the Study of Reading, Urbana–Champaign.

Sulzby, E. (1992). Research directions: Transitions from emergent to conventional writing. *Language Arts, 69,* 290–297.

Sulzby, E., & Teale, W. H. (1991). Emergent literacy. In R. Barr, M. L. Kamil, P. B. Mosenthal, & P. D. Pearson (Eds.), *Handbook of reading research* (Vol. 2, pp. 727–758). New York: Longman.

Taylor, B. M., Frye, B. J., Short, R., & Shearer, B. (1990). *Early intervention in reading: Preventing reading failure among low-achieving first-grade students.* Unpublished manuscript, University of Minnesota.

Tharp, R., & Gallimore, R. (1988). *Rousing minds to life: Teaching, learning, and schooling in social context.* New York: Cambridge University Press.

Tierney, R. J. (1990). Redefining reading comprehension. *Educational Leadership, 47,* 37–42.

Tunmer, W. E. (1989, October). *Does Reading Recovery work?* Professorial inaugural lecture, Massey University.

Tunmer, W. E., & Nesdale, A. R. (1985). Phonemic segmentation skill and beginning reading. *Journal of Educational Psychology, 77,* 417–427.

Valencia, S., McGinley, W., & Pearson, P. D. (1990). Assessing reading and writing: Building a more complete picture. In G. G. Duffy (Ed.), *Reading in the middle school* (2nd ed., pp. 124–156). Newark, DE: International Reading Association.

Weiner, B. (1972). *Theories of motivation from mechanism to cognition.* Chicago: Rand McNally.

Weiner, B., & Kukla, A. (1970). An attributional analysis of achievement motivation. *Journal of Personality and Social Psychology, 15,* 1–20.

Whipple, G. M. (Ed.). (1925). *Twenty-fourth yearbook of the National Society for the Study of Education: Report of the National Committee on Reading* (Vol. 24). Bloomington, IL: Public School Publishing Co.

Whipple, G. M. (Ed.). (1937). *Thirty-sixth yearbook of the National Society for the Study of Education: The teaching of reading: A second report* (Vol. 36). Bloomington, IL: Public School Publishing Co.

Wigfield, A., & Asher, S. R. (1984). Social and motivational influences on reading. In P. D. Pearson, R. Barr, M. L. Kamil, & P. Mosenthal (Eds.), *Handbook of reading research* (pp. 423–452). New York: Longman.

Winne, P. (1991). Motivation and teaching. In H. Waxman & H. Walberg (Eds.), *Effective teaching: Current research* (pp. 295–314). Berkeley, CA: McCutchan.

Wixson, K. K. (1986). Vocabulary instruction and children's comprehension of basal stories. *Reading Research Quarterly, 21,* 317–329.

VI PUBLISHERS' PERSPECTIVES

17 Consensus Emerging, But a Way to Go

James R. Squire
Silver Burdett and Ginn

Forty years after Dora V. Smith and NCTE's Commission on the English Curriculum (Smith & The Commission, 1952) called for integrated language arts in the elementary school, reading is emerging with the richness of a real language art rather than remaining a separate skill-oriented subject. This is the overriding impression one receives from the chapters in this volume. Whereas the Commission called for genuine communication in the classroom, not quite the "meaning making" preferred today, the ultimate intent seems similar, particularly given the stress on literature for children and on thematic and topical units to provide an ideational framework that marked the work of the earlier commission (see Mackintosh, 1954). Some differences remain unresolved in the profession, particularly with respect to the kinds of instruction needed by young people and the ways in which instruction is most effectively introduced; but even the most militant whole language advocate seems now to recognize the importance of planning help for some children, whether by coaching, conferencing, scaffolding, reciprocal teaching, instructional conversations, or even direct teaching. And researchers concerned about skill development seem newly aware of such matters as children's need to read widely, of the importance of linking oral language and writing to reading, of the power of reading literature aloud, and of the importance of talking about books. Sharp differences remain, especially with respect to the when, why, and how of phonics, but, clearly, leaders in the profession are moving to resolve the baffling clash between those who stress instructional design and those who cultivate language experience.

Yet questions must be raised about certain issues in the emerging consensus. Here I comment on eight such issues:

1. Recognition of the role that publishers play in the continuing education of teachers. Chapters such as those by Copeland, Winsor, and Osborn and Pearson and Stallman suggest the value and significance of establishing a partnership between instructional staffs and those who provide instructional materials. Demonstrations on videotape of outstanding teachers in action, as Stephens suggests, provide modelling, of course, but offer only one avenue to strengthening teachers' instructional repertoire. Of even greater importance, perhaps, is the role of the outside consultant in stimulating groups of teachers to consider new ideas. Indeed, the interaction so praised in many primary school classrooms for its contribution to children's learning seems equally critical in teacher education. Only recently, Brown (1991) has reported that engaging teachers in higher order thinking and discussion experiences is a necessary prerequisite to engaging students in such activity. We need to think more deeply about the implications of such findings.

2. Distinguishing more clearly how learning occurs outside the classroom and how it can be most efficiently provided within the schooling process. Stephens distinguishes carefully between the "dominant" response and the "emergent" response. Yet, do not children need both? "Real-life" learning is admittedly impressive, but what evidence have we that it is so superior to learning occurring within the classroom that teachers should do little more than replicate inside what occurs outside?

3. An overemphasis on the uses of narrative and on what children can learn from a story seems characteristic of much of the recent concern with reading and writing and particularly with literature-centered reading programs. Trabasso provides a valuable presentation of such views. But unless the content of literature is redefined to include nonfictional expository–informational prose, and unless school writing programs consciously provide planned instructional experience with expository prose—particularly the prose associated with science, technology, and history—our young people may find that school language arts programs fail to prepare them for the full range of literacy tasks (see Venezky, Kaestle, & Sum, 1987). Certainly Rosenblatt, one of the leading advocates of literature-based programs, has for years stressed the difference between aesthetic reading and what she calls efferent reading activity, the reading of informational prose (Rosenblatt, 1978). Reading "maketh a full man" in the real Baconian sense only if our Janes and Johnnies have instructional experience with all important modes of writing and reading, not just narrative alone.

4. The importance of redesigning instructional materials and teacher manuals to enhance the opportunities for decision making by teachers is a theme that runs through many of the chapters. Well and good, of course, if teachers are prepared for making such decisions! But surely one option that must remain open to teachers is the option of using instructional materials that provide some form of explicit instruction—whether the learning of skills or the discovery of strategies

be the goal. Among the decisions that teachers must be free to make is the decision to use traditional basal reading materials.

5. Competence in word attack skills and in word understandings (vocabulary) is important for all young readers. As both Gaskins and Stahl note, research and experience repeatedly suggest that at-risk children benefit from more structured approaches. Research also continues to demonstrate that competence in decoding is a necessity (see Chall, 1985), and that for many children it must be taught as one way of unlocking the meaning of the text. Overemphasis on isolated instruction and isolated workbook skill drills has been widespread, but what seems to be needed is greater awareness of teacher strategies that can provide instruction or guidance with individual words or word parts within a total context. The Reading Recovery program discussed by Pinnell shows us one way of providing children with explicit help in a meaning-oriented context but requires specialized teacher preparation and a tutorial context. What is needed are similar strategies that might be employed by regular classroom teachers.

6. Recognition that competence in reading involves more than the mastery of discrete skills should not lead to rejection of the concept of skill itself. Too many researchers of whatever persuasion tend to avoid the word itself, preferring references to the more global "strategies" or "processes." Yet skills there are that must be acquired even within the context of total process or strategy. The problem for teachers and those who design instructional materials is how to provide for skill instructions and skill reinforcement within meaning-making activities.

7. Those who recognize that the whole language classroom calls for different kinds of instructional materials seem too prone to discard the baby with the bathwater if they see no future use for basal reading programs. Less death than transformation of basals seems the likely consequence of new insights into literary experience and teacher decision making. Indeed, among the changes most likely to emerge in basal programs are: modular organizations to encourage flexibility in planning; a deemphasis on extensive skill drills coupled with greater emphasis on oral language activity and writing in relation to reading; clustering of literary selections around topics and themes of interest to large numbers of children; provision for alternative forms of assessment. Some of these emphases along with strengthened literary content are already characteristic of newer basals. Providing strong support for the instructional program, albeit in more flexible contexts, will likely remain a unique contribution of basal programs.

8. Widespread independent reading with easy access to many books in the classroom remains one essential of a reading program on which both supporters of whole language and of phonics-based programs agree. Long supported by research (see, e.g., LaBrant, 1936), wide reading became endangered in the early television–mastery learning days of the 1960s and 1970s, when passing tests, not reading books, seemed the ultimate goal. Not until the publication of *Becoming a Nation of Readers* (Anderson, Hiebert, Scott, & Wilkinson, 1985)

was the value of wide reading so strongly reinforced. Further research in emergent literacy and in interactive learning, as discussed by Kerr and Mason, has sharpened awareness of the significance of writing and talking about the books read.

CONCLUSION

The learning of language is so complex that no one single point of view or single scholarly inquiry seems likely to embrace it fully—not behaviorism, not cognitive science, not linguistics, not socio or psycholinguistics. The richness of the chapters in this volume demonstrates how research and analysis of many kinds can contribute to better teaching and learning. Indeed, providing teachers as well as learners with a variety of strategies for reading from which they may choose should be a vital dimension of the curricula in reading and in reading education (Siegler, 1991).

REFERENCES

Anderson, R. C., Hiebert, E. H., Scott, J. A., & Wilkinson, I. A. G. (1985). *Becoming a nation of readers: The report of the Commission on Reading.* Champaign, IL: Center for the Study of Reading, Washington, DC: National Institute of Education.

Brown, R. (1991). *Schools of thought: How the politics of literacy shape thinking in the classroom.* San Francisco: Jossey–Bass.

Chall, J. S. (1985). *Growth in reading ability.* New York: McGraw–Hill.

LaBrant, L. (1936). *An evaluation of the free reading program in grades ten, eleven, and twelve.* Columbus, OH: The Ohio State University.

Mackintosh, H. (1954). *Language arts for today's children.* New York: Appleton–Century–Crofts.

Rosenblatt, L. (1978). *The reader, the text, and the poem.* Carbondale: Southern Illinois University Press.

Siegler, R. S. (1991). Strategy choice and strategy discovery. *Learning and Instruction, 1,* 89–102.

Smith, D. V., & The Commission on the English Curriculum. (1952). *The English language arts.* New York: Appleton-Century-Crofts.

Venezky, R., Kaestle, C. F., & Sum, A. M. (1987). *The subtle danger.* Princeton, NJ: Educational Testing Service.

18 Children, Adults, Books: Implications for Publishers

John T. Ridley
Houghton Mifflin

Three chapters in this volume offer perspectives on interactions among children, adults, and books. Two of the chapters, those by Kerr and Mason and by Pinnell, speak to the importance of children taking an active role in reading and to the positive impact that this has on children's learning to read. A third chapter, that by Meyer and Wardrop, presents findings on certain home and school influences on learning to read in kindergarten through second grade and, among other findings, reveals unexpected results that reinforce the vital nature of active as opposed to passive reading. My purpose here is to review all three chapters from a publisher's perspective for implications offered for materials published for students and teachers in the 21st century.

Kerr and Mason present a number of valuable insights into the activity of reading aloud to children. They cast the activity within a Vygotskian theoretical framework and offer many examples of how parents and children are involved in highly interactive activities during read-aloud events. They note that, whereas the amount of research available on the effects of teachers' reading aloud to students is more restricted, there is a growing body of evidence to suggest that a teacher's reading aloud of books to groups of students has a beneficial effect on their abilities that are related to reading and literacy. Kerr and Mason go beyond reviewing research supporting the positive effects of reading aloud to children and begin to specify the manner in which the beneficial effect takes place. They note several important areas that are beneficially affected by read-aloud events—written language awareness, vocabulary and concept development, learning letter names, and word identification.

The probable implications of the Kerr and Mason chapter for publishers of instructional materials seem fairly straightforward. Certainly, teachers should be urged, in materials designed to help them plan their instruction, to use read-aloud events on a regular basis. Further, those techniques that make reading aloud far more interactive, such as pointing to words as they are being read, focusing attention on specific words, dealing with the left-to-right directionality of reading, stressing key vocabulary, and relating the ideas of the book to the child's real-life experiences, should be suggested as important instructional aspects of the read-aloud process.

The interactive activities used in reading aloud to children also seem closely related to concepts that are part of shared-reading activities. For example, there is a growing body of evidence that indicates that multiple readings of the same text result in improved student learning. Specifically, research in the area of vocabulary development strongly suggests that repeated readings of the same text, in itself, has a beneficial effect on vocabulary acquisition. This same research, however, suggests that teachers can further children's vocabulary development by making the activity more interactive—that is, by at least briefly discussing some of the words that are part of the shared-reading experience.

Finally, this chapter offers implications for the kinds of books that need to be published for use in the beginning stages of learning to read. For example, the study by Mason, Peterman, Powell, and Kerr (1989) cited in the chapter suggests an interaction between teacher practices and the types of materials being used. Because of the nature of the text used and the kinds of activities that teachers engage in, students appear to understand narrative texts better. It is important, however, that students also gain the ability to understand expository, or nonfiction materials, even at an early age. There appears to be the need for increasing the amount of expository materials available at these early levels and also a need to investigate further and suggest strategies that will help children more adequately understand expository text.

In her chapter, Pinnell adds a different perspective on complex interactions, providing a concise description of the widely praised Reading Recovery program and detailing specifically the interactions between a teacher and a child. It seems likely that the documented success of Reading Recovery stems from the extensive training that the tutors in this program receive. An essential part of Reading Recovery is the active decision making that teachers engage in as they interact with students and use their responses to support and improve their approach to being successful readers.

Pinnell's chapter has several implications for publishers. First, it reminds us that the teaching of reading is a very complex phenomenon, and that it is impossible to specify exactly what teachers should do and how they should do it. Publishers of instructional materials for the teaching of reading should offer a variety of suggestions, with the expectation that teachers will choose from these suggestions and modify them as they actively and professionally interact with students.

Second, Pinnell's chapter demonstrates the need for a wide variety of published materials for students. The books that are used in the Reading Recovery program, although varying in level of difficulty, do not employ the excessive rules with respect to vocabulary control and repetition that until recently have been applied to widely used instructional materials. Nevertheless, Reading Recovery does indicate the need for materials with which children will experience substantial success. Children do need to begin to experience reading with texts that are relatively simple and progress through increasing levels of challenge.

Third, the materials used in Reading Recovery offer some suggestions as to how the level of difficulty might be monitored. The easiest books are quite predictable and are supported with pictures. Later books use increasingly complex language and vocabulary and systematically withdraw external context clues such as pictures. This, too, has immediate implications for publishers of materials for children. A wide variety of materials needs to be available, and the level of complexity does need to vary. However, Reading Recovery principles also suggest that there can be no simple formula for determining the difficulty level of a text. Instructional materials designed for teacher use need to make clear that teachers will constantly need to evaluate the textual difficulty of a book in terms of what they know about the children with whom they are working. Indeed, Pinnell describes a circumstance in which a book that was chosen for a child was found during use to be inappropriate. She reminds us as publishers and teachers that even a highly skilled professional using good instructional materials will sometimes err in instructional decisions and should be willing and able to modify the use of materials or reject them as the circumstances warrant.

Fourth, principles, practices, and materials used in Reading Recovery offer suggestions for the types of materials that publishers need to prepare for use in the assessment of reading. Materials that are published to support teachers' instructional efforts should offer many suggestions for the way in which assessment can be built naturally into ongoing reading and writing instructional activities. Assessment materials that closely match the materials used in instruction also seem to have the greatest degree of validity and utility.

The instructional framework for the daily lessons used in Reading Recovery also offers some interesting implications for publishers of instructional and children's materials. First, there is a structure to the activities used in Reading Recovery. It seems likely that many teachers indeed would profit from having a framework suggested, and that many students would find a well-crafted framework and pattern of activities to be reassuring and worthwhile.

In addition, the sequence of activities used in Reading Recovery seems to have some implications for publishers and curriculum developers. Students begin by engaging in activities that are designed to provide them with success. Assessment procedures are then built into the sequence of activities, and writing activities are used to reinforce reading skills. Writing then becomes a response to the reading the students are doing. Next, students are presented with new and challenging reading experiences. This seems a sequence that deserves to be considered as publishers prepare materials to help teachers make important instructional decisions, particularly decisions about materials for use with students experiencing reading difficulty.

Finally, Reading Recovery procedures point to the need for connecting school and home literacy events. Students who are tutored using Reading Recovery procedures take home the sentences that they have written, and the tutorial session ends with the student selecting a book to take home from the collection of books previously read. Publishers of instructional materials need to offer many suggestions for building such school–home ties and to publish relatively inexpensive versions of quality literature that children can take home.

The third chapter that provides perspectives on child–adult–book interactions is by Meyer and Wardrop. By far the most ambitious and far-ranging in scope, this chapter stems from a longitudinal study involving approximately 650 students that examined the effects of various home and school influences on reading achievement in the early grades.

The results of this study, reported in the Meyer and Wardrop chapter, are somewhat difficult to interpret. The chapter clearly only partly reflects the results of the larger study; therefore, details such as the full criteria for which activities were contained in a particular category are omitted. The study demonstrates the complexity involved in ferreting out factors that have a substantial influence on student reading achievement. One of the most consistent findings was that the socioeconomic status of children had a substantial influence on their achievement. This is not a particularly useful finding, however, as we need to have high aspirations for all children regardless of their socioeconomic background. Another finding, that knowledge of letter names predicted kindergarten reading achievement, is not surprising and is in line with a large body of research.

One of the discouraging findings reported in this chapter is that there are very few instructional factors that seem to make a difference in children's reading achievement. Some of the findings about instructional influences are also difficult to interpret. For example, in some cases, the amount of teacher feedback encouraging students to reconsider an incorrect response shows a negative relationship with student achievement; why this would be the case is unclear. It seems that the nature of this interaction needs to be much more carefully defined and more closely studied, perhaps through further analysis of the tape recordings made of teachers' lessons.

Among the most difficult findings to interpret in the chapter is the lack of relationship between, or the negative relationship between, reading aloud to children and their achievement in reading. This finding is at variance with a rather substantial body of previous research and reviews of the literature. For example, in *Becoming a Nation of Readers,* Anderson, Hiebert, Scott, and

Wilkinson (1985) concluded, "The single most important factor for building the knowledge required for eventual success in reading is reading aloud to children" (p. 23). Using almost identical words in *Beginning to Read,* Adams (1990) concluded, "The single most important activity for building the knowledge and skills eventually required for reading is that of reading aloud to children" (p. 86). The authors of both books, however, recognize that simply reading to children is not enough. Anderson and his colleagues put it this way: "The benefits [of reading to children] are greatest when the child is an active participant, engaging in discussions about stories, learning to identify letters and words, and talking about the meanings of words" (p. 23). Adams argued that:

> It is not just reading to children that makes the difference, it is enjoying the books with them and reflecting on their form and content. It is developing and supporting the children's curiosity about text and the meanings it conveys. It is encouraging the children to examine the print. It is sometimes starting and always inviting discussions of the meanings of the words and the relationships of the text's ideas to the world beyond the book. (p. 87)

Meyer and Wardrop, however, suggest that parents are more likely to help their children in reading if they have the children read to them rather than doing the reading themselves. This, they suggest, is because having a child read the material is more active and reading to the child is more passive.

The problem with this notion is that it is quite easy to imagine that a child who simply reads page after page to a parent might be engaged in a relatively passive activity. Interactivity, not passivity, is the key to meaningful reading. The implication for publishers is that they must continue to provide materials that offer activities that involve truly interactive reading.

Meyer and Wardrop's findings about the amount of reading children do at home is congruent with findings from other research, including a study by Anderson, Wilson, and Fielding (1988). Publishers of instructional materials certainly have a responsibility to remind teachers periodically of the importance of independent reading and to make many suggestions for independent reading that complement the instructional program that the children are receiving.

Their finding that children spend relatively small amounts of time reading in school is also congruent with findings from other research (Anderson et al., 1985). Again, publishers need to encourage teachers to develop a schedule that includes generous amounts of time for the continuous reading of text by students. Such materials need to offer abundant suggestions for books that will be suitable for such activities.

One final comment seems in order. The longitudinal study on which Meyer and Wardrop base their chapter was begun almost a decade ago. In the intervening years our understanding of the reading process, the nature of instruction, and the quality of reading instruction material have all improved, and they will continue to improve as we publish and teach in the 21st century.

REFERENCES

Adams, M. J. (1990). *Beginning to read: Thinking and learning about print.* Cambridge, MA: The MIT Press.

Anderson, R. C., Hiebert, E. H., Scott, J. A., & Wilkinson, I. A. G. (1985). *Becoming a nation of readers: The report of the Commission on Reading.* Champaign, IL: Center for the Study of Reading; Washington, DC: National Institute of Education.

Anderson, R. C., Wilson, P., & Fielding, L. (1988). Growth in reading and how children spend their time outside of school. *Reading Research Quarterly, 23,* 285–303.

Mason, J. M., Peterman, C. L., Powell, B. M., & Kerr, B. M. (1989). Reading and writing attempts by kindergartners after book reading by teachers. In J. M. Mason (Ed.), *Reading and writing connections* (pp. 105–120). Boston: Allyn & Bacon.

Author Index

Subject Index

A

Affix(es), 47, 48, 51, 52, 54-57
Africa
  and literacy, 220, 224, 225, 227-230,
    233, 234
Alphabetic principle, 10, 29, 30, 40
Alphabetic script, 5, 6, 12, 13, 15, 16,
  28
Asia
  and literacy, 224, 225, 228, 230
Assessment, 239-250, 289
  evolution of, 241-245
Automaticity, 9, 12, 13, 18, 19

B

Background knowledge, 56, 118, 136,
  144, 261-262
Basal reading programs, 77, 80, 84,
  115-117, 119, 120, 124, 271
  and children's literature, 26
  criticism of, 79, 81, 83, 85, 87, 121,
    122, 211
  effectiveness of, 101-110, 121, 122,
    285
  phonemic awareness, instruction in,
    26, 36-41
  structural analysis, instruction in, 52-
    54, 56
  tests, 239, 240, 243, 248
Base, words, 47, 48, 54
Basic Studies on Reading, 59
Becoming a Nation of Readers, 80, 82,
  83, 86, 133, 253, 254, 262, 265, 266,
  268, 270-273, 290

Beginning reading, 3-20, 25-42, 45-57,
  59-71, 77-87, 101-113, 125, 127,
  133, 165-184, 265-267
*Beginning to Read: Thinking and
  Learning about Print,* 60, 291
Behaviorist philosophy, 77, 78, 80, 90,
  285
Benchmark School, 115-128
Beyond Freedom and Dignity, 77
Blending, 30, 32, 34, 37, 38, 40, 66-68

C

California Reading Initiative, 83
Chapter 1 programs, 242, 243
Children's literature, 26, 84, 121
  multiculturalism and, 201-212
  and reading instruction, 84, 117, 121,
    122, 201, 211
China, People's Republic of
  and literacy, 220-222, 225, 226
Cognitive psychology, 60, 90, 285
Commission on Reading, 80, 82, 83,
  253, 254
Comprehension, 7, 10, 11, 13, 16, 18,
  20, 27, 60, 64, 65, 67, 97, 103, 105,
  106, 111, 125, 126, 196, 254, 259-
  265
Concepts About Print test, 151
Context processor, 8, 9
Cooperative learning, 94, 120
*Counterpoint and Beyond: A Response
  to Becoming a Nation of Readers,*
  82
Criterion-referenced tests, 243